Oxford International Resources

Maths

Workbook

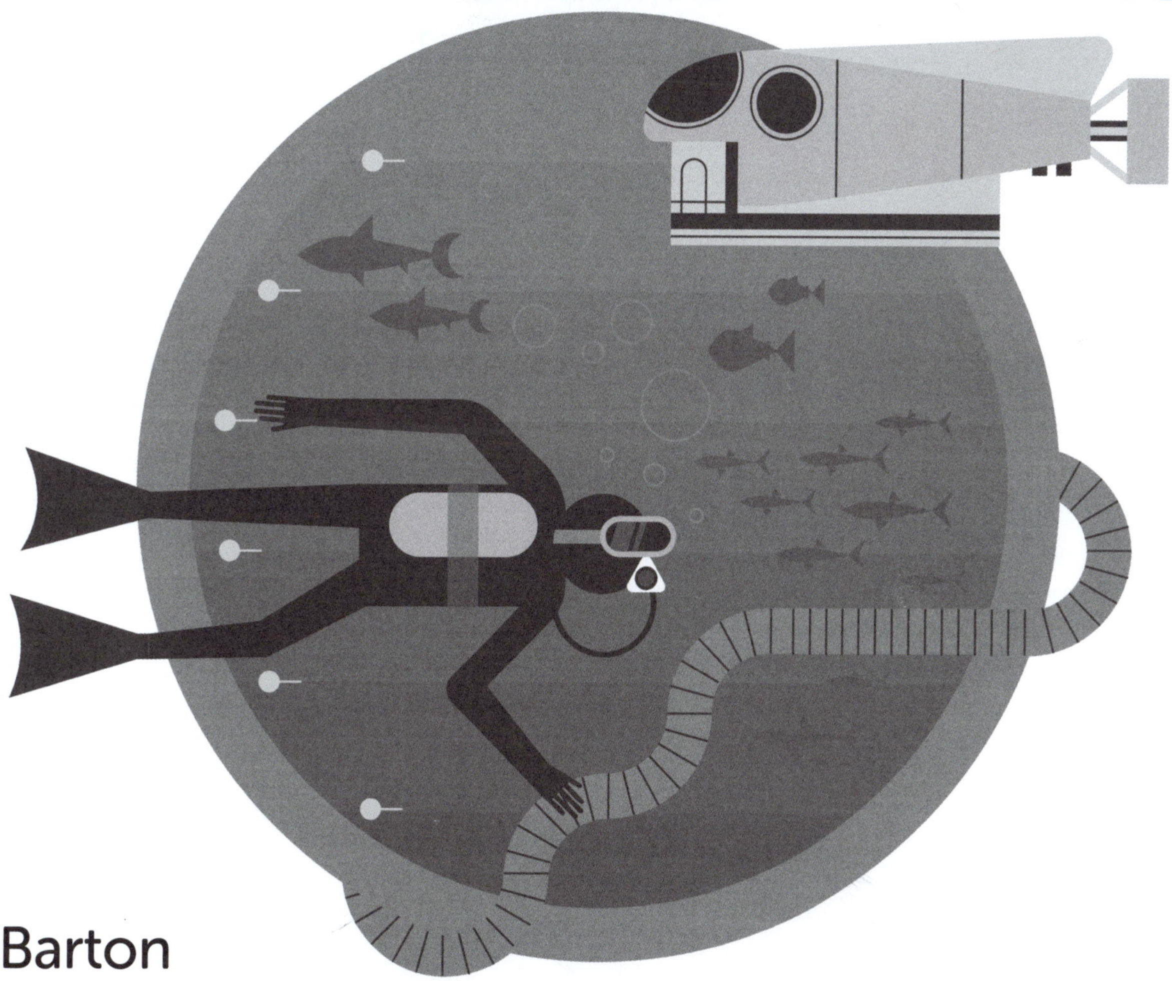

Craig Barton

Charlotte Hawthorne

Jemma Sherwood

Dan Draper

Katie Wood

Helen Konstantine

Paulo Ferro

Sudeep Gokarakonda

OXFORD UNIVERSITY PRESS

OXFORD
UNIVERSITY PRESS

Great Clarendon Street, Oxford, OX2 6DP, United Kingdom

Oxford University Press is a department of the University of Oxford. It furthers the University's objective of excellence in research, scholarship, and education by publishing worldwide. Oxford is a registered trade mark of Oxford University Press in the UK and in certain other countries.

First published in 2026

British Library Cataloguing in Publication Data

Data available

978-1-382-07217-5

10 9 8 7 6 5 4 3 2 1

The manufacturing process conforms to the environmental regulations of the country of origin.

Printed in India by Multivista Global Pvt. Ltd

The manufacturer's authorised representative in the EU for product safety is Oxford University Press España S.A. of el Parque Empresarial San Fernando de Henares, Avenida de Castilla, 2 - 28830 Madrid (www.oup.es/en or product.safety@oup.com). OUP España S.A. also acts as importer into Spain of products made by the manufacturer.

Acknowledgements
Written by Craig Barton, Charlotte Hawthorne, Jemma Sherwood, Dan Draper, Katie Wood, Helen Konstantine, Paulo Ferro, Sudeep Gokarakonda

Cover: Patrick Hruby.

Artwork by Aptara Inc., QBS Learning, Thomson Digital, Pantek Arts Ltd, PDQ Media, and Oxford University Press.

Every effort has been made to contact copyright holders of material reproduced in this book. Any omissions will be rectified in subsequent printings if notice is given to the publisher.

MIX
Paper | Supporting responsible forestry
FSC® C199630
FSC www.fsc.org

Contents

About this Workbook

This write-in Workbook is for use with *Oxford International Maths: Student Book 8 (Lower Secondary)*. It can be used for extra practice in class or for homework activities.

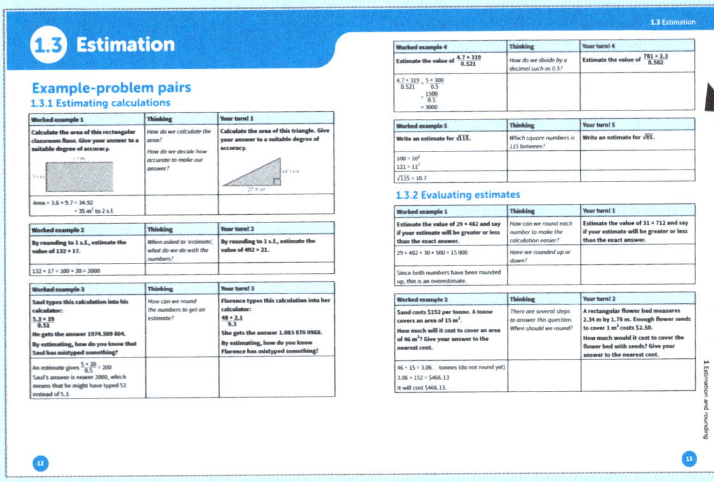

The example-problem pair exercises from the Student Book are included for you to write your working and answers on. There are also additional example-problem pairs to help you build your confidence.

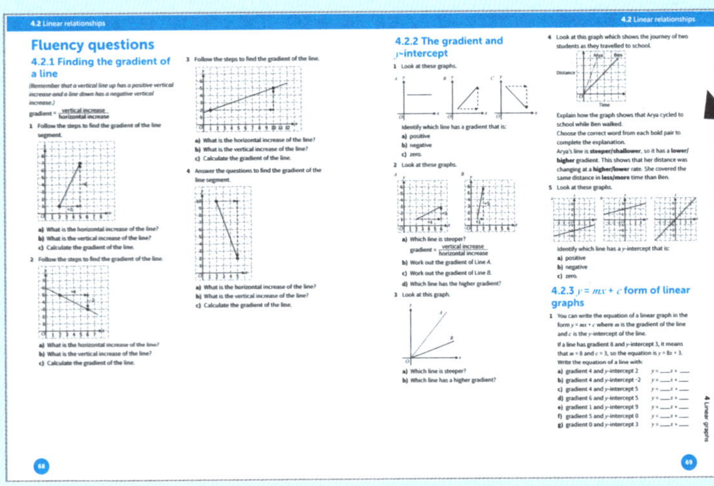

The extra fluency questions in this book are designed to support your fluency for each subsection from the Student Book.

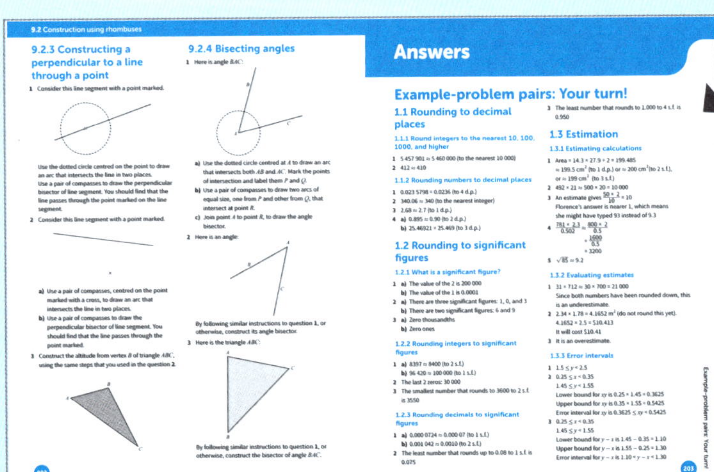

The answers are included at the back of the book, so you can easily check your own work and find out how you are doing.

How to use example-problem pairs

Example-problem pair (EPP) grids are a special type of worked example that help you understand what you are doing at each step and why.

There are lots of different ways you can use the example-problem pairs. Here is one possible way:

1 Start with the **Worked example** on the left.

2 Think about each line of working using the questions in the **Thinking** column.

Worked example	Thinking	Your turn!
Write $8 \times 8 \times 8 \times 8 \times 8$ in index notation.	*Are we repeatedly multiplying the same number?* Yes, so I need to count how many times 8 has been multiplied	**Write $9 \times 9 \times 9 \times 9 \times 9$ in index notation.**
There are 5 copies of the number 8 being multiplied	*How many times are we multiplying that number?* I counted the number of 8s that were written	
8 is the base number and 5 is the exponent	*Which value is the exponent and which is the base number?* The number being multiplied is the base number and the number of copies is the exponent	
So $8 \times 8 \times 8 \times 8 \times 8 = 8^5$		

3 Try to predict what the next line of working will be before you look at it.

4 Once you have thought about the example on the left, move to the **Your turn!** question on the right. This question will be very similar to the example you have just studied.

You can use the same thinking ideas to answer this question one step at a time.

The questions in the **Thinking** column help you think more generally about the example, so that you understand how to answer a different question.

The **Your turn!** question lets you apply the new idea with some support, so that you can be confident in what you need to do before you move on to the **Fluency** questions.

The example-problem pairs tables in this workbook are shown slightly differently to the ones in the Student Book so that more exercises can be included.

1.1 Rounding to decimal places

Example-problem pairs

1.1.1 Rounding integers to the nearest 10, 100, 1000, and higher

Worked example 1	Thinking	Your turn! 1
Round 795 602 to the nearest 10 000.	*Which digit do we look at when rounding?*	**Round 5 457 901 to the nearest 10 000.**
79⑤602 ≈ 800 000	*What does this digit tell us to do?*	

Worked example 2	Thinking	Your turn! 2
Round 538 to the nearest 10.	*Which digit do we look at when rounding?*	**Round 412 to the nearest 10.**
53⑧ ≈ 540	*What does this digit tell us to do?*	

1.1.2 Rounding numbers to decimal places

Worked example 1	Thinking	Your turn! 1
Round 0.015 862 to 4 decimal places.	*Which column do we look at to decide whether to round up or down?*	**Round 0.023 5798 to 4 decimal places.**
0.015 8⑥2 ≈ 0.0159 (to 4 d.p.)		

Worked example 2	Thinking	Your turn! 2
Round 16.53 to the nearest integer.	*Which digit tells us how to round to the nearest integer?*	**Round 340.06 to the nearest integer.**
16.⑤3 ≈ 17		

Worked example 3	Thinking	Your turn! 3
Round 5.734 to 1 decimal place.	*What digit do we look at to round to 1 decimal place?* *What does this digit tell us to do?*	**Round 2.68 to 1 decimal place.**
5.7③4 ≈ 5.7 (to 1 d.p.)		

Worked example 4	Thinking	Your turn! 4
Round: **a) 12.307 to 2 decimal places.**	*What digit do we look at to round to 2 decimal places?* *What does this digit tell us to do?*	**Round:** **a) 0.895 to 2 decimal places.**
12.30 ⑦ ≈ 12.31 (to 2 d.p.)		
b) 0.7195 to 3 decimal places.	*What digit do we look at to round to 3 decimal places?*	**b) 25.469 21 to 3 decimal places.**
0.719 ⑤ ≈ 0.720 (to 3 d.p.)	*What does this digit tell us to do?*	

Fluency questions

1.1.1 Round integers to the nearest 10, 100, 1000, and higher

1 Use the number lines to round each number to the nearest 10.

a) 5

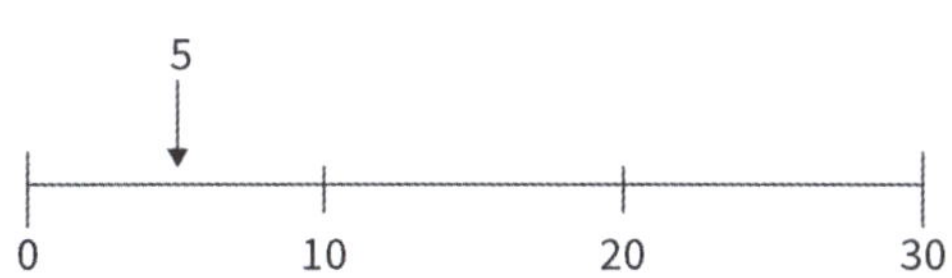

b) 467

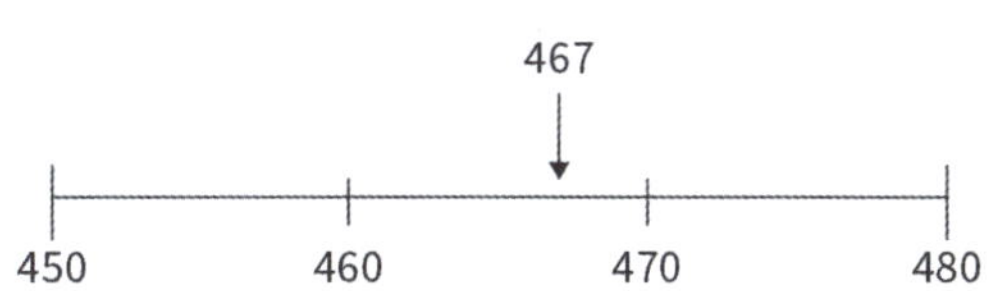

2 Use the number lines to round each number to the nearest 100.

a) 75

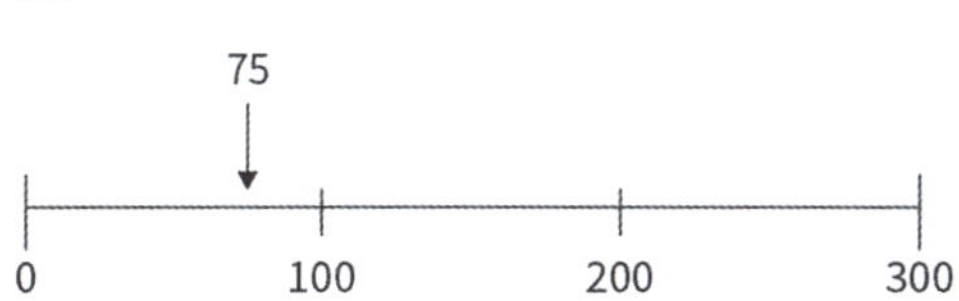

b) 7350

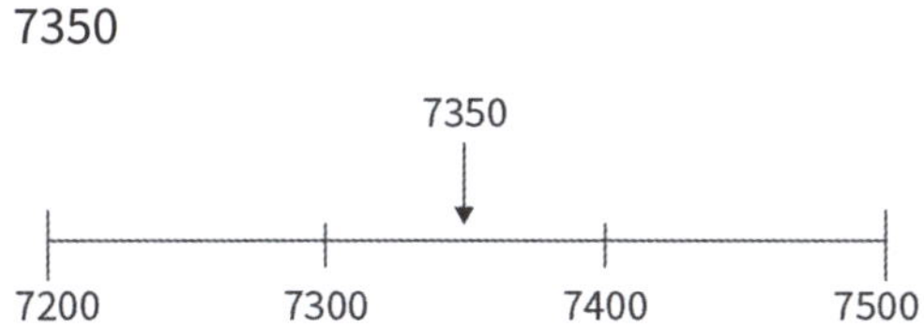

3 Use the number lines to round each number to the nearest 1000.

a) 850

b) 12 300

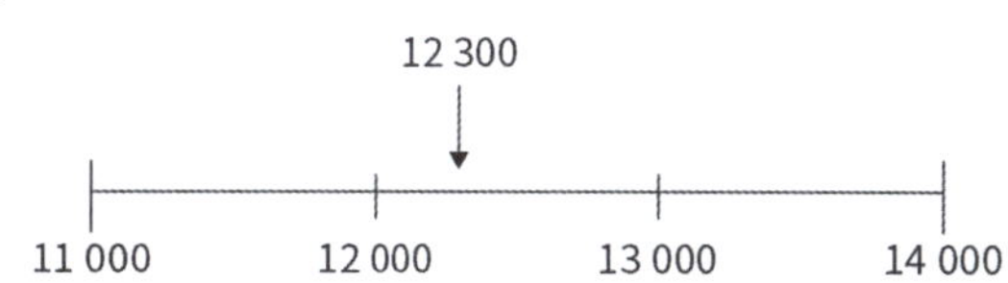

4 Use the number lines to round each number to the nearest 10 000.

a) 13 500

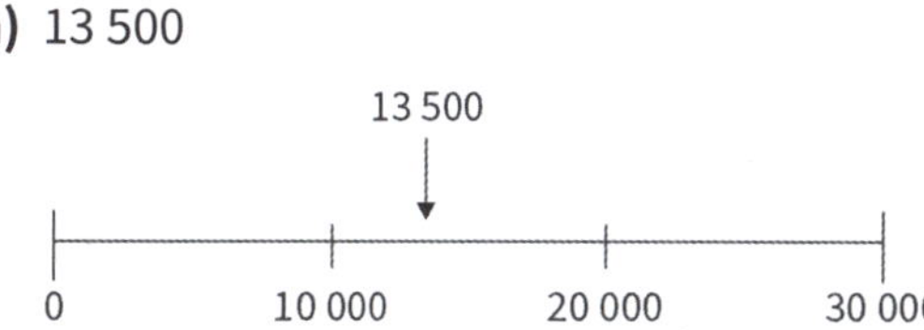

b) 848 500

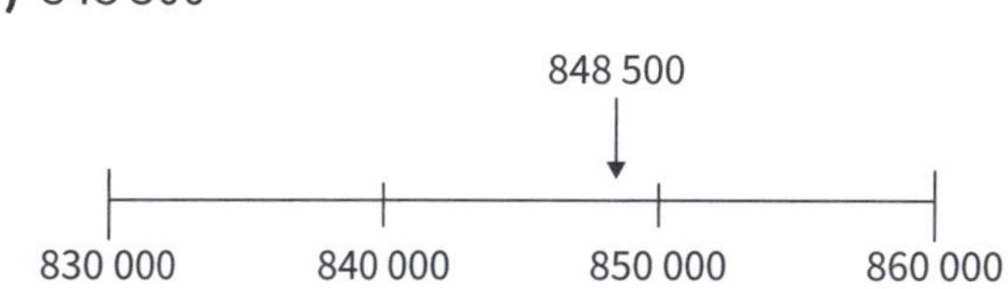

1.1.2 Rounding numbers to decimal places

1 Use the number lines to round each number to 1 decimal place.

a) 3.18

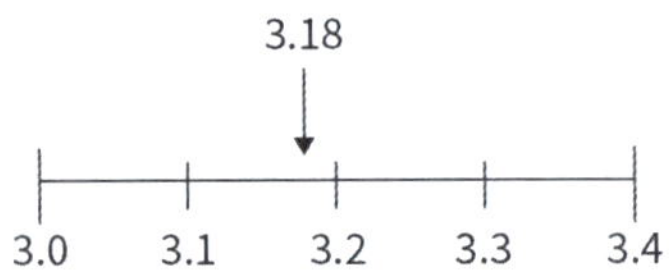

b) 0.85

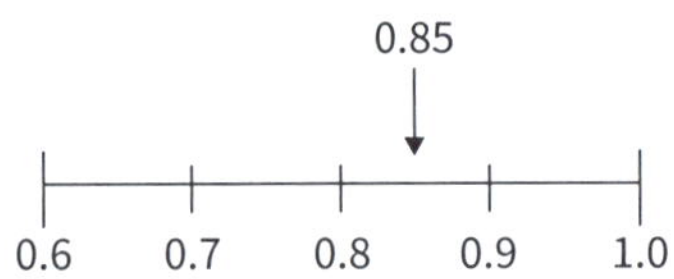

c) 16.425

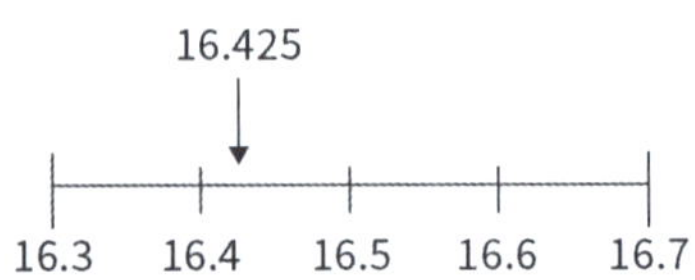

2 Use the number lines to round each number to 2 decimal places.

a) 28.365

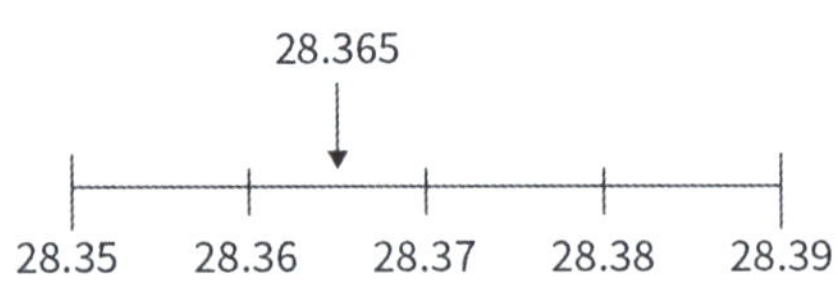

b) 6.028

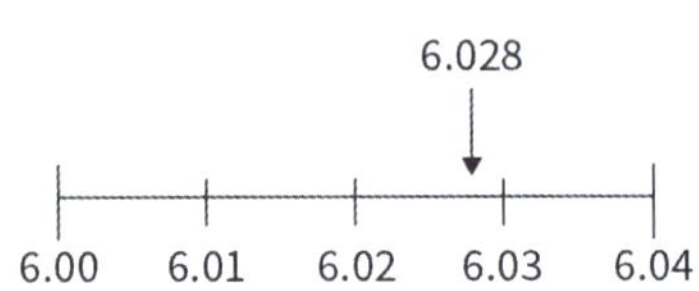

c) 0.8925

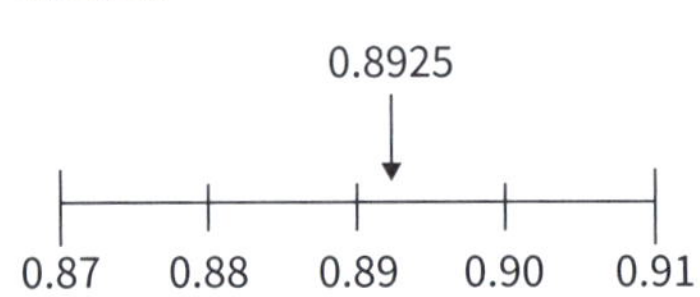

3 Use the number lines to round each number to 3 decimal places.

a) 7.9214

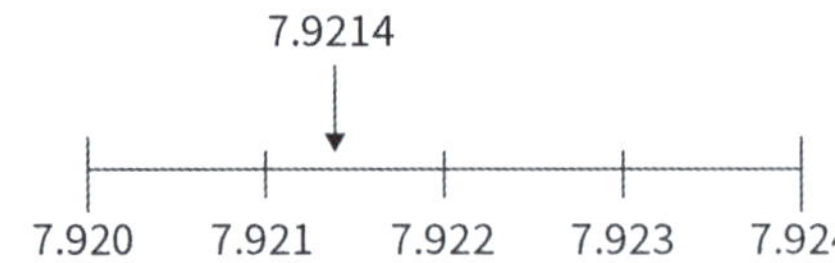

b) 0.3225

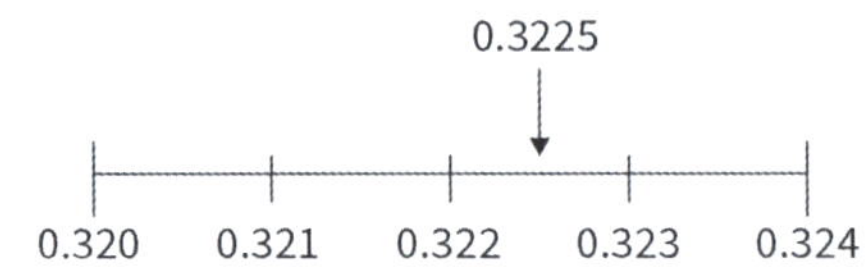

c) 150.428 75

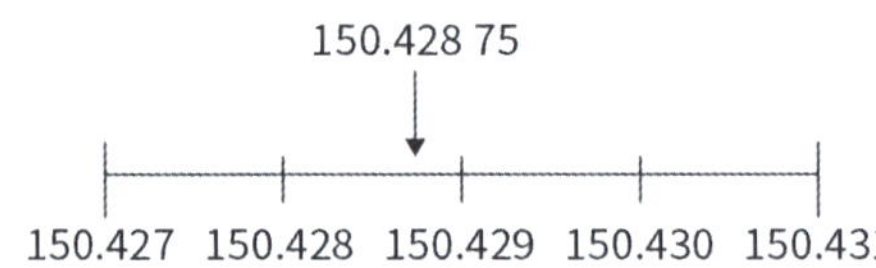

4 Use the number lines to round each number to 4 decimal places.

a) 0.189 55

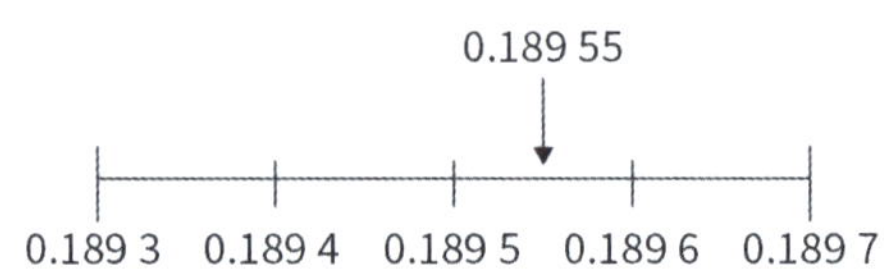

b) 2.761 89

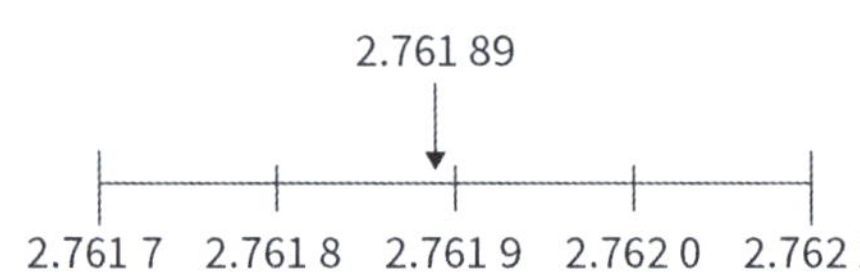

c) 10.489 525

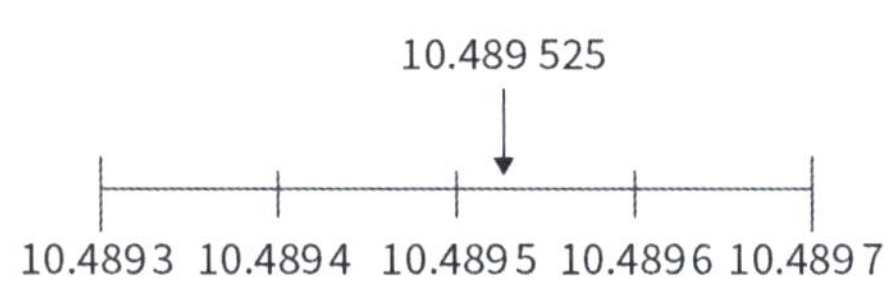

1.2 Rounding to significant figures

Example-problem pairs

1.2.1 What is a significant figure?

Worked example 1	Thinking	Your turn! 1
Copy each number and circle the first significant figure. **Write the value of the significant figure.** **a) 38 024** **b) 0.007 91**		**Copy each number and circle the first significant figure.** **Write the value of the significant figure.** **a) 260 512** **b) 0.000 104**
a) (3) 8 024 The value of the 3 is 30 000.	*Where is the first non-zero digit in the number?*	
b) 0.00(7) 91 The value of the 7 is 0.007.	*Where is the first non-zero digit in this decimal number?*	

Worked example 2	Thinking	Your turn! 2
How many significant figures are there in each number? **a) 0.004 785** **b) 0.010 503**	*Which digits are significant, and which are placeholders?*	**How many significant figures are there in each number?** **a) 0.0103** **b) 0.0069**
a) There are 4 significant figures: 4, 7, 8, and 5.		
b) There are 5 significant figures: 1, 0, 5, 0, and 3.		

Worked example 3	Thinking	Your turn! 3
What is the value of the first significant zero in each number? **a) 38 024** **b) 0.010 503**	*Which zeros are significant, and which are placeholders?*	**What is the value of the first significant zero in each number?** **a) 0.0103** **b) 90.060**
a) 38(0)24 Zero hundreds		
b) 0.01(0)503 Zero thousandths		

1.2.2 Rounding integers to significant figures

Worked example 1	Thinking	Your turn! 1
Round: **a) 45 680 to 2 significant figures** **b) 987 to 1 significant figure.**	*What are the first two significant figures and what is their value?*	**Round:** **a) 8397 to 2 significant figures** **b) 96 420 to 1 significant figure.**
a) 45 680 ≈ 46 000 (to 2 s.f.)	*How do we decide to round up or down?*	
b) 987 ≈ 1000 (to 1 s.f.)	*What is the first significant figure and what does the next figure tell us? How many placeholders will we need?*	

Worked example 2	Thinking	Your turn! 2
A number is rounded to give 6000 to 3 significant figures. **Which digits are not significant figures?**	*How many digits are significant and what does that leave us with?*	**A number is rounded to give 30 000 to 3 significant figures.** **Which digits are not significant figures?**
600⓪		

Worked example 3	Thinking	Your turn! 3
A number is rounded to 2 significant figures to get 720. **What is the smallest the original number could be?**	*What digits would round up a number?* *What digits would round down a number?*	**A number is rounded to 2 significant figures to get 3600.** **What is the smallest the original number could be?**
The smallest number that rounds to 720 to 2 s.f. is 715.		

1.2.3 Rounding decimals to significant figures

Worked example 1	Thinking	Your turn! 1
a) Round 0.003 712 to 1 significant figure.	*What is the first significant figure?*	**a) Round 0.000 0724 to 1 significant figure.**
0.003 712 ≈ 0.004 (to 1 s.f.)	*Do we need to round up or down?*	
b) Round 0.080 25 to 2 significant figures.	*How many significant figures do we need to write in our answer?*	**b) Round 0.001 042 to 2 significant figures.**
0.080 25 ≈ 0.080 (to 2 s.f.)		

Worked example 2	Thinking	Your turn! 2
A number is rounded to 0.0023 to 2 significant figures. **What is the least the number could have been?**	*What numbers would round up to the given number?*	**A number is rounded to 0.08 to 1 significant figure.** **What is the least the number could have been?**
The least number that rounds up to 0.0023 to 2 s.f. is 0.002 25.		

Worked example 3	Thinking	Your turn! 3
A number is rounded to 4 significant figures to get 14.04. **What is the least the number could have been?**	*What numbers would round down to the given number?*	**A number is rounded to 4 significant figures to get 1.000.** **What is the least the number could have been?**
The least number that rounds up to 14.04 to 4 s.f. is 14.035.		

Fluency questions

1.2.1 What is a significant figure?

Circle the first significant figure in each number.

1 30

2 10 000.4

3 705

4 2.05

5 0.05

6 0.0001

7 0.000 4002

8 0.000 007 502

1.2.2 Rounding integers to significant figures

1 Round the number 652 to:

a) 1 significant figure

b) 2 significant figures.

2 Round the number 8127 to:

a) 1 significant figure

b) 2 significant figures

c) 3 significant figures.

3 Round the number 14 815 to:

a) 1 significant figure

b) 2 significant figures

c) 3 significant figures

d) 4 significant figures.

4 Round the number 215 639 to:

a) 1 significant figure

b) 2 significant figures

c) 3 significant figures

d) 4 significant figures

e) 5 significant figures.

1.2.3 Rounding decimals to significant figures

1 Round each number to 1 significant figure.

a) 26

b) 2.6

c) 0.26

d) 0.026

e) 0.0026

f) 0.000 26

g) 0.000 026

2 Round each number to 1 significant figure.

a) 0.72

b) 0.045

c) 1.263

d) 0.008 92

e) 2300.158

1.3 Estimation

Example-problem pairs

1.3.1 Estimating calculations

Worked example 1	**Thinking**	**Your turn! 1**
Calculate the area of this rectangular classroom floor. Give your answer to a suitable degree of accuracy. 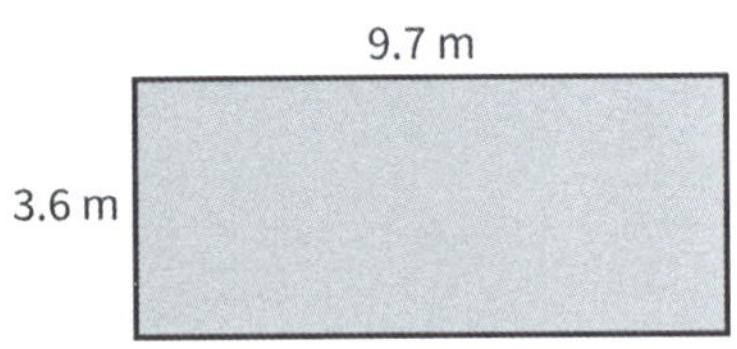	*How do we calculate the area?* *How do we decide how accurate to make our answer?*	**Calculate the area of this triangle. Give your answer to a suitable degree of accuracy.** 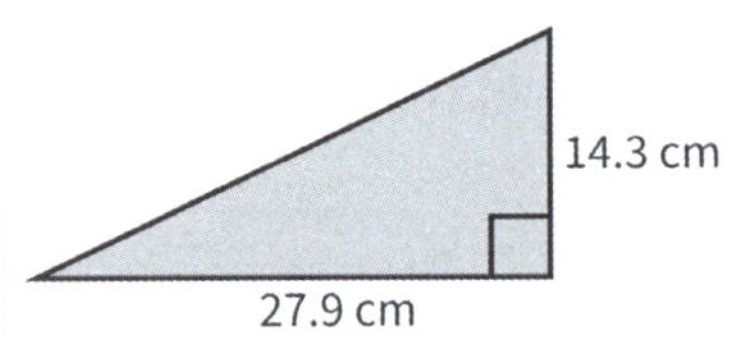
Area = $3.6 \times 9.7 = 34.92$ $= 35\ \text{m}^2$ to 2 s.f.		

Worked example 2	**Thinking**	**Your turn! 2**
By rounding to 1 s.f., estimate the value of 132 × 17.	*When asked to 'estimate', what do we do with the numbers?*	**By rounding to 1 s.f., estimate the value of 492 × 21.**
$132 \times 17 \approx 100 \times 20 = 2000$		

Worked example 3	**Thinking**	**Your turn! 3**
Saul types this calculation into his calculator: $\dfrac{5.3 \times 19}{0.51}$ **He gets the answer 1974.509 804.** **By estimating, how do you know that Saul has mistyped something?**	*How can we round the numbers to get an estimate?*	**Florence types this calculation into her calculator:** $\dfrac{48 \times 2.1}{9.3}$ **She gets the answer 1.083 870 0968.** **By estimating, how do you know Florence has mistyped something?**
An estimate gives $\dfrac{5 \times 20}{0.5} = 200$ Saul's answer is nearer 2000, which means that he might have typed 53 instead of 5.3.		

Worked example 4	Thinking	Your turn! 4
Estimate the value of $\frac{4.7 \times 319}{0.521}$	*How do we divide by a decimal such as 0.5?*	**Estimate the value of $\frac{781 \times 2.3}{0.502}$**
$\frac{4.7 \times 319}{0.521} \approx \frac{5 \times 300}{0.5}$ $= \frac{1500}{0.5}$ $= 3000$		

Worked example 5	Thinking	Your turn! 5
Write an estimate for $\sqrt{115}$.	*Which square numbers is 115 between?*	**Write an estimate for $\sqrt{85}$.**
$100 = 10^2$ $121 = 11^2$		
$\sqrt{115} \approx 10.7$		

1.3.2 Evaluating estimates

Worked example 1	Thinking	Your turn! 1
Estimate the value of 29 × 482 and say if your estimate will be greater or less than the exact answer.	*How can we round each number to make the calculation easier?*	**Estimate the value of 31 × 712 and say if your estimate will be greater or less than the exact answer.**
$29 \times 482 \approx 30 \times 500 = 15\,000$	*Have we rounded up or down?*	
Since both numbers have been rounded up, this is an overestimate.		

Worked example 2	Thinking	Your turn! 2
Sand costs \$152 per tonne. A tonne covers an area of 15 m^2. **How much will it cost to cover an area of 46 m^2? Give your answer to the nearest cent.**	*There are several steps to answer this question. When should we round?*	**A rectangular flower bed measures 2.34 m by 1.78 m. Enough flower seeds to cover 1 m^2 costs \$2.50.** **How much would it cost to cover the flower bed with seeds? Give your answer to the nearest cent.**
$46 \div 15 = 3.06\ldots$ tonnes (do not round yet) $3.06 \times 152 = \$466.13$ It will cost \$466.13.		

Worked example 3	Thinking	Your turn! 3
Druv wants to estimate the answer to $\frac{21}{\sqrt{45}}$. **Druv approximates this to $\frac{21}{\sqrt{49}} = \frac{21}{7} = 3$.** **Is Druv's answer an overestimate or an underestimate?**	*How does the direction of rounding the root affect the answer?*	**Sofia wants to estimate the answer to $\frac{50}{\sqrt{27}}$.** **Sofia approximates this to $\frac{50}{\sqrt{25}} = \frac{50}{5} = 10$.** **Is Sofia's answer an overestimate or an underestimate?**
It is an underestimate.		

1.3.3 Error intervals

Worked example 1	Thinking	Your turn! 1
A number, x, rounds to 80 to the nearest 10. **Write the error interval for this number.**	*What is the first number that rounds up to this value?* *When do numbers stop rounding down to this value?*	**A number, x, rounds to 2 to the nearest 10.** **Write the error interval for this number.**
75 is the lower bound.		
85 is the upper bound.	*What symbols do we write in an error interval?*	
$75 \leq x < 85$		

Worked example 2	Thinking	Your turn! 2
$x = 80$ to one significant figure. **$y = 320$ to two significant figures.** **What is the error interval for xy?**	*What are the error intervals for x and y?*	**$x = 0.3$ to one significant figure.** **$y = 1.5$ to two significant figures.** **What is the error interval for xy?**
$75 \leq x < 85$ $315 \leq y < 325$	*How do we work out the lower and upper bounds for a multiplication?*	
Lower bound for xy is $75 \times 315 = 23\,625$ Upper bound for xy is $85 \times 325 = 27\,625$ Error interval for xy is $23\,625 \leq xy < 27\,625$		

Worked example 3	Thinking	Your turn! 3
$x = 80$ to one significant figure. **$y = 320$ to two significant figures.** **What is the error interval for $y - x$?**	*What are the error intervals for x and y?*	**$x = 0.3$ to one significant figure.** **$y = 1.5$ to two significant figures.** **What is the error interval for $y - x$?**
$75 \le x < 85$ $315 \le y < 325$	*How do we work out the lower and upper bounds for a subtraction?*	
Lower bound for $y - x$ is $315 - 85 = 230$ Upper bound for $y - x$ is $325 - 75 = 250$	*Which inequality symbols should we use?*	
Error interval for $y - x$ is $230 < y - x < 250$		

Fluency questions

1.3.1 Estimating calculations

1 A group of students take some measurements to compare their hand spans. Which set of results use the most sensible degree of accuracy?

a) 14.262 cm, 12.827 cm, 12.183 cm (to 5 significant figures)

b) 14.26 cm, 12.82 cm, 12.18 cm (to 4 significant figures)

c) 14.2 cm, 12.8 cm, 12.1 cm (to 3 significant figures)

d) 14 cm, 12 cm, 12 cm (to 2 significant figures)

e) 10 cm, 10 cm, 10 cm (to 1 significant figure)

2 We can use rounding to help us to estimate calculations. First, you round the numbers to a sensible degree of accuracy and then you estimate the calculation.

For example:

$$205 \times 5.82 \approx 200 \times 6 = 1200$$

Fill in the blanks to complete each estimate.

a) $452 \div 9.61 \approx 500 \div 10 =$ ______.

b) $3187 + 9025 \approx 3000 +$ ______ $=$ ______.

c) $18.42 \times 1201 \approx$ ______ $\times 1000 =$ ______.

d) $581.045 - 249.968 \approx 580 -$ ______ $=$ ______.

e) $1.4983 + 0.5204 \approx$ ______ $+$ ______ $=$ ______.

f) $8.968 \times 3241.2 \approx$ ______ $\times$ ______ $=$ ______.

g) $121.02 \div 19.9983 \approx$ ______ $\div$ ______ $=$ ______.

h) $74\,925 - 4989.65 \approx$ ______ $-$ ______ $=$ ______.

1.3.2 Evaluating estimates

1 State whether each estimate is an overestimate or an underestimate.

a) $392 + 98 \approx 400 + 100 = 500$

b) $2530 + 1029 \approx 2500 + 1000 = 3500$

c) $7560 + 1002 \approx 8000 + 1000 = 9000$

2 State whether each estimate is an overestimate or an underestimate.

a) $3031 \times 2.142 \approx 3000 \times 2 = 6000$

b) $482 \times 9.792 \approx 500 \times 10 = 600$

c) $2471 \times 4.989 \approx 2000 \times 5 = 10\,000$

1.3.3 Error intervals

1 a) For each number, write down whether or not it rounds to 500 to 1 significant figure.

- **i.** 499
- **ii.** 550
- **iii.** 501
- **iv.** 549.99
- **v.** 599
- **vi.** 449.99
- **vii.** 450

b) Using the numbers in part **a**, write down:

- **i.** the lowest number that rounds to 500 to 1 significant figure
- **ii.** the highest number that rounds to 500 to 1 significant figure.

2 a) For each number, write down whether or not it rounds to 300 to 2 significant figures.

- **i.** 299
- **ii.** 301
- **iii.** 305
- **iv.** 291
- **v.** 295
- **vi.** 304.99
- **vii.** 294.99

b) Using the numbers in part **a**, write down:

- **i.** the lowest number that rounds to 300 to 2 significant figures
- **ii.** the highest number that rounds to 300 to 2 significant figures.

3 a) For each number, write down whether or not it rounds to 800 to 3 significant figures.

- **i.** 801
- **ii.** 800.5
- **iii.** 798.5
- **iv.** 800.49
- **v.** 799.49
- **vi.** 810.21
- **vii.** 799.5

b) Using the numbers in part **a**, write down:

- **i.** the lowest number that rounds to 800 to 3 significant figures
- **ii.** the highest number that rounds to 800 to 3 significant figures.

2.1 Solutions to linear equations

Example-problem pairs

2.1.1 What is a linear equation?

Worked example 1	Thinking	Your turn! 1
Decide whether each of these mathematical statements is a linear equation.		**Decide whether each of these mathematical statements is a linear equation.**
a) $2 + 3x = 70$	*Is there an equals symbol?*	**a)** $7 + 2x = 12$
The equals symbol means it is an equation.	*What is the exponent of the unknown?*	
x has an exponent of 1, so it is a linear equation.		
b) $7x - 2 + 19$	*Is there an equals symbol?*	**b)** $5x - 12 + 7x - 2$
This is an expression.		
c) $5t(3 + t) = 0$	*Is there an equals symbol?*	**c)** $2x(3x + 1) = 0$
The equals symbol means it is an equation.	*How do we find the exponent of the unknown?*	
Expanding gives: $15t + 5t^2 = 0$ The greatest exponent of t is 2, so this is a non-linear equation.	*What is the greatest exponent of the unknown?*	

Worked example 2	Thinking	Your turn! 2
Decide whether each of these mathematical statements is a linear equation.		**Decide whether each of these mathematical statements is a linear equation.**
a) $5x - 3 = 3(x - 1) + 2x$	*Is there an equals symbol?*	**a)** $7x + 7 - x = 6(x + 2) - 5$
The equals symbol means it could be an equation or an identity.	*How can we check if it is an equation or an identity?*	
Simplify the left-hand side: $3(x - 1) + 2x = 3x - 3 + 2x$ $= 5x - 3$ So, $5x - 3 = 5x - 3$ This is an **identity** because both sides have the same expression.		

b) $2 \geq 7m + 9$	*Is there an equals symbol?*	**b)** $5x - 12 \leq 7x - 2$
No equals symbol means this is not an equation. This is a linear inequality because of the ≥ symbol and because the unknown has an exponent of 1.		

2.1.2 Solutions to equations

Worked example 1	**Thinking**	**Your turn! 1**
By substituting, find out which of the values 2, 3, or 4 is the solution to the equation $7x - 6 = 2x + 9$	*How do we substitute into an equation?*	**By substituting, find out which of the values 2, 3, or 4 is the solution to the equation** $5x - 3 = 3x + 5$
Try $x = 2$ $7 \times 2 - 6 = 2 \times 2 + 9$ $14 - 6 = 4 + 9$ $8 \neq 13$ so $x = 2$ is not the solution.	*In which order do we carry out the operations?*	
Try $x = 3$ $7 \times 3 - 6 = 2 \times 3 + 9$ $21 - 6 = 6 + 9$ $15 = 15$ so $x = 3$ is the solution to the equation.	*How do we know when we have found the correct solution?*	

Worked example 2	**Thinking**	**Your turn! 2**
Is $x = 6$ the solution to each equation?		**Is $x = 9$ the solution to each equation?**
a) $x - 2 = \frac{x}{2} + 1$	*How do we substitute into the equation?*	**a)** $x - 3 = \frac{x}{3} + 2$
Substitute $x = 6$ on both sides.	*How do we substitute into the fractional term?*	
$6 - 2 = \frac{6}{2} + 1$ $4 = 3 + 1$ $4 = 4$ So $x = 6$ is the solution.	*In which order to we carry out the operations?*	
b) $2x + 8 = 4x - 6$		**b)** $3x + 10 = 5x - 8$
Substitute $x = 6$ on both sides. $2 \times 6 + 8 = 4 \times 6 - 6$ $12 + 8 = 24 - 6$ $20 \neq 18$ So $x = 6$ is not the solution.	*How do we know when we have found the correct solution?*	

Worked example 3	Thinking	Your turn! 3
Decide whether each equation has no solutions, one solution or many solutions.	*How do we decide how many solutions an equation has?*	**Decide whether each equation has no solutions, one solution or many solutions.**
a) $4x + 3 = 11$	*How many unknowns does the equation have?*	**a)** $p + 2q = 8$
One solution, $x = 2$. A linear equation with one unknown has one solution.		
b) $m + 5 = m$	*Can we solve this equation?*	**b)** $2a = 4a$
No solutions. You cannot add 5 to a number and get the number you started with.		
c) $a + b = 11$	*How many unknowns does the equation have?*	**c)** $3x + 12 = 3x$
Many solutions. There are infinitely many pairs of numbers that sum to 11.		

2.1.3 Maintaining equality

Worked example 1	Thinking	Your turn! 1
Decide whether the step performed between the two equations has maintained equality or not.		**Decide whether the step performed between the two equations has maintained equality or not.**
a) $2x + 7 = 18$ ↓ $2x + 9 = 20$	*What happened to the term on both sides?*	**a)** $4x - 2 = 10$ ↓ $4x - 5 = 13$
2 was added to both sides, so equality is maintained.		
b) $6 + 7x = 2 - 3x$ ↓ $6 + 9x = 2 - 5x$		**b)** $3x + 7 = 15$ ↓ $4x + 7 = 15 + x$
$2x$ was added on the left, but $-2x$ was added on the right so equality is not maintained.	*How could equality have been maintained?*	
c) $3x + 5 = x + 2$ ↓ $9x + 15 = 3(x + 2)$		**c)** $5x + 1 = x - 3$ ↓ $20x + 1 = 4x - 12$
Both sides were multiplied by 3, so equality is maintained.		

Worked example 2	Thinking	Your turn! 2
Here is an equation: $2n - 4 = 10$ **Write down three more examples of equations that have the same solution.**	*How can we find a family of equations?*	**Here is an equation:** $3a + 5 = 11$ **Write down three more examples of equations that have the same solution.**
$2n - 4 = 10$ $+5 \downarrow \quad \downarrow +5$ $2n + 1 = 15$	*How do we maintain equality?*	
$2n - 4 = 10$ $-1 \downarrow \quad \downarrow -1$ $2n - 5 = 9$		
$2n - 4 = 10$ $\times 3 \downarrow \quad \downarrow \times 3$ $6n - 12 = 30$		

Worked example 3	Thinking	Your turn! 3
Decide whether the step performed between the two equations has maintained equality or not.		**Decide whether the step performed between the two equations has maintained equality.**
a) $3x - 6 = x$ $\downarrow$ $x - 2 = \frac{x}{3}$	*What has happened to the terms on both sides?*	**a)** $5x = x + 15$ $\downarrow$ $x = \frac{x}{5} + 3$
Both sides have been divided by 3, so equality has been maintained.		
b) $2x + 5 = 3x + 2$ $\downarrow$ $5 - x = 2$		**b)** $4x + 2 = 3x + 7$ $\downarrow$ $2 - x = 7$
$3x$ has been subtracted from both sides, so equality has been maintained.		
c) $2x + 7 = 13$ $\downarrow$ $2x + 6 = 14$	*What has happened to the terms on both sides?*	**c)** $3x + 4 = 8$ $\downarrow$ $3x + 6 = 10$
$2x + 7 = 13$ $-1 \downarrow \quad \downarrow +1$ $2x + 6 \neq 14$	*How could equality have been maintained?*	
1 has been subtracted on the left, but 1 has been added on the right. Equality has not been maintained.		

Fluency questions

2.1.1 What is a linear equation?

1 Circle the symbol(s) that **must** be found in an equation.

a) +
b) =
c) ×
d) <

2 Tick (✓) the statements that are equations.

a) $3p + 2 - 5$ ☐
b) $4y - 2 = 0$ ☐
c) $1.8x = 5x - \frac{1}{2}$ ☐
d) $8z - 2 < 12$ ☐
e) $7 \neq 15 - 6x$ ☐
f) $2a = 4b - 3$ ☐

3 Look at this equation and answer the questions about it.

$$2 - 5y = 8x + 7$$

a) Write down any terms in the equation that contain a variable. __________

b) Do any of those terms have a variable with an exponent bigger than 1? __________

c) Do any of those terms have variables multiplied together? __________

d) Linear equations cannot have variables with exponents bigger than 1 or have variables multiplied together. Is this equation linear?

____

4 Look at this equation and answer the questions about it.

$$3x^2 + 4y = 2xy + 5$$

a) Write down any terms in the equation that contain a variable. __________

b) Do any of those terms contain a variable with an exponent bigger than 1? __________

c) Do any of those terms contain variables multiplied together? __________

d) Linear equations cannot have variables with exponents bigger than 1 or have variables multiplied together. Is this equation linear?

____

2.1.2 Solutions to equations

1 If the number 5 is put in the empty box, will it make these statements true?

a) $7 \times \square = 29 + 6$ Yes/ No

b) $2 \times 3 = \square - 1$ Yes/ No

c) $\frac{40}{\square} = \frac{56}{7}$ Yes/ No

d) $2 \times (5 + \square) = 4 \times \square$ Yes/ No

e) $2 \times (\square + 2) = (\square - 3) \times 6$ Yes/ No

2 Work out whether 2, 3, or 5 should go in the empty box(es) to make each statement true.

a) $\square + 4 \times \square = 11 + 14$ ______

b) $3 \times \square - 4 = \frac{15}{3}$ ______

c) $\frac{30}{\square} = \square + 1$ ______

d) $\square + 6 = \square \times 3$ ______

e) $\square + 8 = 2 \times (\square + 3)$ ______

3 Work out the number that goes in each empty box to make these statements true.

a) $\square - 6 = 14$ ______

b) $48 = \square \times 12$ ______

c) $3 \times 6 = 2 + \square$ ______

d) $25 - 4 = \square \times 3$ ______

e) $\frac{\square}{4} = \frac{48}{6}$ ______

2.1.3 Maintaining equality

1 Answer true or false to each statement.

a) $x = 6$ is the solution to the equations $x + 2 = 8$ and $x + 5 = 10$.

____

b) $x = 8$ is the solution to the equations $24 = 3x$ and $\frac{24}{x} = 3$.

____

c) $x = 2$ is the solution to the equations $x + 4 = 6$ and $2x + 8 = 12$.

____

d) $x = 4$ is the solution to the equations $5x = 20$ and $5x - 2 = 22$.

____

e) $x = 3$ is the solution to the equations $5x = 15$, $x = \frac{15}{5}$, and $x - 2 = 1$.

____

2 Starting with the equation $x + 3 = 10$, a student performs an operation to get the new equation $x = 10 - 3$

a) Is $x = 7$ the solution to the equation $x + 3 = 10$? Yes / No

b) Is $x = 7$ the solution to the equation $x = 10 - 3$? Yes / No

c) Has equality been maintained? Yes / No

3 Starting with the equation $6x = 24$, a student performs an operation to get the new equation $6 = \frac{24}{x}$

a) Is $x = 4$ the solution to the equation $6x = 24$? Yes / No

b) Is $x = 4$ the solution to the equation $6 = \frac{24}{x}$? Yes / No

c) Has equality been maintained? Yes / No

4 Starting with the equation $2x + 1 = 7$, a student performs an operation to get the new equation $2x + 5 = 10$

a) Is $x = 3$ the solution to the equation $2x + 1 = 7$? Yes / No

b) Is $x = 3$ the solution to the equation $2x + 5 = 10$? Yes / No

c) Has equality been maintained? Yes / No

2.2 One-step linear equations

Example-problem pairs

2.2.1 Additive steps

Worked example 1	Thinking	Your turn! 1
Solve the equation $12.6 = 7.8 + g$	*What can we add to isolate the unknown?*	**Solve the equation $8.7 = 3.9 + v$**
$12.6 = 7.8 + g$ $12.6 - 7.8 = 7.8 - 7.8 + g$ $4.8 = g$		

Worked example 2	Thinking	Your turn! 2
Solve the equation $f + 9 = 17$	*What can we add to isolate the unknown?*	**Solve the equation $t + 11 = 19$**
$f + 9 = 17$ $f + 9 - 9 = 17 - 9$ $f = 8$	*How can we check the solution?*	
Check: left-hand side = 8 + 9 = 17 left-hand side = right-hand side		

Worked example 3	Thinking	Your turn! 3
Solve the equation $15 = h - 7$	*What can we add to isolate the unknown?*	**Solve the equation $8 = w - 11$**
$15 = h - 7$ $15 + 7 = h - 7 + 7$ $22 = h$	*How can we check the solution?*	
Check: right-hand side = 22 − 7 = 15 left-hand side = right-hand side		

Worked example 4	Thinking	Your turn! 4
Solve:		**Solve:**
a) $y - 5 = 4 \times 4 - 6$	*How can we simplify the equation?*	**a)** $b + 4 = 15 - 2 \times 3$
$y - 5 = 4 \times 4 - 6$ $y - 5 = 16 - 6$ $y - 5 = 10$	*Which operation do we do first?*	
$y - 5 + 5 = 10 + 5$ $y = 15$	*What can we do to isolate the unknown?*	
b) $x + 2(3 + 5) = 20$	*How can we simplify the equation?*	**b)** $p + 1 + 4^2 = 10$
$x + 2(3 + 5) = 20$ $x + 2(8) = 20$ $x + 16 = 20$	*Which operation do we do first?*	
$x + 16 - 16 = 20 - 16$ $x = 4$	*What can we do to isolate the unknown?*	

2.2.2 Multiplicative steps

Worked example 1	Thinking	Your turn! 1
Solve $5x = 24$	*How can we isolate* x*?*	**Solve** $4x = 14$
$5x = 24$ $\frac{5x}{5} = \frac{24}{5}$ $x = 4.8$		

Worked example 2	Thinking	Your turn! 2
Solve $4x = 5 \times 2 - 2$	*How can we simplify the equation?*	**Solve** $3a = 4(7 - 1)$
$4x = 5 \times 2 - 2$ $4x = 10 - 2$ $4x = 8$	*Which operation do we do first?*	
$\frac{4x}{4} = \frac{8}{4}$ $x = 2$	*What can we do to isolate the unknown?*	

Worked example 3	Thinking	Your turn! 3
Solve $\frac{x}{3} = 18$	*How can we isolate x?*	**Solve $\frac{x}{5} = 15$**
$\frac{x}{3} \times 3 = 18 \times 3$ $x = 54$	*How can we check that the solution is correct.*	

Worked example 4	Thinking	Your turn! 4
Solve $\frac{x}{3} = 4.1 \times 3 - 2.5 \times 2$	*How can we simplify the equation?*	**Solve $\frac{x}{5} = 7^2 - 8.1 \times 6$**
$\frac{x}{3} = 4.1 \times 3 - 2.5 \times 4$ $\frac{x}{3} = 12.3 - 10$ $\frac{x}{3} = 2.3$	*Which operation do we do first?*	
$\frac{x}{3} \times 3 = 2.3 \times 3$ $x = 6.9$	*What can we do to isolate the unknown?*	

Fluency questions

2.2.1 Additive steps

1 Give the additive inverse of these numbers.

a) 7

b) −4

c) −1

d) 12

2 **Example:** Solve the equation $a + 8 = 10$

To isolate the unknown, you need to add the inverse of +8 to both sides.

The inverse of +8 is −8

Adding −8 to both sides of the equation gives:

$a + 8 - 8 = 10 - 8$

$a = 2$

a) Solve $x + 4 = 9$

I need to add the additive inverse of __________ to both sides:

$x + 4 = 9$ __________

$x =$ __________

b) Solve $y - 2 = 6$

I need to add the additive inverse of __________ to both sides:

$y - 2$ __________ $= 6$ __________

$y =$ __________

3 Solve:

a) $x + 2 = 3$

b) $y - 6 = 12$

c) $x - 14 = 10$

d) $y + 5 = 25$

2.2.2 Multiplicative steps

1 The multiplicative inverse of ÷ 3 is × 3

Give the multiplicative inverse of these:

a) ÷ 9

b) × 2

c) ÷ 10

d) × 12

2 Example: Solve the equation $5a = 10$

$5a$ means $5 \times a$

To isolate the unknown, you need to use the multiplicative inverse of × 5

The inverse of × 5 is ÷ 5

Dividing both sides of the equation by 5 gives:

$$\frac{5a}{5} = \frac{10}{5}$$

$$a = 2$$

Now solve $8x = 32$

__________ both sides of the equation by __________ gives:

$$\frac{8x}{\square} = \frac{32}{\square}$$

$x =$ __________

3 Solve:

a) $3x = 18$

b) $7y = 84$

c) $4x = 26$

d) $10y = 15$

4 **Example:** Solve the equation $\frac{b}{4} = 7$

$\frac{b}{4}$ means $b \div 4$

To isolate the unknown, you need to use the multiplicative inverse of ÷ 4

The inverse of ÷ 4 is × 4

Multiplying both sides of the equation by 4 gives:

$$\frac{b}{4} \times 4 = 7 \times 4$$

$$b = 28$$

a) Solve $\frac{x}{3} = 6$

__________ both sides of the equation by __________ gives:

$\frac{x}{3} \times$ ______ $= 6 \times$ ______

$x =$ ______

b) Solve $\frac{y}{5} = 4$

__________ both sides of the equation by __________ gives:

$\frac{y}{5} \times$ ______ $= 4 \times$ ______

$y =$ ______

2.3 Two-step linear equations

Example-problem pairs

2.3.1 Dealing with a negative coefficient of the unknown

Worked example 1	Thinking	Your turn! 1
Solve $3.1 - 2k = 1.9$	*How can we isolate the unknown?*	Solve $9.7 - 3x = 2.8$
$3.1 - 2k = 1.9$ $3.1 - 3.1 - 2k = 1.9 - 3.1$ $-2k = -1.2$ $\frac{-2k}{-2} = \frac{-1.2}{-2}$ $k = 0.6$	*What other step do we need to do to get the positive unknown?*	

Worked example 2	Thinking	Your turn! 2
Solve $17 - 2x = 1$	*How can we isolate the unknown?*	Solve $19 - 3y = 4$
$17 - 2x = 1$ $17 - 17 - 2x = 1 - 17$ $-2x = -16$	*What other step do we need to do to get the positive unknown?*	
$\frac{-2x}{-2} = \frac{-16}{-2}$ $x = 8$		

Worked example 3	Thinking	Your turn! 3
Solve $\frac{9}{5} - 3x = \frac{4}{5}$	*How can we isolate the unknown?*	Solve $\frac{1}{2} - 4q = -\frac{3}{2}$
$\frac{9}{5} - 3x = \frac{4}{5}$ $\frac{9}{5} - \frac{9}{5} - 3x = \frac{4}{5} - \frac{9}{5}$ $-3x = \frac{-5}{5}$ $-3x = -1$	*What other step do we need to do to get the positive unknown?*	
$\frac{-3x}{-3} = \frac{-1}{-3}$ $x = \frac{1}{3}$		

Worked example 4	Thinking	Your turn! 4
Solve 1.3 = 3.7 − 1.2k	*How can we isolate the unknown?*	**Solve 0.9 = 5.3 − 1.1d**
$1.3 = 3.7 - 1.2k$ $1.3 - 3.7 = 3.7 - 3.7 - 1.2k$ $-2.4 = -1.2k$	*What other step do we need to do to get the positive unknown?*	
$\frac{-2.4}{-1.2} = \frac{-1.2k}{-1.2}$ $2 = k$		

Worked example 5	Thinking	Your turn! 5
Solve 27 = 18.2 − m	*How can we make the coefficient of the unknown positive?*	**Solve 23 = 14.6 − y**
$27 = 18.2 - m$ $27 \times -1 = (18.2 - m) \times -1$ $-27 = -18.2 + m$ $-27 + 18.2 = -18.2 + 18.2 + m$ $-8.8 = m$	*Is the solution negative or positive? Does this make sense?*	

Worked example 6	Thinking	Your turn! 6
Solve 6 = 14 − x	*How can we make the coefficient of the unknown positive?*	**Solve 11 = 5 − x**
$6 = 14 - x$ $6 \times -1 = (14 - x) \times -1$ $-6 = -14 + x$	*How can we isolate the unknown?*	
$-6 + 14 = -14 + 14 + x$ $8 = x$	*Is the solution negative or positive? Does this make sense?*	

Worked example 7	Thinking	Your turn! 7
Solve 3.9 = −1.3x	*How can we make the coefficient of the unknown positive?*	**Solve −5.6 = −1.4t**
$3.9 = -1.3x$ $3.9 \times -1 = -1.3x \times -1$ $-3.9 = 1.3x$	*How can we isolate the unknown?*	
$\frac{-3.9}{1.3} = \frac{1.3x}{1.3}$ $-3 = x$	*Is the solution negative or positive? Does this make sense?*	

2.3.2 Solving equations that require more than one step

Worked example 1	Thinking	Your turn! 1
Solve $2x + 3 = 8$	*How can we isolate x?*	**Solve $3x + 2 = 11$**
$2x = 8 - 3$ $2x = 5$	*How do we find the value of one x?*	
$x = \frac{5}{2}$ $x = 2.5$		

Worked example 2	Thinking	Your turn! 2
Solve $5x - 9 + 5 = 13$	*How do we decide on our first step?*	**Solve $2x - 7 + 3 = 11$**
$5x - 9 + 5 = 13$ $5x - 4 = 13$	*How can we isolate the unknown x?*	
$5x - 4 + 4 = 13 + 4$ $5x = 17$	*What is the final step?*	
Divide by 5: $\frac{5x}{5} = \frac{17}{5}$ $\quad x = \frac{17}{5} = 3\frac{2}{5} = 3.4$	*How can we check that the solution is correct?*	
Check: $5x - 9 + 5 = 13$ RHS = 13 LHS = $5 \times 3.4 - 9 + 5$ $= 17 - 9 + 5 = 13$ LHS = RHS, so the solution is correct.		

Worked example 3	Thinking	Your turn! 3
Solve $-22 = 5 - 3x$	*What step could we carry out first?*	**Solve $-16 = 5 - 7x$**
$-22 = 5 - 3x$ $-22 - 5 = 5 - 5 - 3x$ $-27 = -3x$	*How do we find the value of the unknown?*	
$\frac{-27}{-3} = \frac{-3x}{3}$ $9 = x$	*How can we check that the solution is correct?*	
Check: RHS = $5 - 3 \times 9$ $= 5 - 27$ $= -22$ = LHS LHS = RHS, so the solution is correct.		

2.3.3 Unknowns on both sides

Worked example 1	Thinking	Your turn! 1
Solve $3x - 1 = x + 4$	*What can we do so that the unknown appears on only one side?*	**Solve $5x - 3 = 2x + 1$**
$3x - 1 = x + 4$ $3x - x - 1 = x - x + 4$ $2x - 1 = 4$	*How can we isolate the unknown?*	
$2x - 1 + 1 = 4 + 1$ $2x = 5$ $\frac{2x}{2} = \frac{5}{2}$ $x = \frac{5}{2} = 2\frac{1}{2}$ or $x = 2.5$		

Worked example 2	Thinking	Your turn! 2
Solve $2x - 3 = 18 - 3x$	*How can we get the unknown on one side?*	**Solve $5x - 7 = 4 - 3x$**
$2x + 3x - 3 = 18 - 3x + 3x$ $5x - 3 = 18$	*How can we isolate x?*	
$5x - 3 + 3 = 18 + 3$ $5x = 21$ $\frac{5x}{5} = \frac{21}{5}$ $x = \frac{21}{5} = 4\frac{1}{5}$ or $x = 4.2$		

Worked example 3	Thinking	Your turn! 3
Solve $2x - 3 = \frac{1}{3}x + 2$	*How can we remove the fraction?*	**Solve $2x - 1 = \frac{1}{4}x + 6$**
$2x - 3 = \frac{1}{3}x + 2$ $2x \times 3 - 3 \times 3 = \frac{1}{3}x \times 3 + 2 \times 3$ $6x - 9 = x + 6$	*How can we get the unknown on one side?*	
$6x - x - 9 = x - x + 6$ $5x - 9 = 6$	*How can we isolate x?*	
$5x - 9 + 9 = 6 + 9$ $5x = 15$ $\frac{5x}{5} = \frac{15}{5}$ $x = 3$		

Worked example 4	**Thinking**	**Your turn! 4**
Solve $10 - \frac{1}{3}x = \frac{1}{2}x + 5$	*How can we remove both fractions?*	**Solve** $\frac{1}{4}x + 6 = \frac{3}{5}x - 1$
$10 - \frac{1}{3}x = \frac{1}{2}x + 5$ $10 \times 6 - \frac{1}{3}x \times 6 = \frac{1}{2}x \times 6 + 5 \times 6$ $60 - 2x = 3x + 30$	*How can we get the unknown on one side?*	
$60 - 2x + 2x = 3x + 2x + 30$ $60 = 5x + 30$	*How can we isolate x?*	
$60 - 30 = 5x + 30 - 30$ $30 = 5x$ $\frac{30}{5} = \frac{5x}{5}$ $6 = x$		

Worked example 5	**Thinking**	**Your turn! 5**
Solve $4.6 - 0.2x = \frac{1}{2}x + 1.1$	*How can we remove the fraction?*	**Solve** $8.5 + \frac{1}{4}a = 0.9a + 3.3$
$4.6 - 0.2x = \frac{1}{2}x + 1.1$ $4.6 \times 2 - 0.2x \times 2 = \frac{1}{2}x \times 2 + 1.1 \times 2$ $9.2 - 0.4x = x + 2.2$	*How can we get the unknown on one side?*	
$9.2 - 0.4x + 0.4x = x + 0.4x + 2.2$ $9.2 = 1.4x + 2.2$	*How can we isolate x?*	
$9.2 - 2.2 = 1.4x + 2.2 - 2.2$ $7 = 1.4x$ $\frac{7}{1.4} = \frac{1.4x}{1.4}$ $5 = x$		

Fluency questions

2.3.1 Dealing with a negative coefficient of the unknown

1 Work out:

a) $-x \times -1 =$ ________

b) $8 \times -1 =$ ________

c) $-15 \times -1 =$ ________

d) $-y \times -1 =$ ________

2 Fill in the blanks to rewrite each equation so that the coefficient of the unknown is positive.

Example

$$-x + 2 = 5$$
$$(-x \times -1) + (2 \times -1) = 5 \times -1$$
$$(x) + (-2) = -5$$
$$x - 2 = -5$$

a) $8 - x = -3$

$(8 \times -1) + (-x \times -1) = -3 \times -1$

________ + ________ = ________

b) $-y = 3$

$-y \times$ ________ $= 3 \times$ ________

________ = ________

c) $-z - 4 = 9$

$(-z \times$ ________$) + (-4 \times$ ________$) = 9 \times$ ________

________ + ________ = ________

3 Rewrite each equation so that the coefficient of the unknown is positive.

a) $-x = -12$

b) $5 = 7 - y$

c) $-z - 2 = -8$

d) $-x - 20 = 15$

2.3.2 Solving equations that require more than one step

1 Fill in the blanks to solve the equation $3x + 2 = 11$.

a) First, carry out an additive step to isolate $3x$.

Add the inverse of +2 to both sides of the equation:

$3x + 2 +$ ________ $= 11 +$ ________

$3x =$ ________

b) Then carry out a multiplicative step to isolate x.

Do the inverse of × 3 to both sides of the equation:

$$\frac{3x}{\square} = \frac{\square}{\square}$$

$x =$ ________

2 Fill in the blanks to solve the equation $4x - 5 = 15$.

a) First, carry out an additive step to isolate $4x$.

Add the inverse of −5 to both sides of the equation:

$4x - 5 +$ ________ $= 15 +$ ________

$4x =$ ________

b) Then carry out a multiplicative step to isolate x.

Do the inverse of × 4 to both sides of the equation:

$$\frac{4x}{\square} = \frac{\square}{\square}$$

$x =$ ________

3 Solve the equation $2x + 7 = 13$.

a) First, carry out an additive step to isolate $2x$.

Add the inverse of +7 to both sides of the equation.

b) Then carry out a multiplicative step to isolate x.

Do the inverse of ×2 to both sides of the equation.

4 Solve the equation $5x + 10 = 40$.

a) First, carry out a multiplicative step to simplify the equation.

Divide each term in the equation by 5.

b) Then carry out an additive step to isolate x.

Add the inverse of +2 to both sides of the equation.

2.3.3 Unknowns on both sides

1 Fill in the blanks to solve the equations.

a) Solve the equation $x + 12 = 7x$.

i. Use an additive step to rearrange the equation $x + 12 = 7x$ so that only one side has a term with an unknown and only one side has a constant.

Subtract x from both sides:

$x + 12 -$ ________ $= 7x -$ ________

________ $=$ ________ x

ii. Use a multiplicative step to isolate x and solve the equation.

Divide both sides of the equation by 6:

$\frac{\_\_\_\_\_\_\_\_}{6} = \frac{\_\_\_\_\_\_\_\_ x}{6}$

________ $= x$

b) Solve the equation $8y = 5y + 9$.

i. Use an additive step to rearrange the equation $8y = 5y + 9$ so that only one side has a term with an unknown and only one side has a constant.

Subtract $5y$ from both sides:

$8y -$ ________ $= 5y + 9 -$ ________

________ $y =$ ________

ii. Use a multiplicative step to isolate y and solve the equation.

Divide both sides of the equation by 3:

$\frac{\_\_\_\_\_\_\_\_ y}{3} = \frac{\_\_\_\_\_\_\_\_}{3}$

$y =$ ________

c) Solve the equation $2z + 23 = 6z + 3$.

i. Use an additive step to rearrange the equation $2z + 23 = 6z + 3$ so that only one side has a term with an unknown and only one side has a constant.

Subtract $2z$ from both sides:

$2z + 23 -$ ________ $= 6z + 3 -$ ________

$23 =$ ________ $z + 3$

Subtract 3 from both sides: $23 -$ ________ $=$

________ $z + 3 -$ ________

________ $=$ ________ z

ii. Use a multiplicative step to isolate z and solve the equation.

Divide both sides of the equation by 4:

$\frac{\_\_\_\_\_\_\_\_}{4} = \frac{\_\_\_\_\_\_\_\_ z}{4}$

________ $= z$

2 Solve the equations.

a) $m + 18 = 4m$

i. Carry out an additive step to rearrange $m + 18 = 4m$ so that only one side has a term with an unknown and only one side has a constant. Do not solve it.

ii. Use a multiplicative step to isolate m and solve the equation.

b) $9p = 5p + 16$

i. Carry out an additive step to rearrange $9p = 5p + 16$ so that only one side has a term with an unknown and only one side has a constant. Do not solve it.

ii. Use a multiplicative step to isolate p and solve the equation.

c) $3q + 1 = q + 5$

i. Carry out an additive step to rearrange $3q + 1 = q + 5$ so that only one side has a term with an unknown and only one side has a constant. Do not solve it.

ii. Use a multiplicative step to isolate q and solve the equation.

2.4 Linear equations with brackets and fractions

Example-problem pairs

2.4.1 Deciding how to deal with brackets in equations

Worked example 1	**Thinking**	**Your turn! 1**
Solve $6(x + 3) = 25$	*How do we rewrite the equation without a bracket?*	**Solve $5(x - 2) = 3$**
$6(x + 3) = 25$ $6x + 18 = 25$	*How do we isolate the term with the unknown?*	
$6x + 18 - 18 = 25 - 18$ $6x = 7$	*How do we find the value of x?*	
$\frac{6x}{6} = \frac{7}{6}$ $x = \frac{7}{6}$ or $1\frac{1}{6}$		

Worked example 2	**Thinking**	**Your turn! 2**
Solve $7(2x - 5) = 49$	*How do we decide whether to divide first or expand the bracket first?*	**Solve $4(3x + 1) = 28$**
$\frac{7(2x - 5)}{7} = \frac{49}{7}$ $2x - 5 = 7$	*How do we isolate the term with the unknown?*	
$2x - 5 + 5 = 7 + 5$ $2x = 12$	*How do we find the value of x?*	
$\frac{2x}{2} = \frac{12}{2}$ $x = 6$		

2.4.2 Equations with brackets where the unknown is on both sides

Worked example 1	Thinking	Your turn! 1
Solve $2(x + 3) - 5x = 3(x + 3)$	*How can we rewrite the equation without any brackets?*	**Solve $3(x - 6) + x = 2(3 - 4x)$**
$2x + 6 - 5x = 3x + 9$	*How can we simplify the equation?*	
Simplify the left-hand side by collecting like terms. $6 - 3x = 3x + 9$	*How do we rewrite this so the unknown is on only one side?*	
$6 - 3x + 3x = 3x + 3x + 9$ $6 = 6x + 9$	*How do we decide whether to do the additive or multiplicative step next?*	
$6 - 9 = 6x + 9 - 9$ $-3 = 6x$		
$\frac{-3}{6} = \frac{6x}{6}$ $-\frac{1}{2} = x$		

Worked example 2	Thinking	Your turn! 2
a) Expand the brackets and solve $3(x + 2) = 6x - 21$	*How can we expand the brackets?*	**a) Expand the brackets and solve $5(x - 2) = 2x + 5$**
$3x + 6 = 6x - 21$	*How can we simplify the equation?*	
$3x - 3x + 6 = 6x - 3x - 21$ $6 = 3x - 21$	*How do we get the unknown on only one side?*	
$6 + 21 = 3x - 21 + 21$ $27 = 3x$	*Do we do the additive or multiplicative step next?*	
$\frac{27}{3} = \frac{3x}{3}$ $9 = x$		
b) Here is the same equation as in part a: $3(x + 2) = 6x - 21$ **Divide both sides of the equation by 3.** **Does dividing make the equation easier to solve? Explain your answer.**	*Do all of the terms have a common factor?*	**b) Here is the same equation as in part a: $5(x - 2) = 2x + 5$** **Divide both sides of the equation by 5.** **Does dividing make the equation easier to solve? Explain your answer.**
$3(x + 2) = 6x - 21$ $\div 3 \downarrow \quad \downarrow \div 3$ $x + 2 = 2x - 7$	*How can we make sure that equality is maintained?*	
Yes, the equation is now simpler, because the terms had a common factor of 3.	*What steps would we have to carry out to solve the rewritten equation?*	

2.4.3 Equations with fractions

Worked example 1	Thinking	Your turn! 1
Solve $\frac{5x-3}{6}=7$	*How can we rewrite the equation without the fraction?*	**Solve** $\frac{2x-1}{5}=3$
$\frac{5x-3}{6}\times 6=7\times 6$ $5x-3=42$	*Should we do the multiplicative step or the additive step next?*	
$5x-3+3=42+3$ $5x=45$	*How do we find the value of* x*?*	
$\frac{5x}{5}=\frac{45}{5}$ $x=9$		

Worked example 2	Thinking	Your turn! 2
Solve $5+\frac{x}{3}=7$	*How do we decide the first step?*	**Solve** $\frac{x}{4}+3=5$
$\left(5+\frac{x}{3}\right)\times 3=7\times 3$ $15+x=21$	*Why do we need to use brackets here?*	
$15-15+x=21-15$ $x=6$	*How can we isolate the unknown* x*?*	
Check: $5+\frac{x}{3}=7$ LHS $=5+\frac{6}{3}=5+2=7=$ RHS So the solution is correct.	*How can we check the solution is correct?*	

Worked example 3	Thinking	Your turn! 3
Solve $\frac{3x-2}{3}=\frac{1}{4}$	*Do we need to rewrite just one fraction or both, so that they have a common denominator?*	**Solve** $\frac{3x-5}{7}=\frac{5}{4}$
$\frac{3x-2}{3}\times\frac{4}{4}=\frac{4(3x-2)}{12}$ $\frac{1}{4}\times\frac{3}{3}=\frac{3}{12}$	*How do we rewrite the fractions with the common denominator?*	
$\frac{12x-8}{12}=\frac{3}{12}$	*What do we do now?*	
$12x-8=3$		
$12x-8+8=3+8$ $12x=11$ $\frac{12x}{12}=\frac{11}{12}$ $x=\frac{11}{12}$	*How do we isolate the unknown?*	

Worked example 4	Thinking	Your turn! 4
Solve $\frac{2x-4}{5} = \frac{13-3x}{10}$	*How do we write the fractions with a common denominator?*	**Solve** $\frac{2x-1}{6} = \frac{2x+3}{2}$
$\frac{2x-4}{5} \times \frac{2}{2} = \frac{13-3x}{10}$ $\frac{2(2x-4)}{10} = \frac{13-3x}{10}$	*Why do we need to use brackets here?*	
$\frac{4x-8}{10} = \frac{13-3x}{10}$	*The denominators are equal, so what do we know about the numerators?*	
$4x-8=13-3x$	*How do we get the unknown on one side?*	
$4x+3x-8=13-3x+3x$ $7x-8=13$ $7x-8+8=13+8$ $7x=21$ $\frac{7x}{7}=\frac{21}{7}$ $x=3$		

Worked example 5	Thinking	Your turn! 5
Solve $\frac{2x+1}{6} = \frac{5-2x}{4}$	*How do we write the fractions with a common denominator?*	**Solve** $\frac{2x-1}{2} = \frac{4-3x}{3}$
$\frac{2x+1}{6} \times \frac{2}{2} = \frac{5-2x}{4} \times \frac{3}{3}$	*Why does it look like we have multiplied each side by a different amount?*	
$\frac{4x+2}{12} = \frac{15-6x}{12}$	*Now the denominators are equal, what do we do next?*	
$4x+2=15-6x$ $4x+6x+2=15-6x+6x$ $10x+2=15$	*How do we decide what step to take next?*	
$10x+2-2=15-2$ $10x=13$ $\frac{10x}{10}=\frac{13}{10}$ $x=1.3$		

2.4.4 Equations with the unknown in the denominator

Worked example 1	Thinking	Your turn! 1
Solve $\frac{28}{x} + 5 = 9$	*How can we isolate the term with the unknown?*	**Solve $\frac{36}{x} + 12 = 21$**
$\frac{28}{x} + 5 + (-5) = 9 + (-5)$ $\frac{28}{x} = 4$	*How can we make this equation linear?*	
$\frac{28x}{x} = 4$ $28 = 4x$	*How do we know that this equation is now linear?*	
$\frac{28}{4} = \frac{4x}{4}$ $7 = x$		

Worked example 2	Thinking	Your turn! 2
Solve $\frac{21}{5x + 3} = 2$	*How can we rewrite the equation so the unknown is not in the denominator?*	**Solve $\frac{15}{2x + 1} = 3$**
$\frac{21}{5x + 3} \times (5x + 3) = 2 \times (5x + 3)$ $21 = 2(5x + 3)$	*What step should we do next?*	
$21 = 10x + 6$		
$21 - 6 = 10x + 6 - 6$ $15 = 10x$ $\frac{15}{10} = \frac{10x}{10}$ $1.5 = x$	*How can we isolate the unknown?*	

Worked example 3	Thinking	Your turn! 3
Solve $6 = \frac{82}{2x + 1} + 4$	*How do we decide which step to perform first?*	**Solve $10 = \frac{75}{3x + 1} + 7$**
$6 - 4 = \frac{82}{2x + 1} + 4 - 4$ $2 = \frac{82}{2x + 1}$		
$2 \times \frac{2x + 1}{2x + 1} = \frac{82}{2x + 1}$ $\frac{4x + 2}{2x + 1} = \frac{82}{2x + 1}$	*Why is multiplying just one side of the equation allowed here?*	
$4x + 2 = 82$	*Why can we just write the numerators now?*	
$4x + 2 - 2 = 82 - 2$ $4x = 80$		
$\frac{4x}{4} = \frac{80}{4}$ $x = 20$		

Fluency questions

2.4.1 Deciding how to deal with brackets in equations

1 a) Expand $5(x + 4)$.

b) Use your answer to **a** and an additive step to solve $5(x + 4) = 30$.

2 a) Expand $4(2y + 3)$.

b) Use your answer to **a** and an additive step to solve $4(2y + 3) = 36$.

3 a) Expand $3(x - 5)$

b) Use your answer to **a** and an additive step to solve $3(x - 5) = 18$.

4 a) Expand $2(6y + 1)$.

b) Use your answer to **a** to expand and simplify $2(6y - 1) + 5$.

c) Use your answer to **b** and an additive step to solve $2(6y - 1) + 5 = 51$.

2.4.2 Equations with brackets where the unknown is on both sides

1 a) Expand $2(x + 8)$.

b) Expand $3(x + 4)$.

c) Use your answers to **a** and **b** to solve $2(x + 8) = 3(x + 4)$.

2 a) Expand $6(y + 2)$.

b) Expand $5(y + 6)$.

c) Use your answers to **a** and **b** to solve $6(y + 2) = 5(y + 6)$.

3 a) Expand $4(x + 8)$.

b) Expand $7(x + 2)$.

c) Use your answers to **a** and **b** to solve $4(x + 8) = 7(x + 2)$.

4 a) Expand $10(y + 3)$.

b) Expand $8(y + 5)$.

c) Use your answers to **a** and **b** to solve $10(y + 3) = 8(y + 5)$.

2.4.3 Equations with fractions

1 Solve these equations by filling in the blanks.

a) Solve $\frac{x}{2} = 5$

$\frac{x}{2} \times$ ______ $= 5 \times$ ______

$x =$ ______

b) Solve $\frac{y}{7} = 3$

$\frac{y}{7} \times$ ______ $= 3 \times$ ______

$y =$ ______

c) Solve $\frac{z}{4} = -2$

$\frac{z}{4} \times$ ______ $= -2 \times$ ______

$z =$ ______

2 Solve these equations.

a) $\frac{x}{12} = 4$

b) $\frac{y}{9} = 9$

c) $\frac{z}{3} = -5$

2.4.4 Equations with the unknown in the denominator

1 Solve these equations by filling in the blanks.

a) Solve $\frac{10}{x} = 5$

$\frac{10}{x} \times$ ______ $= 5 \times$ ______

$10 =$ ______

$\frac{10}{\_\_} = x$

______ $= x$

b) Solve $\frac{14}{y} = 2$

$\frac{14}{y} \times$ ______ $= 2 \times$ ______

$14 =$ ______

$\frac{14}{\_\_} = y$

______ $= y$

c) Solve $\frac{36}{z} = 4$

$\frac{36}{z} \times$ ______ $= 4 \times$ ______

$36 =$ ______

$\frac{36}{\_\_} = z$

______ $= z$

2 Solve these equations.

a) $\frac{24}{x} = 8$

b) $\frac{36}{y} = 3$

c) $\frac{28}{z} = 7$

3.1 Features of sequences

Example-problem pairs

3.1.1 Continuing sequences

Worked example 1	Thinking	Your turn! 1
Here is a sequence: 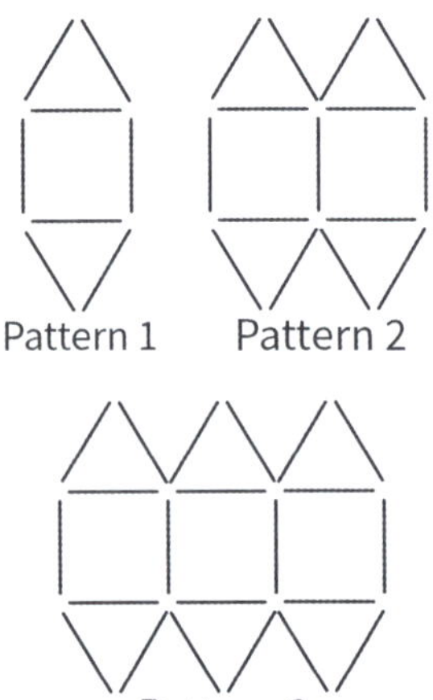 Pattern 1 Pattern 2 Pattern 3		**Here is a sequence:** 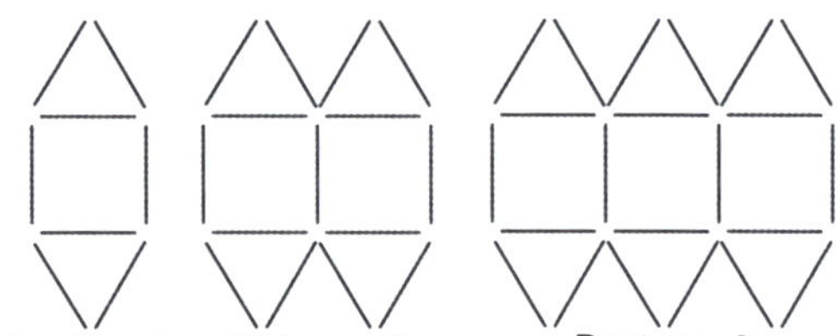 Pattern 1 Pattern 2 Pattern 3
a) Describe in words how the number of sticks in each pattern changes.		**a) Describe in words how the number of sticks in each pattern changes.**
The first pattern uses 6 sticks. Each pattern after this needs 5 more sticks than the previous pattern.	*How do we work out how the patterns are changing each time?*	
b) Draw the next two patterns in the sequence.		**b) Draw the next two patterns in the sequence.**
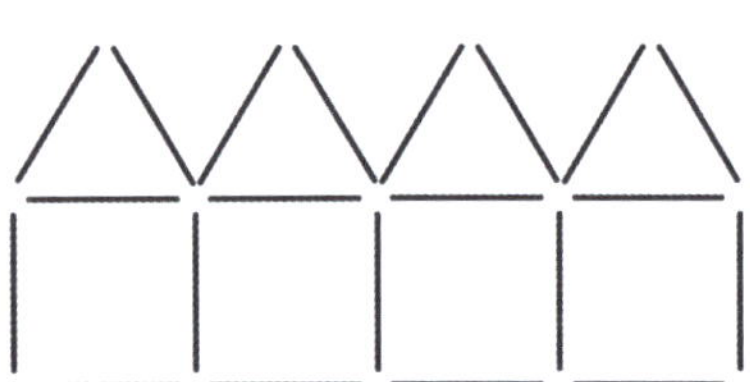 Pattern 4  Pattern 5	*How can we check we have drawn the correct patterns?*	

Worked example 2	Thinking	Your turn! 2
What is the next term in each of these sequences?		**What is the next term in each of these sequences?**
a) 15, 10, 5, ...		**a) 18, 15, 12, ...**
15, 10, 5, ... −5 −5 −5 5 is subtracted each time. The next term is 0.	*How do we work out what is happening to each term in the sequence?*	
b) 3, 15, 75, ...		**b) 3, 9, 27, ...**
3, 15, 75, ... ×5 ×5 ×5 Each term is 5 times the previous term. The next term is 75 × 5 = 375.	*What do we do when the same amount is not added to or subtracted from each term?*	

3.1.2 Using term-to-term rules

Worked example 1	Thinking	Your turn! 1
Describe the term-to-term rule for this sequence and find the next three terms. **7, 14, 28, ...**	*How do we find the term-to-term rule?*	**Describe the term-to-term rule for this sequence and find the next three terms.** **2, 20, 200, ...**
The term-to-term rule is to multiply by 2 each time. The first term is 7.	*How do we generate more terms in a sequence?*	
28 × 2 = 56 56 × 2 = 112 112 × 2 = 224 The next three terms are 56, 112, 224.		

Worked example 2	**Thinking**	**Your turn! 2**
Find the missing term in this Fibonacci-style sequence and find the next three terms. **2, □, 7, …**	*What do we know about Fibonacci-style sequences?*	**Find the missing term in this Fibonacci-style sequence and find the next three terms.** **3, □, 11, …**
2, □, 7, … 7 − 2 = 5 So the sequence starts: 2, **5**, 7, …	*How do we continue this sequence?*	
5 + 7 = 12 7 + 12 = 19 12 + 19 = 31 The next three terms are 12, 19, and 31.		

Worked example 3	**Thinking**	**Your turn! 3**
Describe the term-to-term rule for this sequence and find the next three terms. **5, 8, 11, …**	*How do we find the term-to-term rule?*	**Describe the term-to-term rule for this sequence and find the next three terms.** **5, 7, 9, …**
The term-to-term rule is to add 3 each time, starting from 5.	*How do we generate more terms in a sequence?*	
11 + 3 = 14 14 + 3 = 17 17 + 3 = 20 The next three terms are 14, 17 and 20.	*Is this an increasing or decreasing sequence?*	

Worked example 4	**Thinking**	**Your turn! 4**
Here is a sequence: 2, 3, 5, … **Describe two ways to generate the sequence. Write the next two terms in each case.**	*Can we generate this as a Fibonacci-style sequence?*	**Here is a sequence: 3, 4, 7, …** **Describe two ways to generate the sequence. Write the next two terms in each case.**
Add the preceding two terms: 2 + 3 = 5 3 + 5 = 8 5 + 8 = 13 So the next two terms are 8 and 13.	*Can we generate this sequence using addition or multiplication?*	
Multiply by 2 and subtract 1: 2 × 2 − 1 = 3 3 × 2 − 1 = 5 5 × 2 − 1 = 9 9 × 2 − 1 = 17 So the next two terms are 9 and 17.	*Can we think of any other ways to continue this sequence?*	

3.1.3 Using position-to-term rules

Worked example 1	**Thinking**	**Your turn! 1**
Here is a sequence: 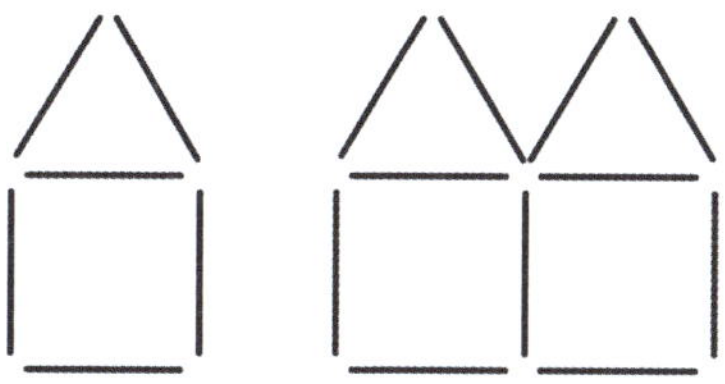 Pattern 1 Pattern 2 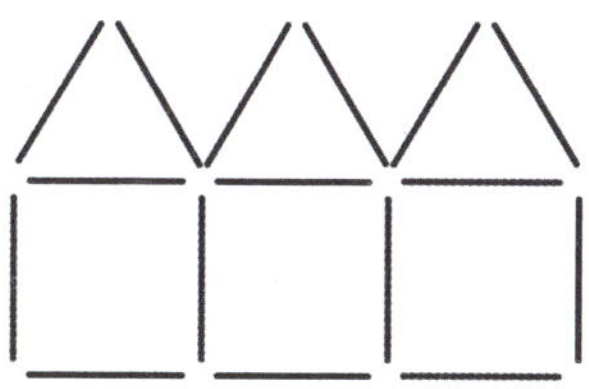 Pattern 3 **How many sticks are needed to make:**		**Here is a sequence:** 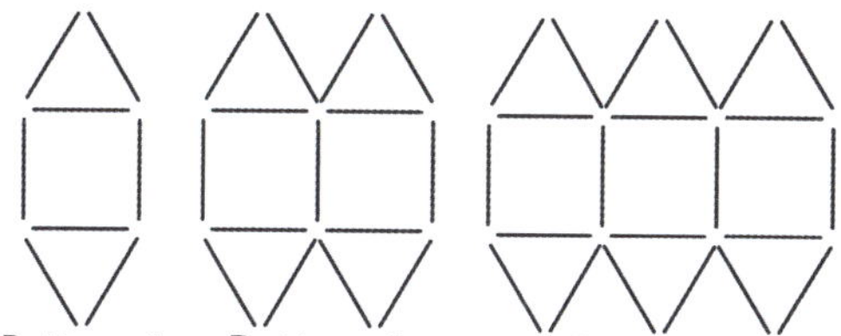 Pattern 1 Pattern 2 Pattern 3 **How many sticks are needed to make:**
a) the 10th pattern		**a) the 10th pattern**
The first pattern has 6 sticks. 5 sticks are added with each new pattern, so 9 times in total. $6 + 9 \times 5 = 51$ The number of sticks needed is 51.	*How many sticks are added each time?*	
b) the 100th pattern in the sequence?		**b) the 100th pattern in the sequence?**
Number of sticks $= 6 + (n - 1) \times 5$ $= 6 + 99 \times 5$ $= 501$	*How do we write an equation to show the rule?*	

Worked example 2	**Thinking**	**Your turn! 2**
What is the position-to-term rule of each of these sequences?		**What is the position-to-term rule of each of these sequences?**
a) 10, 20, 30, 40, …	*How do we write the rule as an equation?*	**a) −1, −2, −3, −4, …**
$10n$		
b) 0.1, 0.2, 0.3, 0.4, …	*How do we write the position-to-term rule?*	**b)** $1, \frac{1}{2}, \frac{1}{3}, \frac{1}{4}, \ldots$
$0.1n$		

Fluency questions

3.1.1 Continuing sequences

1 Look at this sequence made from patterns of dots.

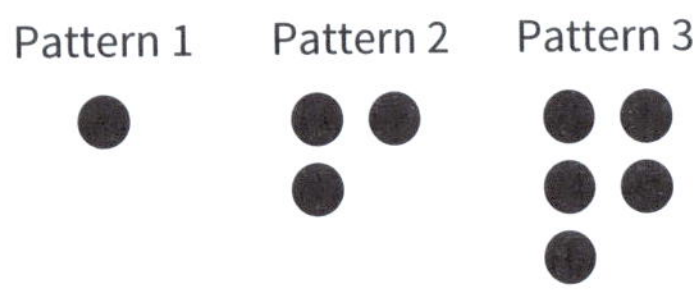

a) Describe how you get from Pattern 1 to Pattern 2.
b) Describe how you get from Pattern 2 to Pattern 3.
c) If the sequence continues in the same way, how many dots would be in Pattern 4?

2 Look at this sequence made from patterns of squares.

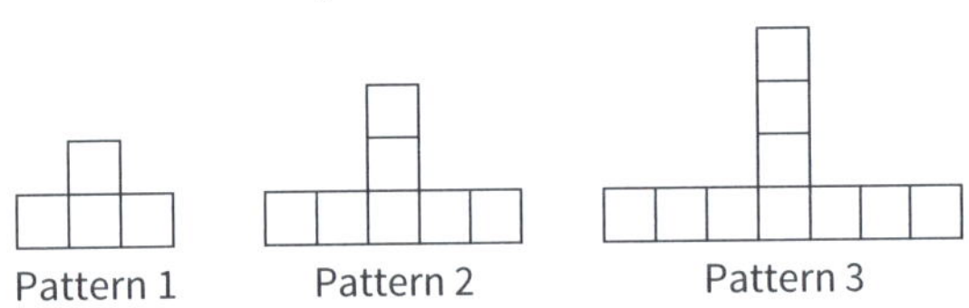

a) Describe how you get from Pattern 1 to Pattern 2.
b) Describe how you get from Pattern 2 to Pattern 3.
c) If the sequence continues in the same way, how many squares would be in Pattern 4?

3 Look at this sequence of numbers: 2, 6, 10, ….
a) Describe how you get from the first number in the sequence to the second number.
b) Describe how you get from the second number in the sequence to the third number.
c) If the sequence continues in the same way, what number will come fourth in the sequence?

4 Look at this sequence of numbers: 3, 8, 13, ….
a) Describe how you get from the first number in the sequence to the second number.
b) Describe how you get from the second number in the sequence to the third number.
c) If the sequence continues in the same way, what number will come fourth in the sequence?

3.1.2 Using term-to-term rules

1 Give the next three terms in each sequence.
a) 2, 4, 6, 8, …
b) 5, 10, 15, 20, …
c) 6, 12, 18, 24, …

2 Here is a sequence of numbers: 2, 5, 8, …
The term-to-term rule is +3. Write the next three terms in the sequence.

3 Here is a sequence of numbers: 13, 11, 9, …
The term-to-term rule is −2. Write the next three terms in the sequence.

4 Here is a sequence of numbers: 2, 4, 8, …
The term-to-term rule is ×2. Write the next three terms in the sequence.

3.1.3 Using position-to-term rules

1 Here is a sequence of patterns made from triangles:

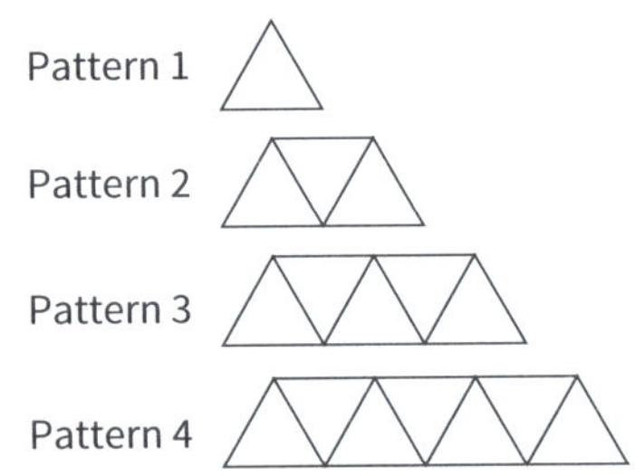

a) How many triangles will there be in Pattern 5?
b) How many triangles will there be in Pattern 7?
c) How many triangles will there be in Pattern 10?

2 Here is a sequence of patterns made from circles:

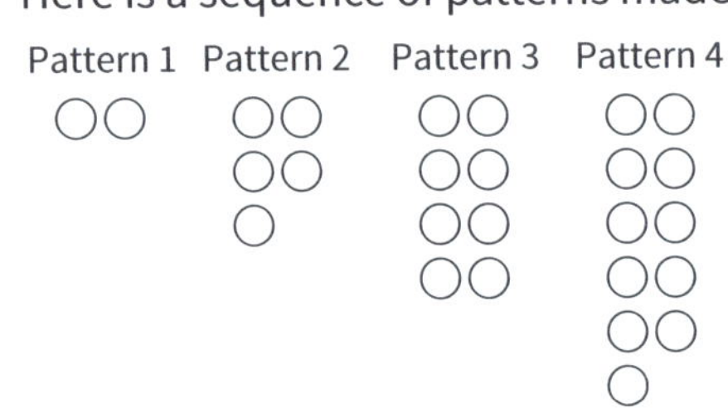

a) How many circles will there be in Pattern 5?
b) How many circles will there be in Pattern 7?
c) How many circles will there be in Pattern 10?

3 Here is a sequence of patterns made from sticks:

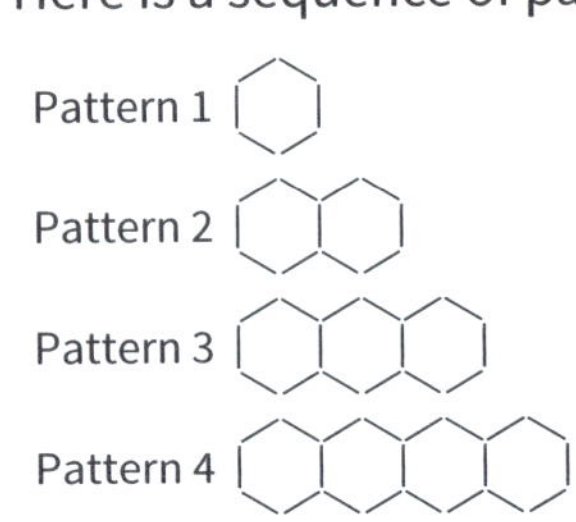

a) How many sticks will there be in Pattern 5?
b) How many sticks will there be in Pattern 7?
c) How many sticks will there be in Pattern 10?

3.2 Arithmetic sequences

Example-problem pairs

3.2.1 Identifying arithmetic sequences

Worked example 1	Thinking	Your turn! 1
Work out whether or not these are arithmetic sequences:		**Work out whether or not these are arithmetic sequences:**
a) 11, 14, 17, 20, ...	*How do we check whether a sequence is arithmetic?*	**a) 2, 4, 6, 10, ...**
11 14 17 20... +3 +3 +3 You add 3 to each term to get the next term. This is an arithmetic sequence.		
b) 8, 7, 5, 2, ...	*Is there a common difference between terms?*	**b) 4, 1, −2, −5, ...**
8 7 5 2... −1 −2 −3 There is not a common difference between consecutive terms. This is not an arithmetic sequence.		
c) 12, 7, 2, −3, ...	*Do arithmetic sequences always have increasing terms?*	**c) 5, 10, 15, 20, ...**
12 7 2 −3 −5 −5 −5 You subtract 5 from each term to get the next term. This is an arithmetic sequence.		

3.2.2 Working out the *n*th term of arithmetic sequences

Worked example 1	Thinking	Your turn! 1
Find the *n*th term rule for this sequence: **2, 8, 14, 20, …**	*What is the first step in finding the nth term rule?*	**Find the *n*th term rule for this sequence:** **4, 11, 18, 25, …**
The difference between each term and the next is 6.	*How do we know which times table to use?*	
$6n$ gives 16, 12, 18, 24, … ↓ −4 2, 8, 14, 20, … *n*th term is $6n - 4$.	*How can we work out how much the times table has moved?*	
Check: 3rd term using $6n - 4$: $6 \times 3 - 4 = 14$	*How do we check our nth term rule is correct?*	

Worked example 2	Thinking	Your turn! 2
Find the *n*th term rule for this sequence: **13, 9, 5, 1, …**	*What is the first step in finding the nth term rule?*	**Find the *n*th term rule for this sequence:** **7, 5, 3, 1, …**
The difference between each term and the next is −4.	*What is different about a decreasing sequence?*	
$-4n$ gives −4, −8, −12, −16, … ↓ +17 13, 9, 5, 1, … The *n*th term is $-4n + 17$.	*How can we work out how much the times table has moved?*	
Check: 3rd term using $-4n + 17$: $-4 \times 3 + 17 = 5$	*How do we check that our nth term rule is correct?*	

3.2.3 Using the *n*th term

Worked example 1	Thinking	Your turn! 1
Write the first five terms of the sequence with nth term $3n - 5$.		**Write the first five terms of the sequence with nth term $10n + 3$.**
1st term $3 \times 1 - 5 = -2$ 2nd term $3 \times 2 - 5 = 1$ 3rd term $3 \times 3 - 5 = 4$ 4th term $3 \times 4 - 5 = 7$ 5th term $3 \times 5 - 5 = 10$ The sequence is −2, 1, 4, 7, 10, …	*What is the first step in finding terms in the sequence?* *Is there another method we could use?*	

Worked example 2	Thinking	Your turn! 2
Write the first five terms of the sequence with nth term $6 - 5n$.		**Write the first five terms of the sequence with nth term $2 - 3n$.**
1st term $6 - 5 \times 1 = 1$ 2nd term $6 - 5 \times 2 = -4$ 3rd term $6 - 5 \times 3 = -9$ 4th term $6 - 5 \times 4 = -14$ 5th term $6 - 5 \times 5 = -19$ The sequence is 1, −4, −9, −14, −19, …	*How can we tell if the sequence is increasing or decreasing?*	

Worked example 3	Thinking	Your turn! 3
Find these terms of the sequence with nth term $7n + 6$.		**Find these terms of the sequence with nth term $4n + 7$.**
a) 50th term		**a) 50th term**
$n = 50$ $7 \times 50 + 6 = 350 + 6$ $= 356$	*How do we use the formula for the nth term?*	
b) 100th term		**b) 100th term**
$n = 100$ $7 \times 100 + 6 = 700 + 6$ $= 706$		
c) 101st term		**c) 101st term**
101st term = 100th term + 7 $706 + 7 = 713$	*Can we get from one term to the next?*	

Worked example 4	Thinking	Your turn! 4
Here is a sequence: **26, 23, 20, 17, ...** **Find the** **a) 10th and** **b) 100th term of the sequence.**	*How can we find any term in a sequence?*	**Here is a sequence:** **27, 23, 19, 15, ...** **Find the** **a) 10th and** **b) 100th term of the sequence.**
The constant difference is −3 so the sequence is related to the −3 times table but starts at 26. So the nth term is $-3n + 29$.		
a) $n = 10$ $-3 \times 10 + 29$ $= -30 + 29$ $= -1$		
b) $n = 100$ $-3 \times 100 + 29$ $= -300 + 29$ $= -271$	*How do we find the 100th term in a sequence?*	

3.2.4 Finding terms of arithmetic sequences

Worked example 1	Thinking	Your turn! 1
Is 38 in the sequence $4n + 2$? **If it is, what is its term number?**	*How do we check whether a number is a term in a sequence?*	**Is 38 in the sequence $5n - 2$?** **If it is, what is its term number?**
$4n + 2 = 38$ $4n = 36$ $n = 9$	*How does this tell us whether the number is in the sequence?*	
38 is a term in the sequence. It is the 9th term.		

Worked example 2	Thinking	Your turn! 2
A sequence has the nth term $7n + 6$. **a) What position is 55 in this sequence?** **b) Is 77 a number in this sequence?**	*How can we use an equation to find the position number?*	**A sequence has the nth term $7 - 6n$.** **a) What position is −23 in this sequence?** **b) Is −77 a number in this sequence?**
a) $7n + 6 = 55$ $7n = 49$ $n = 7$ The position number is 7.		
b) $7n + 6 = 77$ $7n = 71$ $n = 10.14$ n is not a positive integer so 77 is not a number in this sequence.	*How can we use an equation to test whether a number is in a sequence?*	

Fluency questions

3.2.1 Identifying arithmetic sequences

1 Write the common difference between terms in each of these sequences.

a) 4, 8, 12, 16, …
b) 7, 14, 21, 28, …
c) 4, 7, 10, 13, …
d) 1, 6, 11, 16, …
e) 2.5, 5.0, 7.5, 10, …

2 Choose the correct option to complete the sentence.

To move from term to term in an arithmetic sequence you…

… add or subtract different numbers each time.
… add or subtract the same number each time.
… multiply or divide by different numbers each time.
… multiply or divide by the same number each time.

3.2.2 Working out the *n*th term of arithmetic sequences

1 Look at this sequence with a common difference of 3:

3, 6, 9, 12,…

1st term = 3 = 3
2nd term = 6 = 3 + 3
3rd term = 9 = 3 + 3 + 3
4th term = 12 = 3 + 3 + 3 + 3

a) How many 3s are added to make the 1st term?
b) How many 3s are added to make the 2nd term?
c) How many 3s are added to make the 3rd term?
d) How many 3s would need to be added to make the 17th term?
e) How many 3s would need to be added to make the *n*th term?
f) Write the *n*th term rule for this sequence.

2 Look at this sequence with a common difference of 3:

4, 7, 10, 13, …

Comparing this sequence with the 3 times table, you can see that the times table has been shifted by +1 (each term has 1 added to it).

3 times table, 3*n*	3	6	9	12
This sequence	4	7	10	13

+1

So, you can write out the sums as in question 1 but then add 1 to each term:

1st term = 4 = 3 + 1
2nd term = 7 = 3 + 3 + 1
3rd term = 10 = 3 + 3 + 3 + 1
4th term = 13 = 3 + 3 + 3 + 3 + 1

a) How many 3s are added to 1 to make the 1st term?
b) How many 3s are added to 1 to make the 2nd term?
c) How many 3s are added to 1 to make the 3rd term?
d) How many 3s would need to be added to 1 to make the 17th term?
e) How many 3s would need to be added to 1 to make the *n*th term?
f) Write the *n*th term rule for this sequence.

3 Look at this sequence with a common difference of 5:

7, 12, 17, 22, …

Compare this sequence with the 5 times table:

5 times table, 5*n*	5	10	15	20
This sequence	7	12	17	22

a) Complete the following sentence:
The times table has been shifted by ________

b) Complete the sums below to show how each term can be written using a sum of 5s.
1st term = 7 = ________ + 2
2nd term = 12 = ________________ + 2
3rd term = 17 = ________________________ + 2
4th term = 22 = ________________________________ + 2

c) How many 5s are added to 2 to make the 1st term?
d) How many 5s are added to 2 to make the 2nd term?
e) How many 5s are added to 2 to make the 3rd term?
f) How many 5s would need to be added to 2 to make the 17th term?
g) How many 5s would need to be added to 2 to make the *n*th term?
h) Write the *n*th term rule for this sequence.

4 Look at this sequence with a common difference of 4:

3, 7, 11, 15,...

Compare this sequence with the 4 times table:

4 times table, $4n$	4	8	12	16
This sequence	3	7	11	15

a) Complete the following sentence:
The times table has been shifted by ______

b) Complete the sums below to show how each term can be written using a sum of 4s:
1st term = 3 = ______ − 1
2nd term = 7 = ______ − 1
3rd term = 11 = ______ − 1
4th term = 15 = ______ − 1

c) How many 4s are added to −1 to make the 1st term?

d) How many 4s are added to −1 to make the 2nd term?

e) How many 4s are added to −1 to make the 3rd term?

f) How many 4s would need to be added to −1 to make the 17th term?

g) How many 4s would need to be added to −1 to make the nth term?

h) Write the nth term rule for this sequence.

3.2.3 Using the nth term

1 Write the first terms of the sequence with nth term $2n + 3$.

Complete the working.

1st term	2	×	1	+	3	=	5
2nd term	2	×	2	+	___	=	___
3rd term	2	×	___	+	3	=	___
4th term	2	×	___	+	___	=	___
5th term	___	×	___	+	___	=	___

The sequence is ___, ___, ___, ___, ___, ...

2 The nth term of a sequence is $3n + 4$

a) Work out the 1st term of the sequence ($n = 1$).

b) Work out the 2nd term of the sequence ($n = 2$).

c) Work out the 3rd term of the sequence ($n = 3$).

d) Work out the 4th term of the sequence ($n = 4$).

e) Work out the 5th term of the sequence ($n = 5$).

3 The nth term of a sequence is $6n + 1$.

Write the first five terms of the sequence.

4 The nth term of a sequence is $3n - 2$.

Write the first five terms of the sequence.

3.2.4 Finding terms of arithmetic sequences

1 Here are four statements:

- The numbers end in 1 or 6.
- The numbers are all even.
- The numbers are all multiples of 7.
- The numbers are all odd.

Match the statements with these sequences.

a) 10, 16, 22, 28, ... ______

b) 7, 14, 21, 28, ... ______

c) 15, 19, 23, 27, ... ______

d) 1, 6, 11, 16, ... ______

2 A sequence starts 6, 14, 22, 30, ...

a) What do the terms in this sequence all have in common?

b) Is 77 a term in the sequence? Explain your answer.

3 A sequence starts 12, 17, 22, 27, ...

a) What do the terms in this sequence all have in common?

b) Is 55 a term in the sequence? Explain your answer.

c) Is 77 a term in the sequence? Explain your answer.

4 A sequence starts 25, 21, 17, 13, ...

a) What do the terms in this sequence all have in common?

b) Is 8 a term in the sequence? Explain your answer.

c) Is 43 a term in the sequence? Explain your answer.

4.1 Connect coordinates, equations, and graphs

Example-problem pairs

4.1.1 When to join points on a graph

<table>
<tr><th>Worked example 1</th><th>Thinking</th><th>Your turn! 1</th></tr>
<tr>
<td>The table shows the first five terms of the sequence with the nth term $2n + 3$.
<table>
<tr><th>Term number (n)</th><td>1</td><td>2</td><td>3</td><td>4</td><td>5</td></tr>
<tr><th>Term (T)</th><td>5</td><td>7</td><td>9</td><td>11</td><td>13</td></tr>
</table>
</td>
<td>How have the terms of the sequence been generated?</td>
<td>The table shows the first five terms of the sequence with the nth term $3n - 2$.
<table>
<tr><th>Term number (n)</th><td>1</td><td>2</td><td>3</td><td>4</td><td>5</td></tr>
<tr><th>Term (T)</th><td>1</td><td>4</td><td>7</td><td>10</td><td>13</td></tr>
</table>
</td>
</tr>
<tr>
<td>a) Draw and label a suitable set of axes and plot the terms of the sequence.

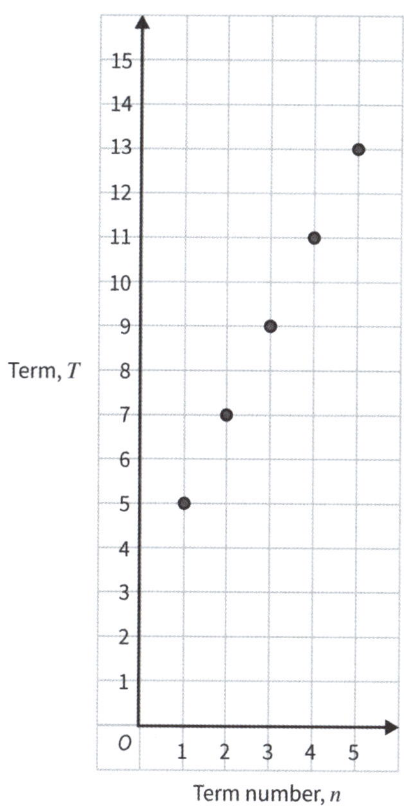

</td>
<td>How could we use the table of values to work out what size axes to draw?</td>
<td>a) Draw and label a suitable set of axes and plot the terms of the sequence.

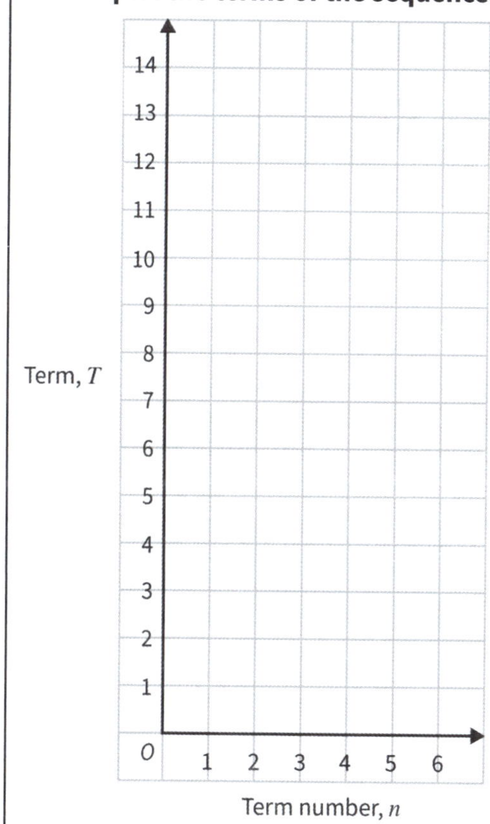

</td>
</tr>
<tr>
<td>b) Should you join the points with a line?</td>
<td>Would it be sensible to have 1.5 as a value for n?</td>
<td>b) Should you join the points with a line?</td>
</tr>
<tr>
<td>No, sequences have integer term numbers so you should not join the points.</td>
<td></td>
<td></td>
</tr>
</table>

4.1.2 Using a rule to find coordinates

Worked example 1

a) **Use the table of values to plot the points on a set of axes and draw a straight line through them.**

x	0	1	2	3	4
y		5		9	11

Thinking: How do we work out which points to plot?

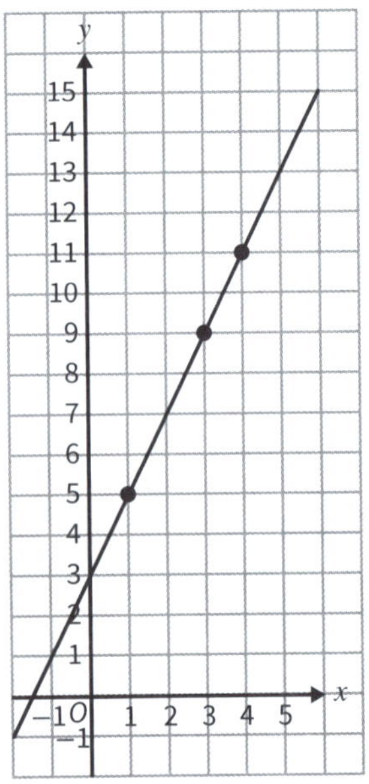

Thinking: Why is it useful to connect the coordinates with a straight line?

b) **Use the graph to fill in the missing coordinates in the table.**

x	0	1	2	3	4
y	3	5	7	9	11

Thinking: How can we find the missing values?

How else could we work out the missing coordinates?

c) **Write a rule that connects the y- and x-coordinates.**

Thinking: How can we work out what the coefficient of x should be in the rule?

$y = 2x + ?$

Thinking: How can we work out the rest of the rule?

Each y-coordinate is double the x-coordinate plus 3: $y = 2x + 3$

Your turn! 1

a) **Use the table of values to plot the points on a set of axes and draw a straight line through them.**

x	0	1	2	3	4
y	−1		5	8	

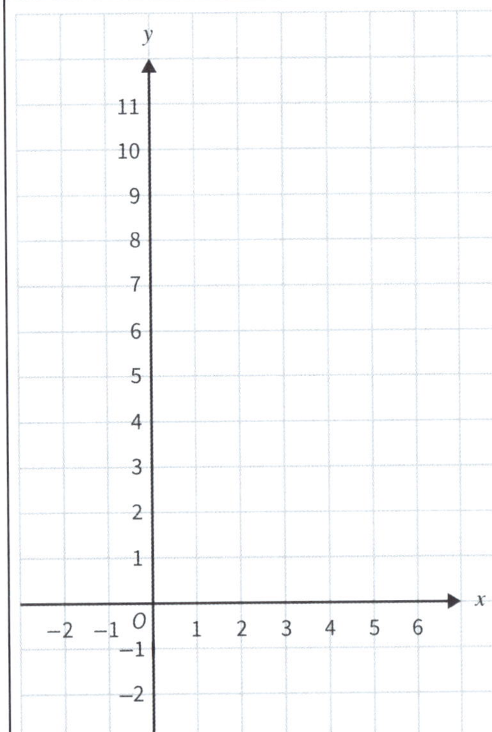

b) **Use the graph to fill in the missing coordinates in the table.**

c) **Write a rule that connects the y- and x-coordinates.**

Worked example 2	Thinking	Your turn! 2
a) A line has equation $y = 3x - 5$. Complete the table of values. x: −2, −1, 0, 1, 2, 3 y: (blank)	*How do we use the equation to complete a table of values?*	**a) A line has equation $y = 2x - 3$. Complete the table of values.** x: −2, −1, 0, 1, 2 y: (blank)
x: −2, −1, 0, 1, 2, 3 y: −11, −8, −5, −2, 1, 4		
b) Plot the points and draw a straight line through them. 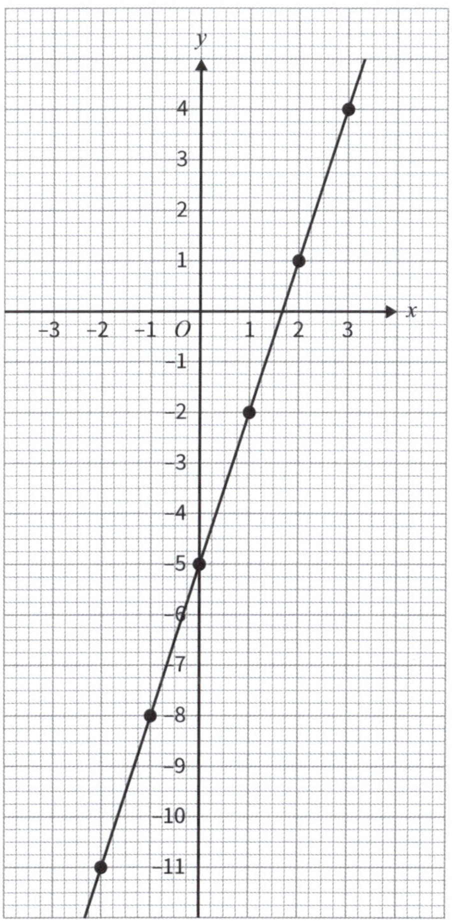	*How long should we draw the line?*	**b) Plot the points and draw a straight line through them.** 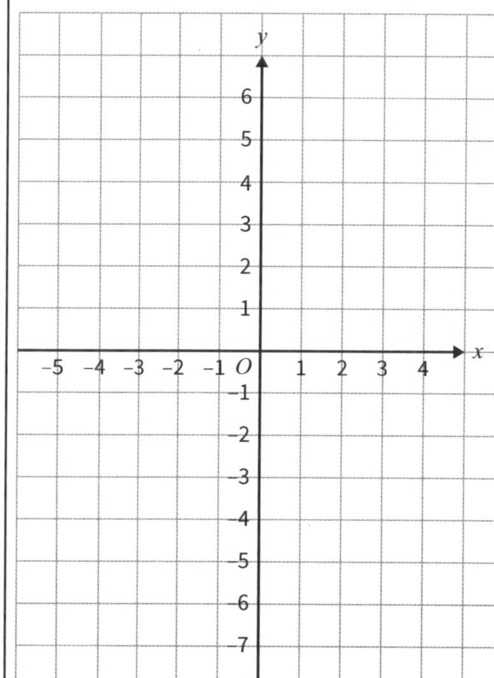
c) Explain whether or not the point (10, 35) lies on the line.	*How can we test if a point lies on the line?*	**c) Explain whether or not the point (10, 17) lies on the line.**
The x-coordinate is 10. Using the equation, the y-coordinate should be: $y = 3x - 5 = 3 \times 10 - 5 = 25$ So (10, 35) does not lie on the line.		

Worked example 2 a) table:

x	−2	−1	0	1	2	3
y						

x	−2	−1	0	1	2	3
y	−11	−8	−5	−2	1	4

Your turn! 2 a) table:

x	−2	−1	0	1	2
y					

Fluency questions

4.1.1 When to join points on a graph

1 A sequence has the nth term $3n - 1$.
The first four terms of the sequence are:

Term number n	1	2	3	4
Term T	2	5	8	11

The terms are plotted as points on a graph.

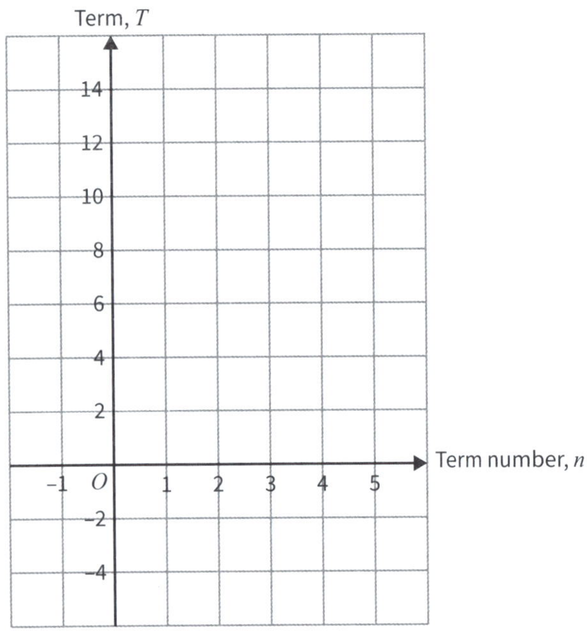

a) Could these points possibly be terms in the sequence?

i. (5, 14)

ii. (2.5, 6.5)

iii. (−1, −4)

b) Should the points on the graph be joined with a straight line?

2 The equation $y = 3x - 1$, is satisfied by these pairs of values:

x	1	2	3	4
y	2	5	8	11

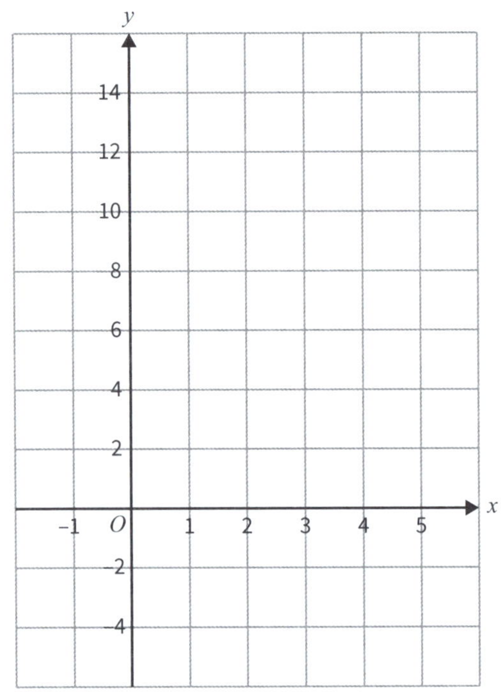

a) Could these points fit the relationship given by the equation?

i. (5, 14)

ii. (2.5, 6.5)

iii. (−1, −4)

b) Should the points on the graph be joined with a straight line?

3 Complete the sentence.
When a line is used to join the points on a graph, it means that …

a) … some points on that line fit the relationship given in the equation.

b) … any integer points on the line fit the relationship given in the equation.

c) … any point on that line fits the relationship given in the equation.

4.1.2 Using a rule to find coordinates

1 x and y are related by the equation $y = x + 4$.

a) Complete this table to show the relationship.

x	1	2	3	4	5
y					

b) Draw a graph to show the relationship.

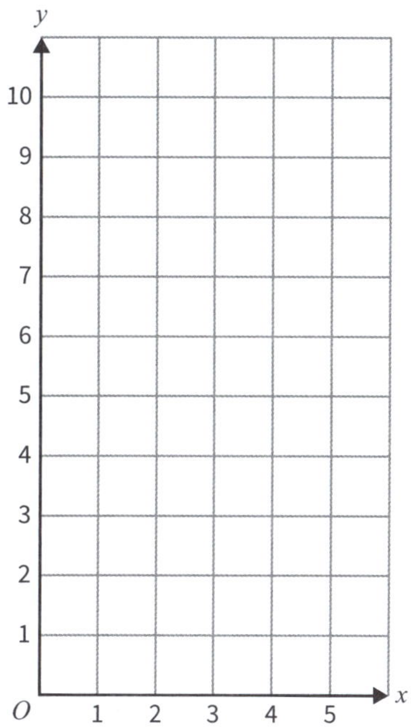

2 x and y are related by the equation $y = 2x$.

a) Complete this table to show the relationship.

x	1	2	3	4	5
y					

b) Draw a graph to show the relationship.

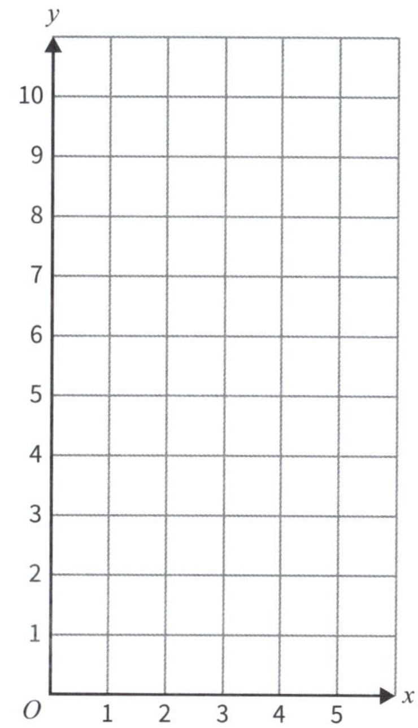

3 A straight line has the equation $y = x - 1$. Decide whether or not the points with these coordinates lie on the line.

a) (1, 2)

b) (3, 2)

c) (10, 12)

d) (15, 14)

4 A straight line has the equation $y = 3x$. Decide whether or not the points with these coordinates lie on the line.

a) (1, 3)

b) (4, 15)

c) (12, 30)

d) (15, 45)

4.2 Linear relationships

Example-problem pairs

4.2.1 Finding the gradient of a line

Worked example 1	Thinking	Your turn! 1
Work out the gradient of the line. 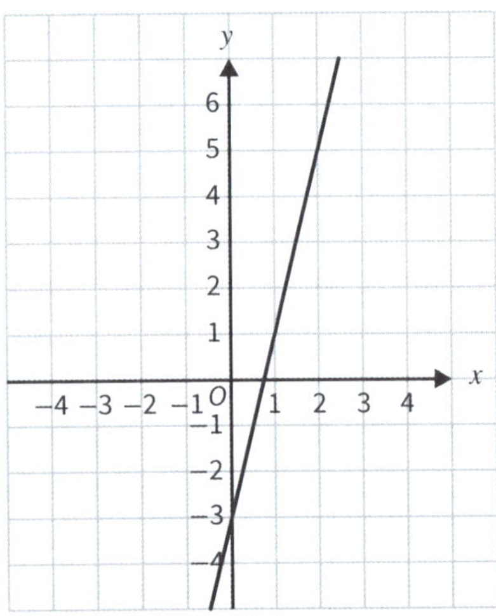	*How can we find values for the horizontal and vertical increases?* *How can we tell if the gradient will be positive or negative*	**Work out the gradient of the line.** 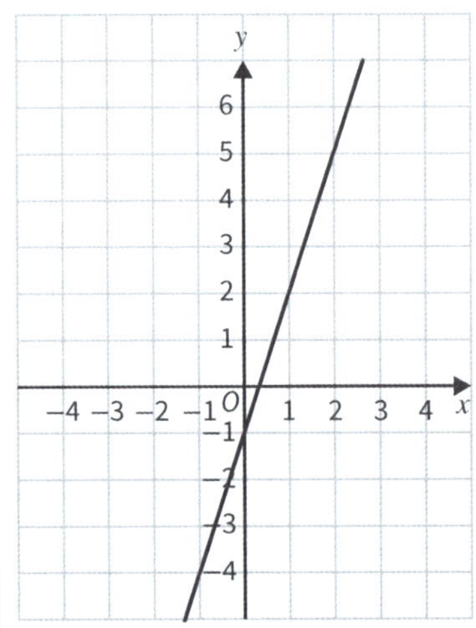
Gradient = $\frac{\text{vertical increase}}{\text{horizontal increase}} = \frac{4}{1} = 4$	*How do we make sure that we divide the numbers correctly?*	

Worked example 2	Thinking	Your turn! 2
Work out the gradient of each line. **a)** 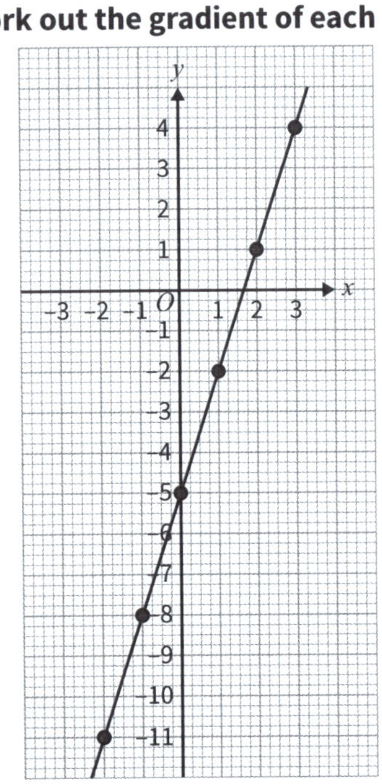	*Where should be the first step?*	**Work out the gradient of each line.** **a)** 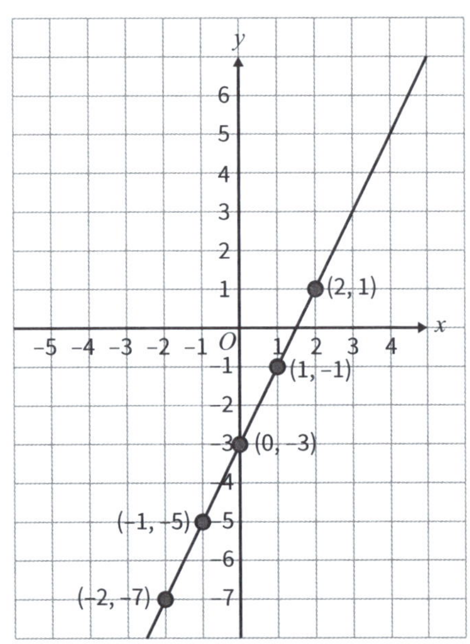

Gradient $= \frac{\text{vertical increase}}{\text{horizontal increase}} = \frac{6}{3} = 2$		
b) 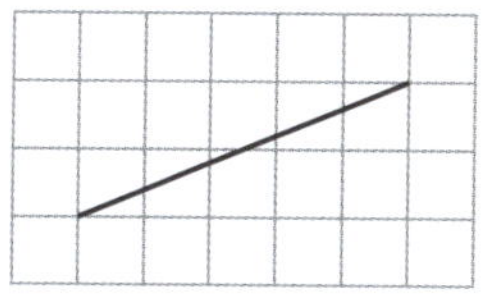	*How do you make sure that you divide the numbers correctly?*	**b)** 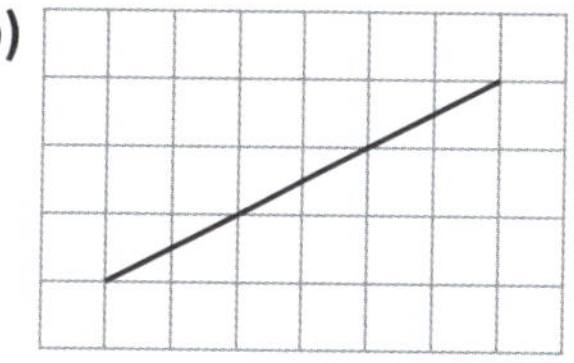
Gradient $= \frac{\text{vertical increase}}{\text{horizontal increase}}$ $= \frac{2}{5} = 0.4$		

Worked example 3	Thinking	Your turn! 3
Work out the gradient of each line. **a)** 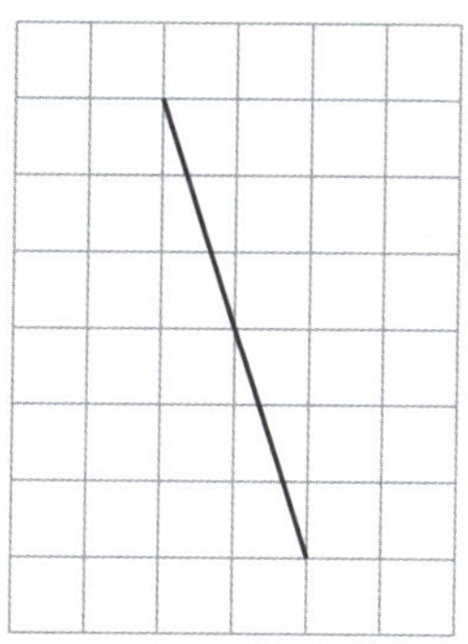	*How do we know if the gradient will be positive or negative?*	**Work out the gradient of each line.** **a)** 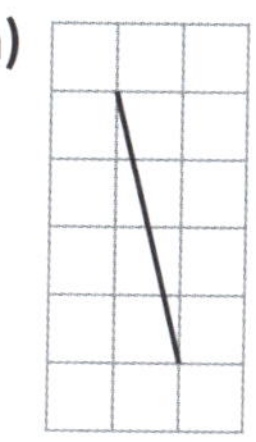
Gradient $= \frac{\text{vertical increase}}{\text{horizontal increase}}$ $= \frac{6}{-2} = -3$		
b) 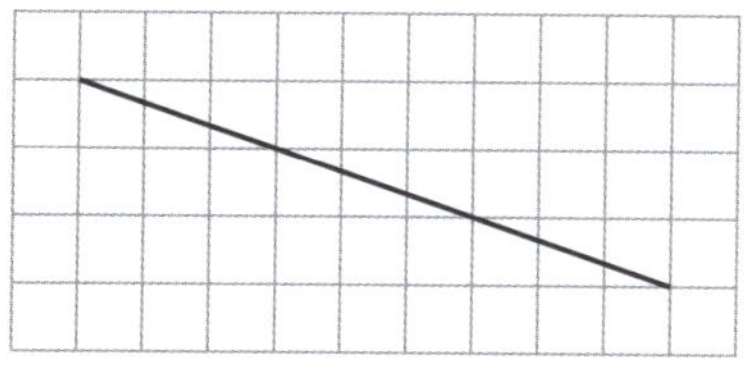	*How do we make sure that we divide the numbers correctly?*	**b)** 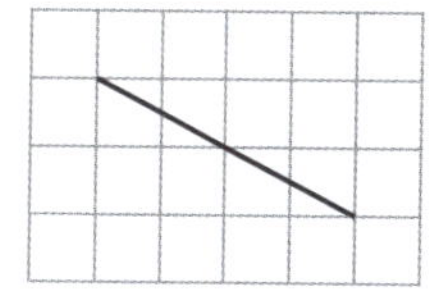
Gradient $= \frac{\text{vertical increase}}{\text{horizontal increase}}$ $= \frac{3}{-9} = -\frac{1}{3}$		

Worked example 4	Thinking	Your turn! 4
Work out the gradient of the line. 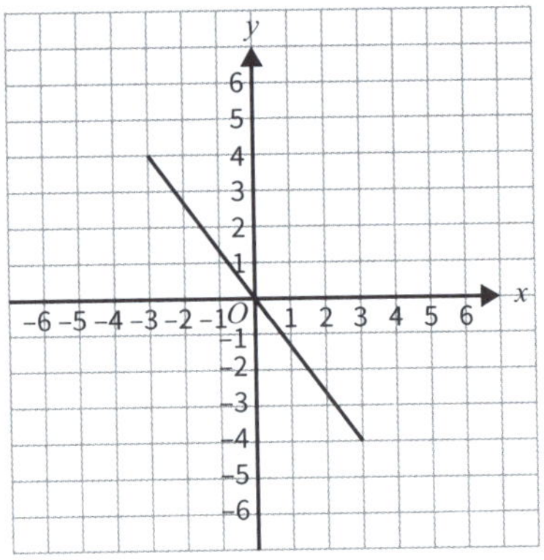	*How can we find values for the horizontal and vertical increases?* *How can we tell if the gradient will be positive or negative?*	**Work out the gradient of the line.** 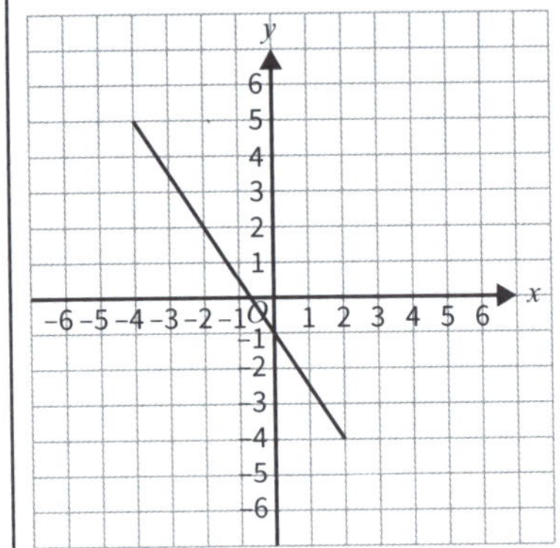
Gradient = $\frac{\text{vertical increase}}{\text{horizontal increase}}$ $= \frac{4}{-3} = -\frac{4}{3}$	*How do we make sure that we divide the numbers correctly?*	

Worked example 5	Thinking	Your turn! 5
Work out the gradient of the line. 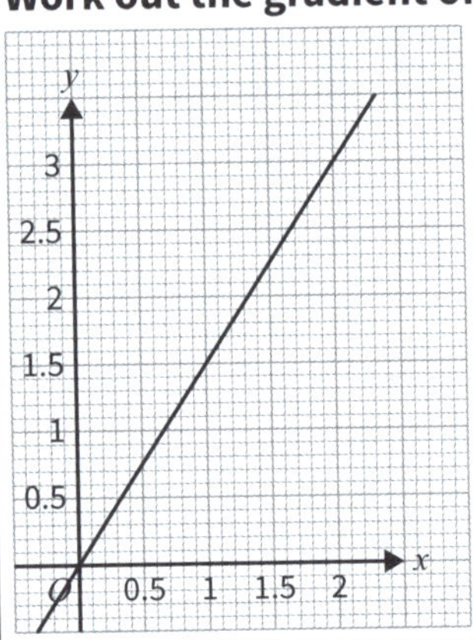	*How can we find values for the horizontal and vertical increases?* *How can we tell if the gradient will be positive or negative?*	**Work out the gradient of the line.** 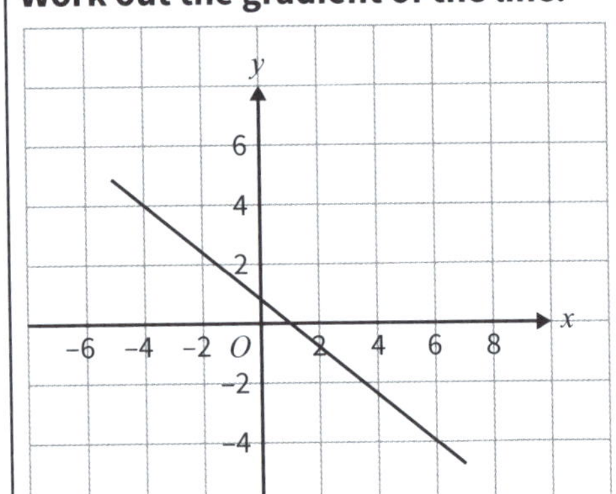
Gradient = $\frac{\text{vertical increase}}{\text{horizontal increase}}$ $= \frac{3}{2} = 1\frac{1}{2} = 1.5$	*How do we make sure that we divide the numbers correctly?*	

Worked example 6	Thinking	Your turn! 6
A line passes through the points (2, −2) and (6, 4). What is its gradient?	*How can we find values for the horizontal and vertical increases?*	**A line passes through the points (5, 2) and (7, −8). What is its gradient?**
The x-value has increased from 2 to 6 so the horizontal increase is $6 - 2 = 4$.		
The y-value has increased from −2 to 4 so the horizontal increase is $4 - (-2) = 6$.	*How do we find the gradient from these two increases?*	
The gradient = $\frac{6}{4} = \frac{3}{2} = 1.5$		

4.2.2 The gradient and y-intercept

Worked example 1	**Thinking**	**Your turn! 1**
On a set of axes draw a line with a gradient of 2 and a y-intercept of −3.	*What does this y-intercept tell us?*	**On a set of axes draw a line with a gradient of 3 and a y-intercept of −1.**
Mark the y-intercept: 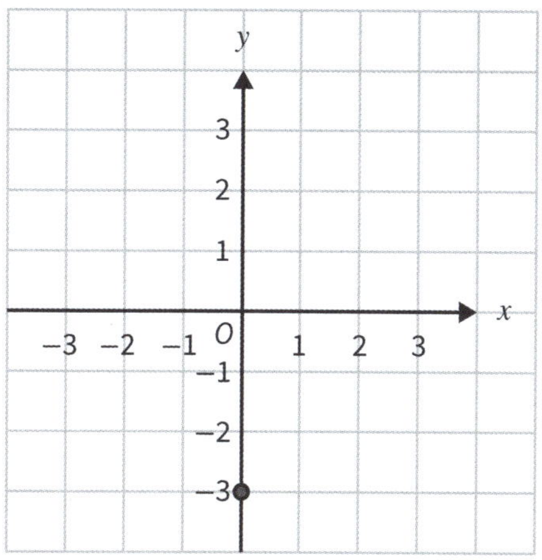	*What does the gradient of a line tell us?*	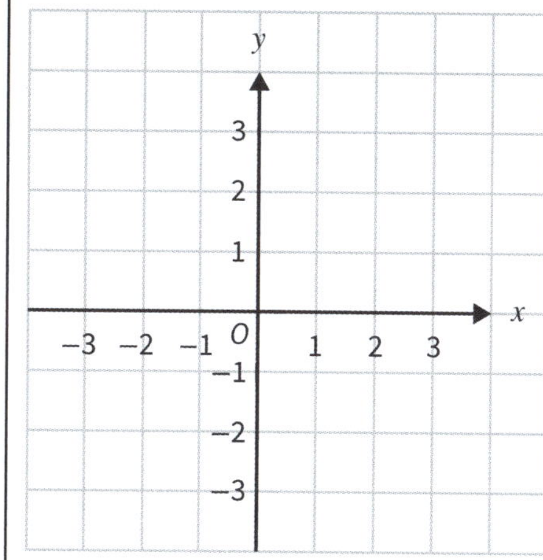
The gradient of +2 means that when the x-value goes up by 1, the y-value goes up by 2.	*How can we use this to find a second point to mark?*	
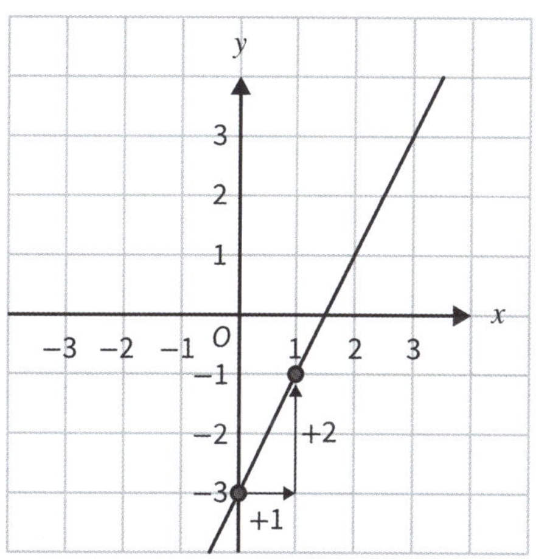	*How do we use the two points to draw the line?*	

Worked example 2	Thinking	Your turn! 2
The graph shows how the distance of three students from their home changed one afternoon on the way back from school. Use the gradients of each to explain which student, A, B, or C: • **stayed at school for a club** • **cycled home** • **walked home?** 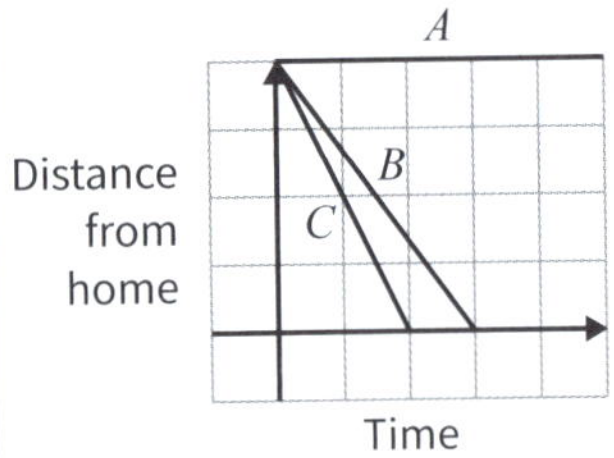	*What does the gradient of a line tell us?*	**The graph shows how the distance of three students from their home changed one morning on the way to school. Use the gradients of each to explain which student, A, B, or C:** • **stayed at home unwell** • **was driven to school** • **walked to school?** 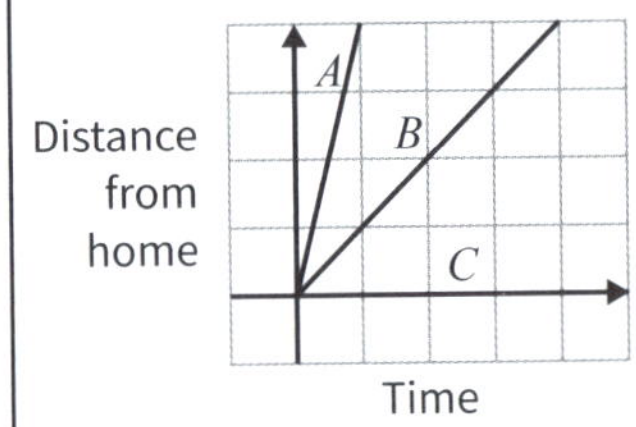
Line *A* has a gradient of zero. So the rate of change of their distance was 0, which means that it did not change. This means that the student stayed in the same place. So student A must have stayed at school for a club.		
Students B and C both changed their distance so must have travelled home.	*How can we compare the two lines?*	
Line *C* is steeper than line *B* so it has a higher gradient. So the rate of change of student C's distance was higher. So both B and C decreased their distance by the same amount, but student C did it in a shorter time. So student C must have cycled home.		
Line *B* is not as steep; it has a lower gradient. So the rate of change of student B's distance is lower.		
So student B covered the same distance but in a longer time. So student B must have walked home.		

Worked example 3	Thinking	Your turn! 3
What is the y-intercept of this graph? 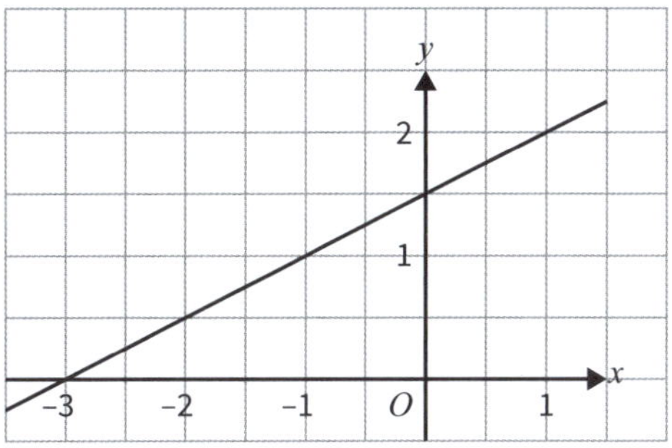	*Where do we look on the graph to find the y-intercept?*	**What is the y-intercept of this graph?** 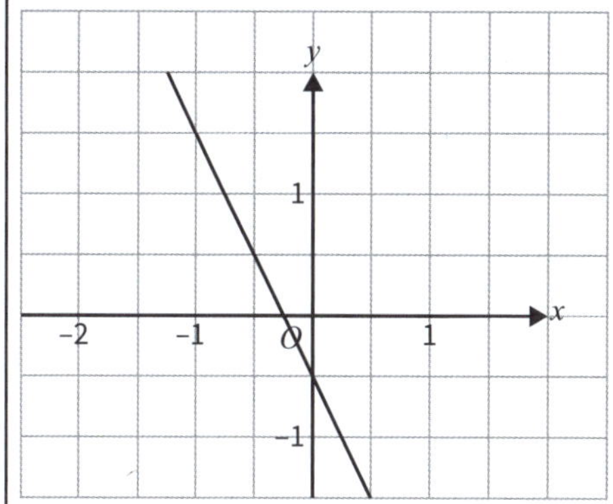
The y-intercept is 1.5.	*In what form do we give the y-intercept?*	

Worked example 4	Thinking	Your turn! 4
Match the lines shown on the graph with the correct gradient and y-intercept in the table. 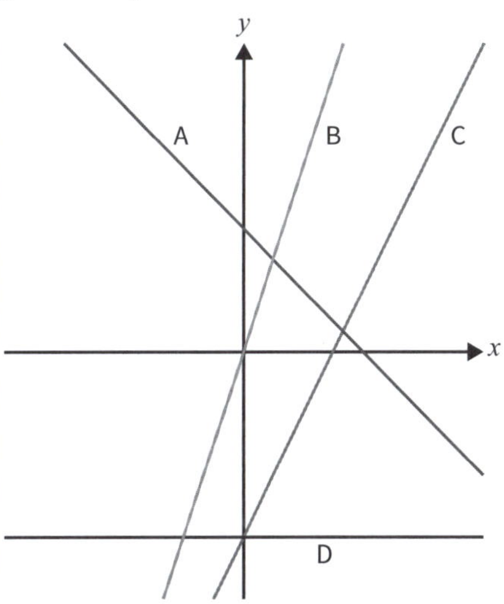	*In what direction will a line with a positive gradient slope?*	**Match the lines shown on the graph with the correct gradient and y-intercept in the table.** 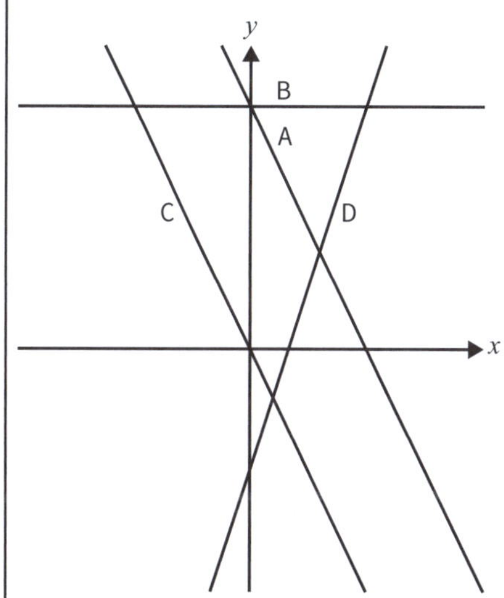

Worked example 4 table:

Line	Gradient	y-intercept
	2	−3
	−1	2
	0	−3
	3	0

Your turn! 4 table:

Line	Gradient	y-intercept
	3	−2
	−2	4
	0	4
	−2	0

The line that matches the first row has a positive gradient and a negative y-intercept. It is line C.	*In what direction will a line with a negative gradient slope?*	
The line that matches the second row has a negative gradient and a positive y-intercept. It is line A.		
The line that matches the third row has a gradient of 0 and negative y-intercept so it is a horizontal line that goes through the negative y-axis. It is line D.	*What does it mean when a line has a gradient of 0?*	
The line that matches the last row has a positive gradient and y-intercept of 0 so it goes through the origin. It is line B.	*What does it mean when a line has a y-intercept of 0?*	

Line	Gradient	y-intercept
C	2	−3
A	−1	2
D	0	−3
B	3	0

Worked example 5	Thinking	Your turn! 5
On a set of axes sketch a line with a gradient of −3 and a y-intercept of 2.	*What does this y-intercept tell us?*	**On a set of axes sketch a line with a gradient of −2 and a y-intercept of −1.**
Mark the y-intercept: 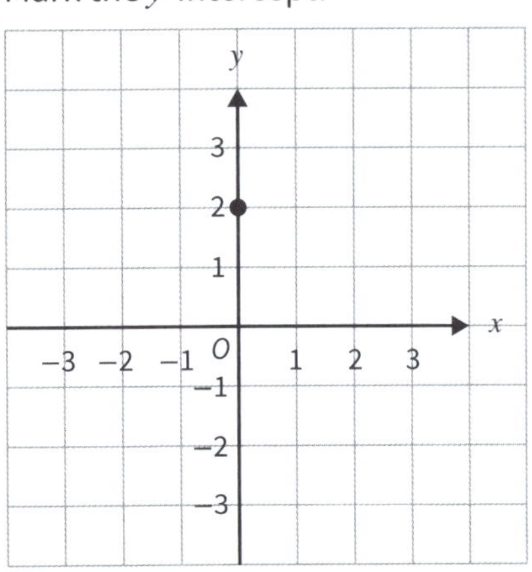	*What does the gradient of a line tell us?* *What does a negative gradient mean?* *How can we use this to find a second point to mark?*	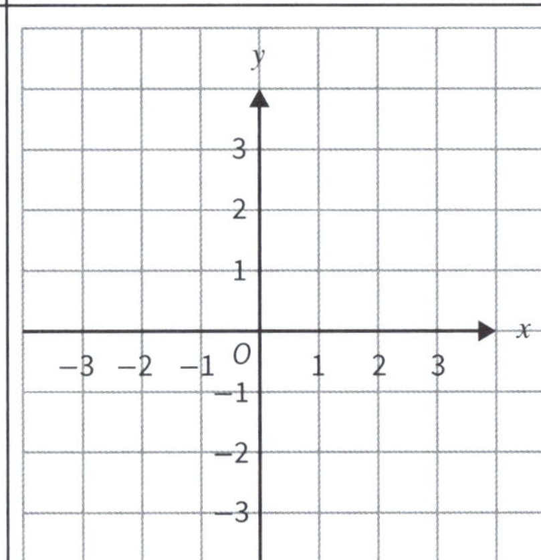
The gradient of −3 means that when the x-value goes up by 1, the y-value goes down by 3.		

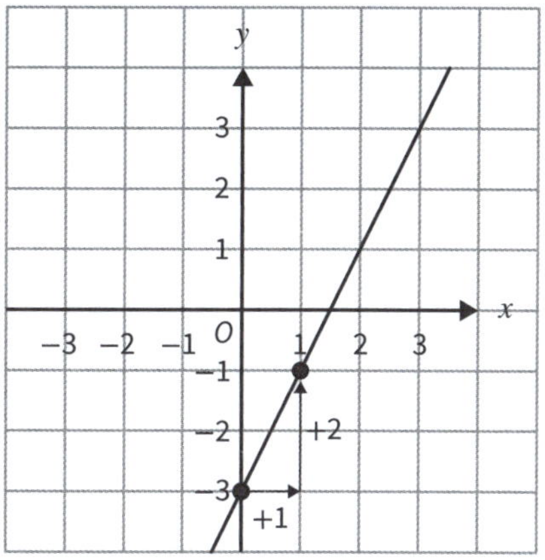	*How do we use the two points to draw the line?*	

Worked example 6	Thinking	Your turn! 6
On a set of axes sketch a line with a gradient of $+\frac{1}{2}$ and a y-intercept of −1.	*What does this y-intercept tell us?*	**On a set of axes sketch a line with a gradient of $+\frac{1}{4}$ and a y-intercept of 1.**
Mark the y-intercept: 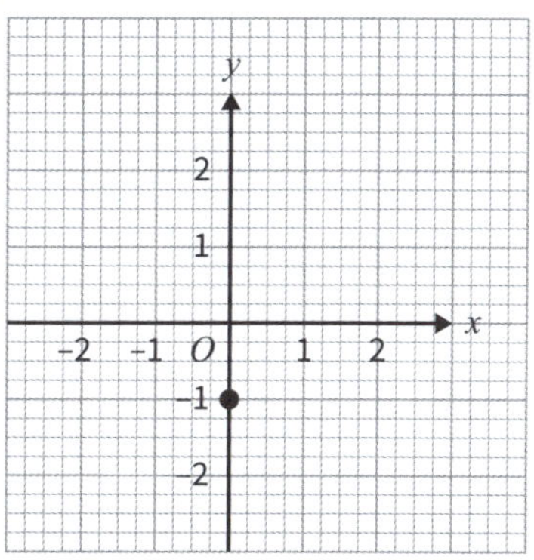	*What does the gradient of a line tell us?* *How can we use this to find a second point to mark?*	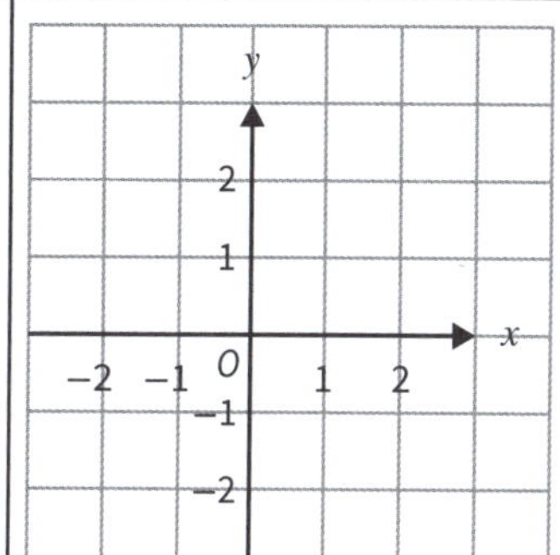
The gradient of $+\frac{1}{2}$ means that when the x-value goes up by 1, the y-value goes up by $\frac{1}{2}$.		
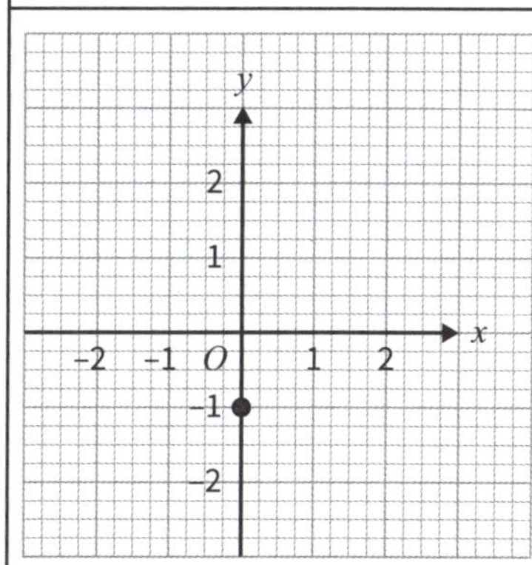	*How do we use the two points to draw the line?*	

4.2.3 $y = mx + c$ form of linear graphs

Worked example 1	Thinking	Your turn! 1
Write the gradient and y-intercept of the line with each of these equations:		**Write the gradient and y-intercept of the line with each of these equations:**
a) $y = 3x - 7$	*Is the equation in gradient-intercept form?*	**a)** $y = 4x - 3$
$y = 3x - 7$ $y = mx + c$ $m = 3$ and $c = -7$	*Which is the gradient, and which is the y-intercept?*	
The gradient is 3. The y-intercept is −7.		
b) $6 - 5x = y$	*Is the equation in gradient-intercept form?*	**b)** $1 - 8x = y$
$6 - 5x = y$ $c + mx = y$ $c = 6$ and $m = -5$	*How can we tell the difference between the gradient and intercept in the equation?*	
The gradient is −5. The y-intercept is 6.		

Worked example 2	Thinking	Your turn! 2
Write the gradient and y-intercept of the line with equation $3y = 6x + 18$.	*Is the equation in gradient-intercept form?*	**Write the gradient and y-intercept of the line with equation $2y = 10x + 6$.**
$\frac{3y}{3} = \frac{6x}{3} + \frac{18}{3}$ $y = 2x + 6$	*What is a possible first step in getting the equation in the form $y = mx + c$* *Is the equation now in gradient-intercept form?*	
$y = 2x + 6$ $y = mx + c$ $m = 2$ and $c = 6$		
The gradient is 2. The y-intercept is 6.		

Worked example 3	Thinking	Your turn! 3
Write the equation of this line.		**Write the equation of this line.**
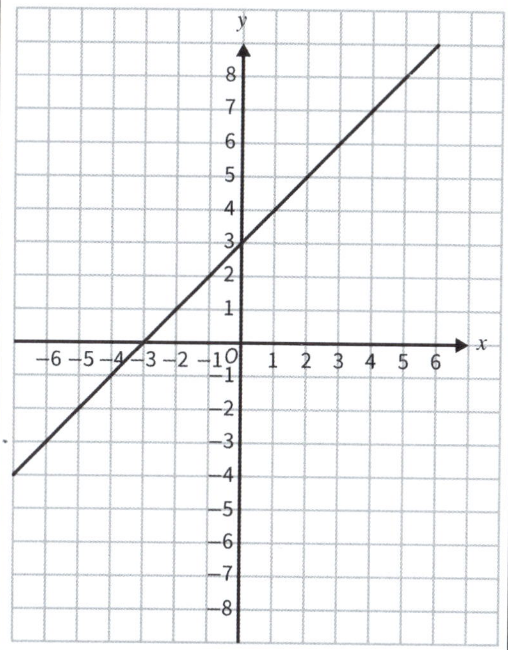	*How do we write the equation of a line from its graph?*	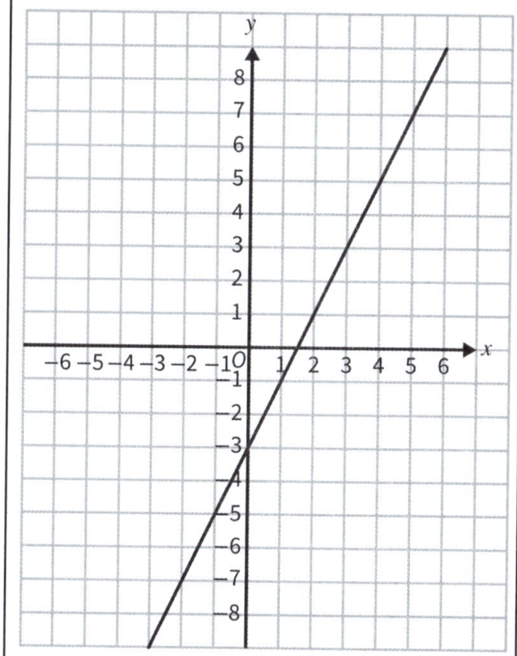
y-intercept = (0, 3), so $c = 3$	*How do we find the gradient?*	
gradient, $m = \frac{\text{vertical increase}}{\text{horizontal increase}}$ $m = \frac{4}{4} = 1$		
So, the equation of the line is $y = 1x + 3 \rightarrow y = x + 3$.		

4.2.4 Solving problems with linear graphs

Worked example 1	Thinking	Your turn! 1
The graph shows the length of a spring as masses are added. 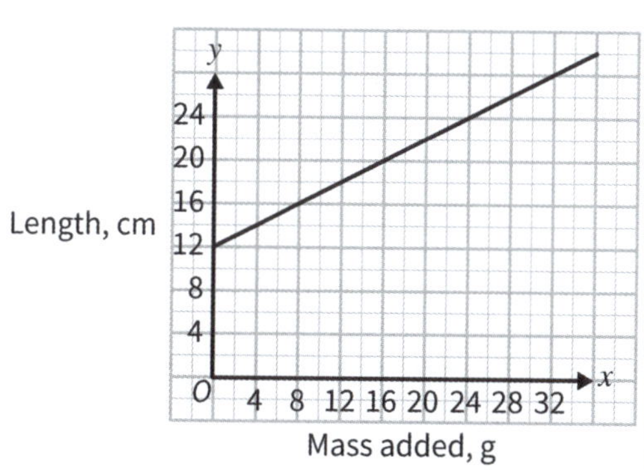		**The graph shows the length of an elastic band as masses are added.** 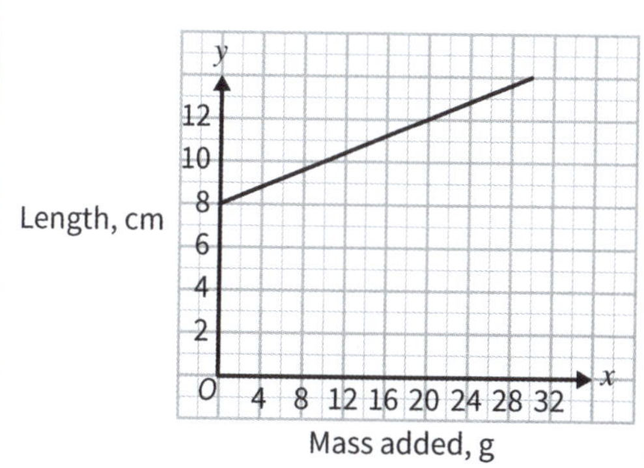
a) Write the y-intercept of the graph.		**a) Write the y-intercept of the graph.**
12		

4 Linear graphs

b) What does the y-intercept represent?	*Which features of the graph tell us what the y-intercept represents?*	**b) What does the y-intercept represent?**
The length of the spring before any masses are added.		
c) Work out the gradient of the line.	*How do we work out gradient?*	**c) Work out the gradient of the line.**
Picking two points from the graph, (0, 12) and (8, 16): Gradient $= \frac{4}{8} = 0.5$		
d) What does the gradient of the line represent?	*What features of the graph tell us what the gradient represents?*	**d) What does the gradient of the line represent?**
For each 1 g in mass added to the spring, the length of the spring increases by 0.5 cm.		

Worked example 2	Thinking	Your turn! 2
A taxi company charges a base rate per journey and then a certain amount per kilometre. The cost of the journey, $$y$, is shown on the graph. Cost, $$y$ 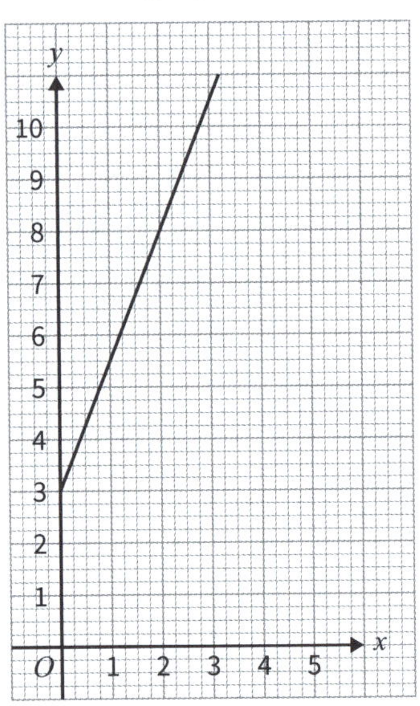 Distance, kilometres		**A taxi company charges a base rate per journey and then a certain amount per kilometre. The cost of the journey, $$y$, is shown on the graph.** Cost, $$y$ 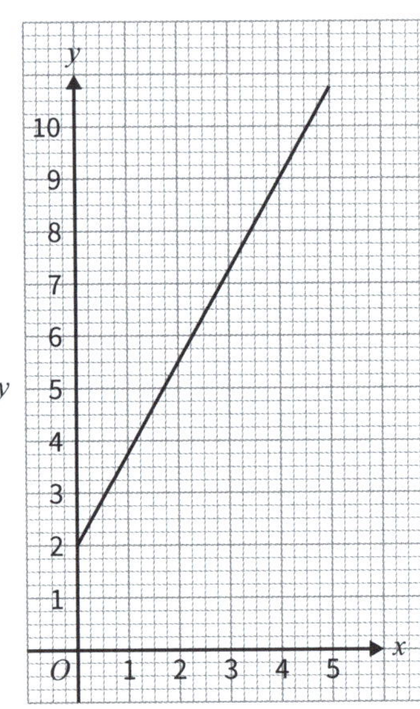 Distance, kilometres
a) What is the base rate charged per journey?	*What represents the base rate?*	**a) What is the base rate charged per journey?**
The cost at 0 kilometres tells us the base rate. This is the y-intercept.		
y-intercept = 3	*Where do we find the units for the base rate?*	
So the base rate at 0 kilometres is $3.		

b) What is the cost per kilometre of a journey?		**b) What is the cost per kilometre of a journey?**
The gradient represents the change in the y-value, the cost, when the x-value, the distance, increases by 1. So it represents the cost per kilometre travelled.	*What feature of the graph represents the cost per mile?*	
Gradient = $\frac{5}{2} = 2.5$	*Where do we find the units to use for the cost per kilometre?*	
So the cost per kilometre is \$2.50.		

Worked example 3	**Thinking**	**Your turn! 3**
Rakesh is having his bedroom decorated. The decorator charges for the cost of the materials and then adds a cost per hour. 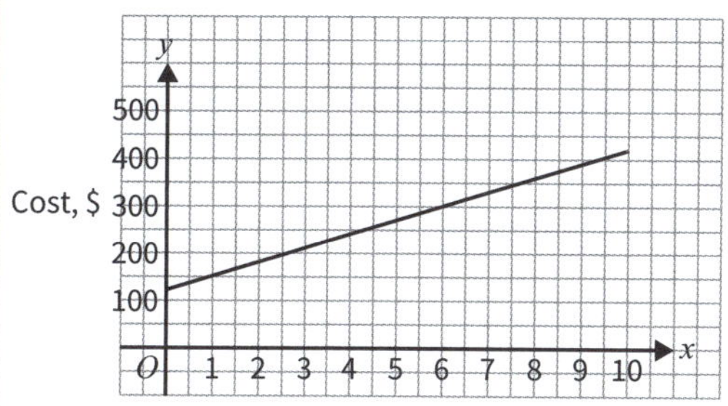	*What feature of the graph represents the cost before any hours of work have been done?* *Where do we find the units to use?*	**Sunita is having her living room decorated. The decorator charges for the cost of the materials and then adds a cost per hour.** 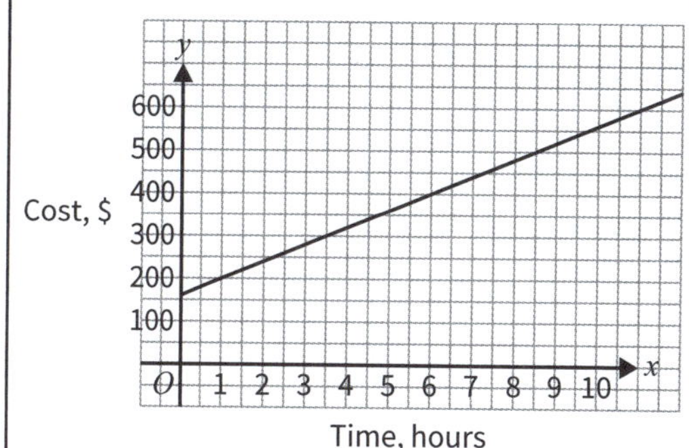
a) How much did the materials cost?		**a) How much did the materials cost?**
The cost at 0 hours tells us the cost of the materials, this is the y-intercept.		
y-intercept = 120		
So the cost of the materials was \$120.		
b) How much does the decorator charge per hour?		**b) How much does the decorator charge per hour?**
The gradient represents the change in the y-value, the cost, when the x-value, the time, increases by 1. So it represents the cost per hour.	*What represents the cost per hour?*	
Gradient = $\frac{150}{5} = 30$	*Where do we find the units?*	
So the cost per hour is \$30.		

Fluency questions

4.2.1 Finding the gradient of a line

(Remember that a vertical line up has a positive vertical increase and a line down has a negative vertical increase.)

$$\text{gradient} = \frac{\text{vertical increase}}{\text{horizontal increase}}$$

1 Follow the steps to find the gradient of the line segment.

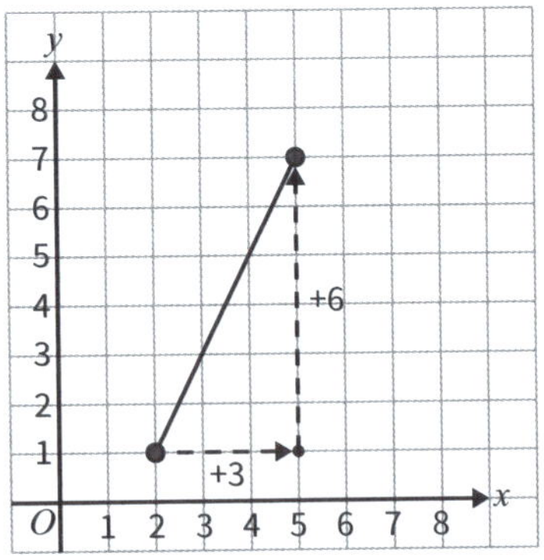

a) What is the horizontal increase of the line?
b) What is the vertical increase of the line?
c) Calculate the gradient of the line.

2 Follow the steps to find the gradient of the line.

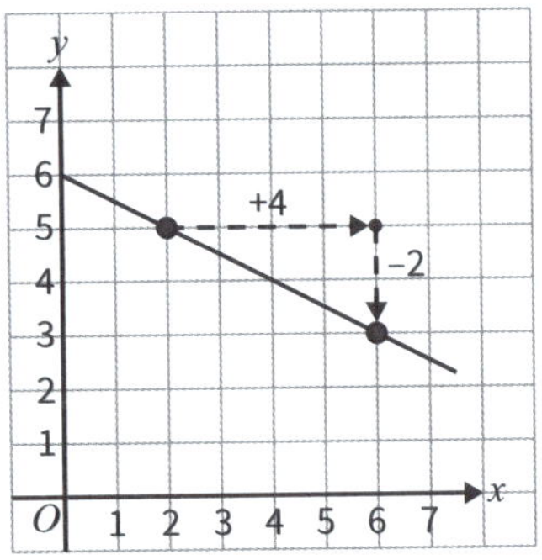

a) What is the horizontal increase of the line?
b) What is the vertical increase of the line?
c) Calculate the gradient of the line.

3 Follow the steps to find the gradient of the line.

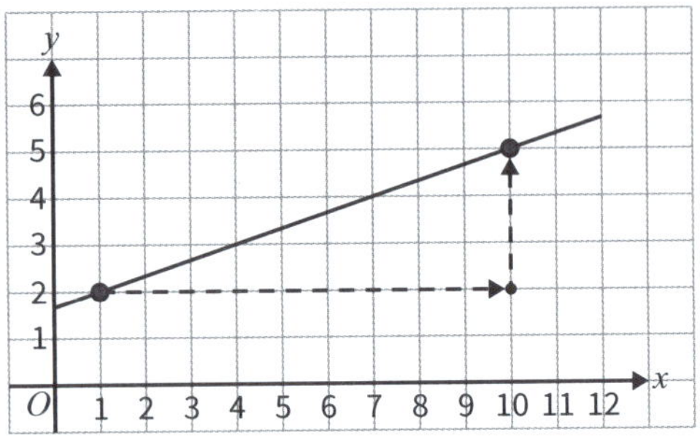

a) What is the horizontal increase of the line?
b) What is the vertical increase of the line?
c) Calculate the gradient of the line.

4 Answer the questions to find the gradient of the line segment.

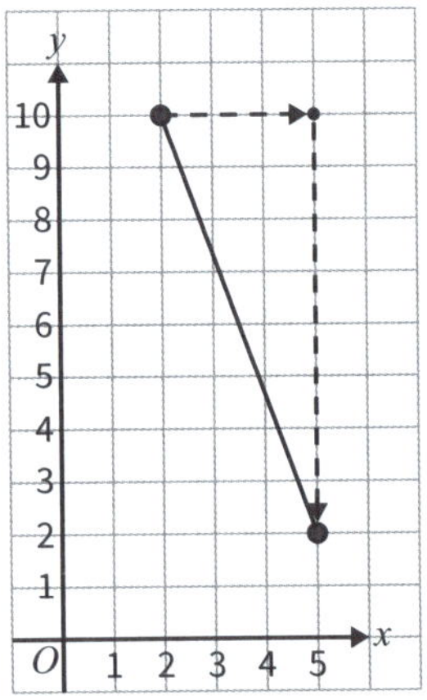

a) What is the horizontal increase of the line?
b) What is the vertical increase of the line?
c) Calculate the gradient of the line.

4.2.2 The gradient and y-intercept

1 Look at these graphs.

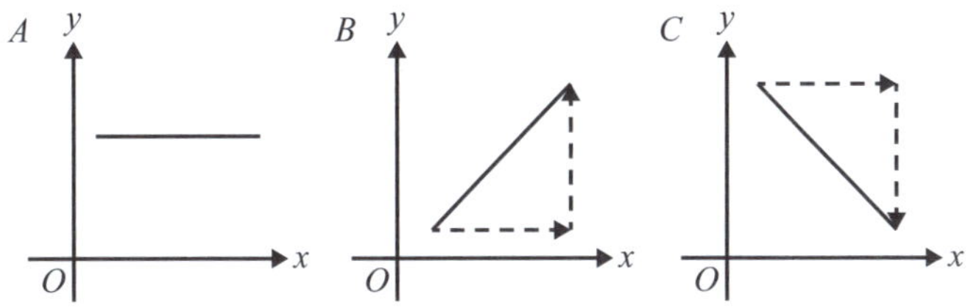

Identify which line has a gradient that is:

a) positive

b) negative

c) zero.

2 Look at these graphs.

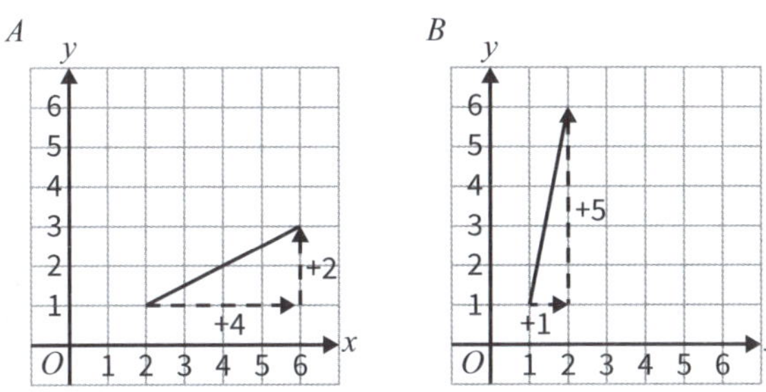

a) Which line is steeper?

gradient = $\dfrac{\text{vertical increase}}{\text{horizontal increase}}$

b) Work out the gradient of Line *A*.

c) Work out the gradient of Line *B*.

d) Which line has the higher gradient?

3 Look at this graph.

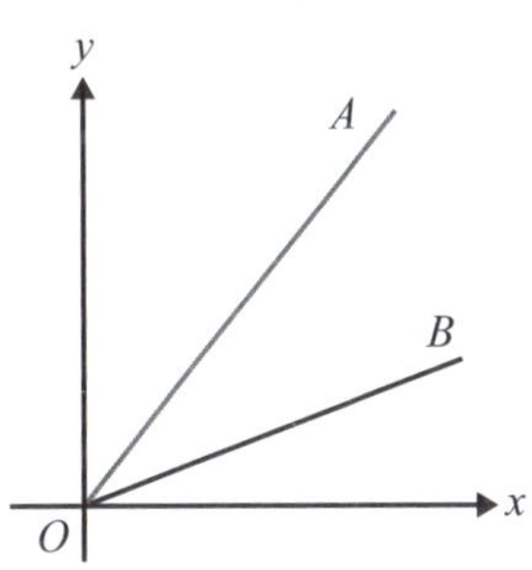

a) Which line is steeper?

b) Which line has a higher gradient?

4 Look at this graph which shows the journey of two students as they travelled to school.

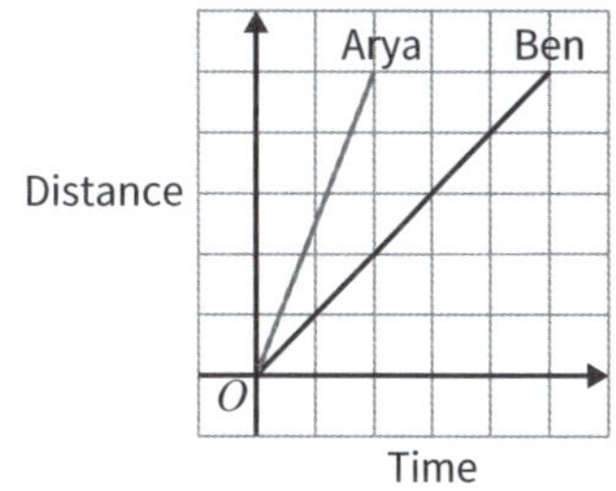

Explain how the graph shows that Arya cycled to school while Ben walked.

Choose the correct word from each bold pair to complete the explanation.

Arya's line is **steeper/shallower**, so it has a **lower/higher** gradient. This shows that her distance was changing at a **higher/lower** rate. She covered the same distance in **less/more** time than Ben.

5 Look at these graphs.

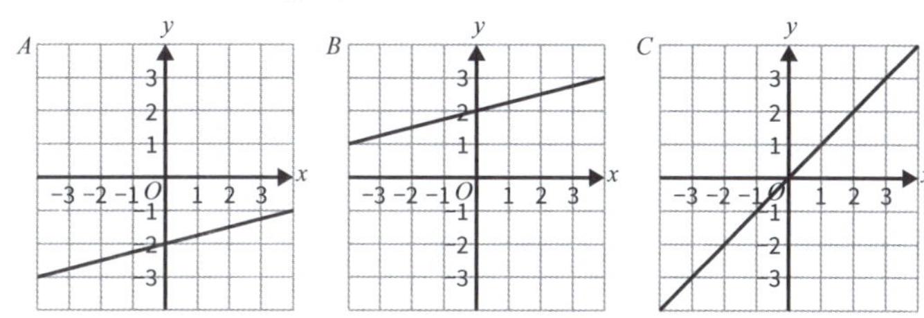

Identify which line has a y-intercept that is:

a) positive

b) negative

c) zero.

4.2.3 $y = mx + c$ form of linear graphs

1 You can write the equation of a linear graph in the form $y = mx + c$ where m is the gradient of the line and c is the y-intercept of the line.

If a line has gradient 8 and y-intercept 3, it means that $m = 8$ and $c = 3$, so the equation is $y = 8x + 3$.

Write the equation of a line with:

a) gradient 4 and y-intercept 2 $y =$ ____$x +$ ____

b) gradient 4 and y-intercept −2 $y =$ ____$x +$ ____

c) gradient 4 and y-intercept 5 $y =$ ____$x +$ ____

d) gradient 6 and y-intercept 5 $y =$ ____$x +$ ____

e) gradient 1 and y-intercept 9 $y =$ ____$x +$ ____

f) gradient 5 and y-intercept 0 $y =$ ____$x +$ ____

g) gradient 0 and y-intercept 3 $y =$ ____$x +$ ____

2 Answer question parts **i–iii** for each of these graphs.

a)

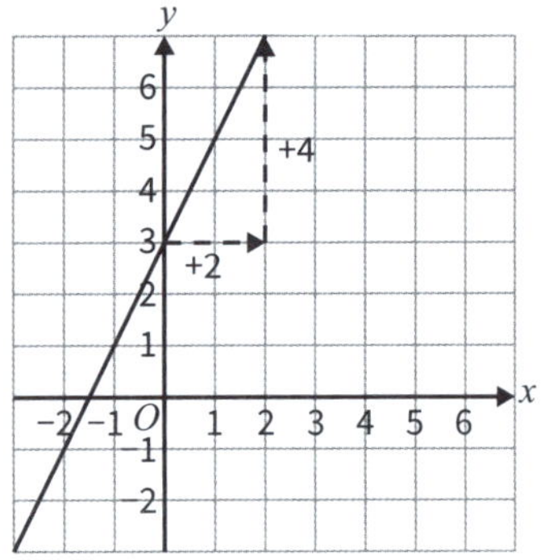

b)

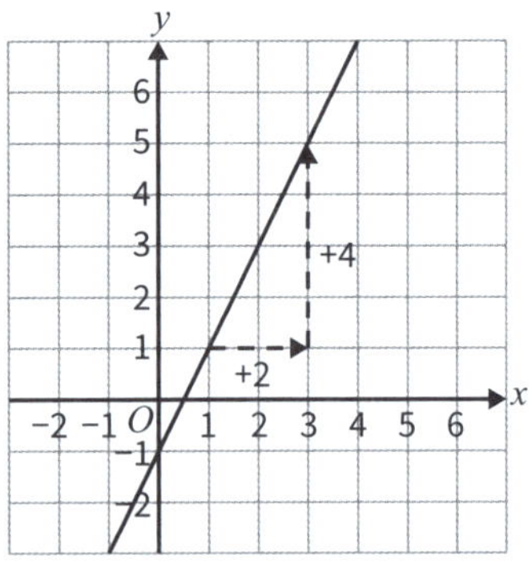

c)

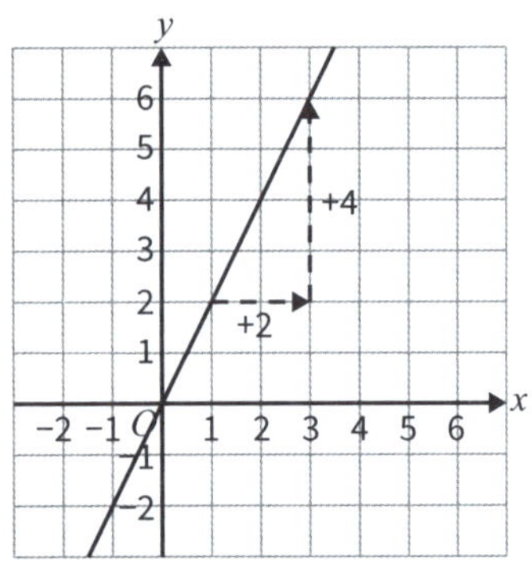

i. Work out the gradient of the line using

$$\text{gradient} = \frac{\text{vertical increase}}{\text{horizontal increase}}$$

ii. Write down the y-intercept of the line.

iii. Substitute your answers for **i** and **ii** into the equation $y = mx + c$ to give the equation of the line.

Remember: m is the gradient **(i)** and c is the y-intercept **(ii)**.

3 Answer question parts **i–iii** for each of these graphs.

a)

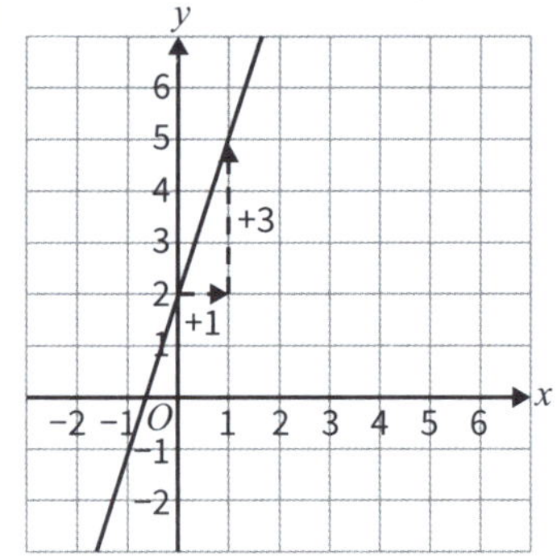

b)

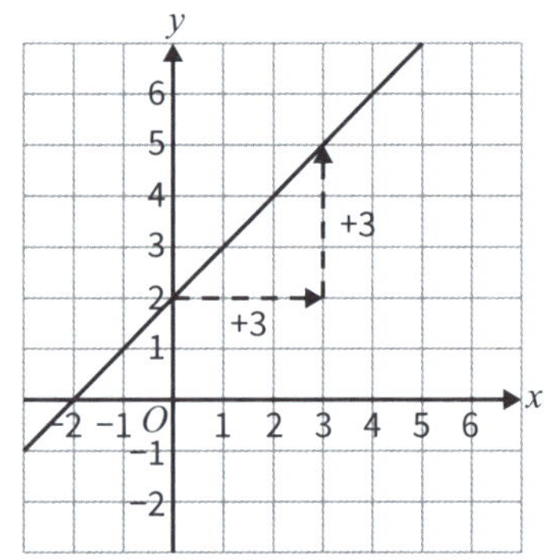

c)

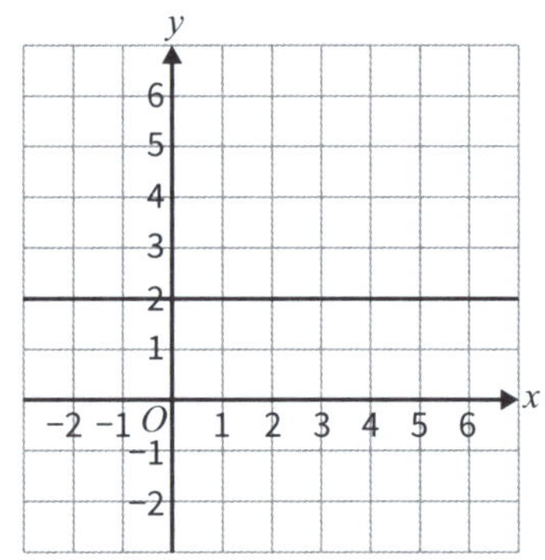

i. Work out the gradient of the line using

$$\text{gradient} = \frac{\text{vertical increase}}{\text{horizontal increase}}$$

ii. Write down the y-intercept of the line.

iii. Substitute your answers for **i** and **ii** into the equation $y = mx + c$ to give the equation of the line.

Remember: m is the gradient **(i)** and c is the y-intercept **(ii)**.

4.2.4 Solving problems involving linear graphs

1 By substituting, work out whether these coordinates could be on the line $y = 3x + 1$.

a) (0, 1)

b) (1, 3)

c) (2, 5)

d) (3, 10)

2 Match each description to the correct graph that represents it.

a) A bath starts off full and then the water level decreases once the plug is removed.

b) The journey of a student sprinting 20 metres.

c) A cold room starts at 12 °C. Then a heater is turned on and the temperature increases.

d) A plumber charges a \$20 callout fee and then charges \$20 per hour for his time.

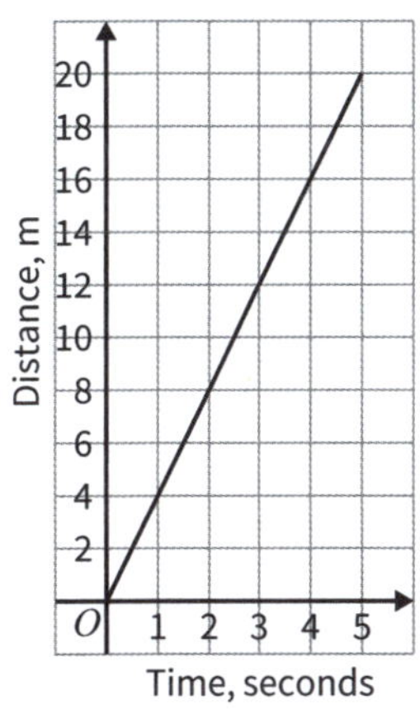

A

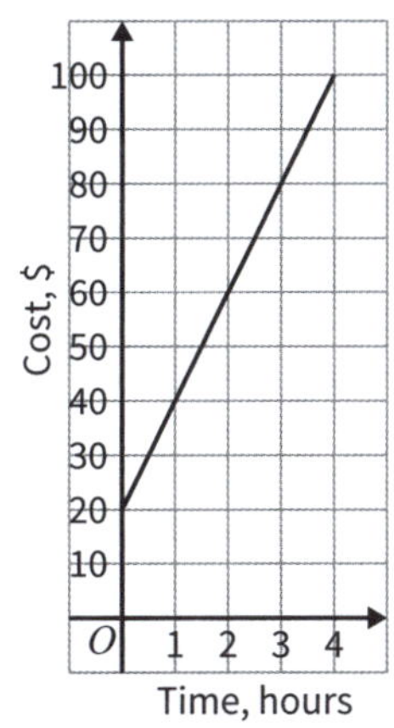

B

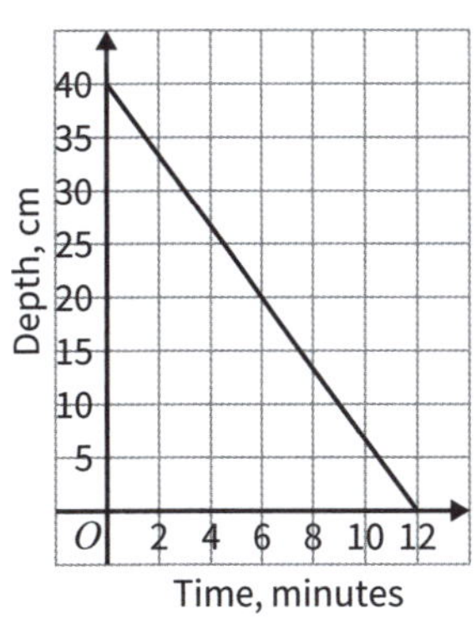

C

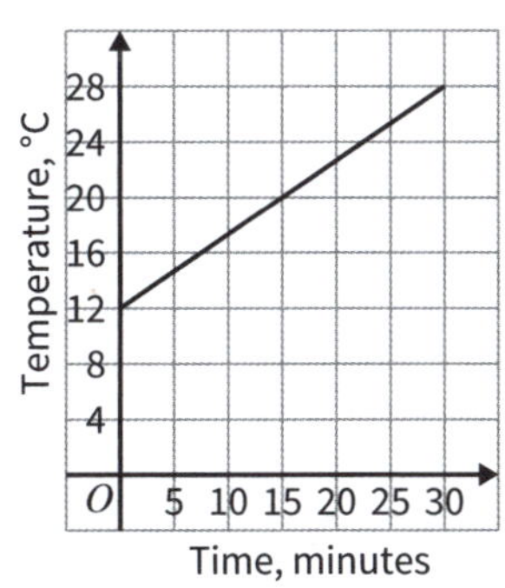

D

3 The graph below shows the cost of a taxi ride for different distances.

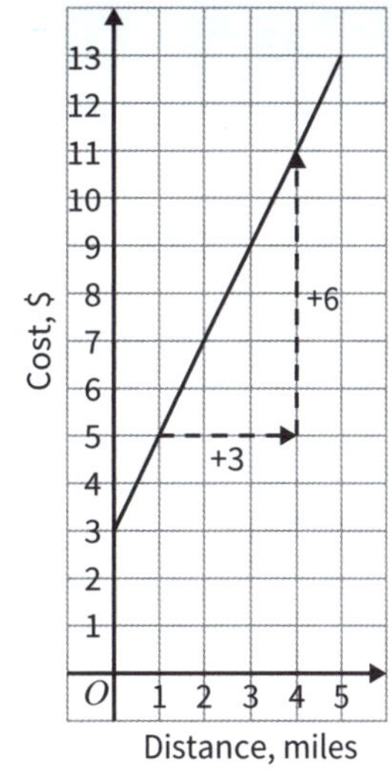

a) What is the y-intercept of the line?

b) Work out the gradient of the line using triangle shown and the following equation:

$$\text{gradient} = \frac{\text{vertical increase}}{\text{horizontal increase}}$$

c) What is the correct equation for the line?

i. $y = 2x$

ii. $y = 2x + 3$

iii. $y = 3x + 2$

iv. $y = 3x + 3$

d) Choose the correct option in each underlined group to complete the sentence.
The **y-intercept/gradient** represents the cost before any distance has been travelled. This means that the taxi driver charges a starting cost of **\$2/\$3/\$6**.

e) Choose the correct option in each underlined group to complete the sentences.
The **y-intercept/gradient** represents the cost per kilometre. It shows that the taxi driver charges **\$2/\$3/\$6** for every 1 kilometre travelled.

5.1 Percentages

Example-problem pairs

5.1.1 Percentages, fractions, and decimals

Worked example 1	Thinking	Your turn! 1
Write 45% as a fraction and a decimal.	*How does the 'per cent' help us to write a fraction?*	**Write 8% as a fraction and a decimal.**
$45\% = \frac{45}{100} = \frac{9}{20}$	*Is the fraction in its simplest form?*	
$45\% = 45 \div 100$ $= 0.45$	*What does a fraction line represent?*	

Worked example 2	Thinking	Your turn! 2
Convert $\frac{1}{6}$ to a percentage.	*What operation does the fraction line represent?* *How can we work this out?*	**Convert $\frac{7}{8}$ to a percentage.**
$6\overline{)1.0\,{}^{4}0\,{}^{4}0\,{}^{4}0}$ with quotient $0.1\;6\;6\;6$	*How do we convert a decimal to a percentage?*	
$0.1666 \times 100\% = 16.66\%$	*How do we represent recurring numbers?*	

Worked example 3	Thinking	Your turn! 3
Convert 162% to a fraction and a decimal.	*How does 'per cent' help us?*	**Convert 220% to a fraction and a decimal.**
$162\% = \frac{162}{100}$		
$\frac{162}{100} = \frac{81}{50} = 1\frac{31}{50}$	*How else can we write an improper fraction?*	
$\frac{162}{100} = 162 \div 100 = 1.62$	*What operation does a fraction line represent?*	

Worked example 4	Thinking	Your turn! 4
Convert 133.3% to a fraction and a decimal.	*How does 'per cent' help us?*	**Convert 142.05% to a fraction and a decimal.**
$133.\dot{3}\% = \frac{133.\dot{3}}{100}$ $= \frac{4}{3}$	*Where have we seen recurring numbers like this in decimals as parts of a whole?*	
$\frac{133.\dot{3}}{100} = 133.\dot{3} \div 100 = 1.\dot{3}$	*What operation does a fraction line represent?*	

5.1.2 Comparing quantities with percentages

Worked example 1	Thinking	Your turn! 1
Write: **a) 30 as a percentage of 48** **b) 48 as a percentage of 30.**	*How can we write a fraction and turn it into a percentage?*	**Write:** **a) 56 as a percentage of 70** **b) 70 as a percentage of 56.**
a) $\frac{30}{48} = 30 \div 48 = 0.625$ $0.625 \times 100\% = 62.5\%$		
b) $\frac{48}{30} = 48 \div 30 = 1.6$ $1.6 \times 100\% = 160\%$	*Is the answer less than or greater than 100%?*	

Worked example 2	Thinking	Your turn! 2
Ayesha got 17 marks out of 20 in Test A and 25 out of 30 in Test B. Which score is better?	*How can we compare both scores on the same scale?*	**Florence got 40 marks out of 50 in Test A and 53 out of 65 in Test B. Which score is better?**
Test A: $\frac{17}{20} = \frac{85}{100} = 85\%$	*Can we make the denominator 100?*	
Test B: $\frac{25}{30} = 25 \div 30 = 0.83 = 83.\dot{3}\%$	*Can we make the denominator 100?*	
Test A is the better score.		

Worked example 3	Thinking	Your turn! 3
The mass of tomatoes in a recipe as a percentage of the mass of pasta is 32%. What is the mass of pasta as a percentage of the mass of tomatoes?	*How can we use reciprocals to help us?*	**The price of Blanket A in a shop is 175% of the price of Blanket B. What is the price of Blanket B as a percentage of the price of Blanket A?**
$32\% = \frac{32}{100}$	*What is the reciprocal of this fraction?*	
$1 \div \frac{32}{100} = \frac{100}{32}$	*What operation does a fraction line represent?*	
$\frac{100}{32} = 25 \div 8 = 3.125$ $= 312.5\%$		

5.1.3 Finding percentages

Worked example 1	Thinking	Your turn! 1
Find 15% of 38.	*What is a useful smaller percentage to find?*	**Find 42% of 65.**
1% is $38 \div 100 = 0.38$	*How can we find larger percentages?*	
15% is $0.38 \times 15 = 5.7$		

Worked example 2	Thinking	Your turn! 2
40% of a number is 36. **What is the number?**	*How can we represent this information?*	**15% of a number is 66.** **What is the number?**
(see table below)	*What multiplications or divisions can we use to find the whole?*	
The number is 90.		

Value	36	9	90
Percentage	40%	10%	100%

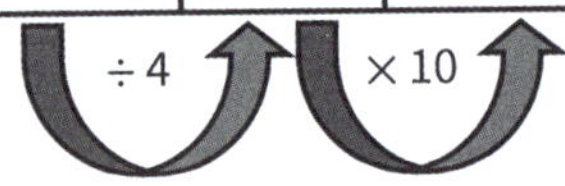

Worked example 3	Thinking	Your turn! 3
25% of a number is 44. **What is 75% of that number?**	*What multiplications or divisions can we use to get from one percentage to another?*	**25% of a number is 35.** **What is 70% of that number?**
75 = 25 × 3	*What do we use the multiplications or divisions on?*	
75% = 44 × 3 = 132		

Worked example 4	Thinking	Your turn! 4
Find 97% of $1500 using a decimal multiplier.	*How do we convert a percentage to a decimal?*	**Find 19% of $589 using a decimal multiplier.**
97% = 0.97		
0.97 × $1500 = $1455	*What can we replace the word 'of' with?*	

Worked example 5	Thinking	Your turn! 5
If you find 10% of a number followed by 20% of the answer, what percentage have you found of the original number?	*How do we combine decimals to show repeated percentage calculations?*	**If you find 80% of a number followed by 15% of the answer, what percentage have you found of the original number?**
0.1 × 0.2 = 0.02 = 2%		

5.1.4 Percentage increase and decrease

Worked example 1	Thinking	Your turn! 1
a) Write a 21% decrease as a fraction and a decimal.	*How can we find a fraction and a decimal that are the same as a percentage decrease?*	**a) Write a 38% decrease as a fraction and a decimal.**
100% − 21% = 79% $= \frac{79}{100}$ = 0.79		

b) Decrease $420 by 21%.	*How do we find a percentage decrease?*	**b) Decrease $500 by 38%.**
0.79 × $420 = $331.80	*What other method could we use?*	
c) Write a 21% increase as a fraction and a decimal.	*How can we find a fraction and a decimal that are the same as a percentage increase?*	**c) Write a 38% increase as a fraction and a decimal.**
100% + 21% = 121% $= \frac{121}{100}$ = 1.21		
d) Increase $420 by 21%.	*How do we find a percentage increase?*	**d) Increase $500 by 38%.**
1.21 × $420 = $508.20	*What other method could we use?*	

Worked example 2	Thinking	Your turn! 2
A shop reduces prices by 25%. What fraction of the original prices are the new prices?	*What is the decimal multiplier for this decrease?*	**A shop reduces prices by 20%. What fraction of the original prices are the new prices?**
100% − 25% = 75% = 0.75	*What fraction is this decimal equivalent to?*	
$0.75 = \frac{75}{100} = \frac{3}{4}$		
The new prices are $\frac{3}{4}$ of the original prices.		

Worked example 3	Thinking	Your turn! 3
A shop reduces prices by 15%, then increases them by 10%. What is the overall percentage change from their starting prices?	*What are the decimal multipliers for these increases and decreases?*	**A shop increases prices by 15%, then reduces them by 10% in a sale. What is the overall percentage change?**
100% − 15% = 85% = 0.85 100% + 10% = 110% = 1.1 0.85 × 1.1 = 0.935 = 93.5%	*What increase or decrease is this percentage equivalent to?*	
100% − 93.5% = 6.5% The overall change is a decrease of 6.5%.		

5.1.5 Finding an original amount

<table>
<tr><th>Worked example 1</th><th>Thinking</th><th>Your turn! 1</th></tr>
<tr><td>a) During a 15% off sale, a TV costs $510. What was the original price?</td><td>How can we represent this information?</td><td>a) During a 10% off sale a TV costs $540. What was the original price?</td></tr>
<tr><td><table><tr><td>Value</td><td>£510</td><td>?</td></tr><tr><td>Percentage</td><td>85%</td><td>100%</td></tr></table>× 0.85</td><td>How can we work backwards to find the original value? 1/2</td><td></td></tr>
<tr><td>$510 ÷ 0.85 = $600
The TV originally cost $600.</td><td></td><td></td></tr>
<tr><td>b) In one year, the price of a house increased by 3% to $247 200. How much did the house cost last year?</td><td>How can we represent this information?</td><td>b) In one year, the price of a house increased by 2% to $183 600. How much did the house cost last year?</td></tr>
<tr><td><table><tr><td>Value</td><td>£247 200</td><td>?</td></tr><tr><td>Percentage</td><td>103%</td><td>100%</td></tr></table>× 1.03</td><td>How do we find the original value?</td><td></td></tr>
<tr><td>$247 200 ÷ 1.03 = $240 000
The house cost $240 000 last year.</td><td></td><td></td></tr>
</table>

<table>
<tr><th>Worked example 2</th><th>Thinking</th><th>Your turn! 2</th></tr>
<tr><td>A shop increases prices by 5% and then has a sale that gives 20% off all prices. If a TV now costs $604.80, how much did it cost originally?</td><td>How can we combine these percentage changes?</td><td>A shop increases prices by 10% and then has a sale that gives 5% off all prices. If a computer now costs $522.50, how much did it originally cost?</td></tr>
<tr><td>÷ 0.84<table><tr><td>Value</td><td>$604.80</td><td>?</td></tr><tr><td>Percentage</td><td>84%</td><td>100%</td></tr></table>× 0.84</td><td>How can we represent the calculations?
What calculation helps us find the unknown amount?</td><td></td></tr>
<tr><td>$604.80 ÷ 0.84 = $720
The TV originally cost $720.</td><td></td><td></td></tr>
</table>

5.1.6 Finding the percentage change

<table>
<tr><th>Worked example 1</th><th>Thinking</th><th>Your turn! 1</th></tr>
<tr><td>The volume of water in a bowl changes from 500 ml to 440 ml. What percentage change is this?</td><td>How can we represent this information?</td><td>The mass of the chocolates in a box changes from 480 g to 600 g. What percentage change is this?</td></tr>
<tr><td>440 ÷ 500 = 0.88

× 0.88
<table><tr><td>Value</td><td>500 ml</td><td>440 ml</td></tr><tr><td>Percentage</td><td>100%</td><td>88%</td></tr></table></td><td>How can we find the multiplier?

What percentage change does this multiplier represent?</td><td></td></tr>
<tr><td>100% − 88% = 12%
The volume has decreased by 12%.</td><td></td><td></td></tr>
</table>

Fluency questions

5.1.1 Percentages, fractions, and decimals

1 Fill in the blanks to answer these questions.

a) Write 70% as a simplified fraction.

$70\% = \frac{\square}{100} = \frac{\square}{\square}$

b) Write 70% as a decimal.

$70\% = \frac{\square}{100} = \square \div 100 = \square$

2 Fill in the blanks to answer these questions.

a) Write 35% as a simplified fraction.

$35\% = \frac{\square}{100} = \frac{\square}{\square}$

b) Write 35% as a decimal.

$35\% = \frac{\square}{100} = \square \div 100 = \square$

3 Write each of these percentages as a:

i. simplified fraction **ii.** decimal.

a) 10% **b)** 15% **c)** 75% **d)** 56%

4 Which of these simplified fractions represents 5%? Circle the correct answer.

a) $\frac{1}{5}$ **b)** $\frac{1}{20}$ **c)** $\frac{1}{2}$ **d)** $\frac{1}{50}$

5 Which of these decimals represents 73%? Circle the correct answer.

a) 0.73 **b)** 7.3 **c)** 0.073 **d)** 73

5.1.2 Comparing quantities with percentages

1 Fill in the blanks to answer these questions.

a) Write 9 as a percentage of 50.

$\frac{9}{50} = \frac{\square}{100} = \square$

b) Write 11 as a percentage of 20.

$\frac{11}{20} = \frac{\square}{100} = \square$

2 Fill in the blanks to answer these questions.

a) Write 13 as a percentage of 52.

$\frac{13}{52} = \square \div 52 = \square$ $\square \times 100\% = \square$

b) Write 60 as a percentage of 75.

$\frac{60}{75} = \square \div 75 = \square$ $\square \times 100\% = \square$

3 Da-young scored 17 out 20 in a Korean spelling test and 41 out 50 in a Japanese spelling test.

a) Write 17 as a percentage of 20.

b) Write 41 as a percentage of 50.

c) Compare the values found in parts **a** and **b**. In which spelling test did Da-young do better?

4 Jabir has two cups. One cup can hold 25 ml and the other cup can hold 30 ml. He poured 18 ml of juice into the first cup and 21 ml into the second cup.

a) Write 18 as a percentage of 25.

b) Write 21 as a percentage of 30.

c) Compare the values found in parts **a** and **b**. In which cup is the percentage of juice lower?

5.1.3 Finding percentages

1 Fill the blanks in these double number lines.

a)

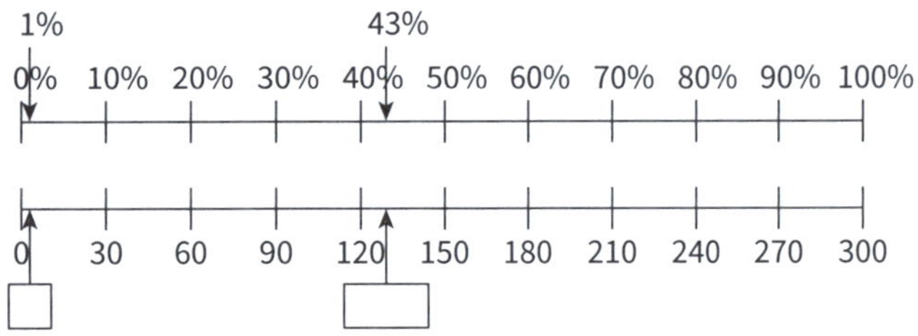

b)

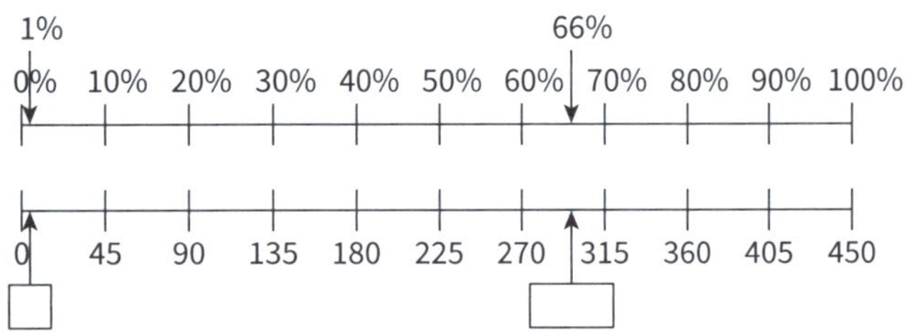

2 Fill in the blank cells and boxes to answer these questions.

a) 25% of a number is 11. What is 75% of that number?

Value	11	
Percentage	25%	75%

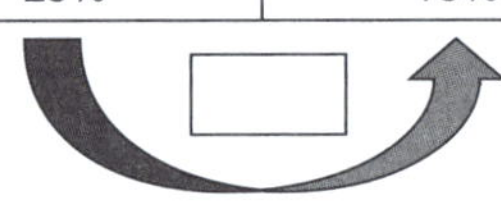

b) 8% of a number is 13. What is 40% of that number?

Value		
Percentage	8%	40%

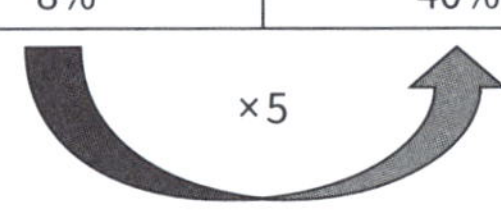

c) 30% of a number is 27.
What is 100% of that number?

Value	27		
Percentage	30%	10%	100%

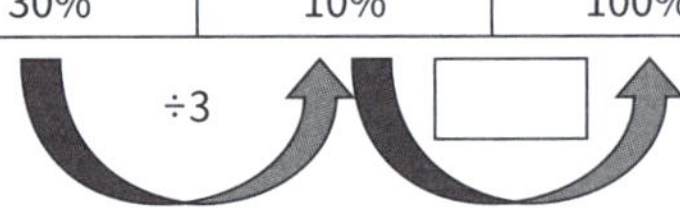

3 What decimal multiplier is equivalent to 57%? Circle the correct answer.

a) 5.7 **c)** 0.57
b) 5.07 **d)** 57

5.1.4 Percentage increase and decrease

1 Fill in the blank cells to answer these questions.

a) Decrease \$80 by 20%.

Value	\$80	
Percentage	100%	80%

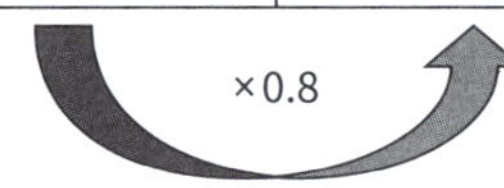

b) Increase \$120 by 10%.

Value	\$120	
Percentage	100%	

2 Fill in the blanks to answer these questions.

a) Write a 20% decrease as a simplified fraction.

$$100\% - 20\% = \square = \frac{\square}{100} = \frac{\square}{\square}$$

b) Write a 20% decrease as a decimal.

$$100\% - 20\% = \frac{\square}{100} = \square \div 100 = \square$$

3 Fill in the blanks to answer these questions.

a) Write a 25% increase as a simplified fraction.

$$100\% + 25\% = \square = \frac{\square}{100} = \frac{\square}{\square}$$

b) Write a 25% increase as a decimal.

$$100\% + 25\% = \frac{\square}{100} = \square \div 100 = \square$$

4 Increase 20 by 10%. Choose the correct answer.

a) 21 **c)** 18
b) 22 **d)** 30

5 Decrease 48 by 25%. Choose the correct answer.

a) 38 **c)** 23
b) 60 **d)** 36

5.1.5 Finding an original amount

1 The number of rabbits in a village in Australia increased by 20% between 2022 and 2023. In 2023, there were 1140 rabbits.

How many rabbits were there in 2022?

2 Fill in the blank cells and boxes to answer the question.

After 10% discount, a bicycle costs $720.
What was the original price of the bicycle?

Value	$720		
Percentage	90%	10%	100%

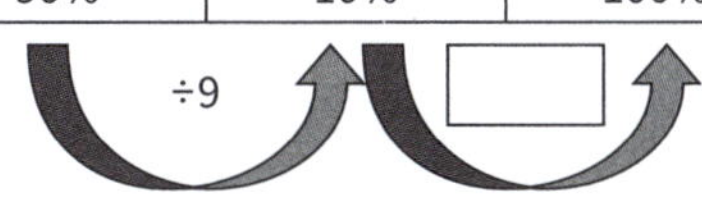

3 In the last month, the number of Americano coffees sold in a café increased by 20% to 6630.

a) What is a 20% increase as a decimal?

b) Draw a ratio table to show the change in the number of Americano coffees sold.

c) How many Americano coffees did the café sell last month?

4 In a 30% off sale, a video game console costs $210.

a) Write a 30% decrease as a decimal.

b) Draw a ratio table to show the change in the cost of the video game console.

c) What was the original price of the video game console before the sale?

5.1.6 Finding the percentage change

1 The volume of water in a tank changed from 10 litres to 14 litres.

What percentage change is this? Is this an increase or a decrease?

2 The number of marbles that Georgio has changed from 50 to 80.
What decimal multiplier represents this change?
Choose the correct answer.

a) 8
b) 8.5
c) 0.625
d) 1.6

3 Fill in the blanks to answer these questions.

a) Write a 25% increase as a decimal multiplier.
25% increase = 100% + ☐ = ☐ = ☐

b) Write a 25% decrease as a decimal multiplier.
25% decrease = 100% − ☐ = ☐ = ☐

4 Fill in the blank cells and boxes to answer these questions.

a) The amount of money in Livia's bank account changed from $1200 to $1500.
What percentage increase is this?

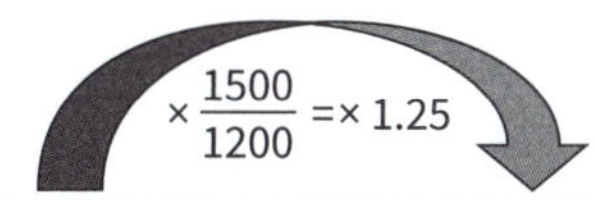

Value	$1200	$1500
Percentage	100%	

The percentage increase is _____%

b) Hans walked 1200 m on Saturday and 960 m on Sunday.
What is the percentage decrease in the distance he walked?

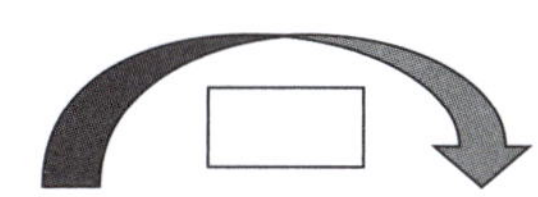

Value	1200 m	960 m
Percentage	100%	

The percentage decrease is __%

5 The volume of air in a balloon changed from 8 litres to 14 litres.

a) Find the decimal multiplier for this change.

b) Draw a ratio table to show the change in volume of the balloon.

c) What is the percentage increase in the volume of the balloon?

6 The number of cookies in a jar changed from 15 to 6.

a) Find the decimal multiplier for this change.

b) Draw a ratio table to show the change in the number of cookies.

c) What is the percentage decrease in the number of cookies?

5.2 Proportionality

Example-problem pairs

5.2.1 Representing multiplicative relationships

<table>
<tr><th>Worked example 1</th><th>Thinking</th><th>Your turn! 1</th></tr>
<tr><td>Draw a graph to show the multiplicative relationship × 4. Write the equation of the graph.</td><td>Can we find some pairs of values that fit this relationship.</td><td>Draw a graph to show the multiplicative relationship × 2. Write the equation of the graph.</td></tr>
<tr><td><table><tr><td>x</td><td>0</td><td>1</td><td>2</td><td>3</td></tr><tr><td>y</td><td>0</td><td>4</td><td>8</td><td>12</td></tr></table></td><td>How do we plot these numbers?</td><td></td></tr>
<tr><td>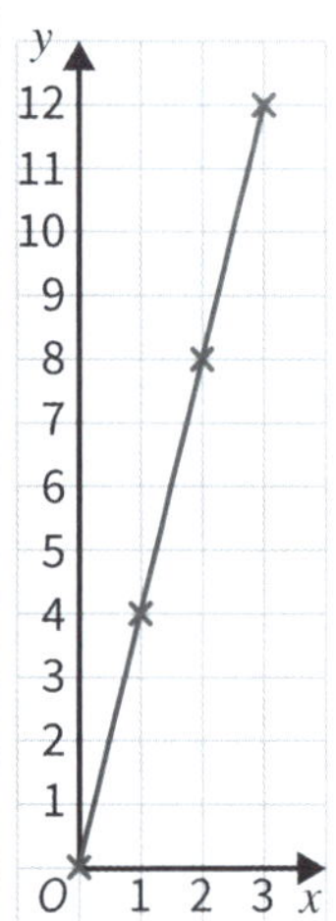
The equation is $y = 4x$.</td><td>What is the gradient and what is the y-intercept of the line?</td><td>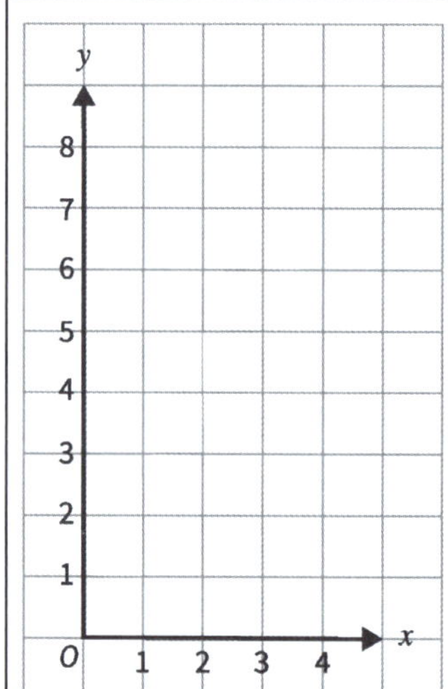</td></tr>
</table>

Worked example 2	Thinking	Your turn! 2
Draw a graph to show the multiplicative relationship 2 : 5. Write the equation of the graph.		**Draw a graph to show the multiplicative relationship 2 : 3. Write the equation of the graph.**
×2 (from $x = 2$ to $x = 4$); ×2.5 (from x to y)	*If we write the ratio in the table, can we find other pairs of values by multiplying?*	
see graph below	*How do we plot these pairs of numbers on coordinate axes?* *What is the gradient and what is the y-intercept of the line?*	see graph below

x	0	**2**	4
y	0	**5**	10

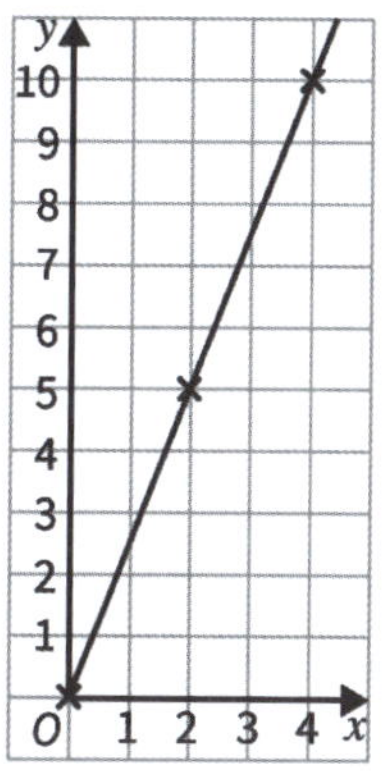

The equation is $y = 2.5x$.

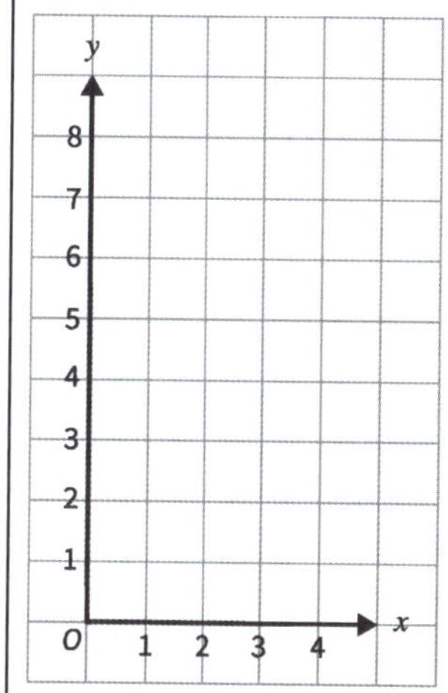

Worked example 3	Thinking	Your turn! 3
4 metres of ribbon cost \$2.80. Draw a graph to show this information and use it to find the cost of 3 metres of ribbon.	*What pairs of values do we know from the question?*	**8 metres of piping cost \$60. Draw a graph to show this information and use it to find the cost of 10 metres of piping.**
see table below	*How far do we need the numbers to go on the axes?*	
see graph below	*How can we use the graph to find different values?*	see graph below

Ribbon (m)	0	4
Cost	\$0	\$2.80

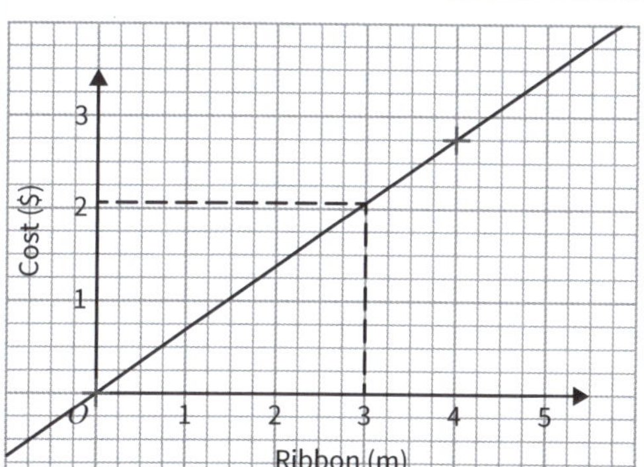

3 metres cost \$2.10.

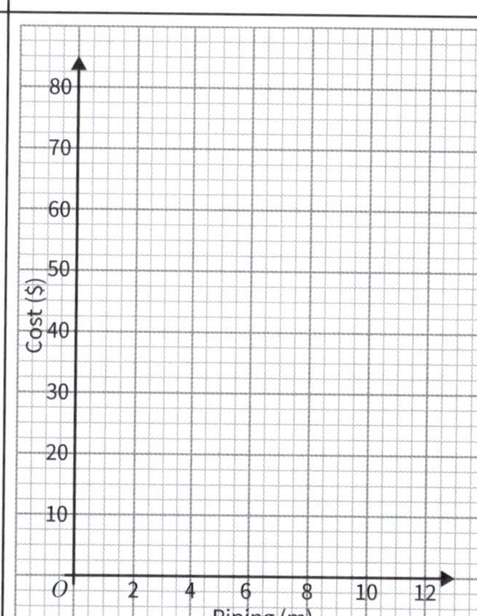

5 Percentages and proportionality

5.2.2 Direct proportion

Worked example 1	Thinking	Your turn! 1
Choose the formulae that represent direct proportion and write each as a ratio in its simplest form. $b = 3a$ $\quad x = \frac{3}{2}y$ $y = 2x + 1$ $c = 0.5d$ $\quad f - 1 = 4e$	*What is the key feature of a directly proportional relationship?*	**Choose the formulae that represent direct proportion and write each as a ratio in its simplest form.** $y = 6x$ $\quad v = w - 2$ $n = \frac{1}{2}m$ $\quad a = b$ $d + 1 = 4e$
These formulae show direct proportion: $b = 3a$ $c = 0.5d$ $x = \frac{3}{2}y$	*How can we turn each formula into a ratio?*	
$a : b = 1 : 3$ $d : c = 1 : 0.5 = 2 : 1$ $y : x = 1 : \frac{3}{2} = 2 : 3$		

Worked example 2	Thinking	Your turn! 2
Give the multiplier of this directly proportional relationship. x: 0, 2, 4, 6 y: 0, 12, 24, 36	*How do we find the constant of proportionality?*	**Give the multiplier of this directly proportional relationship.** x: 0, −3, −6, −9 y: 0, −7, −14, −21
The multiplier is $\frac{12}{2}$ or $\frac{24}{4}$ or $\frac{36}{6}$.		
The multiplier is 6.	*What would the ratio be?*	

Worked example 3	Thinking	Your turn! 3
Choose the formulae that represent direct proportion and write each as a ratio in its simplest form. $b = 0.3a$ $\quad c = \sqrt{2}d$ $y = \frac{1}{2}x - 1$ $\quad x = (25\%)y$	*What is the key feature of a directly proportional relationship?*	**Choose the formulae that represent direct proportion and write each as a ratio in its simplest form.** $y = 5.6x$ $\quad v = w - \sqrt{2}$ $n = (20\%)m$ $\quad \sqrt{3}a = b$
These formulae show direct proportion: $b = 0.3a$ $c = \sqrt{2}d$ $x = (25\%)y$	*How can we turn each formula into a ratio?*	
$a : b = 10 : 3$ $d : c = 1 : \sqrt{2}$ $y : x = 4 : 1$		

Worked example 4	Thinking	Your turn! 4
5 pens cost \$6. If each pen costs the same, write a formula linking the number of pens, n, to the total cost, \$$C$, and write the ratio $n : C$ in its simplest form.	*How do we know that this situation represents direct proportion?*	**4 sweets cost 60c. If each sweet costs the same, write a formula linking the number of sweets, n, to the total cost, C cents, and write the ratio $n : C$ in its simplest form.**
In a ratio table: 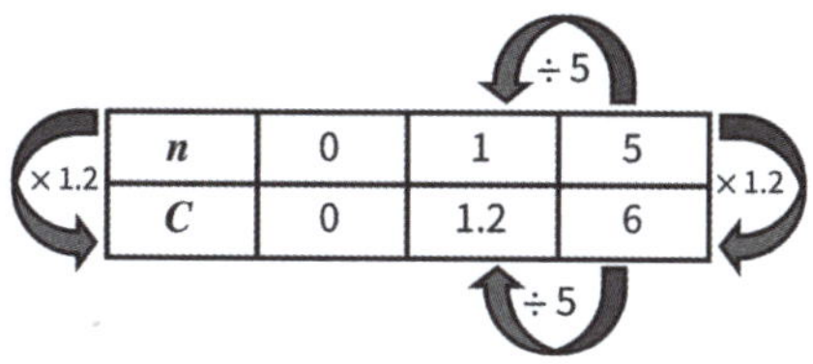	*How can we use the ratio table to find the constant of proportionality?* *How do we use the multiplier?*	
The formula is $C = 1.2n$.		
The ratio is $n : C = 1 : 1.2$ $= 5 : 6$		

Worked example 5	Thinking	Your turn! 5
A cake recipe uses butter (y) to flour (x) in the ratio 3 : 4. Draw a graph of butter against flour.	*If we write the ratio in a table, can we find other pairs of values?*	**A salad dressing uses olive oil (y) to vinegar (x) in the ratio 5 : 3. Draw a graph of olive oil against vinegar.**
In a ratio table: x: 0, 4, 8, 12 y: 0, 3, 6, 9	*How do we plot these pairs of numbers on coordinate axes?*	
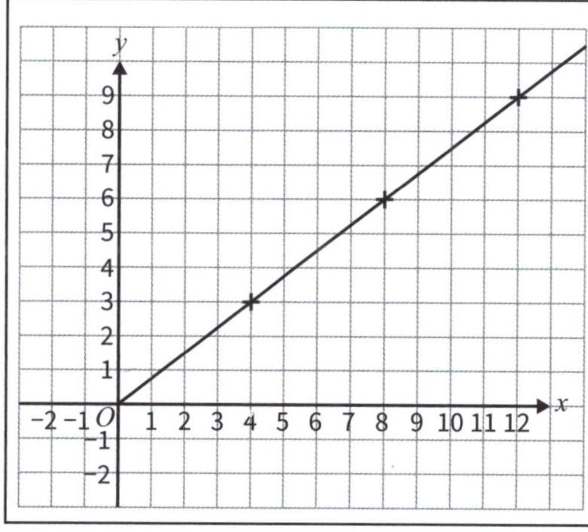		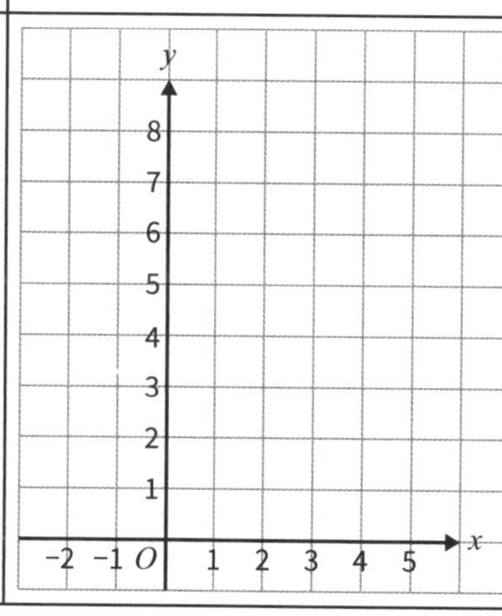

Worked example 6	Thinking	Your turn! 6
The widths of some rectangles are 30% greater than their lengths. Write a formula connecting the width, w, and the length, l, and write the ratio $l : w$.	*How do we increase something by a percentage using a multiplier?*	**The price of some houses this year is 2% higher than last year. Write a formula connecting the new prices, n, and the old prices, p, and write the ratio $p : n$.**
$100\% + 30\% = 130\% = 1.3$, so $w = 1.3l$ $l : w = 1 : 1.3 = 10 : 13$		

5.2.3 Solving problems involving direct proportion

Worked example 1	Thinking	Your turn! 1
A recipe for mashed potato for 4 people uses 1 kg potatoes. **How much potato is needed to serve 6 people?**	*How do we know if this is a question of direct proportion?*	**A recipe for fruit pie filling for 10 people uses 800 g of apples.** **What mass of apples is needed to make fruit pie filling for 4 people?**
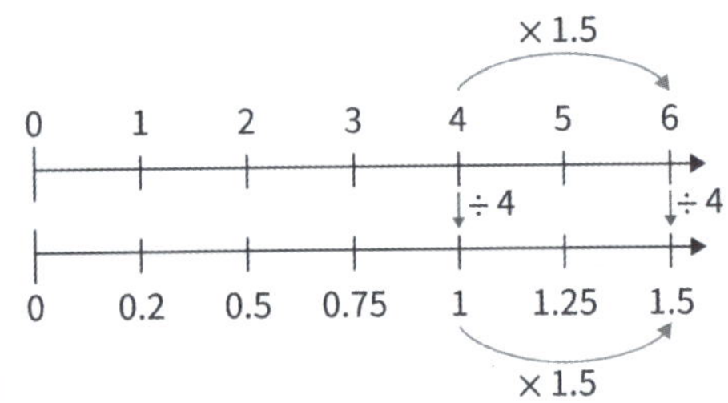	*What multipliers do we use?*	
For 6 people you need 1.5 kg potatoes.		

Worked example 2	Thinking	Your turn! 2
A shop sells two bags of salad. Which bag is better value for money? 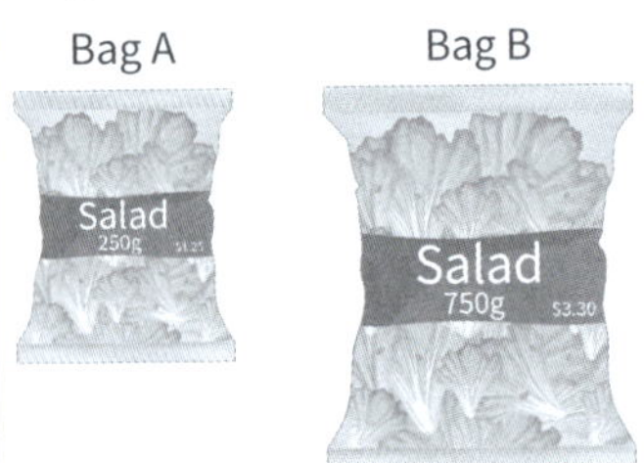	*How can we compare the price of one unit of each?* *How do we find the price of one unit?*	**A shop sells two tubs of butter. Which tub is better value for money?** 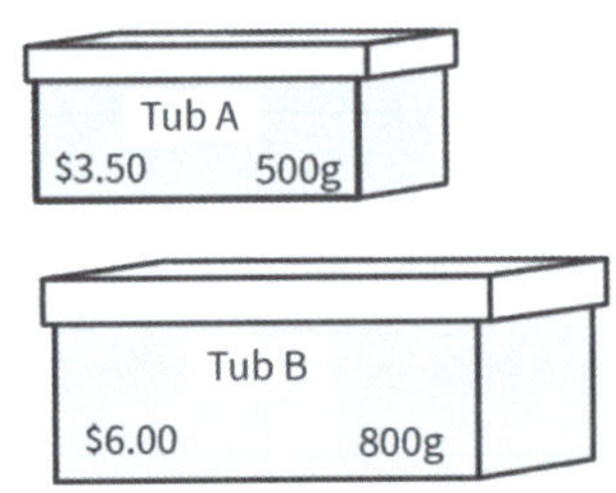

× 4

Bag A	Mass (kg)	0.25	1
	Price ($)	$1.25	$5.00

× 4

÷ 0.75

Bag B	Mass (kg)	0.75	1
	Price ($)	$3.30	$4.40

÷ 0.75

Bag B is better value for money.

5.2.4 Inverse proportion

Worked example 1	Thinking	Your turn! 1
Two people can paint a building in 3 days. How long would it take 1 person working at the same rate?	*How do we know if this is inverse proportion?*	**Three people can build a wall in 5 days. How long would it take 1 person working at the same rate?**
(see diagram below)	*What multipliers do we use?*	
It would take 1 person 6 days.		

÷ 2

People	2	1
Days	3	6

× 2

Worked example 2	Thinking	Your turn! 2
Travelling at a constant 30 km/h, it takes 60 minutes to get from Town A to Town B. How long would it take if you travelled at a constant 45 km/h.	*How can we model inverse proportion?*	**Travelling at a constant 40 km/h, it takes 2 hours to get from Town A to Town B. If the journey instead took 5 hours, at what speed would you be travelling?**
(see diagram below)		
It would take 40 minutes.		

× 1.5

Speed (mph)	30	45
Time (mins)	60	40

÷ 1.5

Worked example 3	Thinking	Your turn! 3
The table shows two quantities, x and y. Are they in inverse proportion?	*What do we need to check for when looking at inverse proportion?*	**The table shows two quantities, x and y. Are they in inverse proportion?**
(see tables below)		
They are in inverse proportion.		

Worked example 3:

x	10	15	7.5
y	45	30	60

× 1.5   ÷ 2

x	10	15	7.5
y	45	30	60

÷ 1.5   × 2

Your turn! 3:

x	12	18	9
y	3	2	1

Fluency questions

5.2.1 Representing multiplicative relationships

1 Consider the graph of the relationship $y = 3x$.

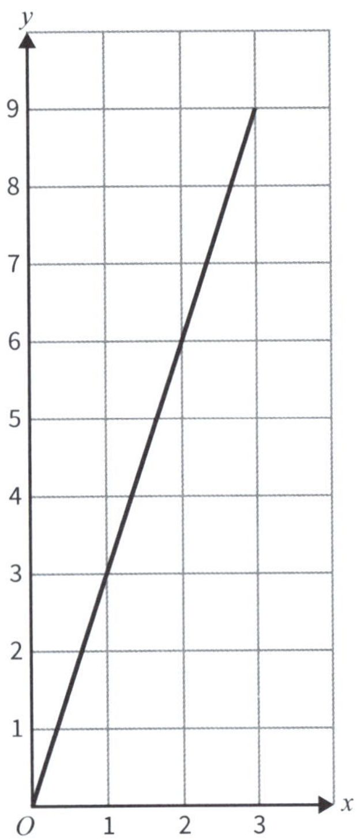

Read the points off the graph and fill in the blank cells of this table.

x	0	1	2	3
y				

2 a) A multiplicative relationship is given as ×2.

Fill in this table to show the relationship.

x	0	1	2	3
y				

b) Fill in the blank boxes of the double number line representing the relationship in part **a**.

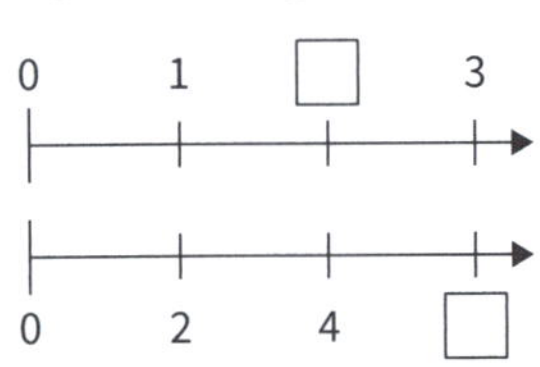

c) Draw a graph to show this relationship.

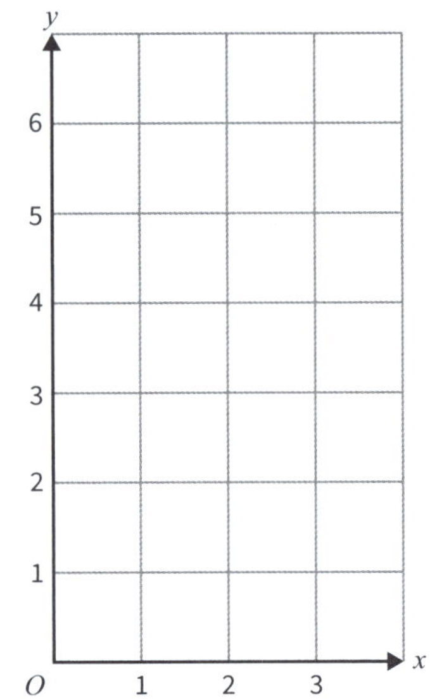

3 a) A multiplicative relationship is given as ×0.5.

Fill in this table to show the relationship.

x	0	2	4	6
y				

× 0.5

b) Fill in the blank boxes of the double number line representing the relationship in part **a**.

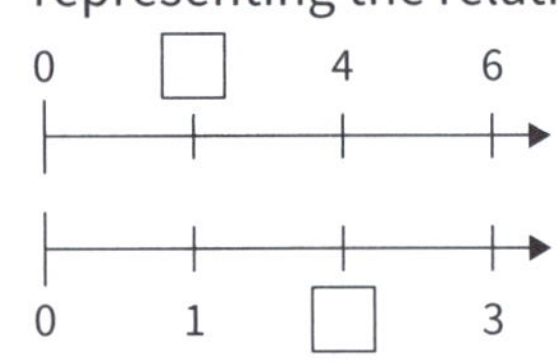

c) Draw a graph to show this relationship.

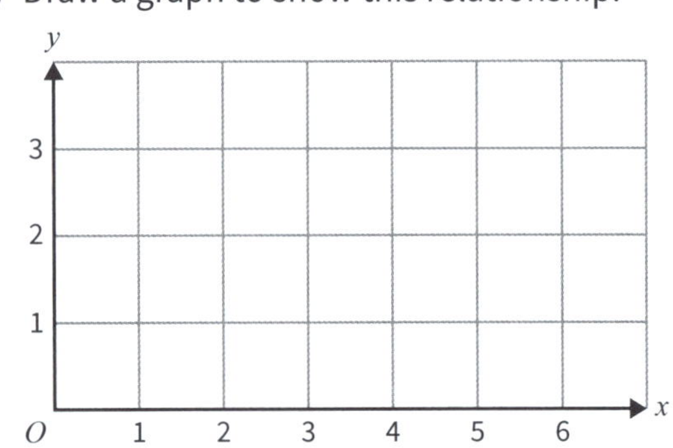

4 Consider the relationship represented in this table.

x	0	1	2	3
y	0	5	10	15

Choose the equation of its graph:

a) $y = 3x$ **c)** $y = 10x$

b) $y = 5x$ **d)** $y = x$

5 Consider the multiplicative relationship represented in this table.

x	0	1	2	3
y	0	6	12	18

What is the multiplier?

a) 6 **c)** $\frac{1}{6}$

b) 3 **d)** $\frac{1}{3}$

5.2.2 Direct proportion

1 Complete the table. The first line has been done.

Directly proportional relationship	Multiplier
$y = 4x$	× 4
$y = 3.5x$	× ________
$y = 0.8x$	× ________
$y =$ ________ x	× 8
$y =$ ________ x	× 5.2

2 Consider the direct proportion represented in the graph below.

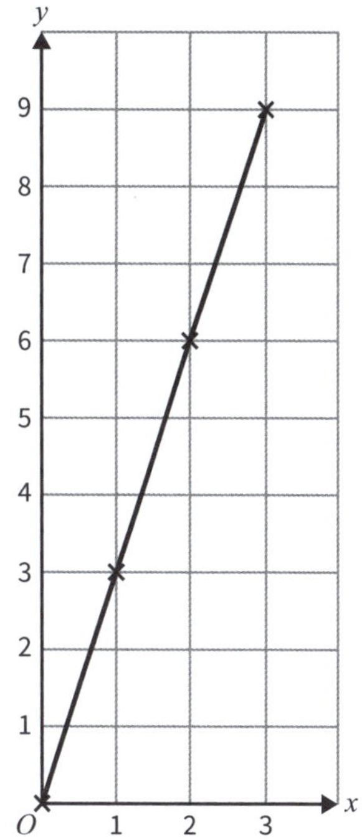

What is the multiplier?

a) $\frac{1}{2}$ **c)** 3

b) 2 **d)** $\frac{1}{3}$

3 Write the directly proportional $y = 5x$ as a ratio in its simplest form.

a) 5 : 1 **c)** 1 : 5

b) 1 : 1 **d)** 5 : 5

4 Consider the relationship represented in this table below.

x	0	2	4	6
y	0	7	14	21

Choose the correct ratio for the relationship.

a) 2 : 5 **c)** 5 : 2

b) 7 : 2 **d)** 2 : 7

5.2.3 Solving problems involving direct proportion

1 Seven pens cost $21.

a) Fill in the blank boxes of the double number line below.

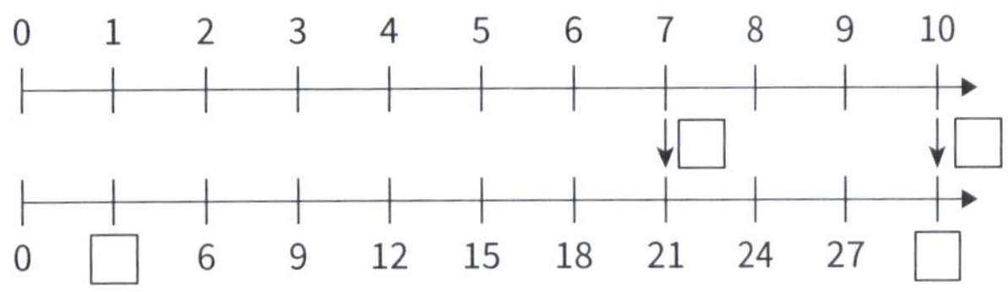

b) How much do 10 pens cost?

2 Four tiles cover an area of 48 square centimetres.

a) Fill in the blank boxes of the double number line below.

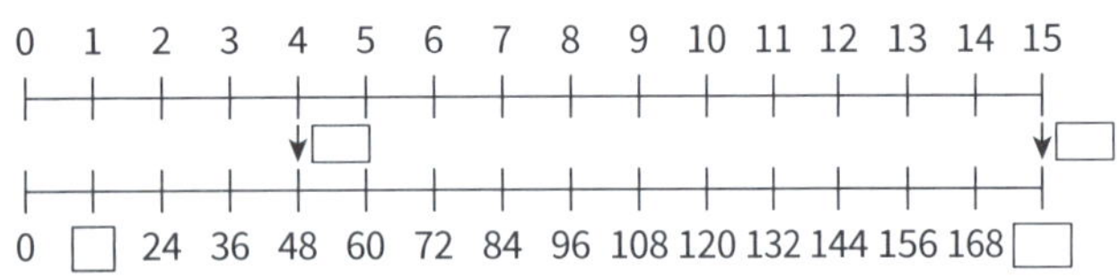

b) How many square centimetres are covered by 15 tiles?

3 A recipe use 125 g of butter to make 25 doughnuts.

a) How much butter is needed to make 1 doughnut?

b) How much butter is needed to make 12 doughnuts?

5.2.4 Inverse proportion

1 It takes 8 days for 24 workers to plant cacao on a plantation.

a) Fill in the blank cells and blank boxes in the ratio table below.

× 2

Workers	12	24
Days		8

b) How long it will take 12 workers to plant cacao on the same plantation?

2 A rectangle has length 15 cm and width 18 cm.

a) Fill in the blank cells and blank boxes in the ratio table below.

Length		15
Width	0.6	18

b) What is the length of a rectangle with the same area and width 0.6 cm?

3 A tap fills a tank in 5 hours at a rate of 20 litres per minute.

a) Fill in the blank cells and blank boxes in the ratio table below.

Hours	5	
Litres	20	80

b) How long will it take to fill the tank at a rate of 80 litres per minute?

4 A car travelling at a constant speed of 30 km/h takes 42 minutes to travel between two cities.

a) Fill in the blank cells and blank boxes in the ratio table below.

Speed (km/h)	30	90
Time (minutes)	42	

b) How long would the same journey take if the car travels at a constant speed of 90 km/h?

6.1 Representing data

Example-problem pairs

6.1.1 Ungrouped frequency tables

<table>
<tr><th>Worked example 1</th><th>Thinking</th><th>Your turn! 1</th></tr>
<tr><td>A primary school records how many accidents happen on the equipment every day for 3 weeks:
0, 2, 1, 4, 2, 0, 0, 0,
1, 2, 2, 2, 1, 0, 1
Represent this data in a frequency table.</td><td>How many rows and columns will we need?</td><td>A youth club records the ages of everyone who attends one week:
11, 13, 14, 12, 13, 14, 12, 13, 14
12, 12, 13, 13, 13, 12, 16, 12, 13
Represent this data in a frequency table.</td></tr>
<tr><td><table>
<tr><th>Number of accidents</th><th>Tally</th><th>Frequency</th></tr>
<tr><td>0</td><td>卌</td><td>5</td></tr>
<tr><td>1</td><td>||||</td><td>4</td></tr>
<tr><td>2</td><td>卌</td><td>5</td></tr>
<tr><td>3</td><td></td><td>0</td></tr>
<tr><td>4</td><td>|</td><td>1</td></tr>
</table></td><td>How can we complete the frequency column?</td><td></td></tr>
<tr><td>5 + 4 + 5 + 1 = 15
There were 15 values in the list, so we have recorded all the data.</td><td>How can we check that we have not missed any values?</td><td></td></tr>
</table>

<table>
<tr><th>Worked example 2</th><th>Thinking</th><th>Your turn! 2</th></tr>
<tr><td>A museum is going to open a gift shop selling souvenirs.
What data should the managers gather to help them with gift sales?</td><td>What information are the museum managers trying to find out?</td><td>An Italian restaurant is going to start a pizza delivery service.
What data should the owner collect to help them to sell pizzas?</td></tr>
<tr><td>• What type of souvenirs museum visitors would want to buy.
• The number of visitors that would buy a souvenir.</td><td></td><td></td></tr>
</table>

Worked example 3	Thinking	Your turn! 3
A school records the ages of students in the canteen during one break time. **The table shows the results.** **Write out the data from the table.**	*What are the possible values of the data?* *What does frequency mean in each row?*	**A pet shop surveys 16 families to find out the number of pets they have.** **The results are shown in the table.** **Write out the data from the table.**

Ages	Frequency
11	6
12	1
13	5
14	6
15	0
16	2

11, 11, 11, 11, 11, 11
12
13, 13, 13, 13, 13
14, 14, 14, 14, 14, 14
16, 16

Number of pets	Frequency
0	4
1	5
2	6
3	0
4	1

6.1.2 Grouped frequency tables

Worked example 1	Thinking	Your turn! 1
These are the times taken for 20 athletes to run 100 m. Represent this data in the frequency table.	*What is the smallest and largest value?* *What could we use for the group intervals?* *How can we work out what interval the values go in?* *How can we fill in the frequency column?*	**These are the times taken for 20 athletes to run 100 m. Represent them in the frequency table.**

Worked example 1 data:

10.38	10.58	10.49	10.60	10.52
10.63	10.56	10.65	10.56	10.67
10.49	10.59	10.52	10.62	10.54
10.64	10.56	10.66	10.57	10.67

Time, x seconds	Tally	Frequency
$10.3 \le x < 10.4$		
$10.4 \le x < 10.5$		
$10.5 \le x < 10.6$		
$10.6 \le x < 10.7$		

How can we check that we have not missed any values?

Time, x seconds	Tally	Frequency
$10.3 \le x < 10.4$	|	
$10.4 \le x < 10.5$	||	
$10.5 \le x < 10.6$	~~||||~~ ||||	
$10.6 \le x < 10.7$	~~||||~~ |||	

Total frequency is $1 + 2 + 9 + 8 = 20$

Your turn! 1 data:

10.66	10.66	10.76	10.51	10.69
10.72	10.70	10.64	10.71	10.67
10.53	10.66	10.68	10.48	10.59
10.64	10.68	10.67	10.75	10.49

Time, x seconds	Tally	Frequency
$10.4 \le x < 10.5$		
$10.5 \le x < 10.6$		
$10.6 \le x < 10.7$		
$10.7 \le x < 10.8$		

6.1.3 Bar charts

Worked example 1	Thinking	Your turn! 1
The bar chart shows the number of drinks a coffee shop sold each day. 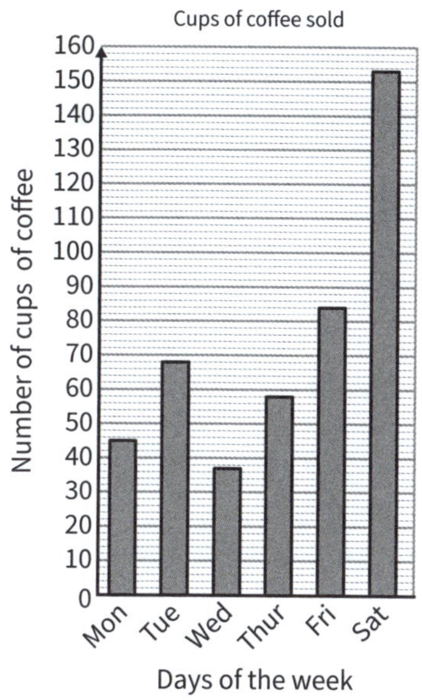 **a) How many cups of coffee were sold in total over the week?**	*How can we use the heights of the bars to find the total frequency?*	**The bar chart shows the number of umbrellas sold by a shop at different times of the year.** 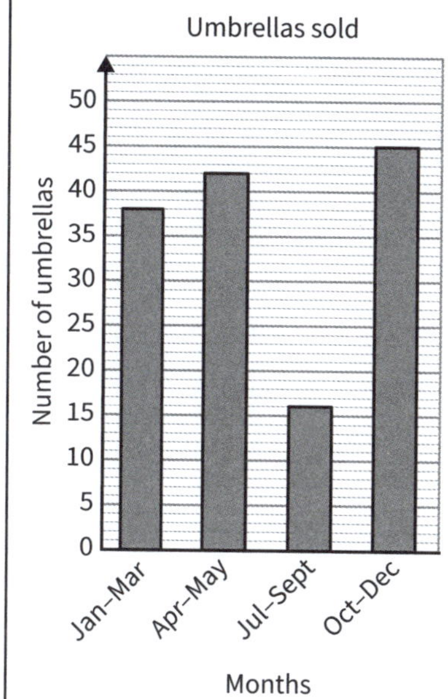 **a) How many umbrellas were sold in total over the year?**
Total number of cups of coffee = 45 + 68 + 37 + 58 + 84 + 153 = 445		
b) Write a sentence about any pattern you notice in the data.		**b) Write a sentence about any pattern you notice in the data.**
The coffee shop sells more cups of coffee on Saturday than on any other day.		

6 Statistics

<table>
<tr><th>Worked example 2</th><th>Thinking</th><th>Your turn! 2</th></tr>
<tr>
<td>The bar chart shows the results when a dice is rolled 30 times.
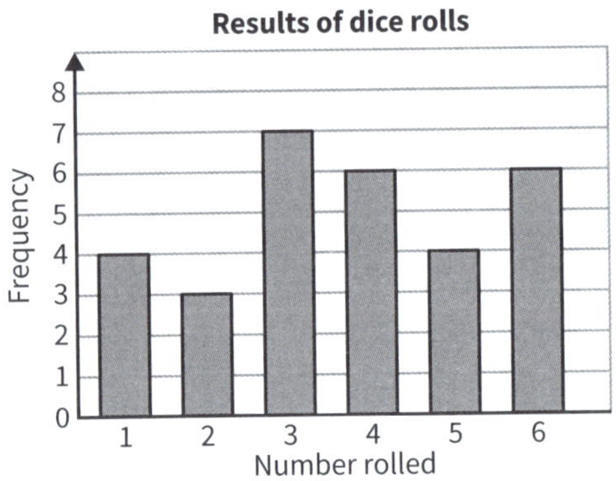

What was the most common result?</td>
<td>How do we know how many times each value occurs?</td>
<td>The bar chart shows the results when a dice is rolled 30 times.
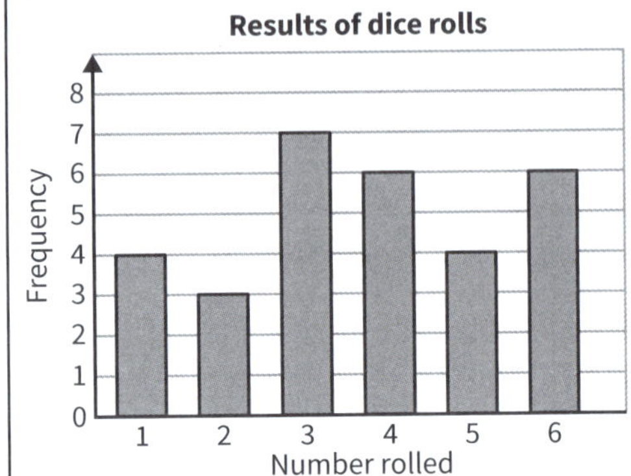

What was the least common result?</td>
</tr>
<tr><td>The most common result was 3, which occurred 7 times.</td><td></td><td></td></tr>
</table>

<table>
<tr><th>Worked example 3</th><th>Thinking</th><th>Your turn! 3</th></tr>
<tr>
<td>The bar chart shows the rainfall in Newcastle and Plymouth in the first week of April.
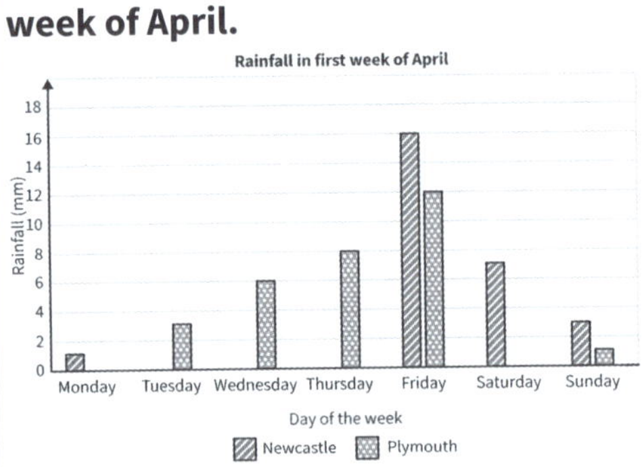

Which day was the wettest? Compare the amount of rain in each city on this day.</td>
<td>How do we know how many times each value occurs?</td>
<td>The bar chart shows the hours of sunshine in Newcastle and Plymouth in the first week of April.
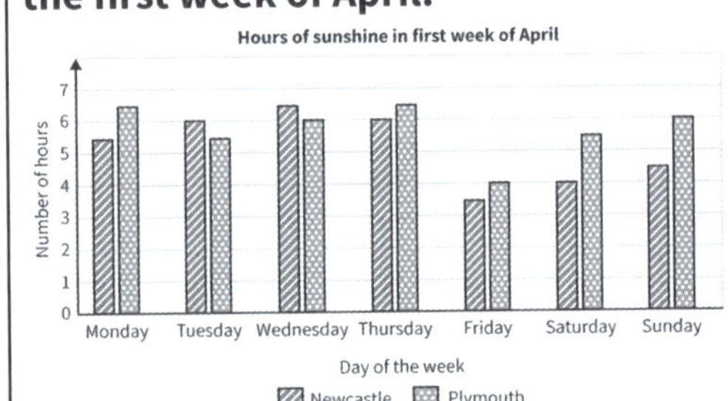

Which day has the least amount of sunshine? Compare the amount of sunshine in each city on this day.</td>
</tr>
<tr><td>The wettest day in both cities was Friday. Newcastle had 4 mm more rain than Plymouth.</td><td></td><td></td></tr>
</table>

6.1.4 Pictograms

Worked example 1	Thinking	Your turn! 1
The table shows the favourite ball sports of a group of people. Construct a pictogram to represent the information.	*What do we need to decide first?* *How can we work out how many symbols to draw for each sport?*	**The table shows the favourite ball sports of a group of people. Construct a pictogram to represent the information.**

Worked example 1 table:

Sport	Frequency
Football	16
Handball	12
Cricket	18
Basketball	8
Other	14

Your turn! 1 table:

Sport	Frequency
Football	60
Handball	20
Cricket	35
Basketball	25
Other	15

Worked example 1	Thinking	Your turn! 1
Use a ball symbol. All of the values in the table are sums of whole, half, or quarter 8s. Use one ball to represent 8 people.		
Football: $16 \div 8 = 2$, so draw 2 balls. Handball: $12 \div 8 = 1.5$, so draw $1\frac{1}{2}$ balls. Cricket: $18 \div 8 = 2.25$, so draw $2\frac{1}{4}$ balls. Basketball: $8 \div 8 = 1$, so draw 1 ball. Other: $14 \div 8 = 1.75$, so draw $1\frac{3}{4}$ balls.	*What must we include with the pictogram?*	
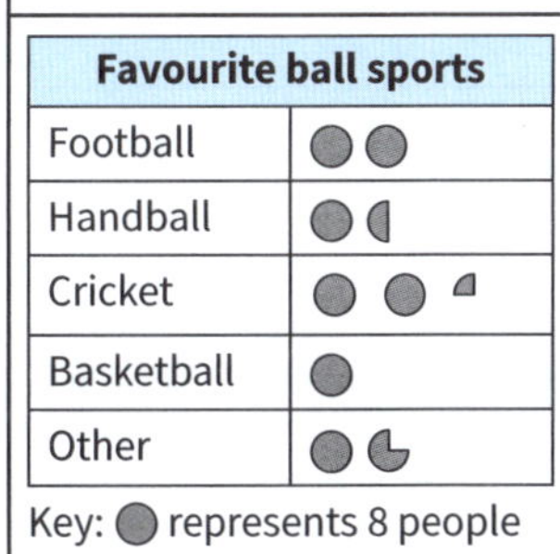		

Worked example 2

The pictogram shows the number of social media posts a group of friends wrote in a week. Work out how many posts each person wrote.

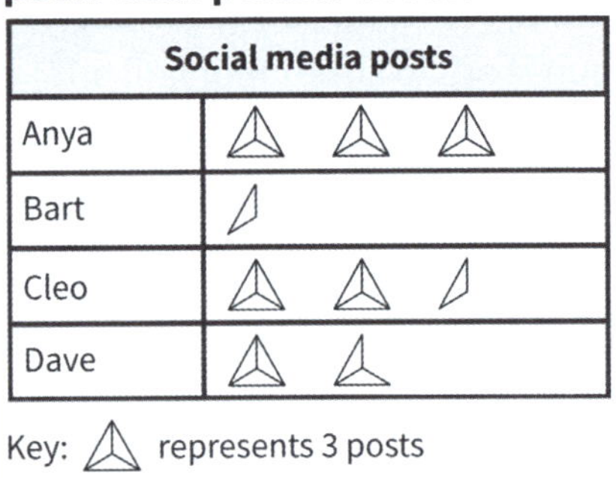

Each icon represents 3 posts, so each section of the icon represents 1 post.

Anya = 3 × 3 = 9 posts

Bart = 1 post

Cleo = 2 × 3 + 1 = 7 posts

Dave = 3 + 2 = 5 posts

Thinking

If we know what each icon represents, how can we work out how many posts each person wrote?

Your turn! 2

The pictogram shows the number of social media posts a group of friends wrote in a week. Work out how many posts each person wrote.

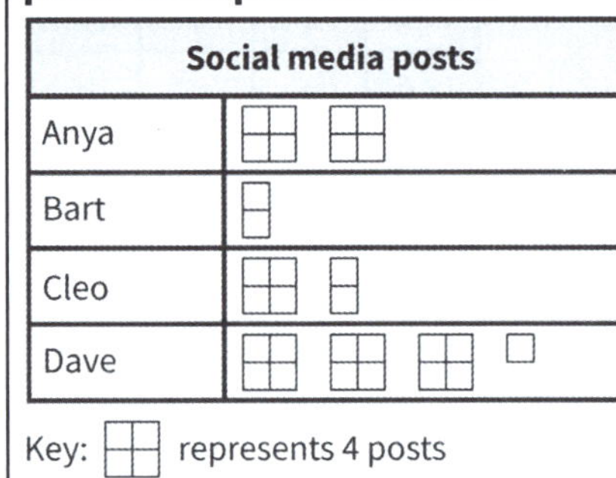

6.1.5 Constructing scatter graphs

Worked example 1

This data shows the goals scored for and against each of 6 teams. Draw a scatter graph to represent the data.

Team	Goals for	Goals against
A	16	31
B	27	37
C	32	16
D	29	25
E	18	26
F	26	36

Thinking

What scales should the axes have?

How do we show the data on the scatter graph?

Your turn! 1

This data shows the goals scored for and against each of 6 teams. Draw a scatter graph to represent the data.

Team	Goals for	Goals against
A	44	8
B	46	12
C	36	20
D	16	20
E	29	22
F	33	42

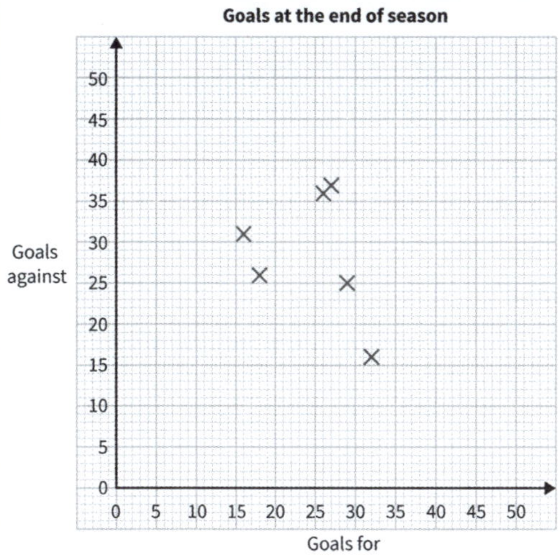

Worked example 2

The data shows the mileage and price of 9 cars. Draw a scatter graph to represent the data.

Key: E = electric, H = hybrid, P = petrol

Type	Mileage (miles, 1000s)	price ($, 1000s)
E	51	11
H	22	26
E	35	17
P	40	6
H	46	16
P	32	10
E	10	17
P	77	3
H	76	8

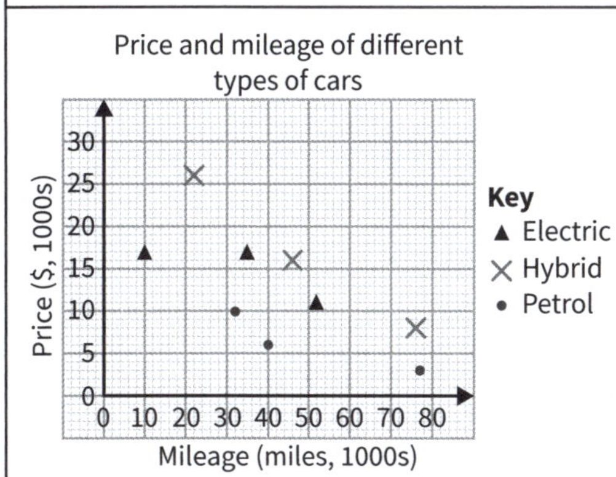

Thinking

What scales should the axes have?

How do we show the different categories on the scatter graph?

Your turn! 2

The data shows the mileage and price of 9 cars. Draw a scatter graph to represent the data.

Key: E = electric, H = hybrid, P = petrol

Type	Mileage (miles, 1000s)	price ($, 1000s)
H	55	13
E	28	19
P	26	11
H	20	19
P	50	7
E	8	24
H	74	9
P	71	11
E	48	12

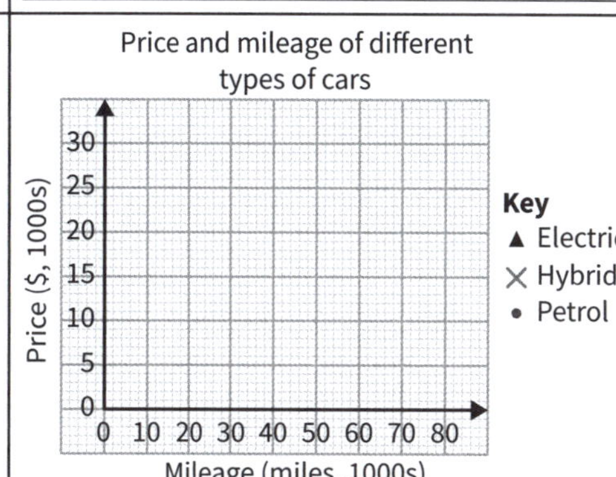

6.1.6 Interpreting scatter graphs

Worked example 1	Thinking	Your turn! 1
The scatter graph shows the results of a group of students who took two tests. Describe the relationship between the results of the two tests. Monthly sales at a bookshop and number of pages in the books 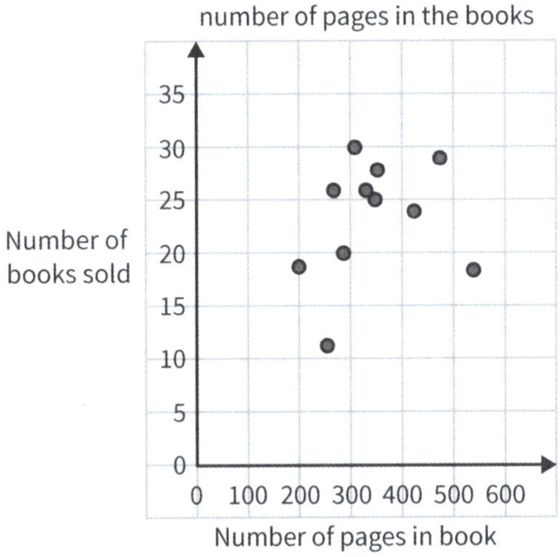	*What relationship do the points have?*	**The scatter graph shows the results of a group of students who took two tests. Describe the relationship between the results of the two tests.** Results of students in two tests 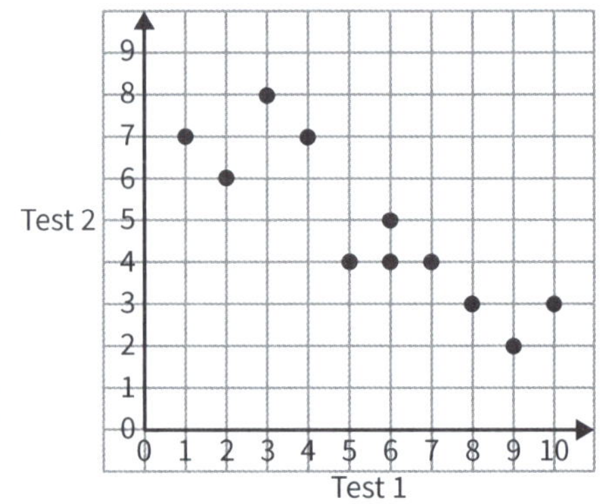
Students with a high score in Test 1 are more likely to have a high score in Test 2.		

Worked example 2	Thinking	Your turn! 2
The scatter graph shows the results of a group of students who took two tests. **Results of students in two tests** 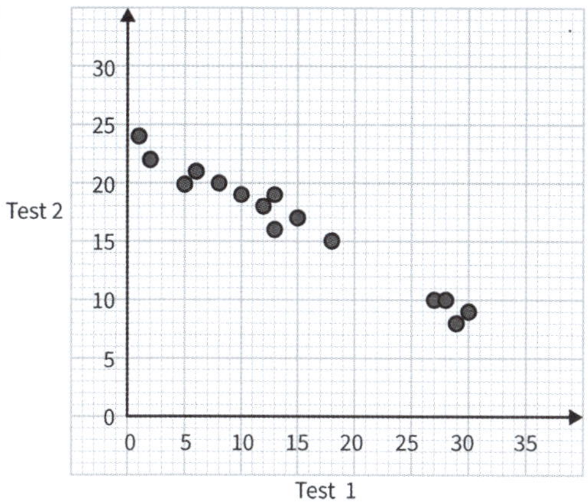 **a) Draw a line of best fit on the graph.**	*What do we need to remember about the line of best fit?*	**The scatter graph shows the results of a group of students who took two tests.** **Results of students in two tests** 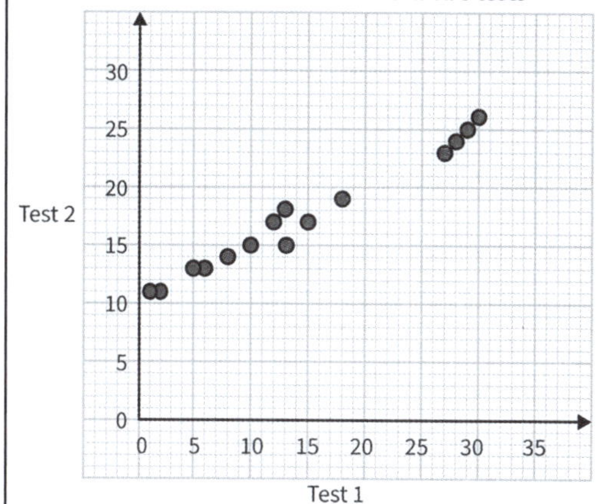 **a) Draw a line of best fit on the graph.**
a) **Result of children in two tests** 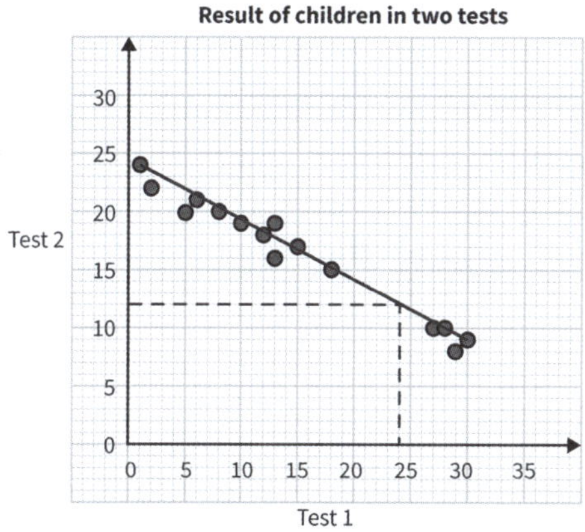		
b) One child was absent for Test 2 but scored 24 marks on Test 1. Use your line of best fit to predict what they would score on Test 2.		**b) One child was absent for Test 2 but scored 22 marks on Test 1. Use your line of best fit to predict what they would score on Test 2.**
b) 12 marks **Result of children in two tests** 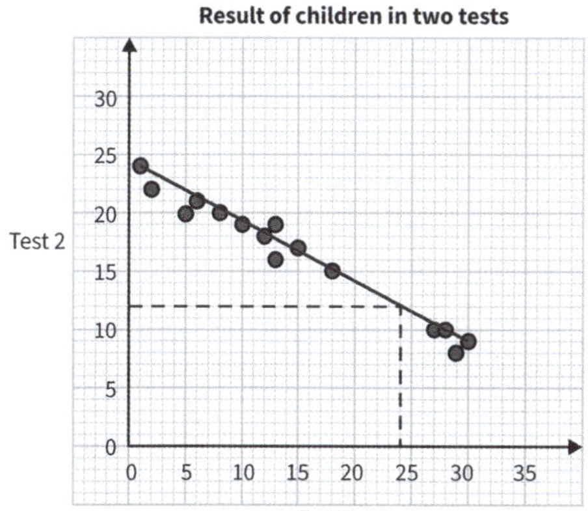		

6 Statistics

Fluency questions

6.1.1 Ungrouped frequency tables

1 A car dealer records the number of cars they sell each day in April

~~0~~	2	3	~~0~~	2	1	3	2	2	~~0~~
1	~~0~~	~~0~~	2	~~0~~	~~0~~	2	3	1	3
1	3	1	2	3	3	2	2	2	1

Use the information above to complete this tally chart.

Number of cars sold	Tally
0	𝍸 ||
1	
2	
3	

2 This frequency table shows the number of goals scored by a football team in the matches they played one season.

Number of goals	Tally	Frequency
0	𝍸 𝍸 ||||	14
1	𝍸 𝍸 |||	
2	𝍸 |||	
3	|||	

a) Complete the table.

b) In how many matches did the team score exactly two goals?

c) How many matches did the team play altogether?

3 A teacher records the number of students absent from class for twenty days.

Number of absent students	Tally	Frequency
0	𝍸 |	6
1	𝍸 |	6
2	||||	4
3	|||	3
4	|	1

Use the information In the table to write a list showing the number of absent students on each of the twenty days.

4 An ice cream seller wants to decide the amount of each flavour to stock. What data should they collect to help them to decide?

6.1.2 Grouped frequency tables

1 These are the marks scored by students in a test.

41	31	33	46	~~27~~	51	35	49	53	38
~~21~~	48	~~22~~	52	49	48	~~26~~	54	32	49

a) Use the information above to complete this frequency table.

Score out of 60	Tally	Frequency
21–30	||||	4
31–40		
41–50		
51–60		

b) The frequency table shows the marks scored by students in a different class. How many students in this class scored 41 or more?

Score out of 60	Tally	Frequency
21–30	𝍸	5
31–40	𝍸 ||||	9
41–50	𝍸 |||	8
51–60	||||	3

c) This incomplete frequency table shows the marks scored by students in another class. There are 22 students in this class.

Complete the table.

Score out of 60	Tally	Frequency
21–30	|	1
31–40	~~||||~~ |	6
41–50	~~||||~~ ~~||||~~	10
51–60		

2 a) Here are the heights (h) of some children in cm.

~~101~~	~~106~~	~~107~~	~~112~~	~~114~~	~~114~~	~~115~~	~~117~~	~~118~~	121
122	123	126	129	131	132	132	134	137	139

Use the information above to complete this frequency table.

Height, h (cm)	Tally	Frequency
$100 \le h < 110$	|||	3
$110 \le h < 120$	~~||||~~ |	6
$120 \le h < 130$		
$130 \le h < 140$		

b) Another student is 130 cm tall. In which category would they belong,
$120 \le h < 130$ or $130 \le h < 140$?

3 A hospital records the masses (m) of new-born babies in grams. Here are the masses of 30 babies

~~2289~~	~~2375~~	~~2473~~	~~2505~~	~~2557~~	~~2625~~	~~2765~~	~~2836~~	~~2956~~	~~3000~~
~~3062~~	~~3149~~	~~3182~~	~~3251~~	~~3343~~	~~3361~~	~~3397~~	~~3424~~	~~3456~~	~~3465~~
~~3476~~	~~3491~~	3570	3651	3805	3834	3904	3944	4104	4397

Use the information above to complete this frequency table.

Mass, m (grams)	Tally	Frequency
$2000 \le m < 2500$	|||	3
$2500 \le m < 3000$	~~||||~~ |	6
$3000 \le m < 3500$	~~||||~~ ~~||||~~ |||	13
$3500 \le m < 4000$		
$4000 \le m < 4500$		

6.1.3 Bar charts

1 In a school, students study one language in addition to English. The table shows the languages chosen by a group of students.

Language	Frequency
French	11
German	6
Spanish	7

Complete the bar chart below.

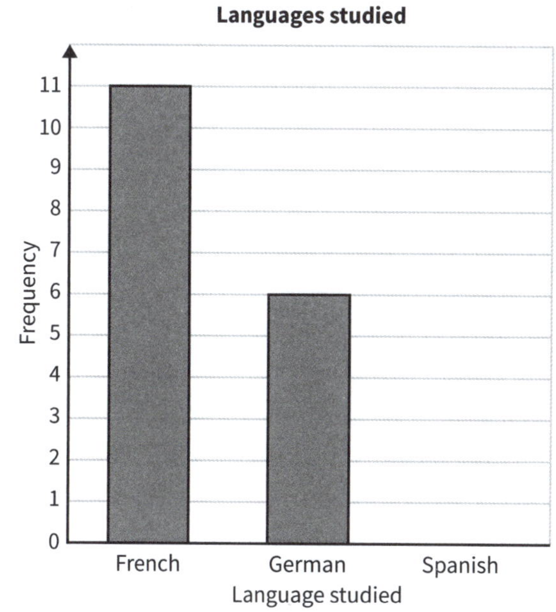

2 The table shows the favourite ice cream flavours of a group of children.

Flavour	Frequency
Vanilla	7
Chocolate	9
Strawberry	4
Other	5

Complete the bar chart below.

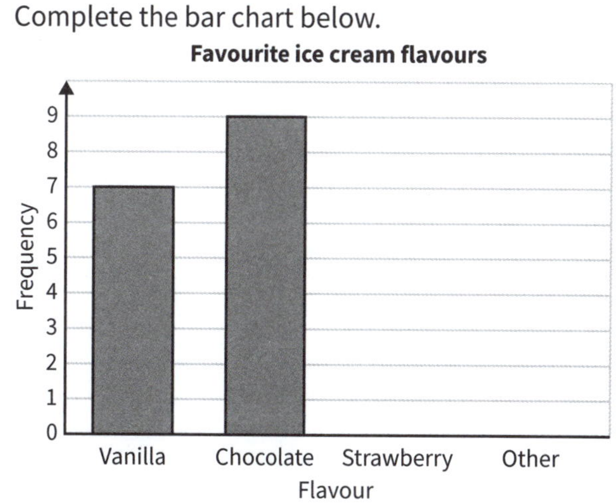

3 The table shows the number of phone calls received by a plumber one week.

Day	Phone calls
Monday	4
Tuesday	7
Wednesday	12
Thursday	7
Friday	8

Complete the bar chart below.

Phone calls received

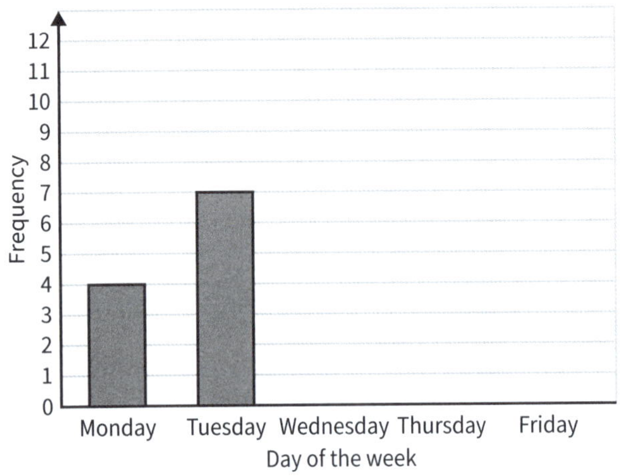

4 This bar chart shows the number of clients seen by a hair stylist each day for a week.

Clients seen

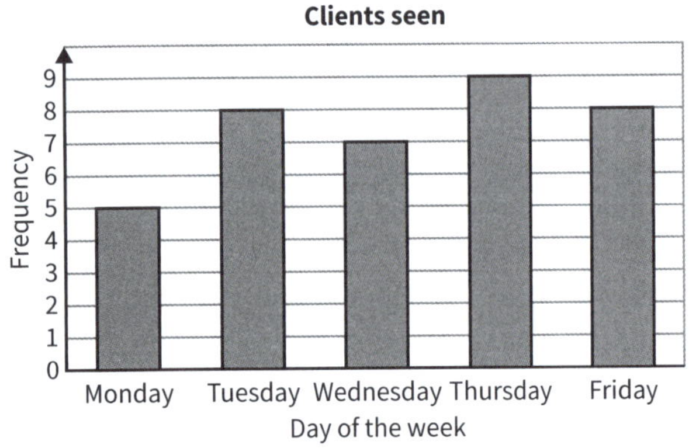

a) On which day of the week did the stylist see the most clients?

b) On which two days of the week did the stylist see eight clients?

5 This bar chart shows the number of postal letters received by a small business one week.

Numbers of Letters received

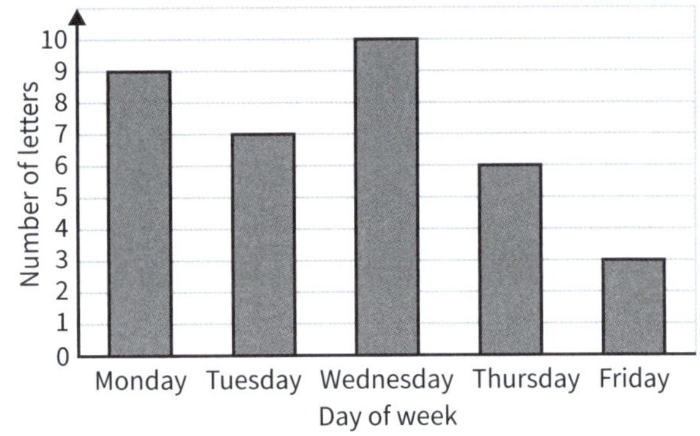

a) How many letters were received on Monday?

b) How many letters were received on Thursday?

c) On which day of the week were the most letters received?

d) On which day of the week were the fewest letters received?

6 A group of twenty people went fishing. The bar chart shows the number of fish caught by each person.

Number of fish caught

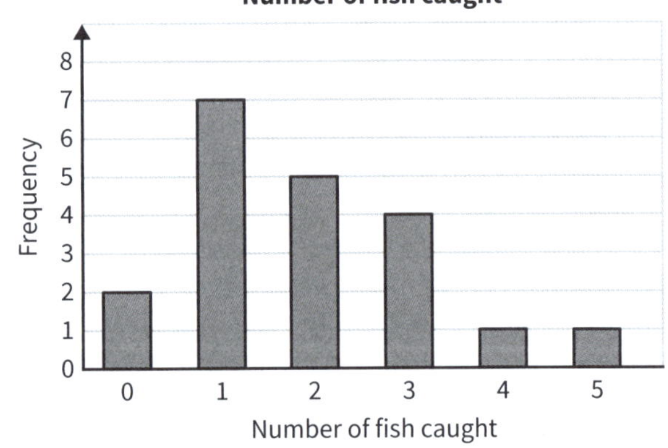

a) How many people caught no fish?

b) How many people caught exactly 1 fish?

c) How many people caught exactly 2 fish?

d) How many people caught 3 or more fish?

6.1.4 Pictograms

1 If the symbol  is used to represent 8 people, how many people are represented by each of the following?

a) 

b)

c) 

d) 

e) 

2 If the symbol  is used to represent 20 cakes, how many cakes are represented by each of the following?

a) 

b) 

c) 

d) 

3 This pictogram shows the number of armchairs sold one week at a furniture shop.

Armchairs sold each day	
Monday	
Tuesday	
Wednesday	
Thursday	
Friday	

Key:  represents 2 armchairs

a) The key states that  represents 2 armchairs.
How many armchairs does  represent?

b) How many armchairs were sold on Tuesday?

c) How many armchairs were sold on Friday?

6.1.5 Constructing scatter graphs

1 The table shows the scores achieved in two video games by six players.

Player	Ali	Bob	Carl	Di	Elif	Fay
Game 1	7	8	6	6	9	3
Game 2	8	5	6	8	7	2

The scatter graph shows the scores for the first five students. Plot Fay's point on the scatter graph.

Scores achieved in two games

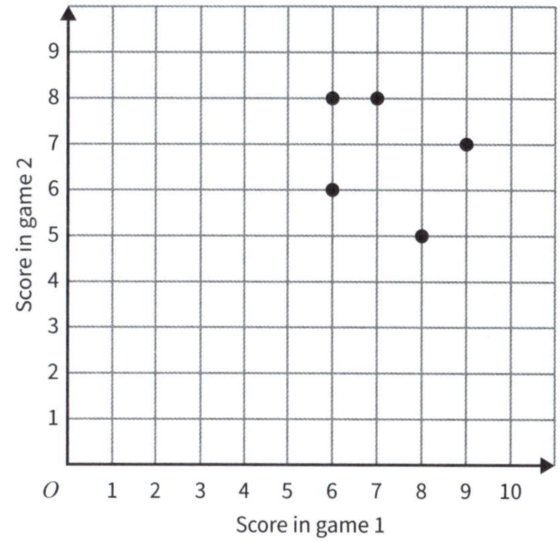

2 The table shows the numbers of ice creams and hot chocolates sold between 10 am and 11 am each morning over an eight-day period.

Day	1	2	3	4	5	6	7	8
Ice creams	9	8	6	6	4	5	2	1
Hot chocolates	2	4	3	4	7	5	10	10

The scatter graph shows the information for the first six days.

Plot the points for days 7 and 8 on the scatter graph.

Ice creams and hot chocolates sold

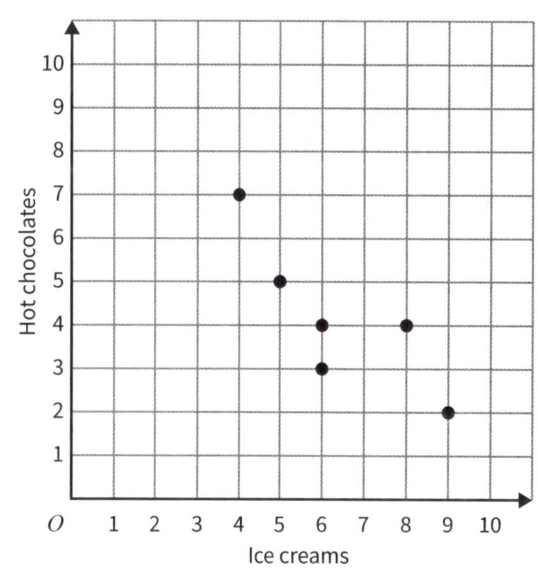

3 The table shows how many years some footballers have been playing the game and the number of goals that they scored during that time.

Years	1	2	3	4	5	7	9
Goals	7	30	19	90	88	100	150

The point representing the footballer who has been playing for 7 years has not been plotted.
Plot this point.

Years of experience and goals scored in a career

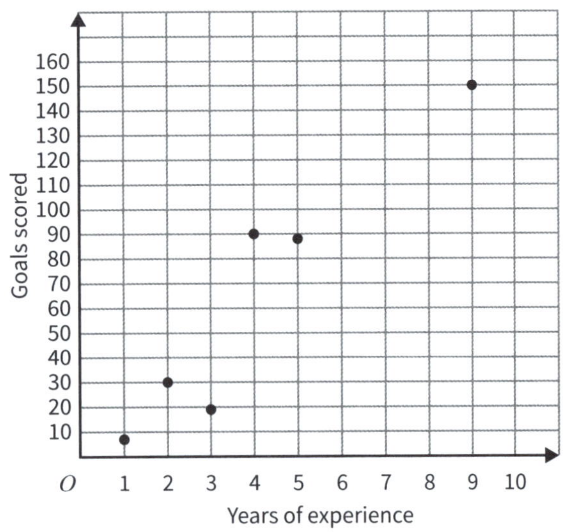

6.1.6 Interpreting scatter graphs

1 This scatter graph shows the money made by seven films and the total number of weeks each film was shown in cinemas.

Weeks film shown and money earned

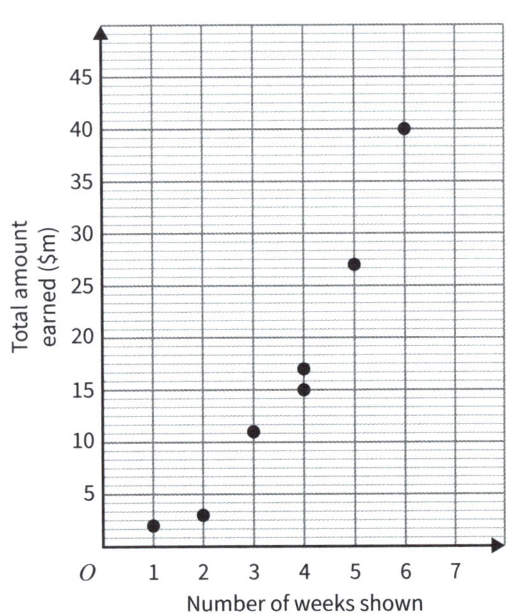

a) How much money was earned by the film that was shown for 6 weeks?

b) How much money was earned by the film that was shown for 3 weeks?

c) One film earned $27m. For how many weeks was this film shown?

d) Two films were shown for the same number of weeks. How much did these two films earn altogether?

2 This scatter graph shows the number of pairs of sunglasses and the number of scarves that a shop sold each month for a year.

Sales of sunglasses and scarves

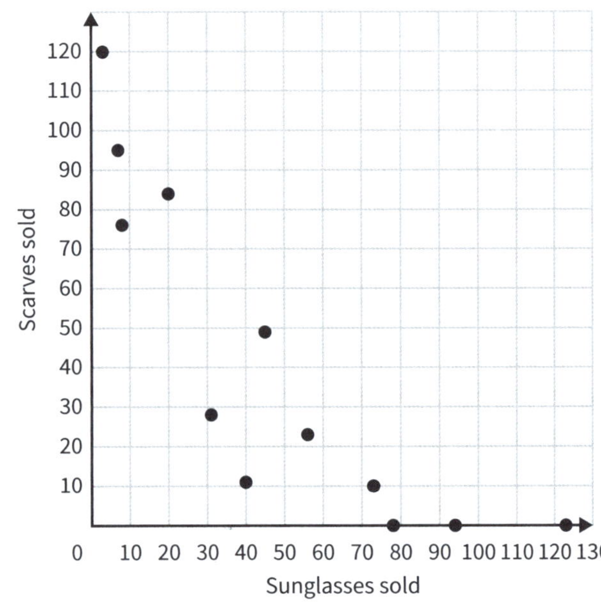

a) In one month, the shop sold 73 pairs of sunglasses.
How many scarves did it sell in that month?

b) In one month, the shop sold 84 scarves.
How many pairs of sunglasses did it sell in that month?

6.2 Pie charts

Example-problem pairs

6.2.1 Fractions of circles

Worked example 1	Thinking	Your turn! 1
The shaded sector is $\frac{3}{8}$ of the whole circle. Work out the angle at the vertex of the shaded sector. 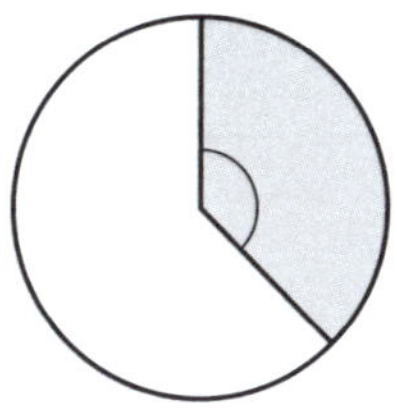	*What fact can we use to work this out?* *What calculation do we need to do?*	**The shaded sector is $\frac{7}{10}$ of the whole circle. Work out the angle at the vertex of the shaded sector.** 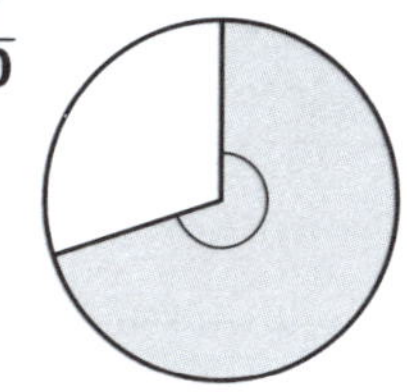
$\frac{3}{8}$ of 360 = 135°		

Worked example 2	Thinking	Your turn! 2
The sector shown is $\frac{1}{3}$ of the circle. Work out the angle at the vertex of the shaded sector. 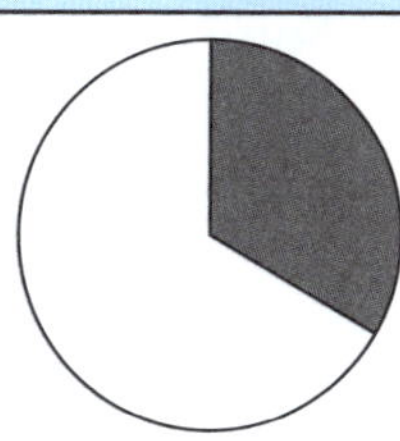	*What fact can we use to work this out?* *How do we calculate the required fraction?*	**The sector shown is $\frac{1}{8}$ of the circle. Work out the angle at the vertex of the shaded sector.** 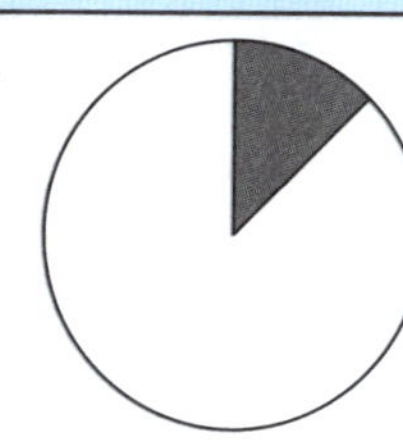
A full turn is 360°.		
$\frac{1}{3}$ of 360 $= \frac{1}{3} \times 360$ $= 360 \div 3$ $= 120°$		

Worked example 3	Thinking	Your turn! 3
The shaded sector is 65% of the whole circle. Work out the angle at the vertex of the shaded sector. 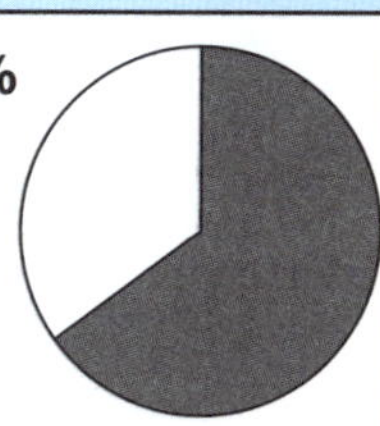	*What fact can we use to work this out?* *What calculation do we need to do?*	**The shaded sector is 30% of the whole circle. Work out the angle at the vertex of the shaded sector.** 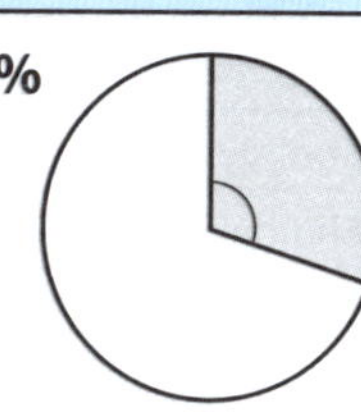
65% of 360 = 0.65 × 360 = 234°	*How do we read the given value from the protractor?*	

Worked example 4	**Thinking**	**Your turn! 4**
Work out what proportion of the circle is shaded. Write your answer as a fraction in its simplest form. 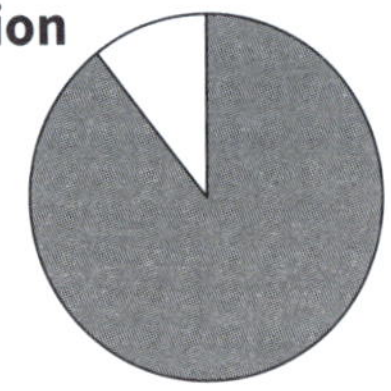	*What do we need to do first?*	**Work out what proportion of the circle is shaded. Write your answer as a fraction in its simplest form.** 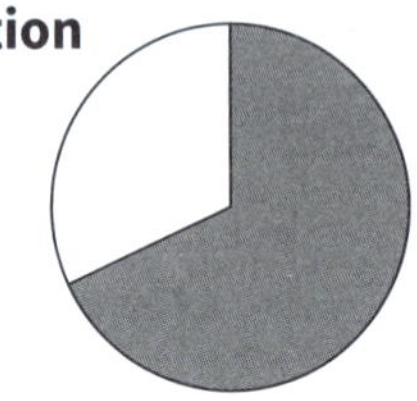
First measure the angle of the non-shaded sector as 38°.	*Then how can we find the angle of the shaded sector?*	
Angle of shaded sector $= 360° - 38° = 322°$	*How do we write the proportion shaded?*	
Proportion shaded $= \frac{322}{360} = \frac{161}{180}$	*Is this in its simplest form?*	

6.2.2 Constructing pie charts

<table>
<tr><th>Worked example 1</th><th>Thinking</th><th>Your turn! 1</th></tr>
<tr><td>Rani asked 72 people what their favourite day of the week is and recorded the results in the table. Draw a pie chart to represent this.
<table>
<tr><th>Day</th><th>Frequency</th></tr>
<tr><td>Friday</td><td>12</td></tr>
<tr><td>Saturday</td><td>30</td></tr>
<tr><td>Sunday</td><td>23</td></tr>
<tr><td>Monday</td><td>7</td></tr>
</table></td>
<td>How many degrees should be used to represent one person?
How do we find the missing angles?</td>
<td>Josh asked 24 people what their favourite season is and recorded the results in a table. Draw a pie chart to represent this.
<table>
<tr><th>Season</th><th>Frequency</th></tr>
<tr><td>Summer</td><td>15</td></tr>
<tr><td>Spring</td><td>1</td></tr>
<tr><td>Autumn</td><td>2</td></tr>
<tr><td>Winter</td><td>6</td></tr>
</table></td></tr>
<tr><td>$\frac{1}{72} \times 360° = 5°$
So, 1 person is represented by 5°.
<table>
<tr><th>Day</th><th>Frequency</th><th>Angle</th></tr>
<tr><td>Friday</td><td>12</td><td>$12 \times 5° = 60°$</td></tr>
<tr><td>Saturday</td><td>30</td><td>$30 \times 5° = 150°$</td></tr>
<tr><td>Sunday</td><td>23</td><td>$23 \times 5° = 115°$</td></tr>
<tr><td>Monday</td><td>7</td><td>$7 \times 5° = 35°$</td></tr>
</table></td>
<td>What check can we do with our values?
How do we begin to construct the first sector on the pie chart?
How do we construct the rest of the pie chart?</td>
<td></td></tr>
<tr><td>Check: $60° + 150° + 115° + 35° = 360°$</td><td></td><td></td></tr>
<tr><td>Favourite day for a group of 72 people
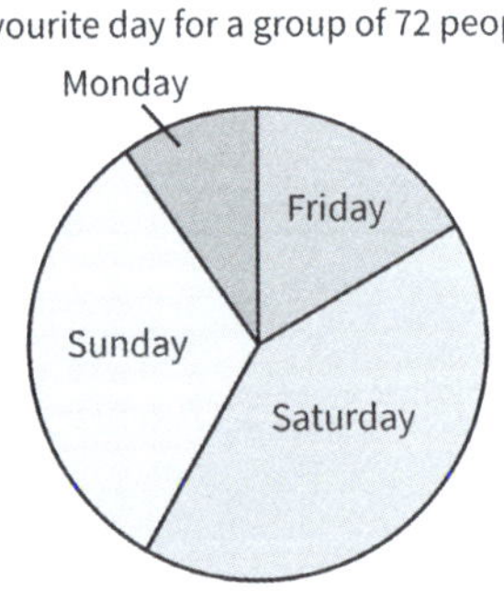
</td>
<td>What do we need to remember to write in each sector?</td>
<td></td></tr>
</table>

6.2.3 Interpreting pie charts

<table>
<tr><th>Worked example 1</th><th>Thinking</th><th>Your turn! 1</th></tr>
<tr><td>Each student at a school studies one foreign language. The foreign languages studied by 40 students are shown on the pie chart.
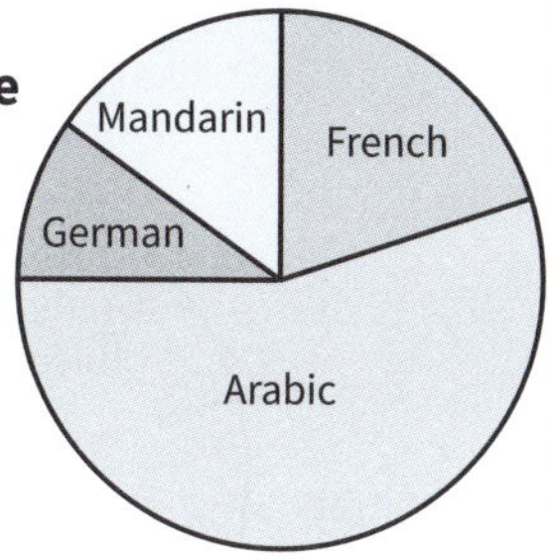
Work out the number of students who study French.</td><td>How can we work out the size of angle that represents one student?</td><td>Each student at a school studies one foreign language. The foreign languages studied by 60 students are shown on the pie chart.
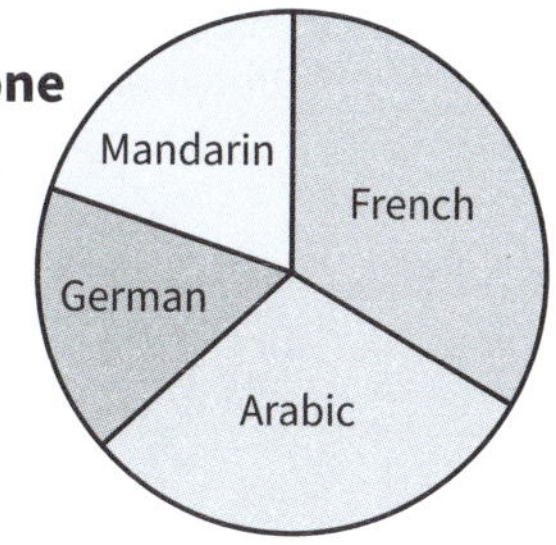
Work out the number of students who study Mandarin.</td></tr>
<tr><td>$\frac{1}{40} \times 360° = 9°$ so each student is represented by 9°.</td><td>What do we need to do now?</td><td></td></tr>
<tr><td>Sector for French = 72°.</td><td></td><td></td></tr>
<tr><td><table><tr><th></th><th>Angle</th><th>Frequency</th><th></th></tr><tr><td>÷ 40</td><td>360°</td><td>40</td><td>÷ 40</td></tr><tr><td></td><td>9°</td><td>1</td><td></td></tr><tr><td>× 8</td><td>72°</td><td>8</td><td>× 8</td></tr></table></td><td>How can we find the number of students that this sector represents?</td><td></td></tr>
<tr><td>$72 \div 9 = 8$
So, 8 students study French.</td><td></td><td></td></tr>
</table>

<table>
<tr><th>Worked example 2</th><th>Thinking</th><th>Your turn! 2</th></tr>
<tr><td>A restaurant owner asks a sample of customers about their favourite pie fillings. The pie chart shows the results.
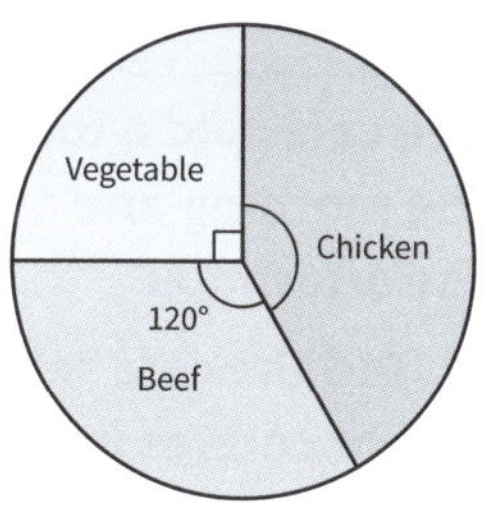
a) Which filling is the most popular?</td><td>Which sector is the largest?</td><td>A restaurant owner asks a sample of customers about their favourite desserts. The pie chart shows the results.

a) Which dessert is the most popular?</td></tr>
<tr><td>Vegetable = 90°
Beef = 120°
Chicken = 360° − 90° − 120° = 150°</td><td>How can we work out which is the biggest sector?</td><td></td></tr>
<tr><td>The largest sector is for chicken, so this is the most popular.</td><td></td><td></td></tr>
<tr><td>b) What fraction of the customers preferred beef pie?</td><td>How many degrees are in the full turn?</td><td>b) What fraction of the customers preferred cheesecake?</td></tr>
<tr><td>Fraction preferring beef pie $= \frac{120}{360}$
$= \frac{1}{3}$</td><td>How can we use this information?</td><td></td></tr>
</table>

6 Statistics

<table>
<tr><th>Worked example 3</th><th>Thinking</th><th>Your turn! 3</th></tr>
<tr>
<td>The pie charts show the drinks ordered in a café in the morning and afternoon.
Drinks ordered in the morning
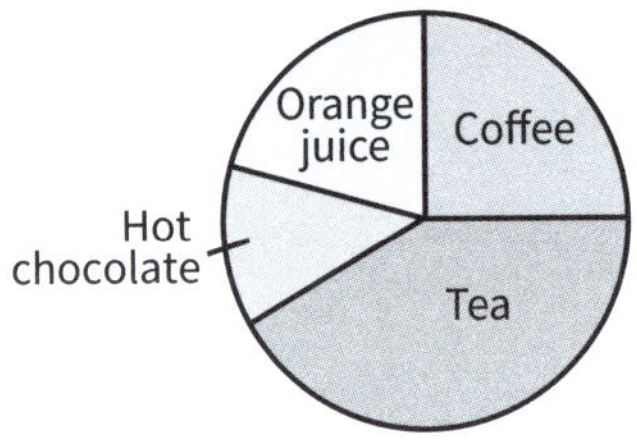

Drinks ordered in the afternoon

a) Did the café sell a higher proportion of tea in the morning or in the afternoon?</td>
<td>What do we need to do to compare proportion?</td>
<td>The pie charts show the drinks ordered in a café in the morning and afternoon.
Drinks ordered in the morning
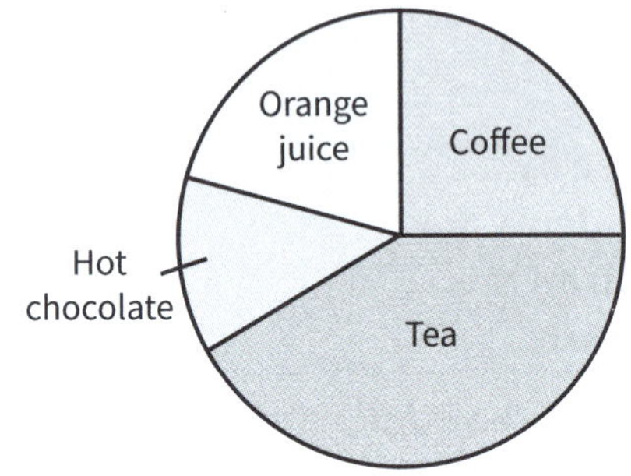

Drinks ordered in the afternoon

a) Did the café sell a higher proportion of orange juice in the morning or in the afternoon?</td>
</tr>
<tr><td>Morning; it has the bigger sector.</td><td></td><td></td></tr>
<tr>
<td>The café sold a total of 160 drinks in the morning and a total of 72 drinks in the afternoon.
b) Did the café sell more coffees in the morning or in the afternoon?</td>
<td>What do we need to do to compare the number of drinks?</td>
<td>The café sold a total of 160 drinks in the morning and a total of 72 drinks in the afternoon.
b) Did the café sell more hot chocolates in the morning or in the afternoon?</td>
</tr>
<tr>
<td>Morning: coffee sector = 90°
Afternoon: coffee sector = 180°</td>
<td>How can we find the number of drinks that each sector represents?</td>
<td></td>
</tr>
<tr>
<td>Morning: $\frac{90}{360} \times 160 = 40$
$\frac{180}{360} \times 72 = 36$
So they sold more coffees in the morning.</td>
<td></td>
<td></td>
</tr>
</table>

Fluency questions

6.2.1 Fractions of circles

1 Work out the following.

a) 360 ÷ 2 **b)** 360 ÷ 3

c) 360 ÷ 4 **d)** 360 ÷ 5

e) 360 ÷ 6 **f)** 360 ÷ 8

g) 360 ÷ 9 **h)** 360 ÷ 10

i) 360 ÷ 12 **j)** 360 ÷ 15

k) 360 ÷ 18

2 What fraction of each circle is shaded? Choose from the following options:

$\frac{1}{3}$ $\frac{1}{5}$ $\frac{1}{6}$ $\frac{1}{9}$ $\frac{1}{10}$ $\frac{1}{12}$

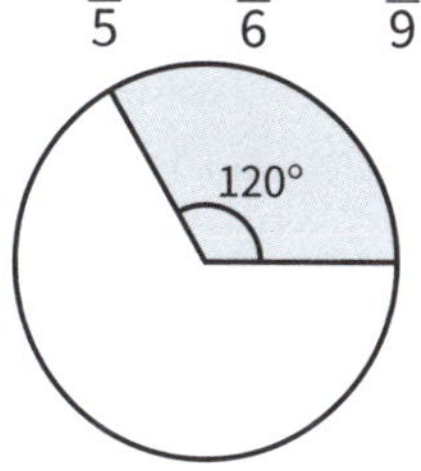

a)

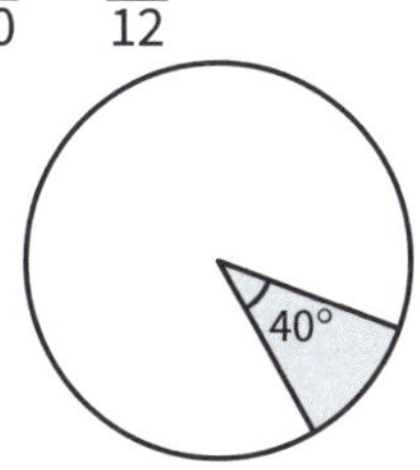

b)

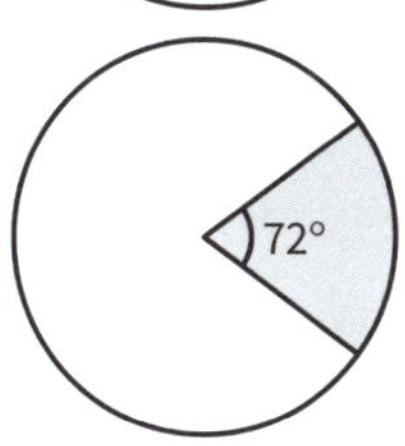

c)

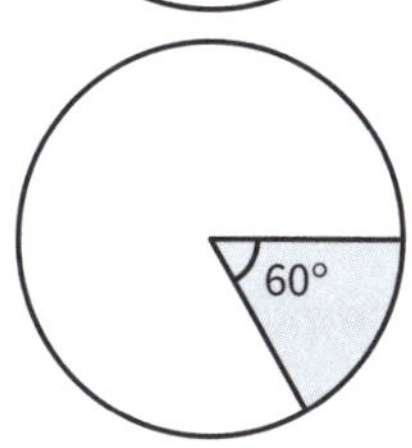

d)

3 Work out the following.

a) $\frac{1}{2}$ of 360 **b)** $\frac{1}{4}$ of 360

c) $\frac{1}{10}$ of 360 **d)** $\frac{3}{10}$ of 360

e) $\frac{1}{5}$ of 360 **f)** $\frac{4}{5}$ of 360

g) $\frac{1}{6}$ of 360

4 Convert each percentage to a fraction in its simplest form.

a) 10%

b) 5%

c) 45%

d) 2%

6.2.2 Constructing pie charts

1 Kendra wants to construct a pie chart showing the favourite colours of 36 children.

Complete the calculation to work out what angle represents one child.

$\frac{1}{36} \times 360° =$ ______°

2 Aleksei wants to construct a pie chart showing the favourite foods of 60 children.

Complete the calculation to work out what angle represents one child.

$\frac{1}{60} \times 360° =$ ______°

3 Zofia opens a pack of sweets. There are 5 strawberry sweets, 7 orange sweets, 3 lemon sweets, 3 lime sweets, and 2 blackcurrant sweets.

Zofia wants to construct a pie chart showing the flavours of sweets in the packet.

Since there are 20 sweets in total, each sweet is represented by an angle of $\frac{1}{20} \times 360° = 18°$

How many degrees should be used to represent the lemon sweets?

4 Matylda wants to construct a pie chart showing the colours of cars in her school's car park.

There are 40 cars in the car park.

She works out that each car must be represented by an angle of 360° ÷ 40 = 9°.

a) Complete the table.

Car colour	Frequency	Angle
White	8	8 × 9° = 72°
Silver	6	6 × 9° = ______°
Red	8	8 × 9° = ______°
Blue	11	11 × 9 = ______°
Other	7	______ × 9° = ______°

b) Complete this pie chart.

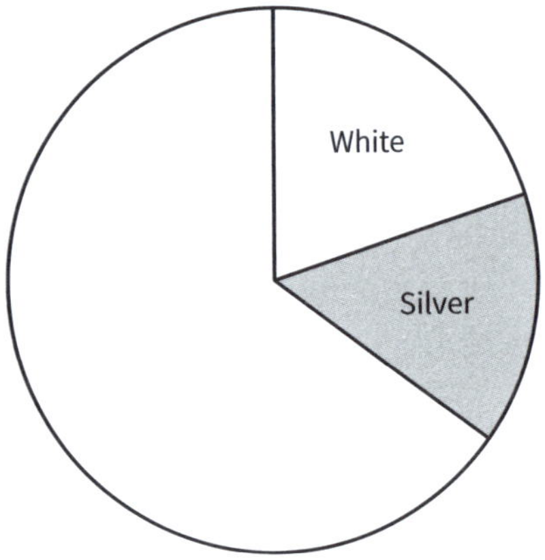

6.2.3 Interpreting pie charts

1 The pie chart shows the fruit chosen by some children at lunch time.

Chosen fruit

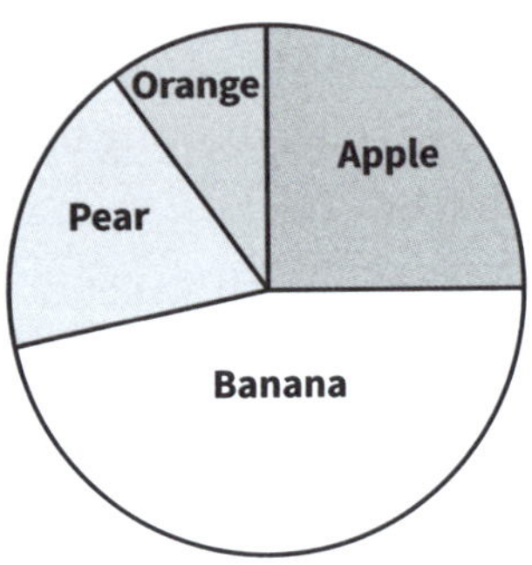

a) Which fruit was most popular?

b) Which fruit was least popular?

2 The pie chart shows the grades achieved by some students in a test.

Grades achieved

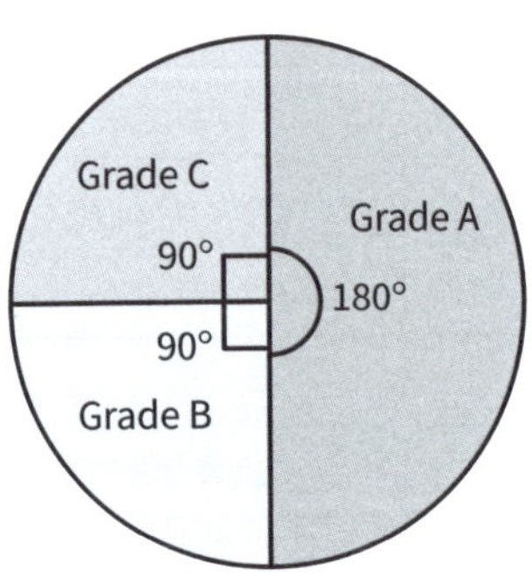

a) What fraction of the circle is the sector for students who achieved grade A?

b) If 20 students took the test, how many achieved grade A?

c) What fraction of the circle is the sector for students who achieved grade B?

d) If 20 students took the test, how many achieved grade B?

3 The pie chart shows the types of bird that visited a garden one day.

Birds visiting the garden

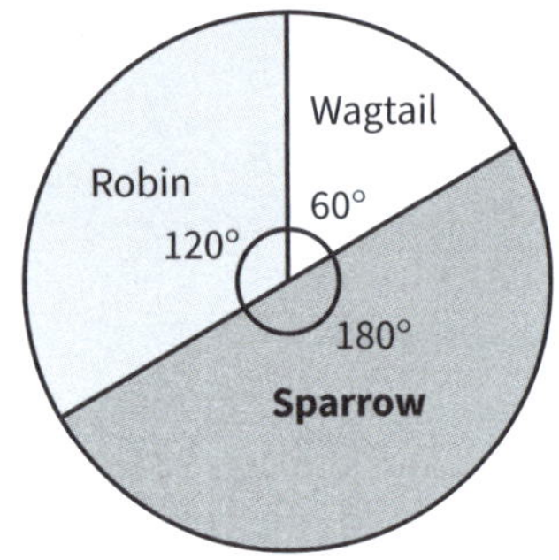

a) What is the angle of the sector representing wagtails?

b) 360° (the full circle) represents all the birds visiting the garden.

Fill in the blanks to find the fraction of the birds that were wagtails, given in its simplest form.

$$\frac{\square}{360} = \frac{\square}{\square}$$

c) In total, 30 birds visited the garden.

Complete the ratio table to work out what angle represents one bird.

	Angle	Number of birds	
÷30	360°	30	÷30
		1	

d) The sector representing robins has an angle of 120°. Complete the ratio table to work out the number of robins visiting the garden.

	Angle	Number of birds	
÷30	360°	30	÷30
		1	
×___	120°		×___

6.3 Measures of average and spread of data

Example-problem pairs

6.3.1 The mean

<table>
<tr><th>Worked example 1</th><th>Thinking</th><th>Your turn! 1</th></tr>
<tr><td>The table shows the ages of 25 children. Work out the mean age.

Ages	Frequency
11	8
12	8
13	3
14	6

</td><td>How do we work out the total of all the values?</td><td>The table shows the ages of 20 children. Work out the mean age.

Ages	Frequency
11	3
12	2
13	1
14	5
15	9

</td></tr>
<tr><td>We can add another column on the table for Age × Frequency.

Ages	Frequency	Age × Frequency
11	8	$11 \times 8 = 88$
12	8	$12 \times 8 = 96$
13	3	$13 \times 3 = 39$
14	6	$14 \times 6 = 84$

</td><td>How do we work out the mean?</td><td></td></tr>
<tr><td>There were 25 children in total, so:

$$\text{mean age} = \frac{88 + 96 + 39 + 84}{25} = \frac{307}{25} = 12.28 \text{ years}$$

</td><td></td><td></td></tr>
</table>

Worked example 2	Thinking	Your turn! 2
20 football players have a mean age of 23 and 30 netball players have a mean age of 28. **What is the mean age of the whole group of 50 people?**	*How do we work out the sum of all the values in the combined group?*	**15 football players have a mean age of 12 and 5 netball players have a mean age of 16.** **What is the mean age of the whole group of 20 people?**
Sum of ages: Football players = 20 × 23 = 460 Netball players = 30 × 28 = 840 Combined group = 360 + 840 = 1300	*How can we use this to work out the mean for the combined group?*	
Mean of whole group = $\frac{\text{sum of values}}{\text{number of values}}$ $= \frac{1300}{50} = 26$		

6.3.2 The median

Worked example 1	Thinking	Your turn! 1
The ages of 12 people are: **17, 11, 50, 23, 66, 65, 13, 18, 9, 27, 66, 4** **Work out the median age.**	*What do we need to do before finding the middle value?*	**The ages of 10 people are:** **14, 71, 29, 31, 75, 40, 42, 5, 15, 14** **Work out the median age.**
The ordered list is: 4, 9, 11, 13, 17, 18, 23, 27, 50, 65, 66, 66	*How can we work out the position of the median?*	
There are 12 values, so the position of the median is given by $\frac{12+1}{2} = \frac{13}{2} = 6.5$ This means that the median is exactly halfway between the 6th and 7th values. The 6th value is 18, the 7th value is 23.	*How do we work out the value halfway between the two middle values?*	
Median age = $\frac{18+23}{2}$ = 20.5 years		

Worked example 2	Thinking	Your turn! 2
The table shows the number of students in 43 different classrooms. Work out the median number of students. (see table A)	*How can we find the position of the median?*	**The table shows the number of students in 39 different classrooms. Work out the median number of students.** (see table B)
$\frac{43+1}{2} = \frac{44}{2} = 22$ The median is the 22nd value.	*How can we work out the value of the median?*	
Add a column with a 'running total' to help work out which row the 22nd value is in. (see table C)		
The 22nd value is 29. Median = 29 students		

Table A (Worked example 2):

Number of students	Frequency
26	3
27	8
28	9
29	14
30	9

Table B (Your turn! 2):

Number of students	Frequency
27	15
28	12
29	6
30	5
31	1

Table C (Worked example 2):

Number of students	Frequency	Running total
26	3	3
27	8	11
28	9	20
29	14	34
30	9	43

Worked example 3

The pictogram shows the number of lessons taught by a group of 20 teachers one day. Work out the median number of lessons.

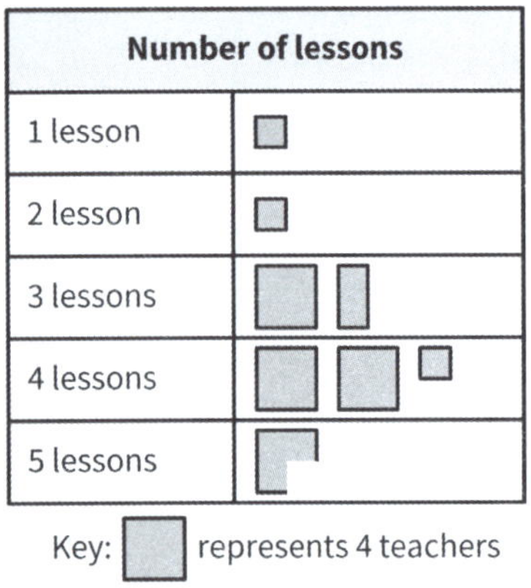

$\frac{20 + 1}{2} = \frac{21}{2} = 10.5$

The median is halfway between the 10th and 11th value.

The 10th value and the 11th value are both 4, so the median is 4.

Thinking

How can we find the position of the median?

Your turn! 3

The pictogram shows the number of lessons taught by a group of 16 teachers one day. Work out the median number of lessons.

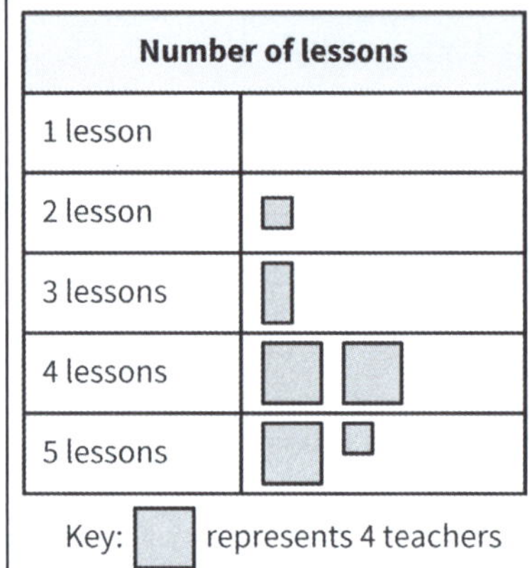

6.3.3 The mode

Worked example 1

16 students in a class were asked how many pens they had. Find the modal number of pens.

Number of pens	Frequency
0	1
1	6
2	8
3	0
4	1

The modal number of pens is 2 because it has the highest frequency.

Thinking

How do we find the modal value?

Your turn! 1

20 students in a class were asked how many pens they had. Find the modal number of pens.

Number of pens	Frequency
0	3
1	12
2	3
3	1
4	0
5	1

Worked example 2	Thinking	Your turn! 2
The pictogram shows the number of pizzas sold by four different restaurants one evening. 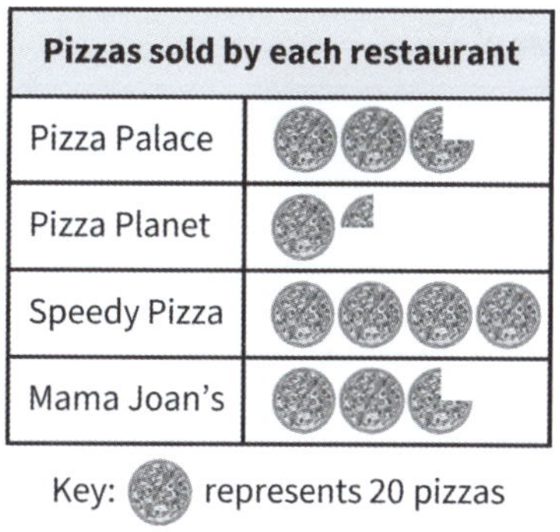 **a) Find the modal restaurant.**	*How do we find the modal value?*	**The pictogram shows the number of pizzas sold by four different restaurants one evening.** 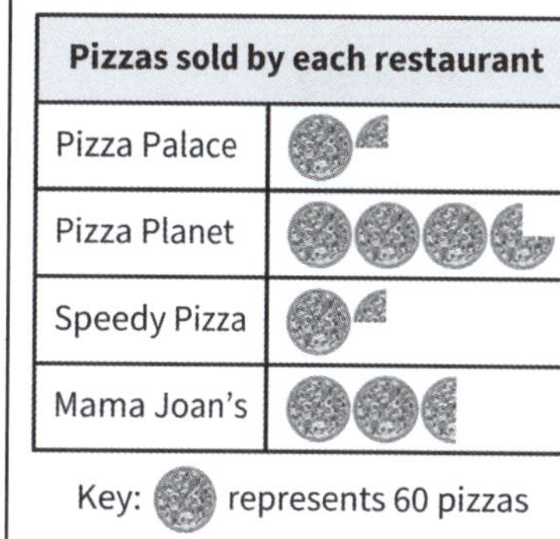 **a) Find the modal restaurant.**
The modal restaurant is Speedy Pizza, as it has the highest frequency.		
b) What is the modal number of pizzas sold? 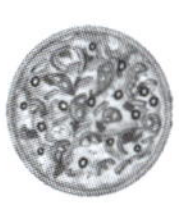 = 20  = 10  = 15  = 5 Number of pizzas at each restaurant: Pizza Palace = 20 + 20 + 15 = 55 Pizza Planet = 20 + 5 = 25 Speedy = 20 + 20 + 20 + 20 = 80 Mama Joan's = 20 + 20 + 15 = 55		**b) What is the modal number of pizzas sold?**
The modal number of pizza sold is 55.		

6.3.4 The range

Worked example 1

The ages of 245 students were recorded. Find the range of their ages.

Age	Frequency
11	38
12	41
13	23
14	45
15	33
16	65

Thinking

What information do we need from the table?

The largest value is 16 and the smallest value is 11.

How do we find the range?

Range = 16 – 11 = 5 years

Your turn! 1

20 people were asked how much sleep they had last night. Find the range of hours of sleep.

Number of hours	Frequency
5	2
6	5
7	9
8	3
9	1

Worked example 2

The bar chart shows the number of spelling mistakes in some students' work. Find the range for the number of spelling mistakes.

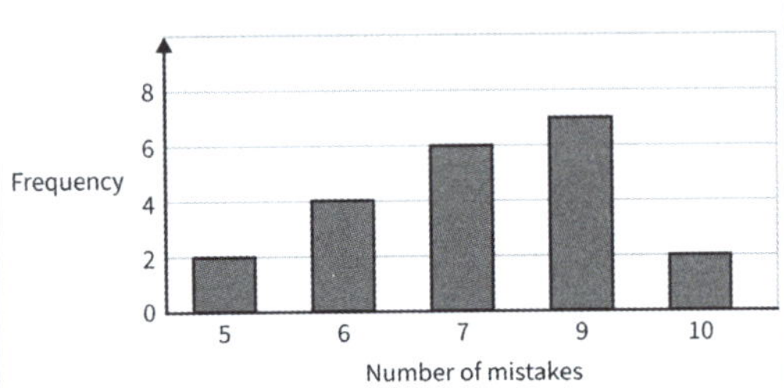

Thinking

What information do we need from the bar chart?

The largest value is 10 and the smallest value is 5.

How do we find the range?

Range = 10 – 5 = 5 mistakes

Your turn! 2

The bar chart shows the number of spelling mistakes in some students' work. Find the range for the number of spelling mistakes.

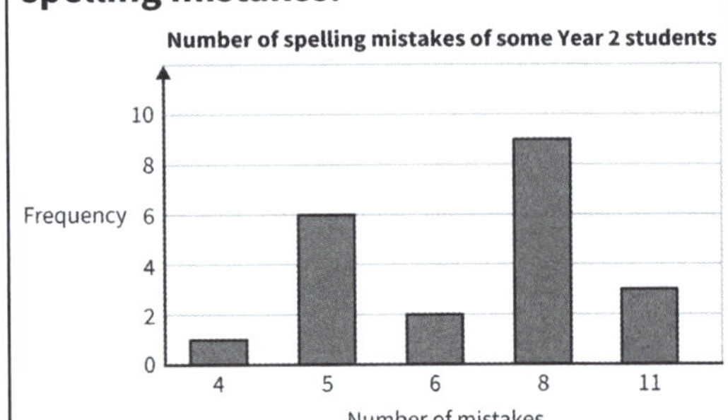

6.3.5 Average and range of grouped data

<table>
<tr><th>Worked example 1</th><th>Thinking</th><th>Your turn! 1</th></tr>
<tr><td>The heights, in metres, of the 16 tallest buildings in the world are shown in the table.
<table>
<tr><th>Height, h (m)</th><th>Frequency</th></tr>
<tr><td>$400 \le h < 500$</td><td>5</td></tr>
<tr><td>$500 \le h < 600$</td><td>7</td></tr>
<tr><td>$600 \le h < 700$</td><td>3</td></tr>
<tr><td>$700 \le h < 800$</td><td>0</td></tr>
<tr><td>$800 \le h < 900$</td><td>1</td></tr>
</table>
a) Write down the modal group.</td><td>How do we find the modal group?</td><td>The heights, in centimetres, of the 16 tallest people who ever lived are shown in the table.
<table>
<tr><th>Height, h (m)</th><th>Frequency</th></tr>
<tr><td>$240 \le h < 250$</td><td>3</td></tr>
<tr><td>$250 \le h < 260$</td><td>8</td></tr>
<tr><td>$260 \le h < 270$</td><td>4</td></tr>
<tr><td>$270 \le h < 280$</td><td>1</td></tr>
</table>
a) Write down the modal group.</td></tr>
<tr><td>The modal group is $500 \le h < 600$ since it has the highest frequency.</td><td></td><td></td></tr>
<tr><td>b) Work out the maximum possible range of the data.</td><td>What do we need from the table to find the maximum range?</td><td>b) Work out the maximum possible range of the data.</td></tr>
<tr><td>We use 900 for the largest value.
The smallest possible value is 400.</td><td>How do we use these values?</td><td></td></tr>
<tr><td>Maximum possible range
$= 900 - 400 = 500$ m</td><td></td><td></td></tr>
<tr><td>c) Work out the median group.</td><td>How do we find the position of the median?</td><td>c) Work out the median group.</td></tr>
<tr><td>$n = 16$
$\frac{16+1}{2} = 8.5$
The median lies halfway between the 8th and 9th values.</td><td>How do we use the table to work out which group these values are in?</td><td></td></tr>
<tr><td>Using a running total, the 8th and 9th values both lie in the second group.
So, the median lies in the group $500 \le h < 600$.</td><td></td><td></td></tr>
</table>

Worked example 2	Thinking	Your turn! 2
The heights, in metres, of the 16 tallest buildings in the world are shown in the table. **Calculate an estimate of the mean. Give your answer correct to 1 decimal place.**	*Which value should we use to approximate the data in each group?*	**The heights, in centimetres, of the 16 tallest people who ever lived are shown in the table.** **Calculate an estimate of the mean. Give your answer correct to 1 decimal place.**
Find the midpoint for each group by adding smallest and largest values for the group and dividing by 2. For the first group: $\frac{400 + 500}{2} = 500$	*How do we find the total of all the values?*	
(table below)	*How do we find the estimate for the mean?*	
Mean = $\frac{2250 + 3850 + 1950 + 0 + 850}{16}$ $= \frac{8900}{16} = 556.3$ m (to 1 decimal place)		

Worked example 2 table:

Height, h (m)	Frequency
$400 \leq h < 500$	5
$500 \leq h < 600$	7
$600 \leq h < 700$	3
$700 \leq h < 800$	0
$800 \leq h < 900$	1

Your turn! 2 table:

Height, h (m)	Frequency
$240 \leq h < 250$	3
$250 \leq h < 260$	8
$260 \leq h < 270$	4
$270 \leq h < 280$	1

Midpoint table:

Height, h (m)	Frequency	Midpoint
$400 \leq h < 500$	5	450
$500 \leq h < 600$	7	550
$600 \leq h < 700$	3	650
$700 \leq h < 800$	0	750
$800 \leq h < 900$	1	850

Frequency × midpoint table:

Height, h (m)	Frequency × midpoint
$400 \leq h < 500$	$5 \times 450 = 2250$
$500 \leq h < 600$	$7 \times 550 = 3850$
$600 \leq h < 700$	$3 \times 650 = 1950$
$700 \leq h < 800$	$0 \times 750 = 0$
$800 \leq h < 900$	$1 \times 850 = 850$

<table>
<tr><th>Worked example 3</th><th>Thinking</th><th>Your turn! 3</th></tr>
<tr><td>The bar chart shows the test scores of 30 students.
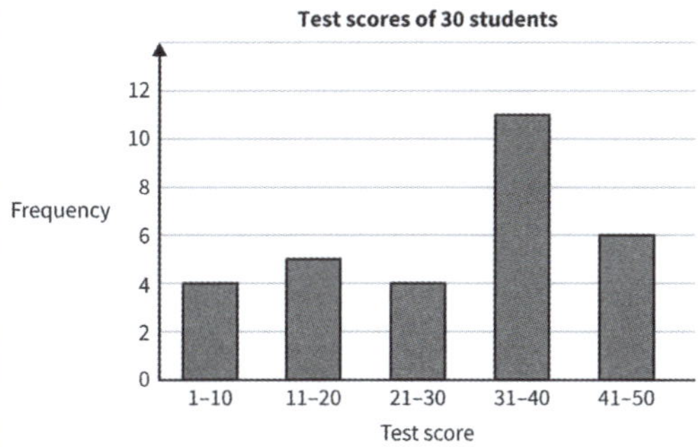

a) Write down the modal group.</td><td>How do we find the modal group?</td><td>The bar chart shows the test scores of 30 students.
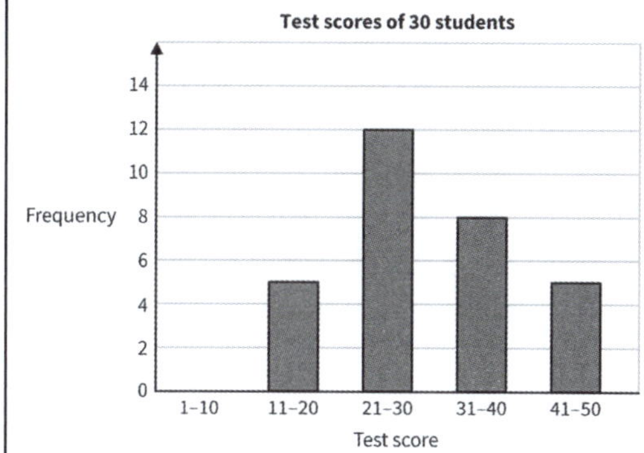

a) Write down the modal group.</td></tr>
<tr><td>The modal group is 31–40, as it has the highest frequency.</td><td></td><td></td></tr>
<tr><td>b) Work out the maximum possible range of the data.</td><td>What do we need from the bar chart to find the maximum range?</td><td>b) Work out the maximum possible range of the data.</td></tr>
<tr><td>The largest possible value is 50.
The smallest possible value is 1.</td><td>How do we find the maximum range?</td><td></td></tr>
<tr><td>Maximum possible range
$= 50 - 1 = 49$</td><td></td><td></td></tr>
<tr><td>c) Work out the median group.</td><td></td><td>c) Work out the median group.</td></tr>
<tr><td>$n = 30$
$\frac{30 + 1}{2} = 15.5$
The median lies halfway between the 15th and 16th values.</td><td>How do we find which position the median would be in?
How can we display the data to make it easier to find the median?</td><td></td></tr>
<tr><td><table>
<tr><th>Test score</th><th>Frequency</th><th>Running total</th></tr>
<tr><td>1–10</td><td>4</td><td>4</td></tr>
<tr><td>11–20</td><td>5</td><td>9</td></tr>
<tr><td>21–30</td><td>4</td><td>13</td></tr>
<tr><td>31–40</td><td>11</td><td>24</td></tr>
<tr><td>41–50</td><td>6</td><td>30</td></tr>
</table></td><td>How do we use the table to work out which group these values are in?</td><td></td></tr>
<tr><td>Using a running total, the 15th and 16th values both lie in the 31–40 group.
The median lies in the group 31–40.</td><td></td><td></td></tr>
<tr><td>d) Calculate an estimate of the mean. Give your answer correct to 1 decimal place.</td><td>Which value approximates the data in each group?</td><td>d) Calculate an estimate of the mean. Give your answer correct to 1 decimal place.</td></tr>
</table>

Test score	Frequency	Midpoint
1–10	4	5.5
11–20	5	15.5
21–30	4	25.5
31–40	11	35.5
41–50	6	45.5

How do we find the total of all the values?

Test score	Frequency × Midpoint
1–10	$4 \times 5.5 = 22$
11–20	$5 \times 15.5 = 77.5$
21–30	$4 \times 25.5 = 102$
31–40	$11 \times 35.5 = 390.5$
41–50	$6 \times 45.5 = 273$

How do we find the estimate for the mean?

$$\text{Mean} = \frac{22 + 77.5 + 102 + 390.5 + 273}{30}$$

$$= \frac{865}{30} = 28.8 \text{ (to 1 decimal place)}$$

Fluency questions

6.3.1 The mean

1 Three students scored 5, 5, and 8 marks in a test. Complete the calculation to find the mean score.

mean score $= \frac{5 + 5 + 8}{3} = \frac{\quad}{3} =$

2 Here is a set of values: 4, 11, 7, 6.

a) Work out the sum of the values.

b) How many values are in the set?

c) Calculate the mean using the formula

$$\text{mean} = \frac{\text{sum of all the values}}{\text{number of values}}$$

d) What is the lowest value in the set?

e) What is the highest value in set?

f) Is the mean value between the lowest and highest values?

3 Calculate the mean of each set of numbers.

a) 6, 8, 5, 11

b) 10, 20, 12

c) 0, 40

d) 14.6, 18.2, 17.1, 14.9, 16.3

4 The bar chart shows information about the number of goals scored by a football team in a tournament.

Goals scored in matches

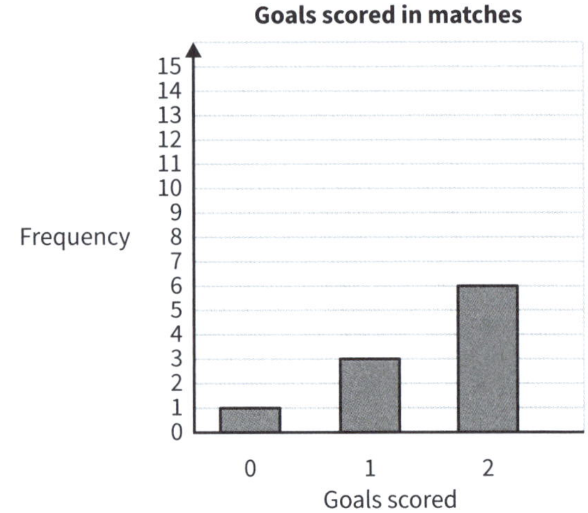

a) In how many matches did the team score 0 goals?

b) In how many matches did the team score 1 goal?

c) In how many matches did the team score 2 goals?

d) What is the total number of goals scored by the team?

e) How many matches did the team play in total?

f) Find the mean number of goals scored by the team per match by using the formula mean number of goals scored per match $= \dfrac{\text{total number of goals scored}}{\text{number of matches played}}$

6.3.2 The median

1 Find the median of each set of values. Each set has already been ordered.

a) 2, 5, 6, 7, 9

b) 1, 3, 3, 4, 4

c) 12, 17, 24, 28, 28, 28, 29

2 Complete the working to find the median of each set of values, which have already been ordered.

Each set has an odd number of values, which means that there are two values in the middle. The two middle values in each set have been underlined.

a) 6, <u>7</u>, <u>9</u>, 13 median $= \dfrac{7+9}{2} =$

b) 2, <u>6</u>, <u>7</u>, 9 median $= \dfrac{6+7}{2} =$

c) 30, 31, <u>42</u>, <u>46</u>, 47, 51 median $= \dfrac{42+46}{2} =$

3 Find the median of each set of numbers.

a) 9, 2, 4, 7, 11

b) 7, 4, 10, 9, 8, 4, 5, 9

4 Eight students take part in a quiz. This bar chart shows information about their scores.

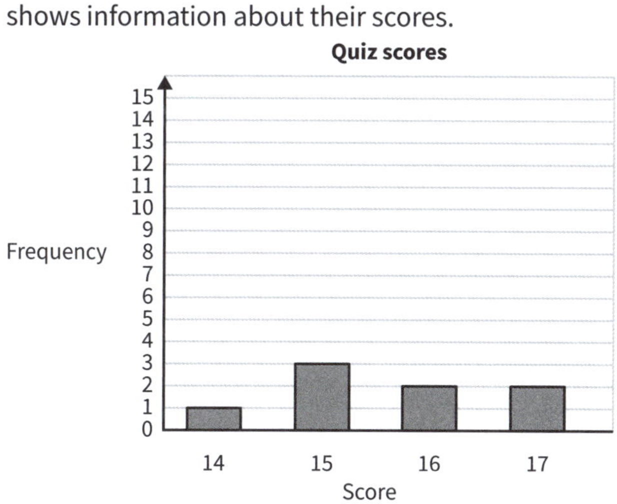

a) How many students scored 14 on the quiz?

b) How many students scored 15 on the quiz?

c) How many students scored 16 on the quiz?

d) How many students scored 17 on the quiz?

e) List the scores achieved by the eight pupils in ascending order.

f) Find the median score.

6.3.3 The mode

1 The pie chart shows the number of cars owned by households on a street.

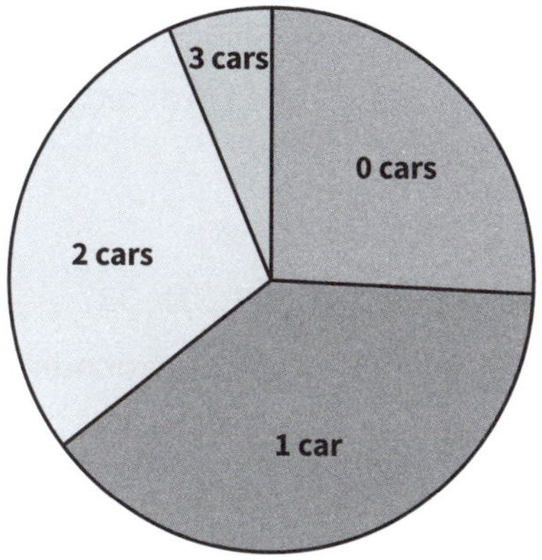

What is the modal number of cars owned?

2 At a diving competition, seven judges award scores to each diver.

One diver is awarded these scores:

8 8.5 8 9 8 8 8.5

What is the modal score?

3 The bar chart shows the number of goals scored by a football team in each match during a season.

What was the modal number of goals scored by the team?

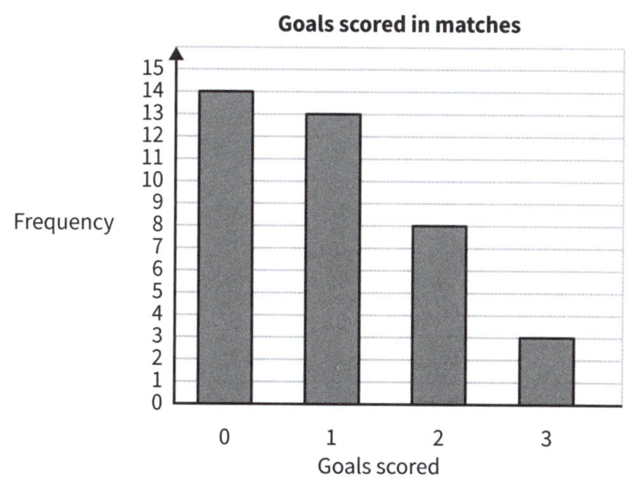

6.3.4 The range

1 A class of students take a test.

The highest score is 19 and the lowest score is 12.

Calculate the range of scores.

2 Here is a set of values: 19, 15, 24, 42, 30, 25

a) Find the lowest value in the set.

b) Find the highest value in the set.

c) Find the range of values in the set.

3 Calculate the range of each set of numbers.

Each set has already been ordered for you.

a) 3, 5, 7, 8, 9

b) 1.2, 3.8, 5.6, 5.9, 6.7, 7.5

c) 230, 271, 299, 304, 305, 319, 337

4 Calculate the range of each set of numbers.

a) 12, 7, 4, 11

b) 80, 72, 47, 55, 27, 64

6.3.5 Average and range of grouped data

1 Fill in the blank with the correct number:

In an ordered list of 15 numbers, the median would be in ______ th position.

2 The frequency table shows the marks scored by a class of students in a test.

Score out of 60	Frequency
21–30	5
31–40	9
41–50	10
51–60	1

a) Write down the modal group of scores.

b) What is the lowest score that a student in this class might have obtained?

Explain why you cannot know for sure whether a student obtained this exact score.

c) What is the highest score that a student in this class might have obtained?

d) i. How many students are in the class?

ii. Fill in the blank with the correct number:

If the scores were listed in order, the median score would be in ______ th position.

3 The frequency table shows the heights of children at a playground.

Height, h (cm)	Frequency
$100 \le h < 110$	3
$110 \le h < 120$	6
$120 \le h < 130$	7
$130 \le h < 140$	1

a) Write down the modal group.

b) How many children were at the playground?

c) If the children were arranged in order of height, in which position would the median child be?

6.4 Analysing and comparing data

Example-problem pairs

6.4.1 Averages and outliers

Worked example 1	Thinking	Your turn! 1
A shop manager collects some data on sales of different size packs of apples and works out these averages: **Mean pack size = 6 apples** **Median pack size = 4.5 apples** **Modal pack size = 4 apples** **The shop manager decides to only stock one size of pack.** **Explain which average they should use to decide what pack size to stock.**	*How do each of the averages summarize the data?*	**A shop manager collects some data on sales of different size bunches of bananas size and works out these averages:** **Mean bunch size = 3.45 bananas** **Median bunch size = 4 bananas** **Modal bunch size = 5 bananas** **The shop manager decides to sell the bananas in bags.** **Explain which average they should use to decide how many bananas to put in a bag.**
They should use the mode since this will be the most popular pack size.		

Worked example 2	Thinking	Your turn! 2
Tej records his score on 5 turns of a computer game. **65, 74, 59, 5, 82**		**Nicky records her score on 5 turns of a computer game.** **83, 79, 84, 80, 99**
a) Explain which score is an outlier and how it affects the range.	*What is meant by an outlier?*	**a) Explain which score is an outlier and how it affects the range.**
5 is an outlier as it is much smaller than the rest of the data. It will increase the range of the data.		
b) Why might Tej choose to use the median to represent his average score instead of the mean?		**b) Why might Nicky choose to use the mean to represent her average score instead of the median?**
The outlier does not affect the median, but it makes the mean smaller. So he might choose the median as it will be bigger.	*Without calculating the mean and median, how do we know which will be bigger?*	

Worked example 3	**Thinking**	**Your turn! 3**
An internet provider claims that their high-speed broadband gives average download speeds of more than 50 Mbps. **The recorded speeds (in Mbps) of a sample of nine downloads are:** **38, 41, 43, 44, 45, 46, 47, 61, 103** **a) Which average has the internet provider used in making this claim?**	*What averages can we find for the data?*	**An electric car manufacturer claims that a car has an average range of 300 miles on a single charge.** **The recorded ranges (in miles) for a sample of seven of their cars are:** **215, 221, 236, 302, 305, 308, 310** **a) Which average has the company used in making this claim?**
No mode. Median: $= \frac{9+1}{2} = 5\text{th value}$ 38, 41, 43, 44, 45, 46 47, 61, 103 So median = 45 Mbps Mean = $\frac{38+41+43+44+45+46+47+61+103}{9}$ $= \frac{468}{9} = 52$ Mbps The internet provider used the mean.		
b) Explain why the claim could be considered misleading.		**b) Explain why the claim could be considered misleading.**
The median download speed is less than 50 Mbps and 7 out of 9 of the recorded speeds are below 50 Mbps.	*How could we use the averages and the data to test the claim?*	

Worked example 4	**Thinking**	**Your turn! 4**
The number of millimetres of rain for each day of a week were: **0.8, 0, 1.2, 0, 3.5, 25, 2.8** **Identify the outlier in the data and explain why you might:** **(i) exclude (ii) include the value from any calculations.**	*What is meant by an outlier?*	**The heights (in metres) of a group of 12-year-old children are:** **1.42, 1.48, 1.36, 1.04, 1.39, 1.48** **Identify the outlier in the data and explain why you might:** **(i) exclude (ii) include the value from any calculations.**
The number 25 is an outlier because it is much larger than the other values.	*We need to think about whether or not the result is an error.*	
(i) We might exclude the value because it could be an error (perhaps it should have been recorded as 2.5).		
(ii) We might include the value because it could have been correct (25 mm of rain is quite possible) and we want to include all the correct data values in our calculations.		

6.4.2 Effect of changing data on measures of average and range

Worked example 1	Thinking	Your turn! 1
The mean length of some cars is 4.2 m. **a) Another car has a length of 4.3 m. Explain the effect on the mean if this value is added to the data set.**	*How can we decide if the mean will increase, decrease, or stay the same when a value is added?*	**The mean length of some bikes is 1.7 m.** **a) Another bike has a length of 1.6 m. Explain the effect on the mean if this value is added to the data set.**
4.3 is greater than the mean of 4.2. So the mean will increase when this value is added to the data set.		
b) One of the cars in the data set was recorded as being 1 m instead of 4.1 m. Explain the effect on the mean if this is corrected.	*How can we decide if the mean will increase or decrease when a value is changed?*	**b) One of the cars in the data set was recorded as being 15 m instead of 1.5 m. Explain the effect on the mean if this is corrected.**
4.1 is higher than 1 so the mean will increase.		

Worked example 2	Thinking	Your turn! 2
The ages of the 7 people who work in a bank are: 24, 39, 43, 45, 49, 53, 66 **a) The age of the youngest person was wrongly recorded. They were actually 34 years old. Explain what effect correcting this value will have on the median.**	*What is meant by the median?*	**The ages of the 8 people who work in a factory are: 18, 19, 23, 25, 37, 54, 58, 92** **a) The age of the oldest person was wrongly recorded. They were actually 62 years old. Explain what effect correcting this value will have on the median.**
The median is the middle term, this will still be 45 when the age is corrected.		
b) A new employee aged 55 joins the bank. Explain what effect this will have on the median age.	*How can we identify the position of the median for the original data?*	**b) A new employee aged 24 joins the factory. Explain what effect this will have on the median age.**
There were 7 employees originally: $\frac{7+1}{2} = \frac{8}{2} = 4$ The median is the 4th worker, so 45.	*How will the position of the median change when the new value is added?*	
There are now 8 employees: $\frac{8+1}{2} = \frac{9}{2} = 4.5$ So the median is exactly halfway between the 4th and 5th values. The new value will be placed after the 6th value of 53. So, the 4th and 5th values are now 45 and 49. Median = 47, so it has increased.		

<table>
<tr><th>Worked example 3</th><th>Thinking</th><th>Your turn! 3</th></tr>
<tr><td>These measures are used to summarize a set of data:
<table><tr><th>Mean</th><th>Median</th><th>Mode</th><th>Range</th></tr><tr><td>25</td><td>26.5</td><td>27</td><td>23</td></tr></table>
Write down the equivalent values if all the values in the data set:</td>
<td>How can we decide if the measures will increase, decrease or stay the same?</td>
<td>These measures are used to summarize a set of data:
<table><tr><th>Mean</th><th>Median</th><th>Mode</th><th>Range</th></tr><tr><td>112</td><td>118</td><td>112</td><td>145</td></tr></table>
Write down the equivalent values if all the values in the data set:</td></tr>
<tr><td>a) have 15 added to them</td><td></td><td>a) have 100 added to them</td></tr>
<tr><td><table><tr><th>Mean</th><th>Median</th><th>Mode</th><th>Range</th></tr><tr><td>25 + 15
= 40</td><td>26.5 + 15
= 41.5</td><td>27 + 15
= 42</td><td>23</td></tr></table></td><td></td><td></td></tr>
<tr><td>b) are multiplied by 2.</td><td></td><td>b) are divided by 10.</td></tr>
<tr><td><table><tr><th>Mean</th><th>Median</th><th>Mode</th><th>Range</th></tr><tr><td>25 × 2
= 50</td><td>26.5 × 2
= 53</td><td>27 × 2
= 54</td><td>23 ×2
= 46</td></tr></table></td><td></td><td></td></tr>
</table>

6.4.3 Comparing sets of data

Worked example 1	Thinking	Your turn! 1
Jen and Leya record their darts scores over 5 rounds. Jen has a median score of 55 and a range of 30. Leya has a median score of 55 and a range of 10. **Compare their scores and explain who you think is the better player.**		**U-jin and Ben record the number of their goals in 5 netball matches. U-jin has mean of 8 and range of 3. Ben has mean of 12 and range of 2.** **Compare their scores and explain who is better at scoring goals.**
Their median scores are the same. The range of Jen's scores is much larger than the range of Leya's scores.	*How could we compare their scores?*	
They have the same average score, but Leya's scores are more consistent, so she is the better player.		

Worked example 2

The table summarizes the ages in years of people in two clubs. Compare the ages of people in the two clubs.

Age (years)	Craft club	Book club
40–49	5	12
50–59	6	13
60–69	9	6
70–79	8	0

Thinking

What may be the best average to use for grouped data?

What do we need to use to work out this average?

Your turn! 2

The table summarizes the ages in years of people in two clubs. Compare the ages of people in the two clubs.

Age (years)	Tennis club	Dance club
20–29	3	0
30–39	16	25
40–49	18	18
50–59	25	31
60–69	1	0

To work out the mean, use the midpoint of each group:

44.5, 54.5, 64.5, 74.5

For craft club, estimate of mean

$= \frac{1726}{28} = 61.6$ years

For book club, estimate of mean

$= \frac{1629.5}{31} = 52.6$

The mean age is higher for craft club than book club.

What other measure could we calculate to compare the ages?

For craft club, maximum range
= 79 − 40 = 39 years

For book club, maximum range
= 69 − 40 = 29 years

The maximum range is larger for craft club than book club.

The members of the craft club are older on average and there is a greater spread of ages.

How could we complete our answer?

Worked example 3

The 400 m race times, in seconds, of 8 competitors are:

53.1	**52.8**	**54.0**	**51.8**
53.8	**55.9**	**25.3**	**54.7**

a) Write down the value(s) of any outliers in the data set.

25.3 seconds

b) Should the outlier(s) identified in part a be included or excluded?

Excluded; it is impossible to run 400 m in 25.3 seconds.

Thinking

How do we decide if a data point is an outlier?

How do we decide if an outlier is an error?

Your turn! 3

The 200 m race times, in seconds, of 8 competitors are:

26.6	**26.1**	**27.0**	**25.7**
37.2	**25.9**	**26.2**	**26.9**

a) Write down the value(s) of any outliers in the data set.

b) Should the outlier(s) identified in part a be included or excluded?

6.4.4 Comparing ways of presenting data

Worked example 1	Thinking	Your turn! 1
For the last year, a pizza delivery company collected data on how many pizzas were in each order, the total cost of the order, how each order was made (in person, by phone, on their app, on the website) and what time the order was placed. **What representation could they use to:**		**For the last year, a cinema collected data on the number of tickets bought in one order, the total cost of food and drink purchased, the genre of movie each ticket was for (comedy, kids, action etc.) and the time of the movie.** **What representation could they use to:**
a) compare the number of pizzas in each order	*What type of data is involved?*	**a) compare the number of tickets bought in each order**
This involves discrete, quantitative data. They could use a bar chart with number of pizzas per order against frequency.	*What representations could we use for this data?*	
b) investigate if there is a relationship between when an order is placed and the total money spent.	*What type of data is involved?*	**b) investigate if there is a relationship between the time of the movie and the money spent on food and drink.**
This involves continuous, quantitative data. They could use a scatter graph of time the order was placed against the total cost.	*What representations could we use for this data?*	

<table>
<tr><th>Worked example 2</th><th>Thinking</th><th>Your turn! 2</th></tr>
<tr><td>Hayley recorded her spending for a month and showed the data in a bar chart and a pie chart.

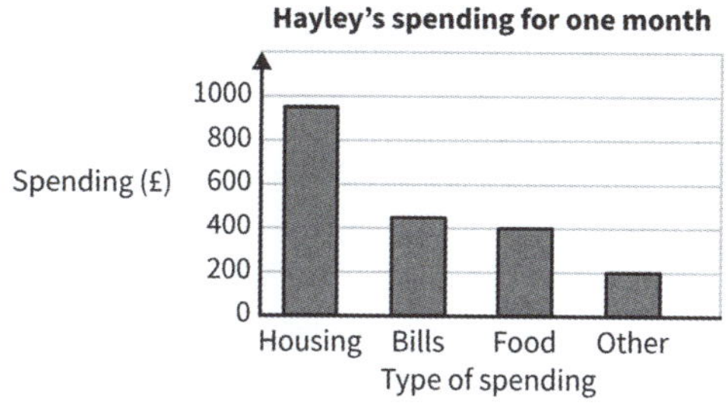

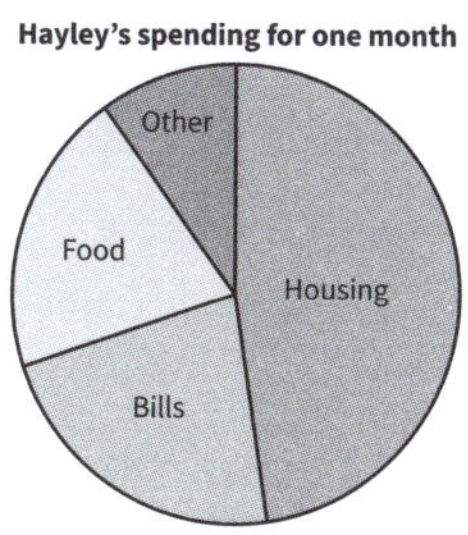

Hayley spent more money on bills than food. Which graph shows this more clearly?</td><td>What are the advantages and disadvantages of each type of chart?</td><td>Tate recorded their spending for a month and showed the data in a bar chart and a pie chart.

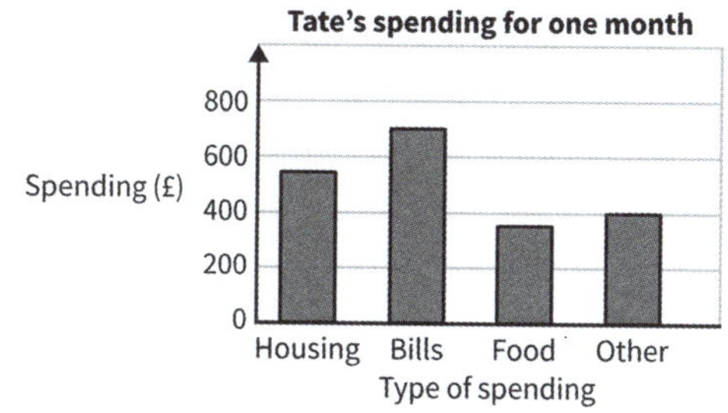

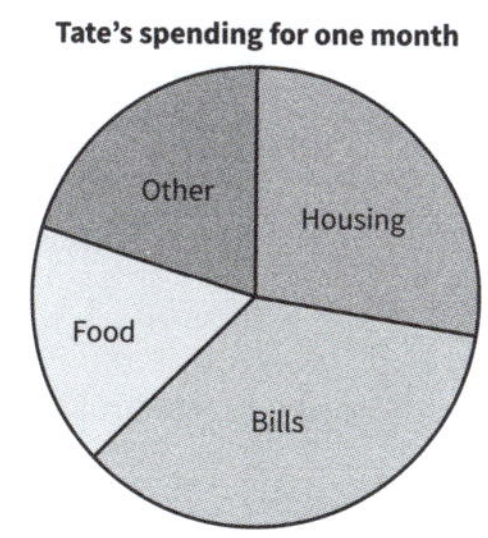

More than a quarter of Tate's monthly spending is on housing. Which graph shows this more clearly?</td></tr>
<tr><td>The bar chart shows this more clearly because the 'bills' bar is taller than the 'food' bar. It is less clear on the pie chart without measuring the angles.</td><td></td><td></td></tr>
</table>

<table>
<tr><th>Worked example 3</th><th>Thinking</th><th>Your turn! 3</th></tr>
<tr><td>A teacher collects data on students' percentage scores in their end of year test and the number of absences from lessons during the year.
What would be the best way to present the data to show:
a) if there is a relationship between number of absences and the score on the end of year test</td><td>What type of data is involved?</td><td>A library collects data on the age of each library member and the number of books they borrowed in a month.
What would be the best way to present the data to show:
a) if there is a relationship between age and the number of books borrowed in a month</td></tr>
<tr><td>A scatter graph of number of absences against the percentage score in the test.</td><td></td><td></td></tr>
<tr><td>b) the test scores of student who were absent for 5 or more lessons?</td><td>What type of data is involved?</td><td>b) the favourite genre of book of members who borrowed more than 8 books a month?</td></tr>
<tr><td>A (grouped) bar chart with percentage score in groups, e.g. 0–20%, 20%–40% etc. against frequency; or a pie chart with sectors representing (groups of) percentage scores.</td><td></td><td></td></tr>
</table>

6.4.5 Using charts and graphs to compare sets of data

Worked example 1	Thinking	Your turn! 1
Two spinners are spun 20 times. The results are shown in the bar charts. Compare the results. 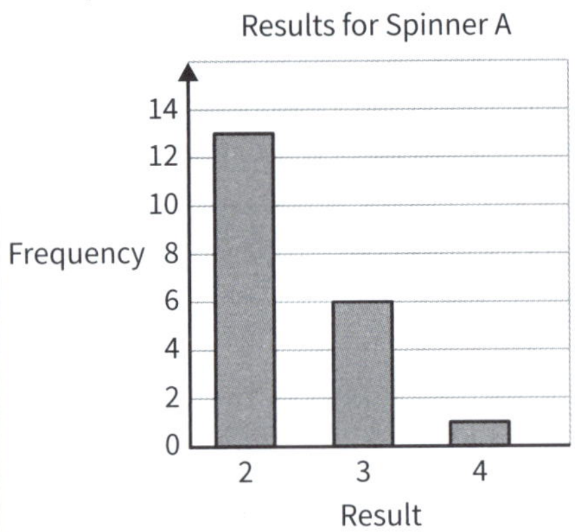 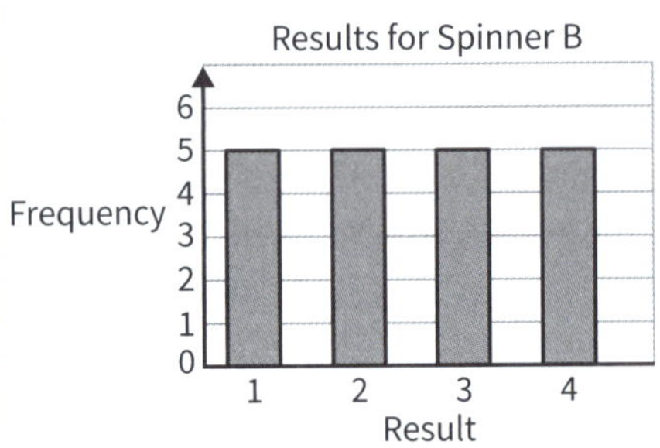	*What average could be the best to use to compare?*	**Riley plays two computer games 18 times each. Her scores are shown in the bar charts. Compare her scores.** 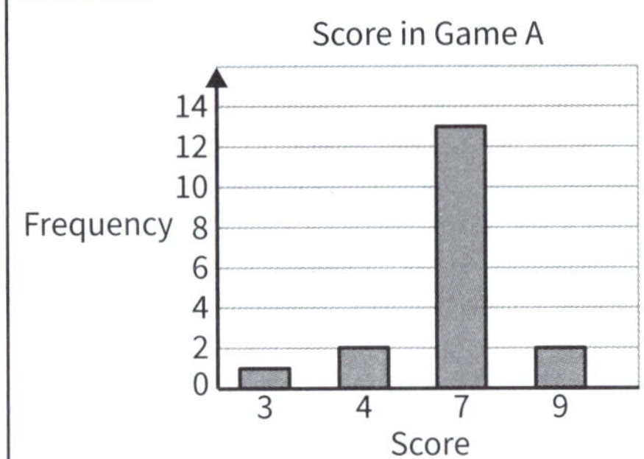 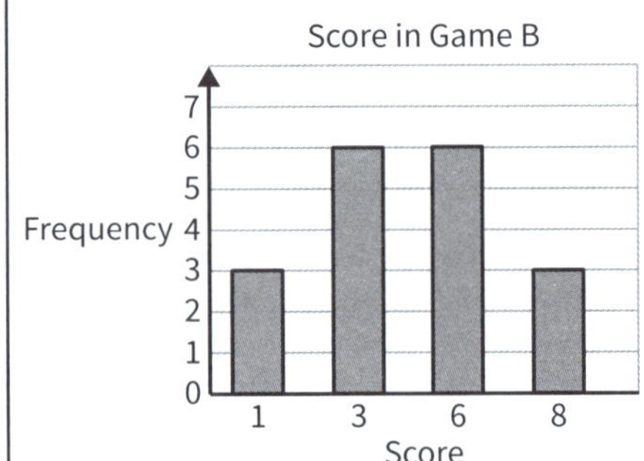
Both data sets have 20 values, so the position of the median is given by $\frac{20 + 1}{2} = 10.5$	*How do we work out the position of the median?*	
Median of spinner A = 2 Median of spinner B = 2.5 The median score for spinner B is higher than for spinner A.	*How do we find the median value?*	
Range of spinner A = 2 Range of spinner B = 3 The range for spinner B is larger than for spinner A.	*What other measure could we use to compare the scores?*	
The score for spinner B is higher on average than for spinner A. The scores for spinner B are also more varied.	*How can we complete our answer?*	

Worked example 2	Thinking	Your turn! 2
Hayley and Tate each recorded how much money they spend each month and showed the data in a pie chart. **Hayley's spending for one month** 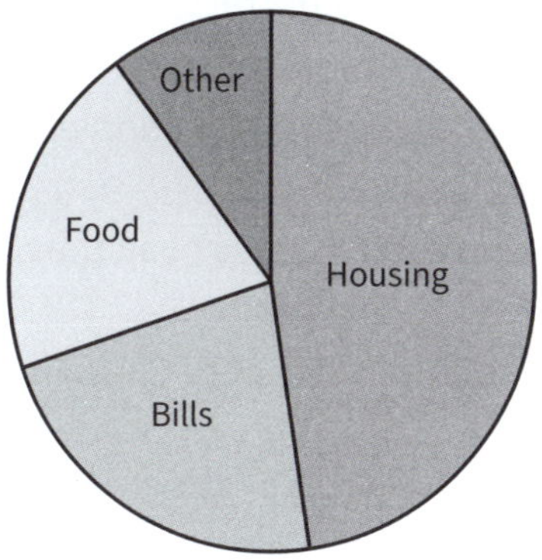 **Tate's spending for one month** 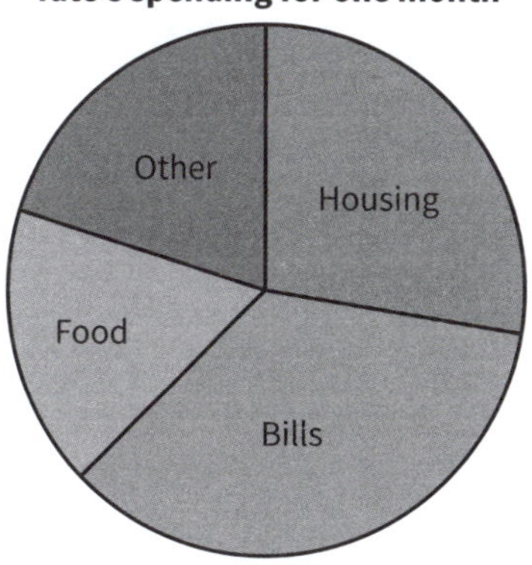 **Compare the two data sets.**	*What are the advantages and disadvantages of each chart?*	**A council recorded how much money they spent in 2022 and 2023 and showed the data in a pie chart.** **2022 council spending** 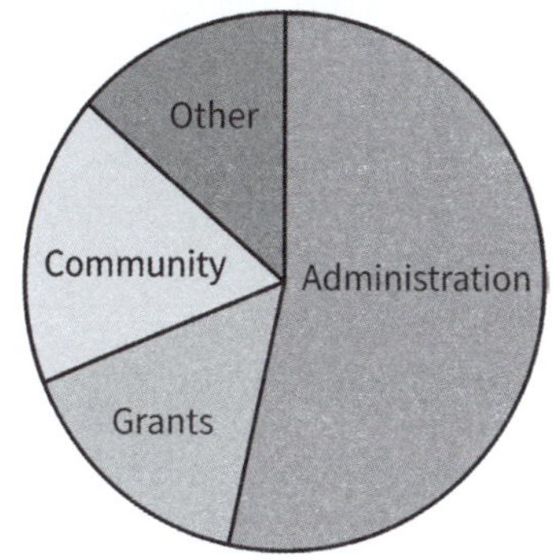 **2023 council spending** 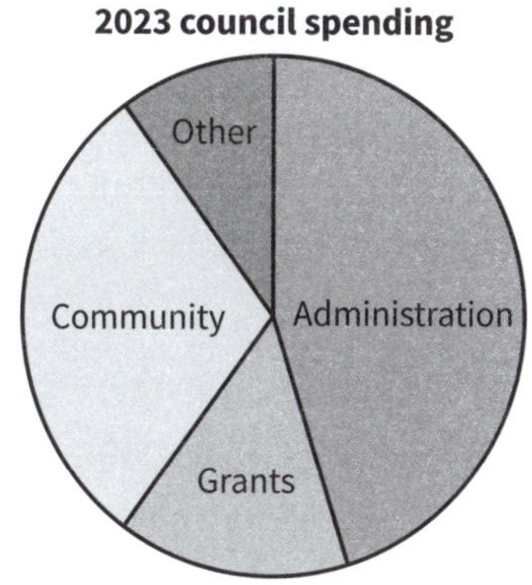 **Compare the two data sets.**
Hayley's modal spending category is housing, Tate's modal spending category is bills. Hayley spends a greater proportion of her money on housing compared with Tate. They spend a similar proportion on food.		

Fluency questions

6.4.1 Averages and outliers

1 Seven people go ten pin bowling.

The list shows the number of pins knocked down by each person on their first bowl.

8 8 3 3 7 8 5

a) What is the mean?

b) What is the median?

c) What is the mode?

d) What is the range?

2 Here are the distances, in metres, achieved by a javelin thrower in eight competitions.

50.18	**48.78**	**50.21**	**49.22**
48.59	**49.62**	**40.72**	**51.09**

a) Which of the eight distances is an outlier?

b) Give a reason for your answer.

3 Here are the annual salaries of the ten employees of an organisation.

\$40 000	\$40 000	\$40 000	\$40 000	\$40 000
\$40 000	\$40 000	\$40 000	\$80 000	\$280 000

a) What is the median salary?

b) What is the mean salary?

Here are the salaries of the ten employees of a different organisation.

\$40 000	\$46 000	\$46 000	\$50 000	\$50 000
\$68 000	\$80 000	\$90 000	\$90 000	\$120 000

c) What is the median salary?

d) What is the mean salary?

4 The average speeds of motorists passing two schools was measured. The roads outside both schools have 20 mph speed limits.

The mean speed outside School A was 19.4 mph.

The mean speed outside School B was 24.1 mph.

The council has enough money to install traffic calming measures outside one of these schools.

The council can choose either School A or School B.

Which school should they choose?

5 A podcaster wants to make podcasts for people to listen to as they commute to work. They need to decide how long the podcasts should be.

The podcaster asks a large group of people two questions:

'How long is your typical commute to work?'

'Do you listen to podcasts?'

Choose an appropriate statistical measure from the following list that would be useful when deciding how long the podcasts should be.

- The median commuting time of people who do not listen to podcasts.
- The range in commuting times of all the people surveyed.
- The mean commuting time of people who do listen to podcasts.
- A pie chart.

6.4.2 Effect of changing data on measures of average and range

1 Here are two lists of numbers.

List 1	4	6	11
List 2	4	6	50

a) i. What is the median of list 1?

ii. What is the median of list 2?

b) i. What is the mean of list 1?

ii. What is the mean of list 2?

c) i. What is the range of list 1?

ii. What is the range of list 2?

2 Here are two lists of numbers. List 2 is the same as list 1, except 16 has been changed to 17.

List 1	10	14	15	15	16
List 2	10	14	15	15	17

a) i. What is the median of list 1?

ii. What is the median of list 2?

iii. Did changing 16 in list 1 to 17 in list 2 have an effect on the median? If so, did the median increase or decrease?

b) i. What is the mean of list 1?

ii. What is the mean of list 2?

iii. Did changing 16 in list 1 to 17 in list 2 have an effect on the mean? If so, did the mean increase or decrease?

c) i. What is the range of list 1?
ii. What is the range of list 2?
iii. Did changing 16 in list 1 to 17 in list 2 have an effect on the range? If so, did the range increase or decrease?

3 Ruben records the number of eggs laid by a group of hens each day for five days. Here are the numbers, listed in order.

13 **13** **13** **14** **15**

He correctly works out the following:

- The mean number of eggs laid is 14.
- The median number of eggs laid is 13.
- The modal number of eggs laid is 13.
- The range in number of eggs laid is 2.

On the sixth day, the hens lay 19 eggs. Ruben updates his list as follows.

13 **13** **13** **14** **15** **19**

a) What is the mean number of eggs laid over the six days?

b) What is the median number of eggs laid over the six days?

c) What is the modal number of eggs laid over the six days?

d) What is the range in number of eggs laid over the six days?

e) For the first five days, the mean number of eggs was 14.

Did including the sixth day's data increase this, reduce it, or have no effect?

f) For the first five days, the range in number of eggs was 2.

Did including the sixth day's data increase this, reduce it, or have no effect?

6.4.3 Comparing sets of data

1 Here are two lists of numbers, presented in order.

List 1	2	4	4	5	7	8	12
List 2	3	3	5	8	8	9	10

a) Which list has the greater median?

b) Which list has the greater mean?

c) Which list has the greater range?

2 The following lists show the number of complaints received by two companies each day for six days.

Company 1	0	2	1	7	2	0
Company 2	5	4	6	3	5	4

a) Which company had the higher mean number of daily complaints?

b) Which company had the higher median number of daily complaints?

c) Which company had the highest number of complaints in a single day?

d) Over the six days, which company do you think performed better?

e) Which company had the higher range of the number of daily complaints?

3 Two five-a-side football teams are playing a match.

The tables show the number of matches that the players of each team have played before this match.

Team A	35	75	29	65	72
Team B	8	43	7	5	57

The mean number of matches played by Team A's players is 55.8.
The mean number of matches played by Team B's players is 24.
The range of the number of matches played by Team A's players is 46.
The range of number of matches played by Team B's players is 52.

a) Which team's players have played more matches on average?

b) Which team's players have a greater spread in the number of matches played?

6.4.4 Comparing ways of presenting data

1 Fill in each blank with one if these three methods of representing data.

scatter graph **pie chart** **bar chart**

a) A ______ shows the proportion of each category.

b) A ______ shows the frequency of each category.

c) A ______ shows the relationship between two sets of numerical data.

2 In a school, students have to choose one sport from football, netball, rounders, and hockey.

Which of the following would be a suitable way to present how popular the sports are?

scatter graph **pie chart**

3 A researcher investigates the relationship between the heights of basketball players and the number of points they score in a season.

Which of the following would be a suitable way to present this relationship?

scatter graph **pie chart** **bar chart**

4 At a wedding reception, there will be three options for the main course of a meal. The caterer wants to know how many of each option to prepare.

Which of these three ways of presenting the information would not be useful to the caterer?

Option	Frequency
Chicken	18
Fish	9
Vegetarian	13

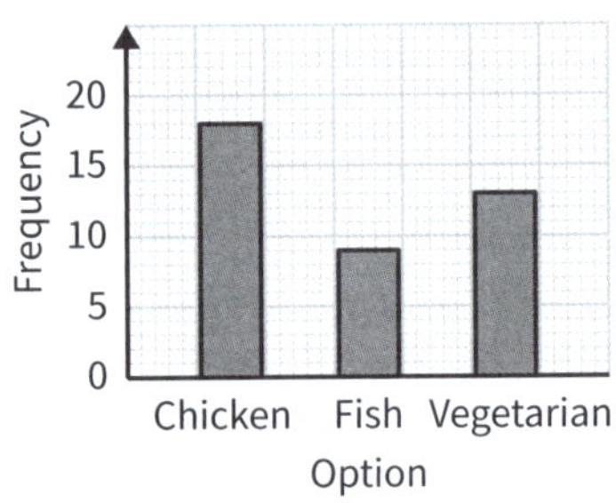

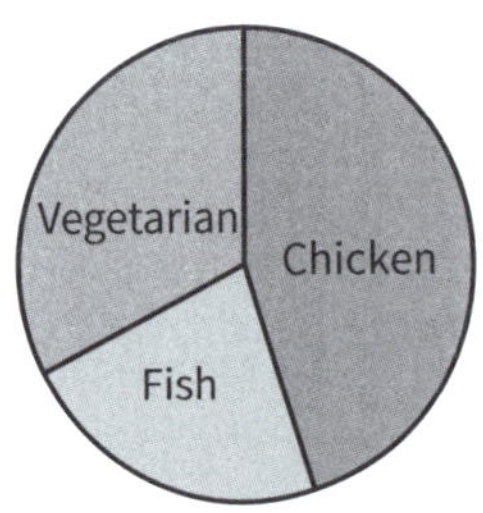

6.4.5 Using charts and graphs to compare sets of data

1 The frequency tables show the number of pets owned by some students in Stage 7 and Stage 8.

Stage 7	
Number of pets	**Frequency**
0	7
1	8
2	4
3	1

Stage 8	
Number of pets	**Frequency**
0	6
1	7
2	8
3	0

a) What is the modal number of pets owned by the Stage 7 students?

b) What is the modal number of pets owned by the Stage 8 students?

c) How many of the Stage 8 students own 3 pets?

d) What is the highest number of pets owned by a Stage 8 student?

e) What is the lowest number of pets owned by a Stage 8 student?

f) Fill in the blanks with 'Stage 7' or 'Stage 8' to form a correct statement.

The modal number of pets in ____________ is higher than in ____________.

2 The bar charts show the number of cars owned by households on one street in a city and one street in a village.

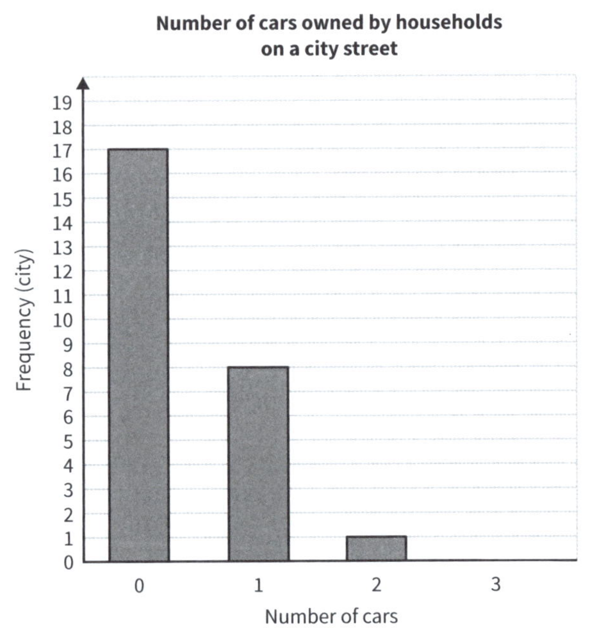

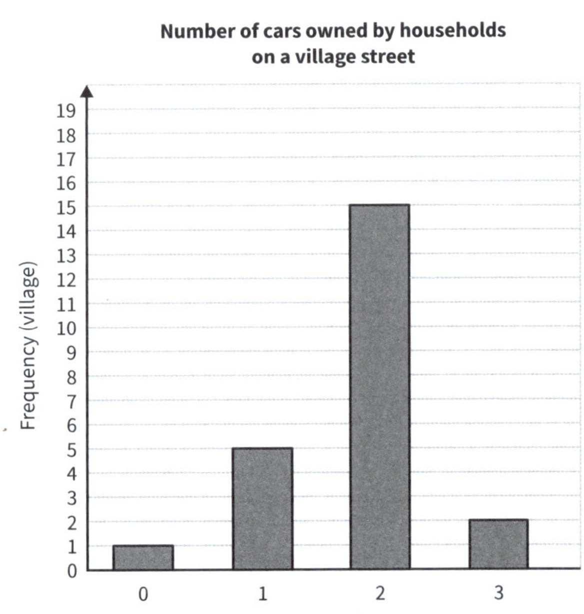

a) What is the modal number of cars owned by city households?

b) What is the modal number of cars owned by village households?

c) Are there any households in the village that own three cars?

d) Are there any households in the village that own more than three cars?

e) What is the lowest number of cars owned by a household in the village?

f) What is the range of the number of cars owned by households in the village?

g) What is the range of the number of cars owned by households in the city?

h) Fill in the blanks with 'city' or 'village' to form two correct statements.

The modal number of cars owned by households is higher in the ______________ than in the ______________. The range of the number of cars owned by households is higher in the ______________ than in the ______________.

3 The pictograms show the number of apples sold at morning break and at lunch break by a school tuck shop.

Apples sold in morning	
Monday	
Tuesday	
Wednesday	
Thursday	
Friday	

Key:  represents 2 apples

Apples sold at lunch	
Monday	
Tuesday	
Wednesday	
Thursday	
Friday	

a) How many apples were sold in morning break on Wednesday?

b) How many apples were sold at lunch break on Friday?

c) What was the mean number of apples sold in the mornings?

d) What was the mean number of apples sold at lunch?

e) What was the highest number of apples sold during a lunch break?

f) What was the lowest number of apples sold during a lunch break?

g) What was the range of the number of apples sold during a lunch break?

h) What was the range of the number of apples sold during a morning break?

i) Fill in the blanks with 'in the mornings' or 'at lunch times' to form two correct statements.

The mean number of apples sold ______________ was lower than the mean number sold ______________. The range in number of apples sold in ______________ was lower than ______________.

6 Statistics

7.1 Perimeter

Example-problem pairs

7.1.1 Circumference of a circle

Worked example 1	Thinking	Your turn! 1
Work out the circumference of a circle with a 10 cm diameter to 1 decimal place. 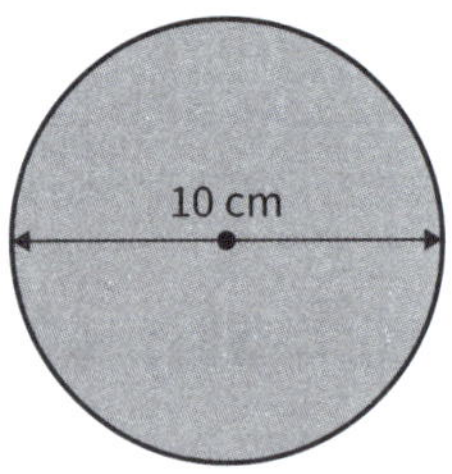 	*What formula can we use to find the circumference?*	**Work out the circumference of a circle with a 9 cm diameter to 1 decimal place.** 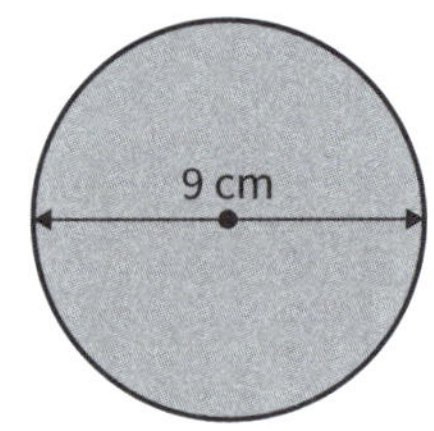
$C = \pi d$ $= \pi \times 10$ $= 31.4$ cm (1 d.p.)	*How should we express the answer?*	

Worked example 2	Thinking	Your turn! 2
Find the circumference of a 6 cm radius circle in terms of π. 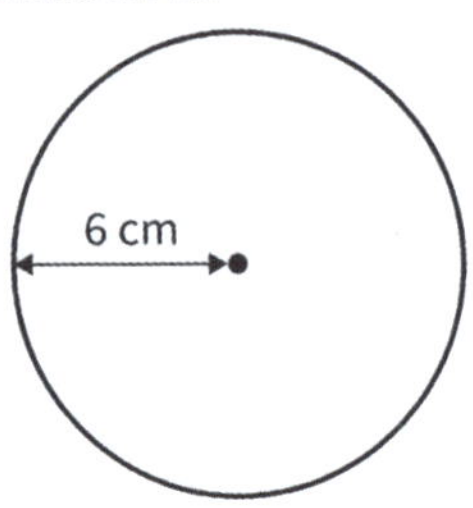 	*What formula can we use to find the circumference?*	**Find the circumference of a 6 cm radius circle in terms of π.** 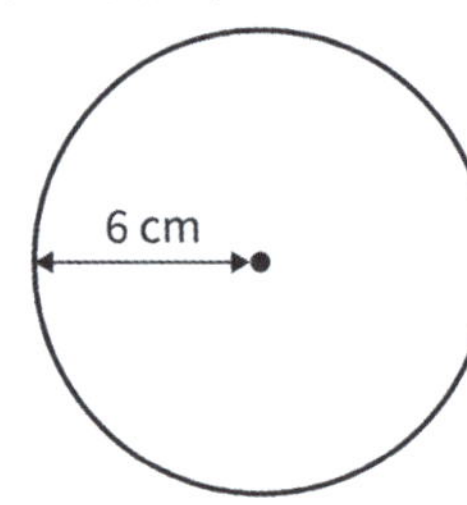
$C = 2\pi r$ $= 2 \times \pi \times 6$ $= 12\pi$ cm	*How should we express the answer?*	

Worked example 3	Thinking	Your turn! 3
The diameter of the wheels on Kabir's bike is 1.5 times the diameter of the wheels on Laila's bike. **When the wheels on Laila's bike rotate 80 times she travels 100 m.** **How far will Kabir travel when his wheels rotate 80 times?**	*How does the distance travelled relate to the circumference and the number of rotations?*	**The diameter of the wheels on Erin's bike is 2 times the diameter of the wheels on Zayden's bike.** **When the wheels on Zayden's bike rotate 30 times he travels 27 m.** **How far will Erin travel when her wheels rotate 30 times?**
Distance travelled = circumference × number of rotations = diameter × π × number of rotations	*How can we use the linear relationship between the diameter and circumference?*	
Laila and Kabir have the same number of rotations but their wheels are different sizes. If the wheel diameter is multiplied by 1.5 then the circumference will be also, and so will the distance travelled. Distance travelled by Kabir = 100 × 1.5 = 150 m		

7.1.2 Perimeter of composite shapes

Worked example 1	Thinking	Your turn! 1
The circle shown has a radius of 3 cm. Find the perimeter of the shaded quarter circle. Give your answer correct to 1 decimal place. 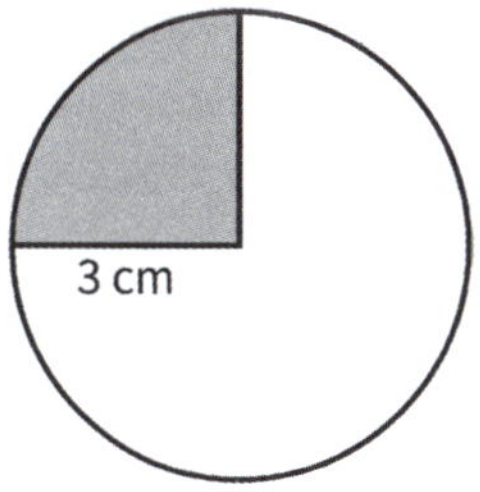 	*How can we find the length of the curved edge of the quarter circle?*	**The circle shown has a radius of 2 cm. Find the perimeter of the shaded quarter circle. Give your answer correct to 1 decimal place.** 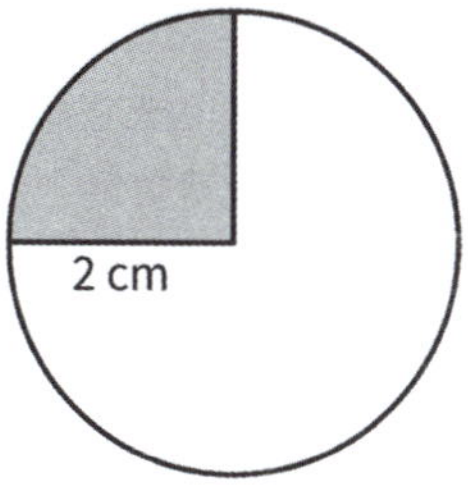
Length of curved edge $= 2\pi r \div 4$ $= 2 \times \pi \times 3 \div 4$ $= 4.71\ldots$ cm		
Perimeter $= 4.71\ldots + 2 \times 3$ = 10.7 cm (to 1 d.p.)	*How can we find the perimeter of the quarter circle?*	

Worked example 2	Thinking	Your turn! 2
The shape shown is formed by a square and a quarter circle. Find the perimeter of the shape. 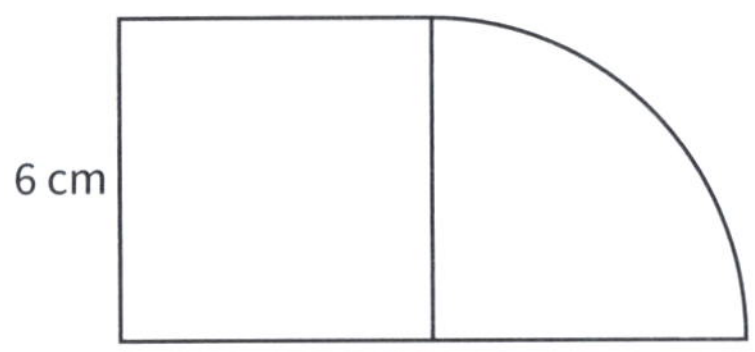	*What is the radius or diameter of the circle part?*	**The shape shown is formed by a rectangle and a semicircle. Find the perimeter of the shape.** 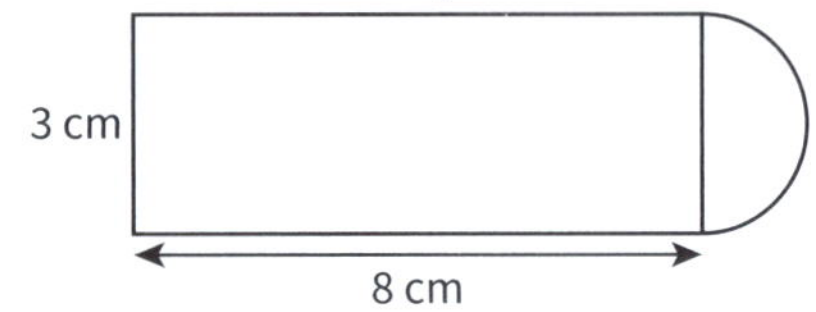
Radius = 6 cm Length of curved edge $= 2 \times \pi \times 6 \div 4$ $= 9.42\ldots$ cm	*How can we find the length of the curved edge?*	
Perimeter $= 9.42\ldots + 4 \times 6$ = 33.4 cm (to 1 d.p.)	*What must we add to this length to find the perimeter?*	

Worked example 3	Thinking	Your turn! 3
Find the diameter of a circle with circumference 28 cm. Give your answer correct to 1 decimal place.	*What formula can we use?*	**Find the diameter of a circle with circumference 37 cm. Give your answer correct to 1 decimal place.**
$C = \pi d$ $28 = \pi d$	*How can we find d?*	
$\frac{28}{\pi} = d$ $d = 8.9$ cm (to 1 d.p.)		

Worked example 4	Thinking	Your turn! 4
The diameter of a semicircle is 15 cm. Find its perimeter. Give your answer correct to 1 decimal place. 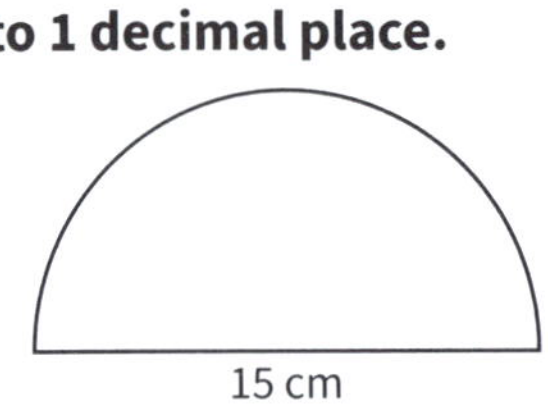	*How can we find the length of the curved edge of the semicircle?*	**The diameter of a semicircle is 13 cm. Find its perimeter. Give your answer correct to 1 decimal place.** 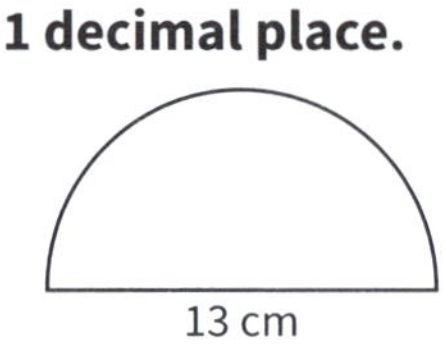
Length of curved edge $= \pi d \div 2$ $= \pi \times 15 \div 2$ $= 23.56\ldots$ cm		
Perimeter $= 23.56\ldots + 15$ = 38.6 cm (to 1 d.p.)	*How can we find the perimeter of the semicircle?*	

Fluency questions

7.1.1 Circumference of a circle

1 Decide whether each of the following statements is true or false.

a) The perimeter of a circle is called its circumference. True / False

b) The radius of a circle is double its circumference. True / False

c) The value of π is exactly 3.14. True / False

2 A circle has a diameter of 9 cm. Without using a calculator, decide which stateme is true. Tick (✓) the correct answer.

The circumference of the circle is:

a) greater than 27 cm ☐

b) exactly 27 cm ☐

c) less than 27 cm ☐

3 The diameters and circumferences (correct to the nearest 0.01 cm) of four circles are given.

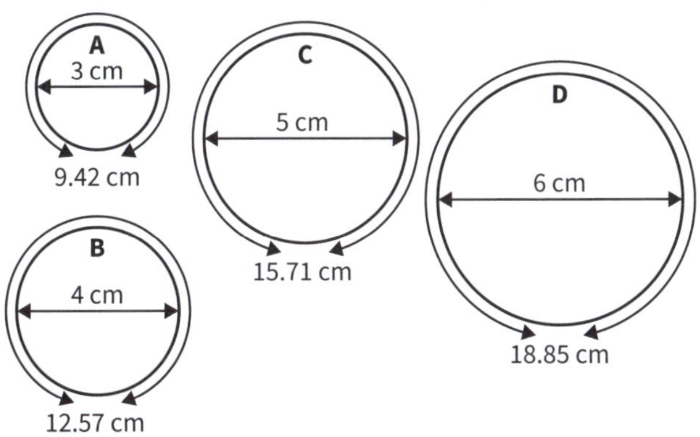

a) Complete the final column of this table.

Round your answers to 2 decimal places.

	Diameter	Circumference	Circumference ÷ Diameter
A	3 cm	9.42 cm	3.14
B	4 cm	12.57 cm	
C	5 cm	15.71 cm	
D	6 cm	18.85 cm	

b) What do you notice?

4 The table shows the radius, diameter, and circumference of three circles.

Fill in the blanks, rounding each value to the nearest 0.1 cm.The first row is completed as an example.

	Radius	Diameter	Circumference
Example	*5 cm*	*10 cm*	*31.4 cm*
a)	4 cm	8 cm	
b)		18 cm	
c)	8.5 cm		

7.1.2 Perimeter of composite shapes

1 The circumference of a circle is 80 cm.

Without using a calculator, decide which of the following is its diameter, correct to the nearest 0.1 cm. Circle the correct answer.

251.3 cm   50.9 cm   25.5 cm   12.7 cm

2 The diameter of a circle is 18 cm. What is its radius?

3 The circumference of a circle is 32 cm.

Without using a calculator, decide which of the following is its radius, correct to the nearest 0.1 cm. Circle the correct answer.

100.5 cm   20.4 cm   10.2 cm   5.1 cm

4 **a)** What is the circumference of a circle with diameter 9 cm?

b) Here is a semicircle with diameter 9 cm.

Complete the working to find the perimeter of the semicircle.

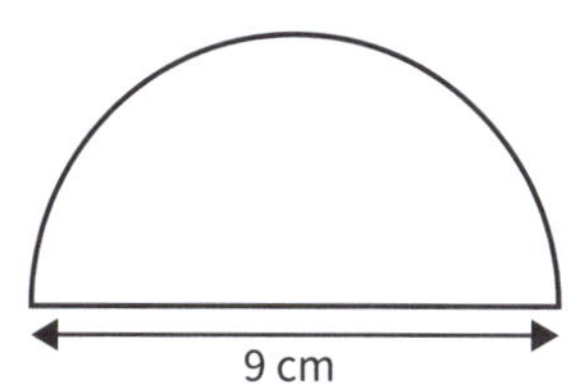

perimeter	=	length of straight side	+	length of curved edge
	=	diameter	+	half of the circumference
	=	_____ cm	+	_____ cm
perimeter	=	_____ cm		

7.2 Area

Example-problem pairs

7.2.1 Area of a circle

Worked example 1	Thinking	Your turn! 1
Work out the area of a circle with radius 11 cm. Give your answer correct to 1 decimal place.	*What formula can we use?*	**Work out the area of a circle with radius 7 cm. Give your answer correct to 1 decimal place.**
$A = \pi r^2$ $= \pi \times 11^2$	*What is the correct order of operations?*	
$A = \pi \times 121$ $= 380.1\text{ cm}^2$ (to 1 d.p.)		

Worked example 2	Thinking	Your turn! 2
Work out the area of a circle with diameter 14 cm. Give your answer as an exact multiple of π.	*How can we find the radius?*	**Work out the area of a circle with diameter 6 cm. Give your answer as an exact multiple of π.**
$r = 14 \div 2$ $= 7\text{ cm}$		
$A = \pi r^2$ $= \pi \times 7^2$	*What formula can we use?*	
$A = \pi \times 49$ $= 49\pi\text{ cm}^2$	*How should we write the answer?*	

7.2.2 Problem solving with area of a circle

Worked example 1	Thinking	Your turn! 1
Find the area of the semicircle. Give your answer in terms of π. 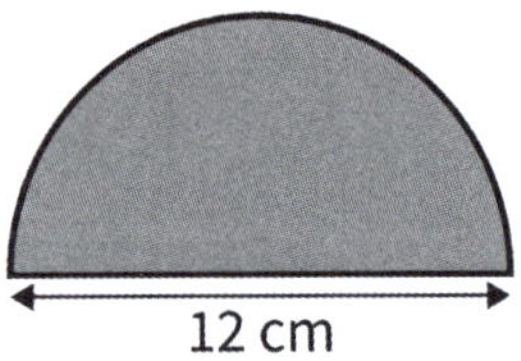 	*What is the first step to finding the area of the whole circle?*	**Find the area of the semicircle. Give your answer in terms of π.** 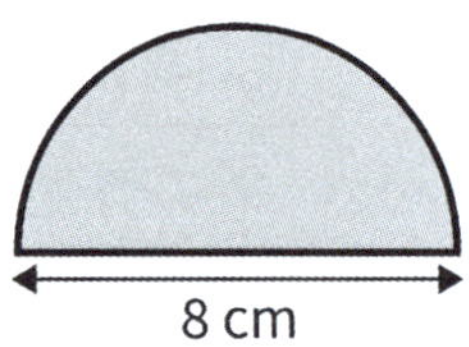
Radius = $12 \div 2 = 6\text{ cm}$		
Area of circle = $\pi \times 6^2$ $= 36\pi\text{ cm}^2$	*How do we find the area of the semicircle?*	
Area of semicircle = $36\pi \div 2$ $= 18\pi\text{ cm}^2$		

Worked example 2	Thinking	Your turn! 2
Work out the area of a quarter circle with a radius of 18 cm. Give your answer correct to 1 decimal place.	*How can we find the area of the whole circle?*	**Work out the area of a quarter circle with a radius of 20 cm. Give your answer correct to 1 decimal place.**
$A = \pi r^2$ Area of circle $= \pi \times 18^2$ $= 1017.876\ldots$	*How can we use this to find the area of the quarter circle?*	
Area of quarter circle $= 1017.876 \div 4$ $= 254.5\text{ cm}^2$ (to 1 d.p.)		

Worked example 3	Thinking	Your turn! 3
This shape is formed by removing a circle from the inside of a square. Work out the area of the shape. Give your answer to 1 decimal place. 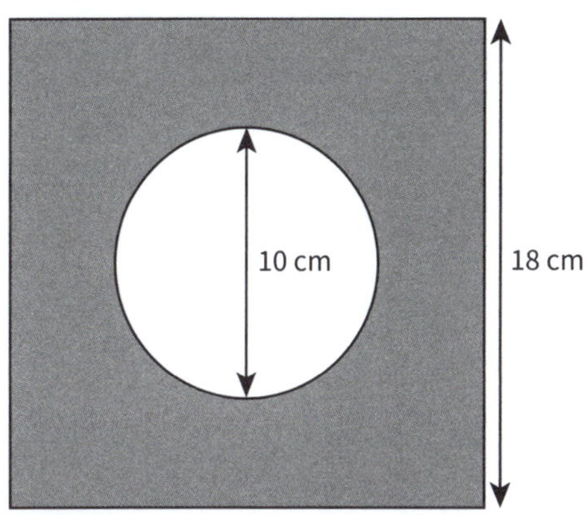	*How can we find the area of the circle or semicircle?*	**This shape is formed by removing a semicircle from the inside of a rectangle. Work out the area of the shape. Give your answer to 1 decimal place.** 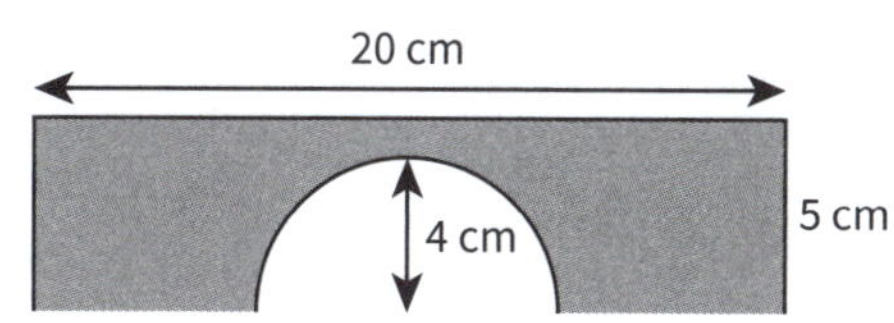
Using $A = \pi r^2$ $r = 10 \div 2 = 5$ Area of circle $= \pi \times 5^2$ $= 25\pi\text{ cm}^2$	*What other area do we need to find?*	
Area of square $= 18^2$ $= 324\text{ cm}^2$	*How can we find the total area of the shape?*	
Total area $= 324 - 25\pi$ $= 245.5\text{ cm}^2$ (to 1 d.p.)		

Worked example 4	**Thinking**	**Your turn! 4**
Work out the diameter of a circle with an area of 12 cm^2. Give your answer correct to 1 decimal place.	*What formula should we substitute into?*	**Work out the diameter of a circle with an area of 37 cm^2. Give your answer correct to 1 decimal place.**
$A = \pi r^2$ $12 = \pi r^2$	*How do we find the value of r?*	
$r^2 = \frac{12}{\pi}$ $r = \sqrt{\frac{12}{\pi}}$ $= 1.954\ldots$ cm	*How can we use r to find the diameter of the circle?*	
Diameter = $2 \times 1.954\ldots$ = 3.9 cm (to 1 d.p.)		

Worked example 5	**Thinking**	**Your turn! 5**
A semicircle has an area of 38 cm^2. Work out its radius. Give your answer correct to 1 decimal place.	*How can we work out the area of a circle with the same radius?*	**A semicircle has an area of 42 cm^2. Work out its radius. Give your answer correct to 1 decimal place.**
Area of circle = 2×38 = 76 cm^2	*What formula should we now substitute into?*	
$A = \pi r^2$ $76 = \pi r^2$		
$r^2 = \frac{76}{\pi}$ $r = \sqrt{\frac{76}{\pi}}$ $= 4.918\ldots$ cm Radius = 4.9 cm (to 1 d.p.)	*How can we solve this equation to find the value of r?*	

Fluency questions

7.2.1 Area of a circle

1 Here is a circle with a 3 cm radius, shown on a square centimetre grid.

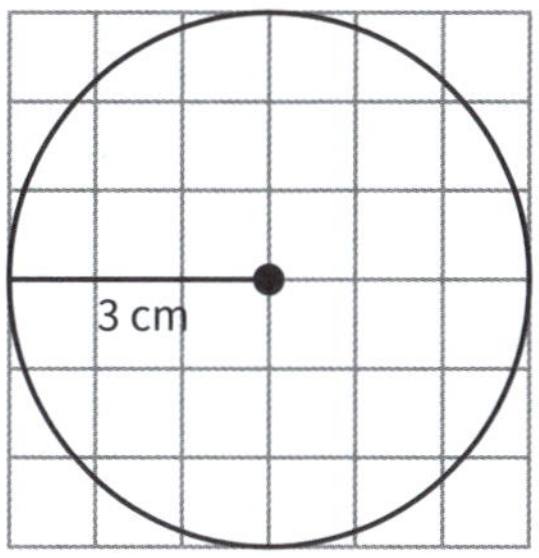

a) Estimate the area of the circle by counting squares.

b) Complete the working to find the area of the circle. Give your answer to 3 significant figures.

$A = \pi r^2$

$= \pi \times 3^2$

$=$ ______ cm^2

2 Complete the working to find the area of this circle. Give your answer to 3 significant figures.

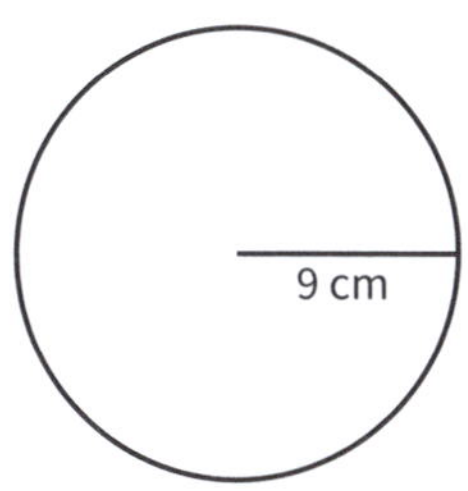

$A = \pi r^2$

$= \pi \times 9^2$

$=$ ______ cm^2

3 Find the area of this circle. Give your answer to 3 significant figures.

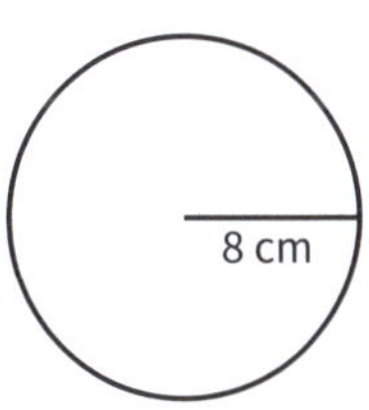

4 Complete the working to find the area of this circle. Give your answer to 3 significant figures.

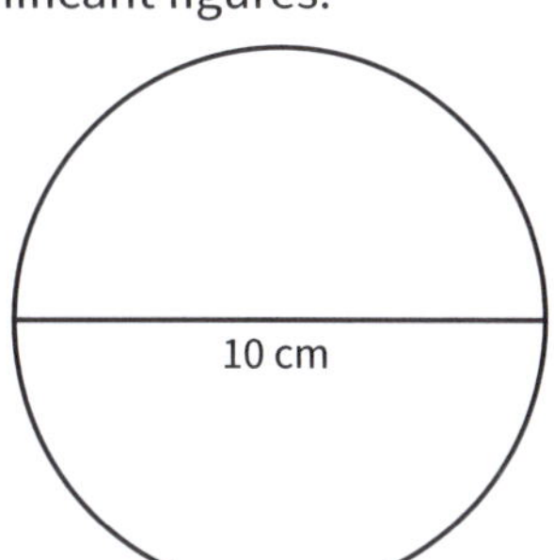

Diameter = 10 cm, so

Radius = ______ cm

$A = \pi r^2$

$= \pi \times$ ______^{2}

$=$ ________ cm^2

7.2.2 Problem solving with area of a circle

1 Complete the working to find the area of this semicircle. Give your answer to 3 significant figures.

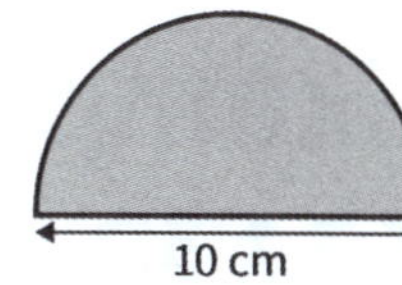

Area of whole circle $= \pi r^2$

$= \pi \times 5^2$

$=$ ______ cm^2

Area of semicircle = ______ cm^2

2 Complete the working to find the radius of a circle with an area of 70 cm^2.
Give your answer to 2 significant figures.

$A = \pi r^2$

$70 = \pi r^2$

$r^2 = \frac{70}{\pi}$

$r =$ ______ cm

3 Calculate the diameter of a circle with area 62 cm^2.
Give your answer to 2 significant figures.

4 This compound shape is made from a square and a quarter circle.
Complete the working to find the area of the compound shape. Give your answer to 3 significant figures.

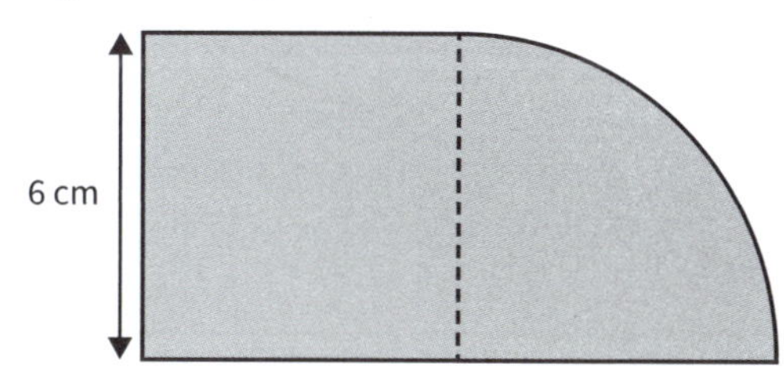

Area of square = ______ cm^2

Area of whole circle $= \pi r^2$

$= \pi \times 6^2$

$=$ ______ cm^2

Area of quarter circle = ______ cm^2

Area of whole compound shape
= area of square + area of quarter circle

$=$ ______ cm^2

7.3 Surface area

Example-problem pairs

7.3.1 3D shapes

Worked example 1	Thinking	Your turn! 1
Write the name of this 3D shape. 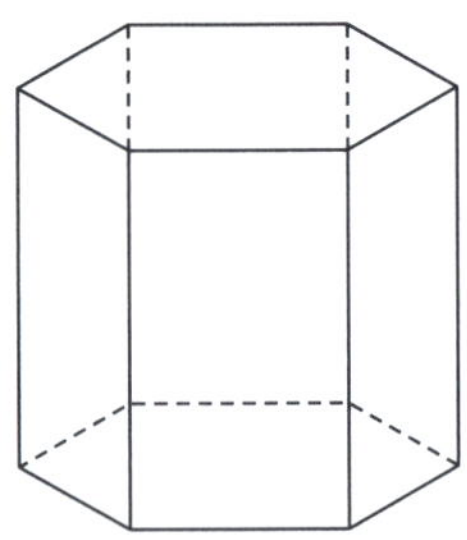	*How can we find what the 3D shape might be?*	**Write the name of this 3D shape.** 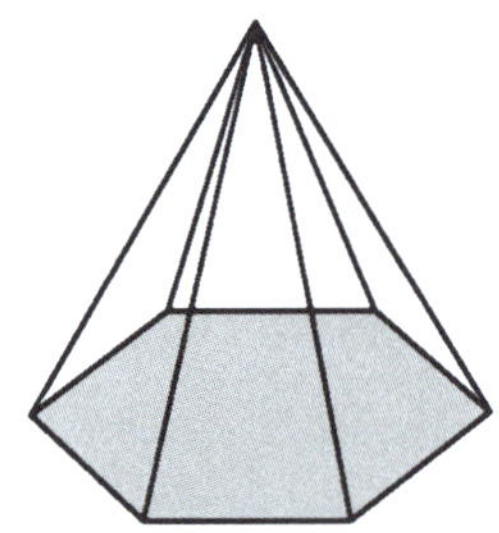
The shape has two identical trapezium faces, and all the other faces are parallelograms. It is a trapezium-based prism.		

Worked example 2	Thinking	Your turn! 2
Sketch the faces of this triangular right prism. Include side lengths in your sketches. 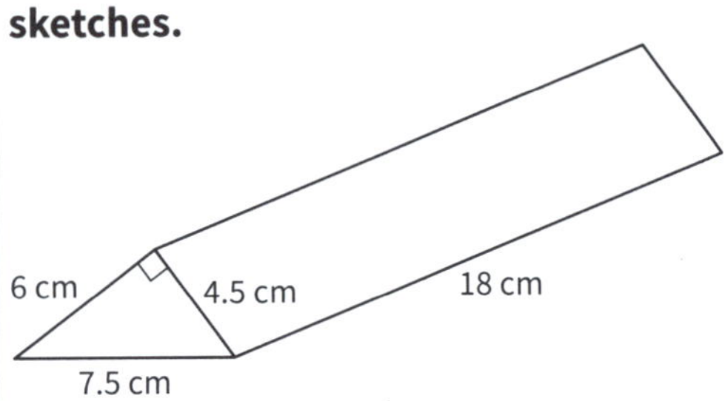	*How many faces does the prism have and what shape are they?*	**Sketch the faces of this triangular right prism. Include side lengths in your sketches.** 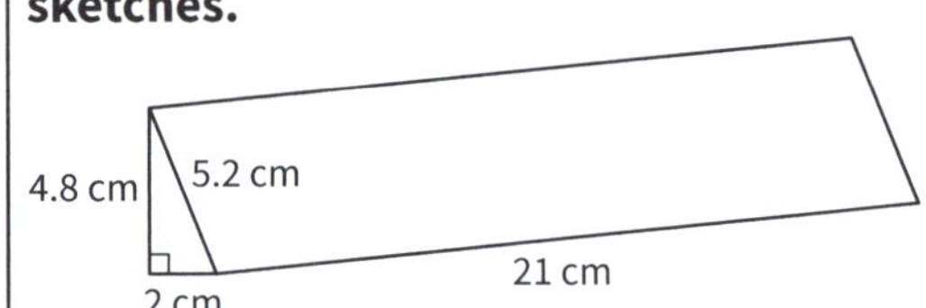
A triangular right prism has 5 faces: 2 identical triangular faces 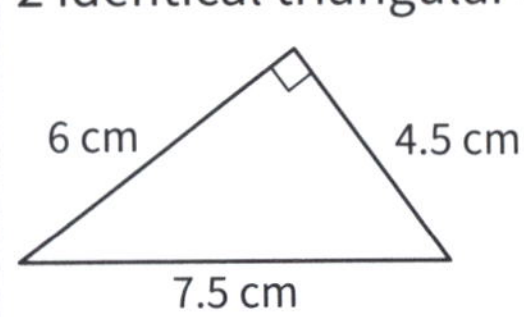	*What are the lengths of all the rectangular faces?*	
and 3 rectangular faces. 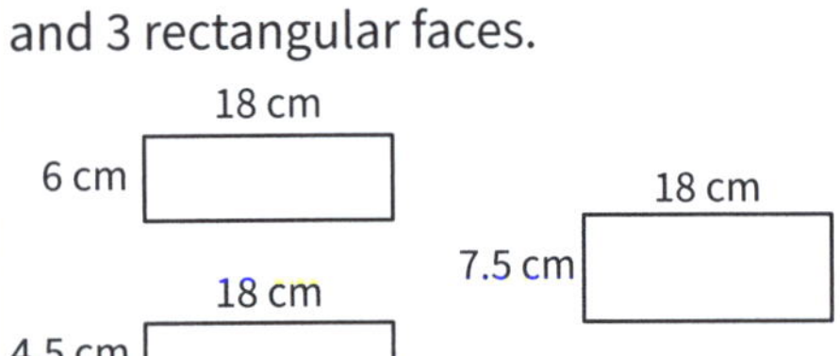		

7.3.2 Cubes and cuboids

Worked example 1	**Thinking**	**Your turn! 1**
A cuboid has width 3 cm, length 5 cm, and height 7 cm. **Work out its surface area.** 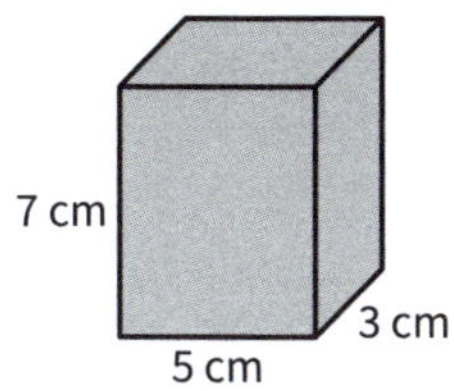 	*How many faces are there and what shapes are they?*	**A cuboid has width 4 cm, length 7 cm, and height 8 cm.** **Work out its surface area.** 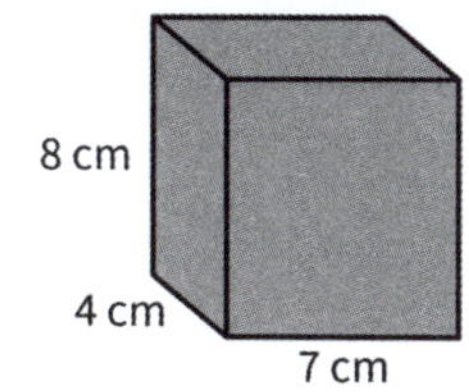
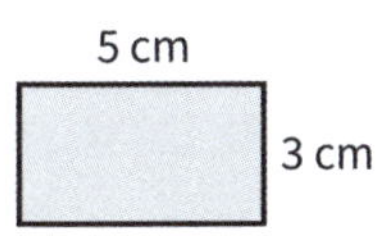 Area = $3 \times 5 = 15$ cm^2 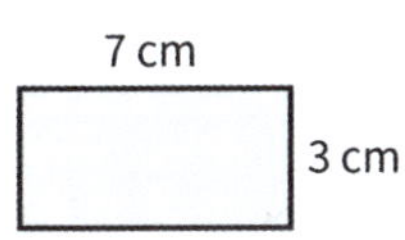 Area = $7 \times 3 = 21$ cm^2 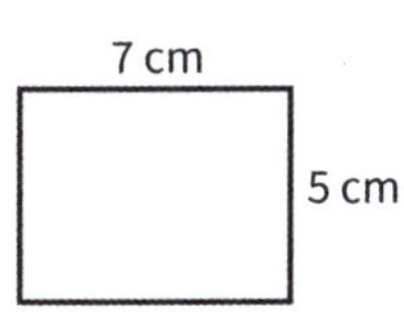 Area = $7 \times 5 = 35$ cm^2	*How can we work out the area of a face?* *How can we use these areas to find the surface area of the cuboid?*	
Surface area = $2 \times (15 + 21 + 35)$ = 142 cm^2		

Worked example 2	Thinking	Your turn! 2
Work out the surface area of the cuboid with this net. 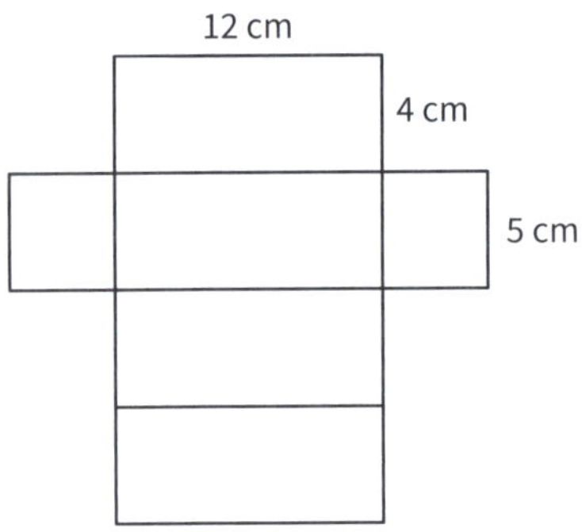	*What is the rule for finding the area of a rectangle?*	**Work out the surface area of the cuboid with this net.** 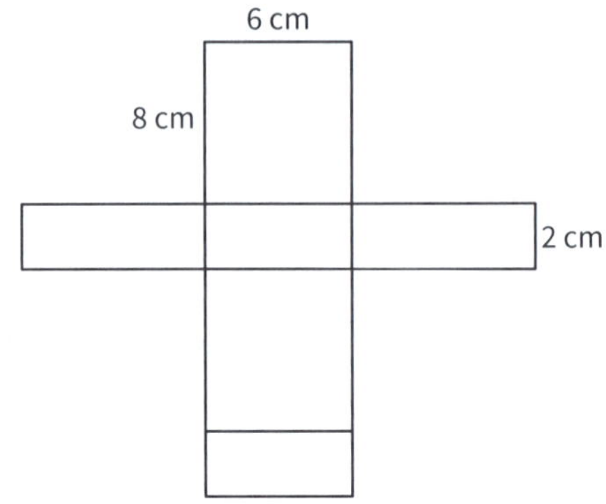
The area of each rectangle is its length multiplied by its width. 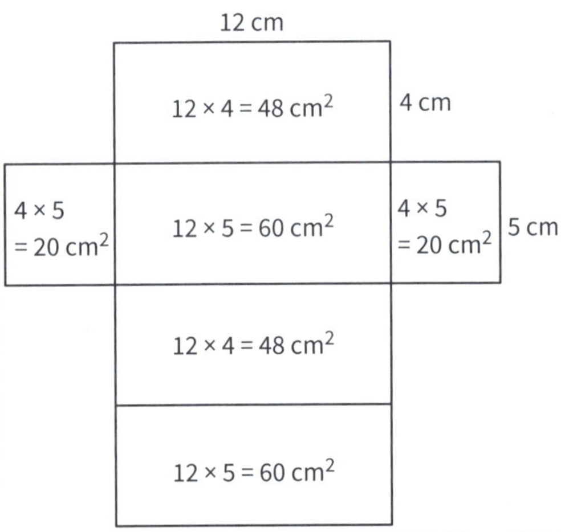	*How can we now find the surface area of the cuboid?*	
Add up all the areas to find the surface area of the cuboid. Surface area = 48 + 20 + 60 + 20 + 48 + 60 = 256 cm^2		

Worked example 3	Thinking	Your turn! 3
A cube has a surface area of 150 cm^2. What is the side length of the cube?	*What do we know about the faces of a cube?*	**A cube has a surface area of 54 cm^2. What is the side length of the cube?**
Area of one face = 150 ÷ 6 = 25 cm^2	*How can we use the area of one face to find the side length?*	
Side length = $\sqrt{25}$ = 5 cm		

Worked example 4	Thinking	Your turn! 4
This solid is formed by a cube placed on top of a cuboid. Work out the surface area of the solid. 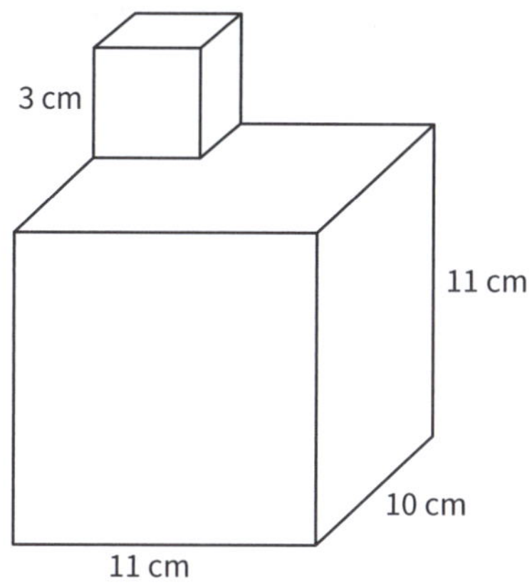	*How can we work out the surface area of the larger cuboid?*	**This solid is formed by two cuboids. Work out the surface area of the solid.** 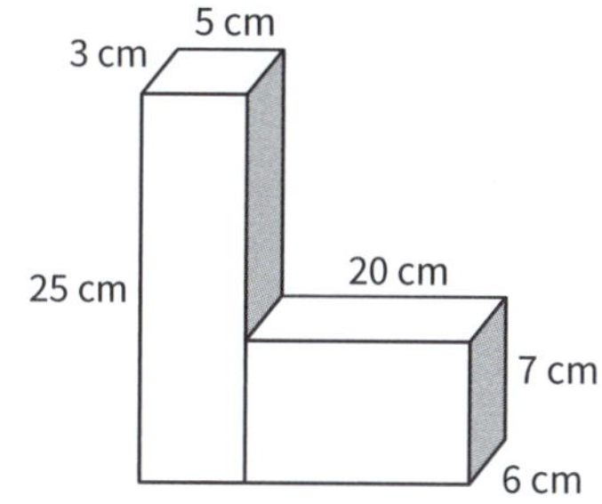
Surface area of cuboid $= 2 \times (11 \times 10 + 11 \times 10 + 11 \times 11)$ $= 2 \times 341$ $= 682\ cm^2$	*Do we need to subtract any surface area of the larger cuboid that is not exposed?*	
Area of cuboid not exposed $= 3 \times 3 = 9\ cm^2$ Therefore, exposed surface area of cuboid $= 682 - 9$ $= 673\ cm^2$	*How can we work out the surface area of the cube?*	
Five faces of the cube are exposed. Exposed surface area of cube $= 5 \times 9$ $= 45\ cm^2$		
Total surface area $= 673 + 45$ $= 718\ cm^2$		

7.3.3 Prisms

Worked example 1	Thinking	Your turn! 1
Work out the surface area of this trapezium-based right prism. 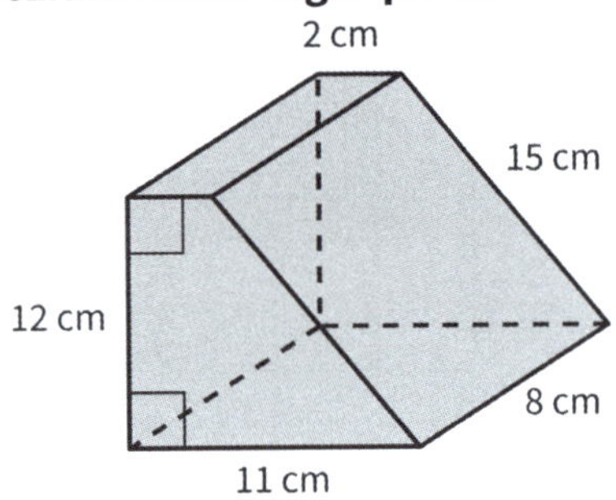 	*Which shape is the base of the prism?*	**Work out the surface area of this parallelogram-based right prism.** 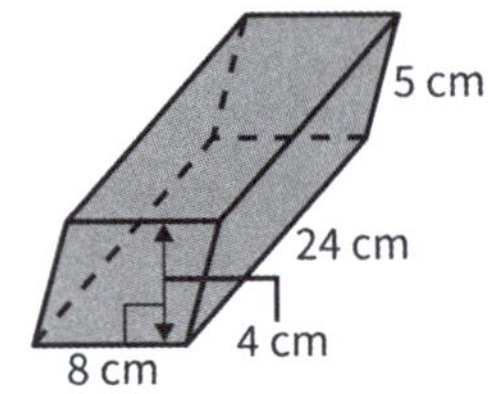
Area of trapezium face $= \frac{1}{2} \times (a + b) \times h$ $= \frac{1}{2} \times (11 + 2) \times 12$ $= 78\text{ cm}^2$ 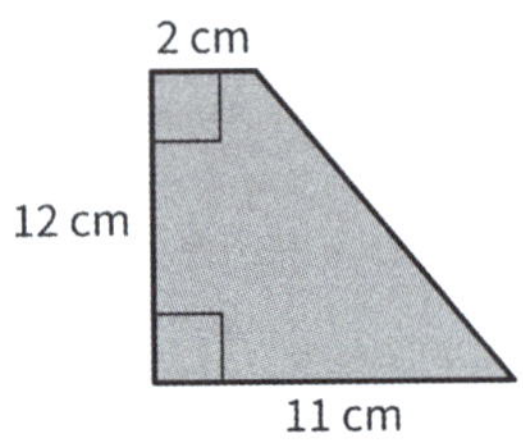 	*How do we work out the area of the other faces?*	
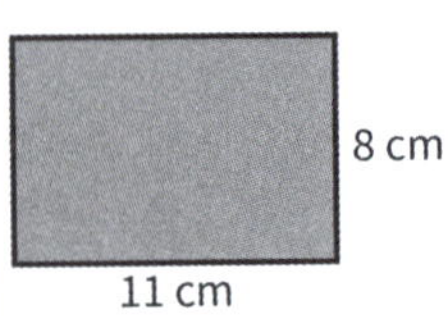 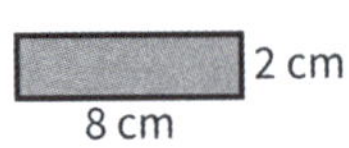 Area $= 8 \times 11 = 88\text{ cm}^2$ Area $= 8 \times 2 = 16\text{ cm}^2$ 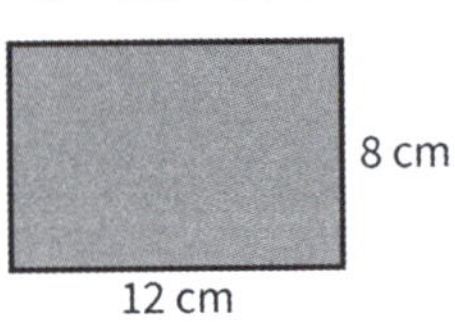 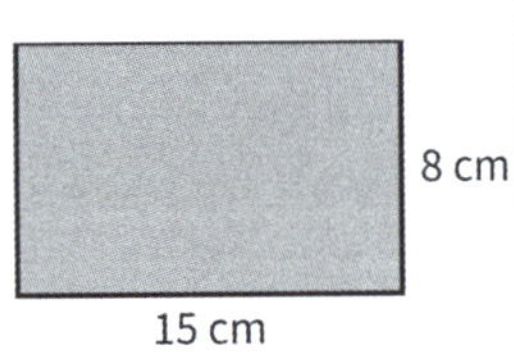 Area $= 12 \times 8 = 96\text{ cm}^2$ Area $= 8 \times 15 = 120\text{ cm}^2$	*How can we find the total surface area?*	
Surface area $= 78 + 78 + 88 + 96 + 16 + 120$ $= 476\text{ cm}^2$		

Worked example 2	Thinking	Your turn! 2
Work out the surface area of this right prism. 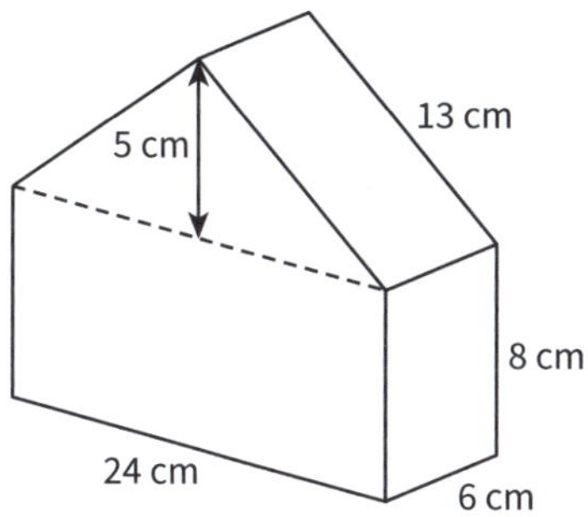	*Which face is the front and how can we find its area?*	**Work out the surface area of this right prism.** 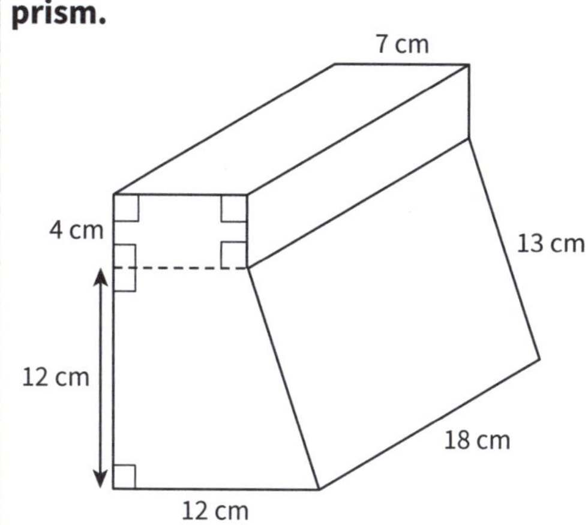
The front face is formed from a rectangle and a triangle. Area of rectangle = $24 \times 8 = 192$ cm^2 Area of triangle = $\frac{1}{2} \times 24 \times 5 = 60$ cm^2 Area of front face = $192 + 60 = 252$ cm^2	*How can we find the area of the other faces?*	
Area of other faces = length of prism × perimeter of base $= 6 \times (24 + 8 + 13 + 13 + 8)$ $= 6 \times 66$ $= 396$ cm^2	*How can we find the total surface area?*	
Surface area = $2 \times 252 + 396$ $= 900$ cm^2		

7.3.4 Cylinders

Worked example 1	Thinking	Your turn! 1
Find the surface area of a cylinder with diameter 16 cm and height 7 cm. Give your answer as an exact multiple of π.	*How can we find the area of the curved surface?*	**Find the surface area of a cylinder with diameter 12 cm and height 15 cm. Give your answer as an exact multiple of π.**
$C = \pi d$ $= \pi \times 16$ $= 16\pi$ cm Area of curved surface = $16\pi \times 7$ $= 112\pi$ cm^2	*How can we find the area of one of the circular faces?*	
The radius is half of the diameter: $r = 16 \div 2 = 8$ cm $A = \pi r^2$ $= \pi \times 8^2$ $= 64\pi$ cm^2	*How can we find the surface area of the cylinder?*	
Surface area = $2 \times 64\pi + 112\pi$ $= 240\pi$ cm^2		

7 Perimeter, area, and volume

Worked example 2	Thinking	Your turn! 2
A solid is formed by removing a cylinder of radius 1 cm from the centre of a cylinder of radius 10 cm and height 30 cm. 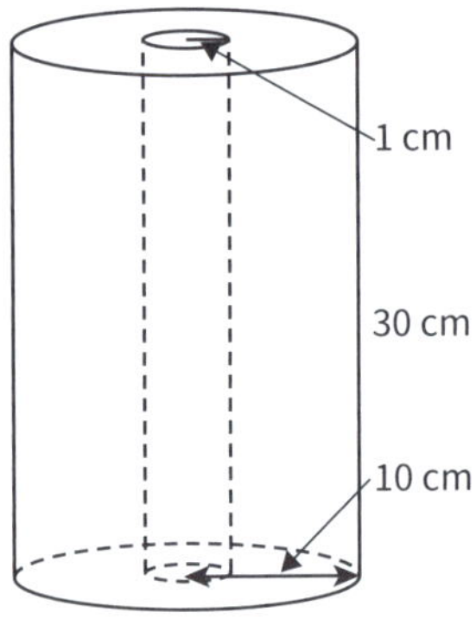 **Calculate the surface area of the solid, including the surface 'inside' the shape. Give your answer correct to 1 decimal place.**	*What areas do we need to find?*	**A solid is formed by removing a cylinder of radius 3 cm from the centre of a cube of side length 8 cm.** 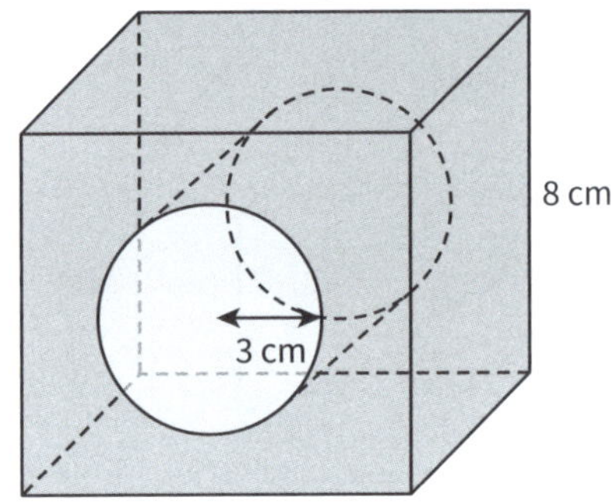 **Calculate the surface area of the solid, including the surface 'inside' the shape. Give your answer correct to 1 decimal place.**
Find the curved surface area of each cylinder and the area of the circular face of each cylinder.	*How do we find the areas of the curved surfaces?*	
For the larger cylinder: Circumference $= 2 \times \pi \times 10$ $= 20\pi$ cm Area of curved surface $= 20\pi \times 30$ $= 600\pi$ cm^2 For the smaller cylinder: Circumference $= 2 \times \pi \times 1$ $= 2\pi$ cm Area of curved surface $= 2\pi \times 30$ $= 60\pi$ cm^2	*How do we find the area of the flat faces?*	
For the larger cylinder: Area of circular face $= \pi \times 10^2$ $= 100\pi$ cm^2 For the smaller cylinder: Area of circular face $= \pi \times 1^2$ $= \pi$ cm^2 So, the area of one of the flat faces is given by: $A = 100\pi - \pi = 99\pi$ cm^2	*How can we use this information to find the surface area?*	
Surface area $= 600\pi + 60\pi + 2 \times 99\pi$ $= 858\pi$ $= 2695.5$ cm^2 (to 1 d.p.)		

Fluency questions

7.3.1 3D shapes

1 **a)** Name this 3D shape.

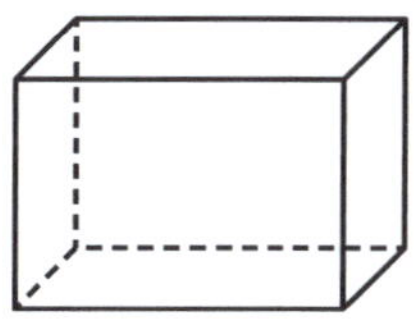

____

b) Name this 3D shape.

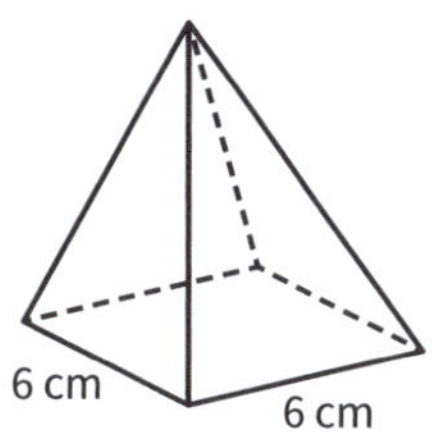

____

c) Here is a triangular prism.

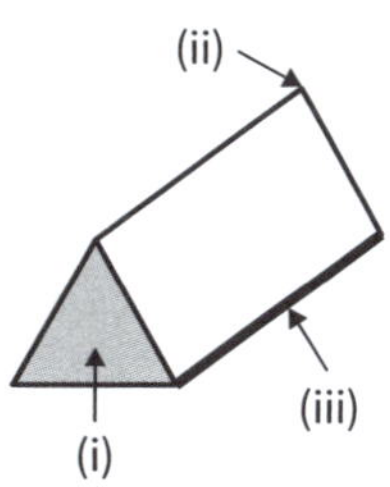

Identify each of the three labelled parts, choosing from these words: vertex edge face

i. ________________

ii. ________________

iii. ________________

2 Here is a pentagonal prism.

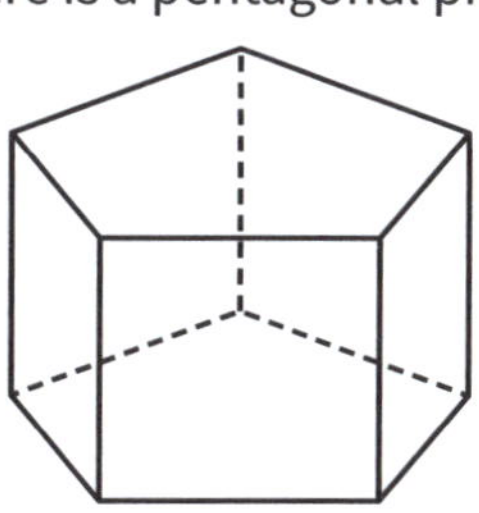

a) How many faces does this shape have? ________

b) How many edges does this shape have? ________

c) How many vertices does this shape have? ______

3 Here is a hexagonal prism.

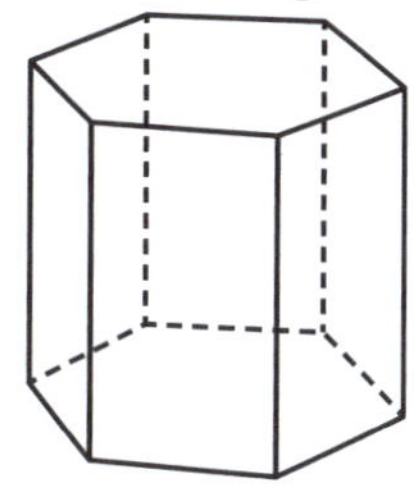

a) How many faces does this shape have? ________

b) How many edges does this shape have? ________

c) How many vertices does this shape have? ______

4 Here is a tetrahedron.

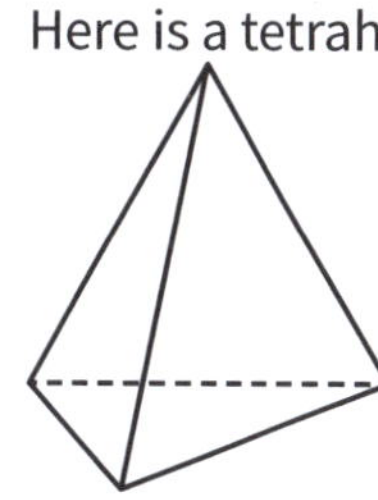

a) How many faces does this shape have? ________

b) How many edges does this shape have? ________

c) How many vertices does this shape have? ______

7.3.2 Cubes and cuboids

1 Here is a net of a cuboid.

The areas of rectangular faces are given.

Find the surface of area of the cuboid.

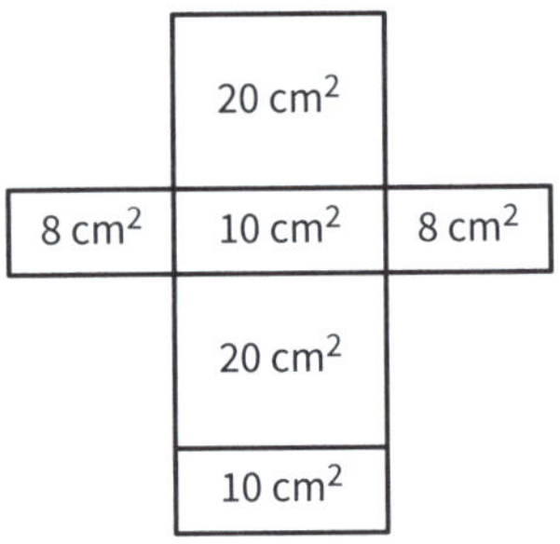

2 Here is the net of a cuboid, with its faces labelled A–F.

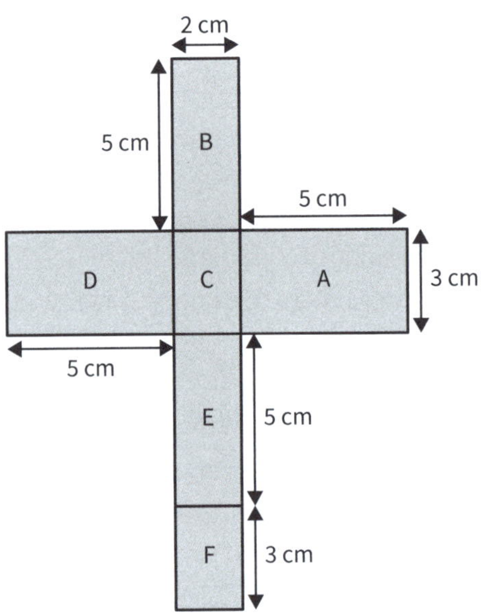

Face	Area
A	15 cm^2
B	
C	
D	
E	
F	

a) Complete the table.

b) Work out the surface area of the cuboid.

3 Find the surface of area of the cuboid made by folding up this net.

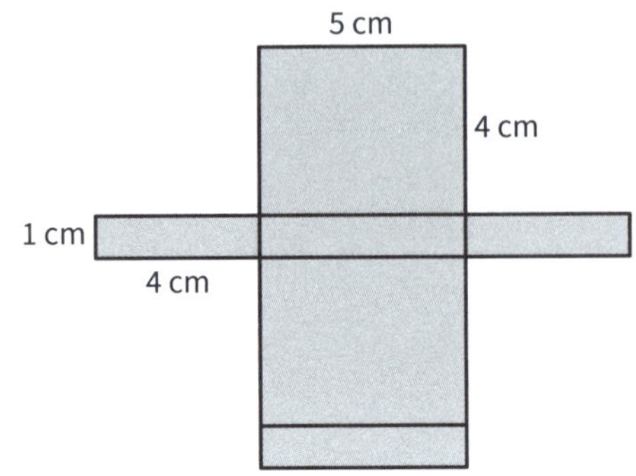

4 A cube has edges of length 5 cm.

a) Work out the area of one face of the cube.

b) How many faces does the cube have?

c) Work out the surface area of the cube.

7.3.3 Prisms

1 Here is a net of a triangular prism.

The area of each face of the prism is given. Find the surface of area of the prism.

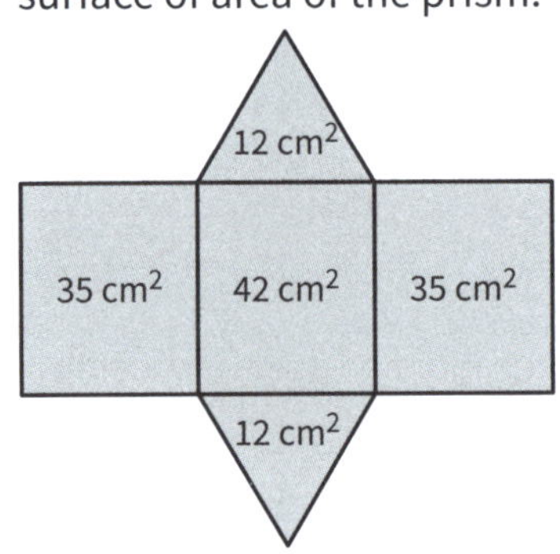

2 Here is a net of a pentagonal prism.
The area each face of the prism is given. Find the surface of area of the prism.

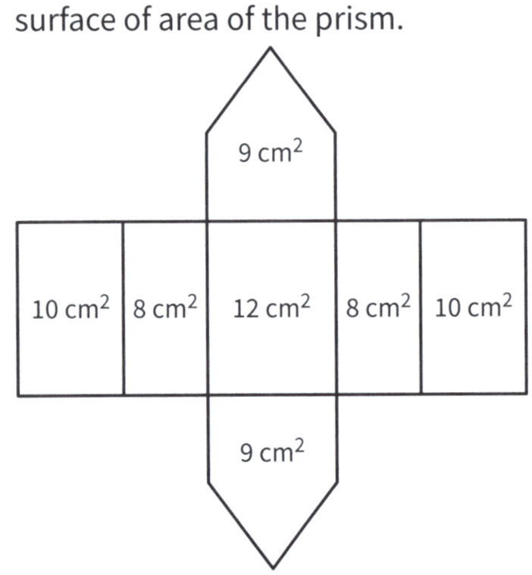

3 Here is a net of a prism.

The area of each face of the prism is given. Find the surface of area of the prism.

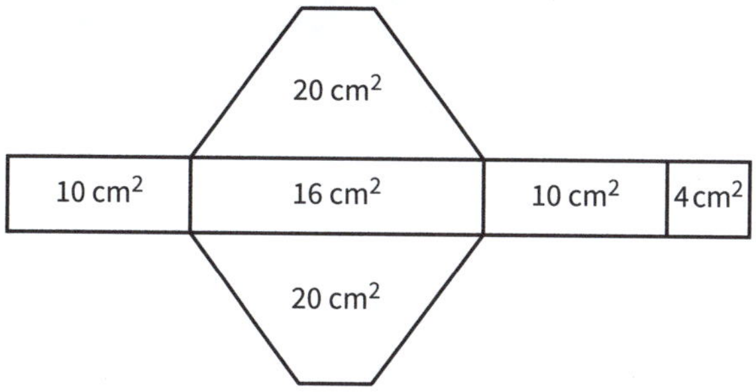

4 Here is a triangular prism, with its faces labelled A–E.

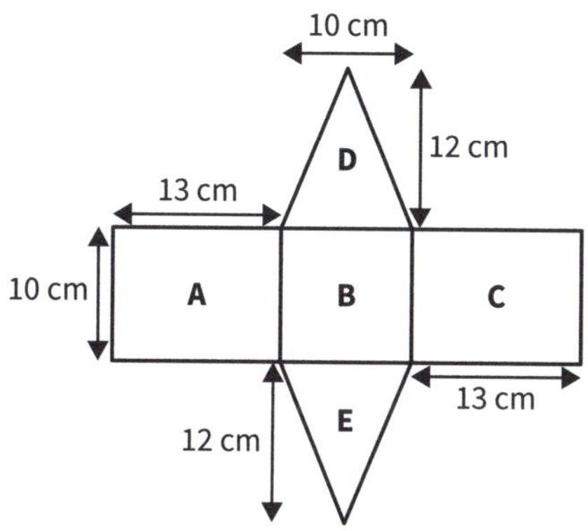

a) Complete the table.

Face	Area
A	130 cm^2
B	
C	
D	
E	

b) Work out the surface area of the triangular prism.

7.3.4 Cylinders

1 Here is a net of a cylinder, formed of a rectangle and two circles. The areas of each part of the net are given, in terms of π.

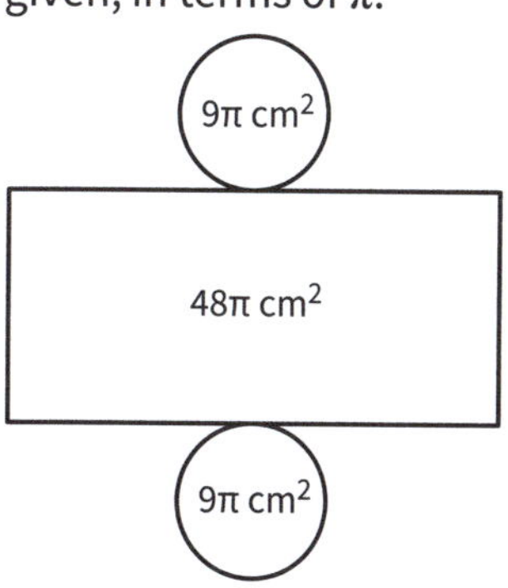

Find the surface area of the cylinder.

Give your answer:

a) in terms of π

b) to 3 significant figures.

2 Here is a net of a cylinder, formed of a rectangle and two circles. The area of the curved surface of the cylinder is $60\pi\text{ cm}^2$, as shown. The circular faces have radius 5 cm^2.

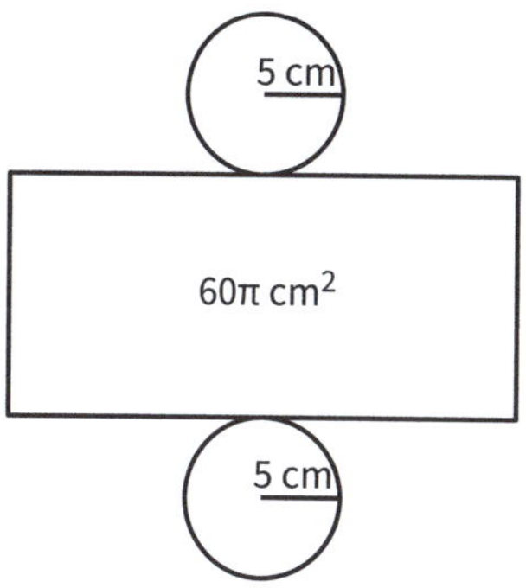

a) Work the area of one circular face, in terms of π.

b) Hence work out the surface area of the cylinder, in terms of π.

3 Here is a net of a cylinder.

Each circular face has radius 5 cm and the length of the cylinder is 7 cm.

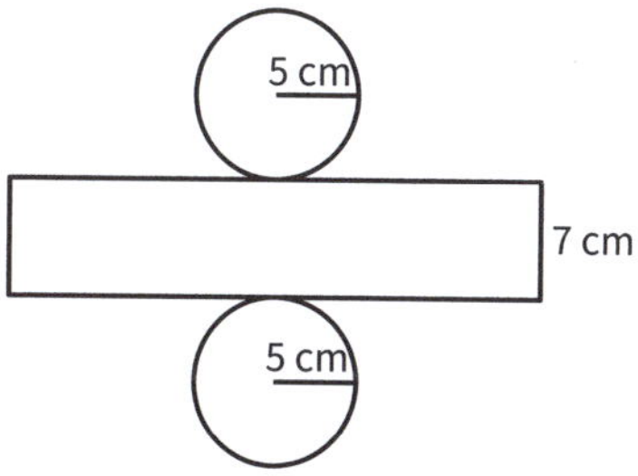

a) Work out the area of one of the circular faces. Give your answer in terms of π.

b) Work out the circumference of one of the circular faces. Give your answer in terms of π.

c) The circumference of the circle matches the length of one pair of sides of the rectangle in the net. Work out the area of this rectangle. Give your answer in terms of π.

d) Hence work out the surface area of the cylinder, writing your answer:

i. in terms of π

ii. to 3 significant figures.

7.4 Volume

Example-problem pairs

7.4.1 Cubes and cuboids

Worked example 1	**Thinking**	**Your turn! 1**
Work out the volume of the cuboid without using a calculator. 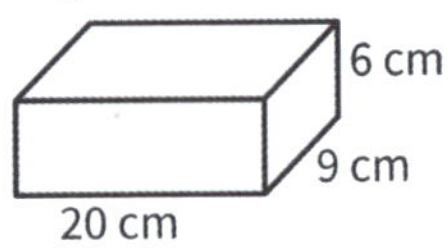	*What formula can we use?*	**Work out the volume of the cuboid without using a calculator.** 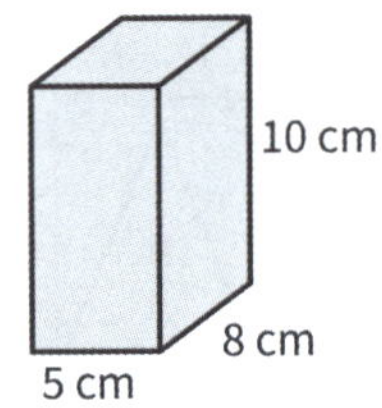
Volume = $6 \times 9 \times 20$ $= 54 \times 20$ $= 1080\ \text{cm}^3$	*How do we work this out?*	

Worked example 2	**Thinking**	**Your turn! 2**
This cuboid is formed from 1 cm cubes. Work out the volume of the cuboid. 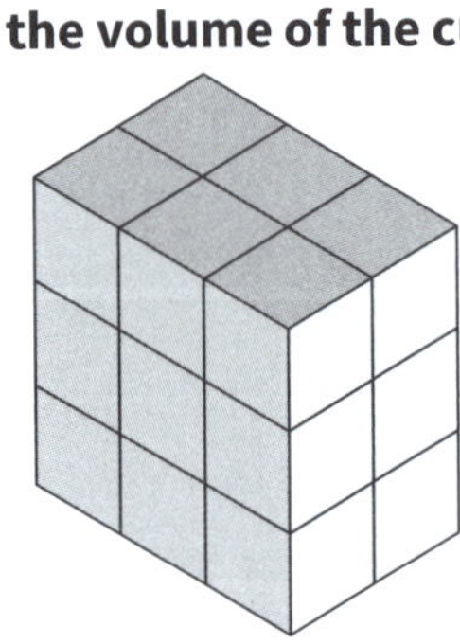	*How many cubes are visible on one face of the cuboid?*	**This cuboid is formed from 1 cm cubes. Work out the volume of the cuboid.** 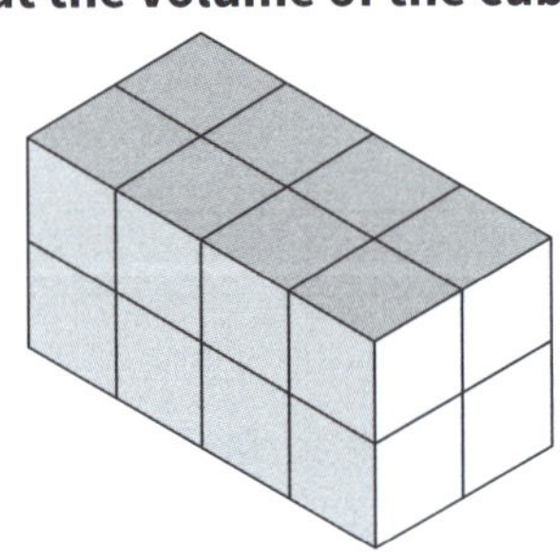
The face on the right has 6 cubes visible.	*How many rows using this number of cubes are there?*	
There are 3 rows of 6 cubes.	*How many cubes are there in total?*	
Total number of 1 cm cubes $= 3 \times 6 = 18$	*How do we write the volume of the cuboid?*	
Volume of cuboid = $18\ \text{cm}^3$		

Worked example 3	Thinking	Your turn! 3
The 3D solid is formed from a cuboid and a cube. Work out its volume. 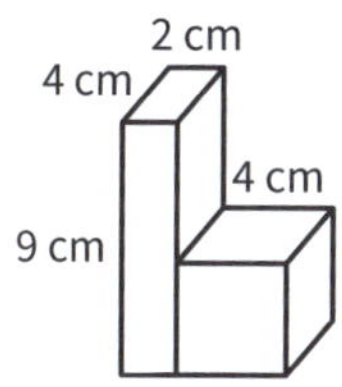	*What formula can we use for the cuboid?*	**The 3D solid is formed from a cuboid and a cube. Work out its volume.** 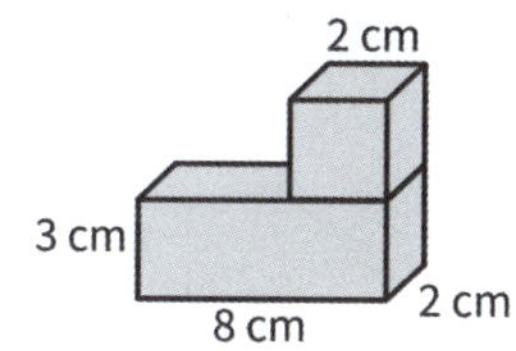
Volume of cuboid $= 9 \times 2 \times 4$ $= 72\ \text{cm}^3$	*What formula can we use for the cube?*	
Volume of cube $= 4^3$ $= 64\ \text{cm}^3$	*How do we find the volume of the whole 3D solid?*	
Volume of solid $= 72 + 64$ $= 136\ \text{cm}^3$		

Worked example 4	Thinking	Your turn! 4
A cuboid has a volume of $350\ \text{cm}^3$. Each side is an integer number of centimetres. Work out two sets of possible side lengths.	*What is the prime factorisation of the volume measurement?*	**A cuboid has a volume of $99\ \text{cm}^3$. Each side is an integer number of centimetres. Work out two sets of possible side lengths.**
$350 = 2 \times 5 \times 5 \times 7$		
One possibility is 2 cm, 5 cm, and 35 cm	*What are two possible side lengths?*	
Another possibility is 1 cm, 25 cm, and 14 cm		

7.4.2 Prisms and cylinders

Worked example 1	Thinking	Your turn! 1
Work out the volume of the triangular prism. 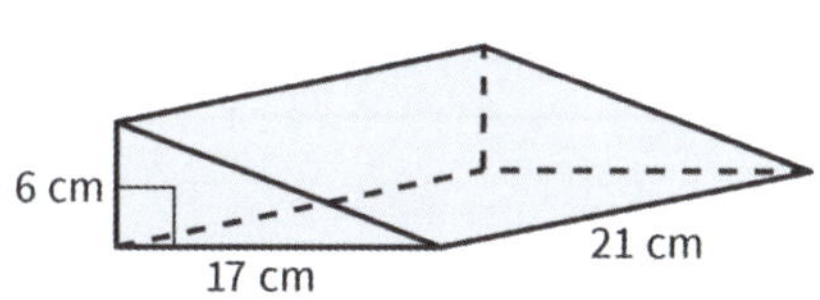	*What do we need to work out first?*	**Work out the volume of the triangular prism.** 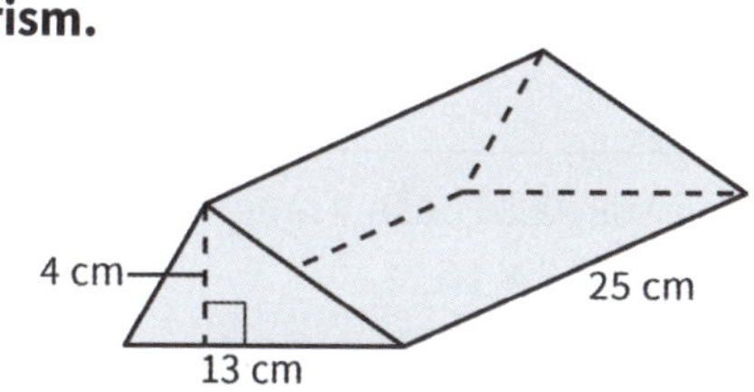
Area of base $= \frac{1}{2} \times 17 \times 6$ $= 51\ \text{cm}^2$	*What rule can we use now?*	
Volume $= 51 \times 21$ $= 1071\ \text{cm}^3$		

Worked example 2	Thinking	Your turn! 2
Work out the volume of the prism given that the area of its base is 24 cm³. 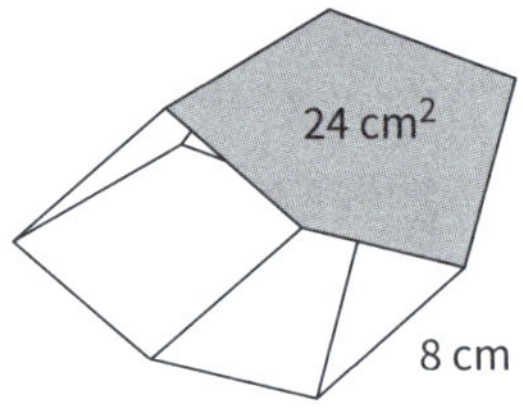	*What rule can we use?*	**Work out the volume of the prism given that the area of its base is 15 cm².** 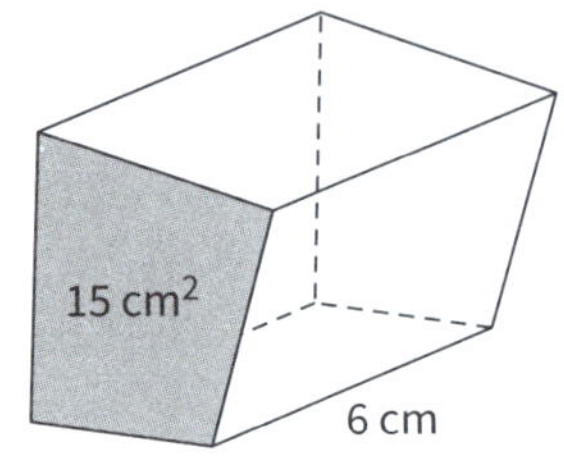
Volume = area of base × length of prism $= 24 \times 8$ $= 192\ \text{cm}^3$		

Worked example 3	Thinking	Your turn! 3
A solid is formed by removing one right-angled triangular prism from the centre of another. Both triangular prisms have a length of 16 cm. **Work out the volume of the solid.** 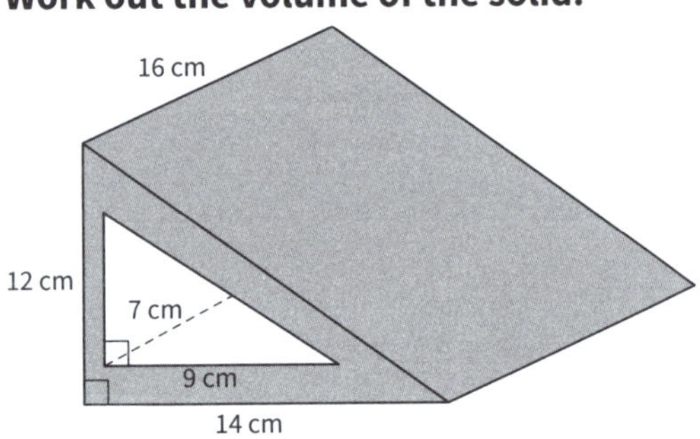	*How can we find the area of the base of the solid?*	**A solid is formed by removing a cuboid from a triangular prism. The cuboid and the triangular prism both have a length of 19 cm.** **Work out the volume of the solid.** 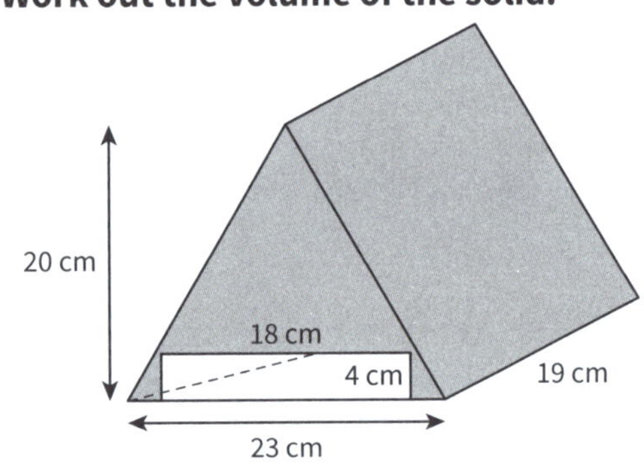
Area of base = area of large triangle − area of small triangle $= \frac{1}{2} \times 14 \times 12 - \frac{1}{2} \times 9 \times 7$ $= 84 - 31.5$ $= 52.5\ \text{cm}^2$	*What rule can we use now?*	
Volume = area of base × length $= 52.5 \times 16$ $= 840\ \text{cm}^3$		

Worked example 4	Thinking	Your turn! 4
Work out the volume of the cylinder. 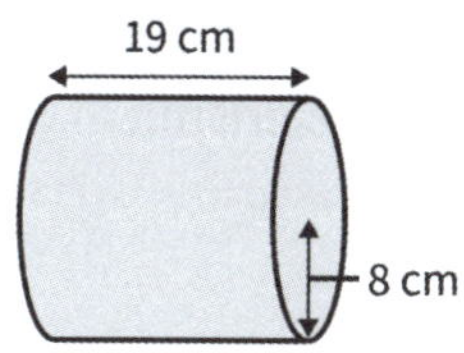	*What dimensions do we need?*	**Work out the volume of the cylinder.** 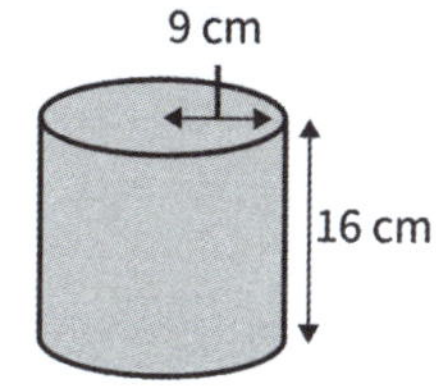
$r = 8$ cm $\quad h = 19$ cm	*What is the formula?*	
$V = \pi \times 8^2 \times 19$		
$V = 1216\,\pi$ cm^3 (in terms of π) = 3820.2 cm^3 (to 1 d.p.)	*What is the answer?*	

Worked example 5	Thinking	Your turn! 5
2.3 litres of water is poured into a cylindrical container with diameter 26 cm. What is the height of water in the container? Give your answer correct to 1 decimal place.	*What is the volume of water?*	**3.5 litres of water is poured into a cylindrical container with diameter 18 cm. What is the height of water in the container? Give your answer correct to 1 decimal place.**
2.3 litres is the same as 2300 cm^3.		
Radius of cylinder = 26 ÷ 2 = 13 cm Volume = $\pi r^2 h$ $= \pi \times 13^2 \times h$ $= 169\pi h$	*How can we work out the volume of a cylinder?*	
$169\pi h = 2300$ $h = \dfrac{2300}{169\pi}$ $h = 4.33\ldots$ Height of water = 4.3 cm (to 1 d.p.)	*How can we use what we have written down so far to find the height of water?*	

Fluency questions

7.4.1 Cubes and cuboids

1 Here is a cuboid made up identical cubes.

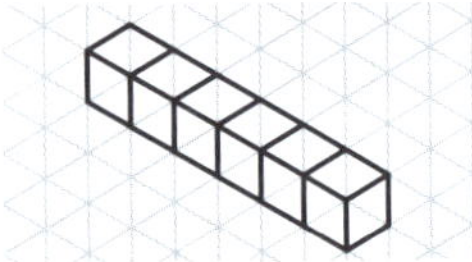

a) How many cubes make up this cuboid?

b) Each of the cubes is one cubic centimetre. Write down the volume of the cuboid.

2 Each cube in this cuboid is one cubic centimetre.

Work out the volume of the cuboid.

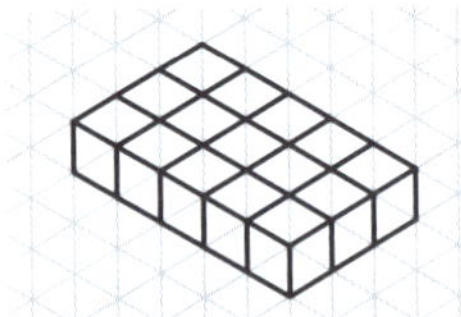

3 Each cube in this cuboid is one cubic centimetre.

Work out the volume of the cuboid.

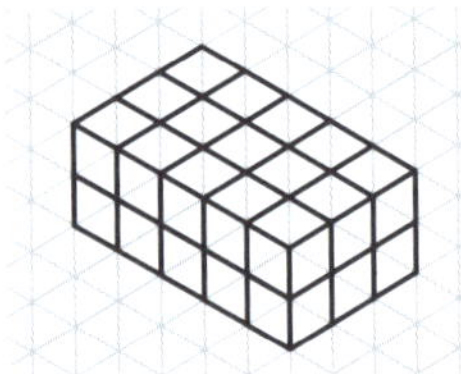

4 Complete the working to find the volume of this cuboid.

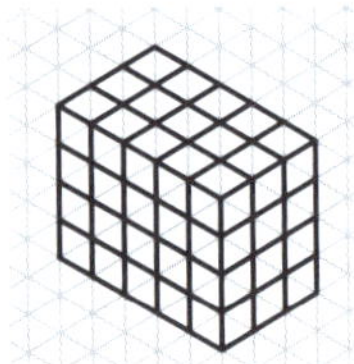

Volume of cuboid = $3 \times 5 \times 4$ = ______ cm^3

7.4.2 Prisms and cylinders

1 Work out the volume of this prism.

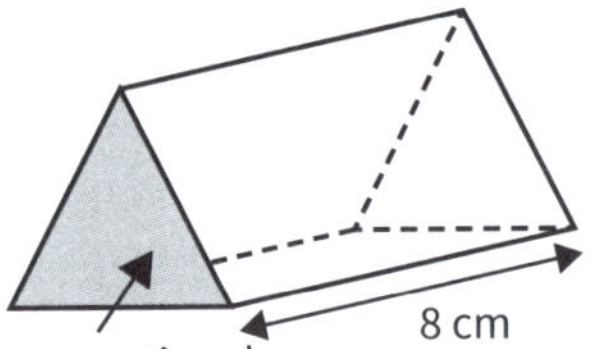

2 Work out the volume of this prism.

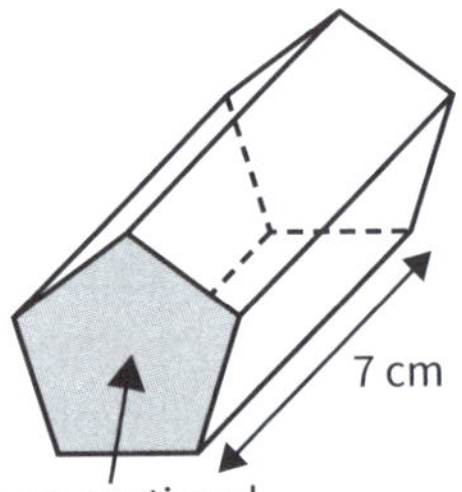

3 Work out the volume of this cylinder.

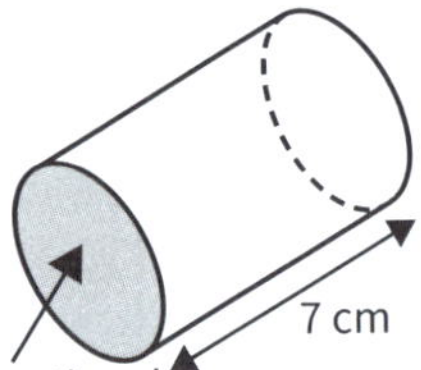

4 Here is a triangular prism.

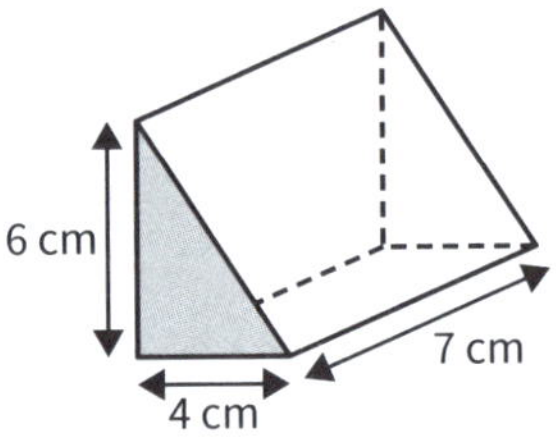

a) Work out the area of the shaded triangular face.

b) Work out the volume of the triangular prism.

8.1 Symmetry

Example-problem pairs

8.1.1 Line symmetry

Worked example 1	**Thinking**	**Your turn! 1**
Complete the polygon so that the dashed lines are lines of symmetry. 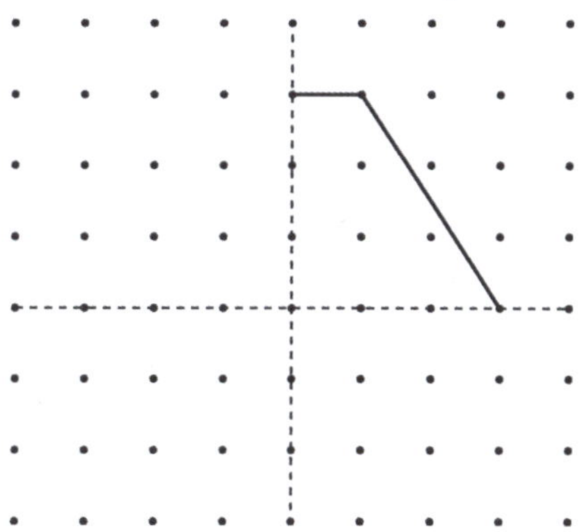	*What is meant by a line of symmetry?*	**Complete the polygon so that the dashed lines are lines of symmetry.** 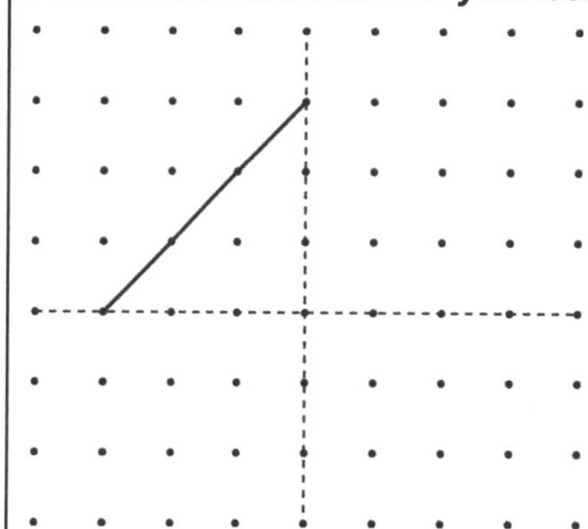
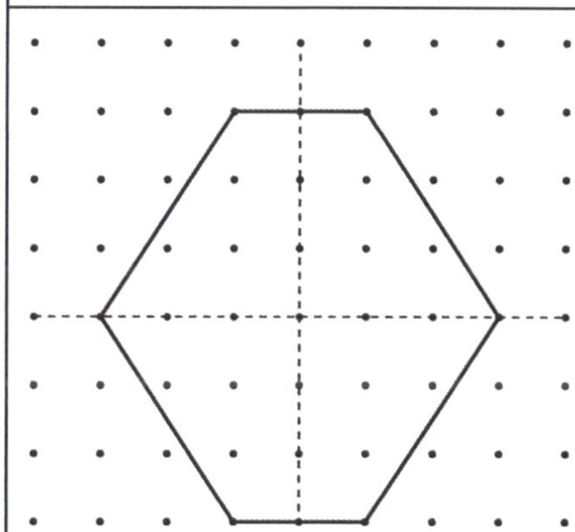	*How do we draw in the missing vertices?*	

Worked example 2	Thinking	Your turn! 2
Complete the polygon so that the dashed line is a line of symmetry. 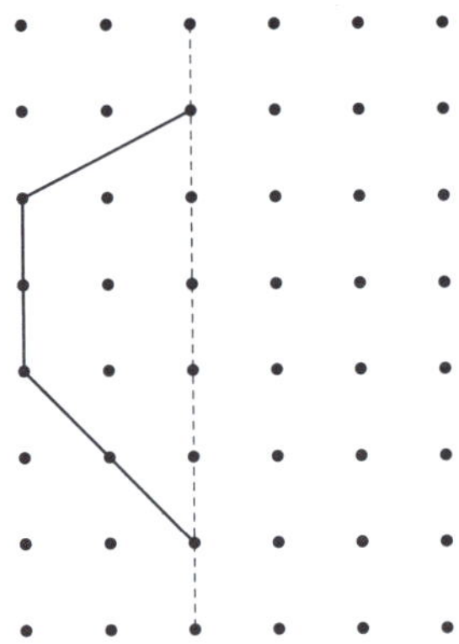	*How is the dashed line the same as a mirror line?*	**Complete the polygon so that the dashed line is a line of symmetry.** 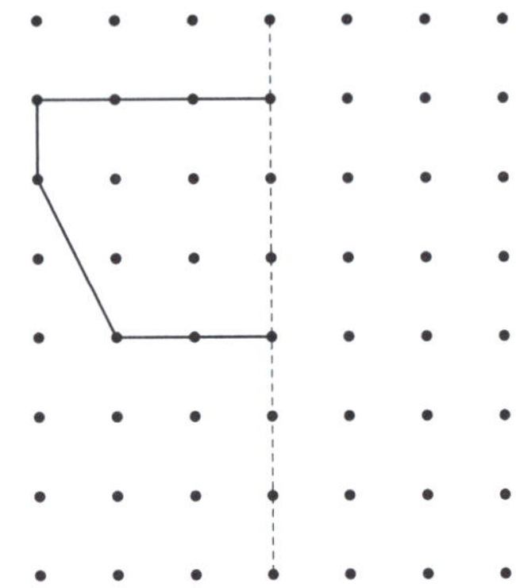
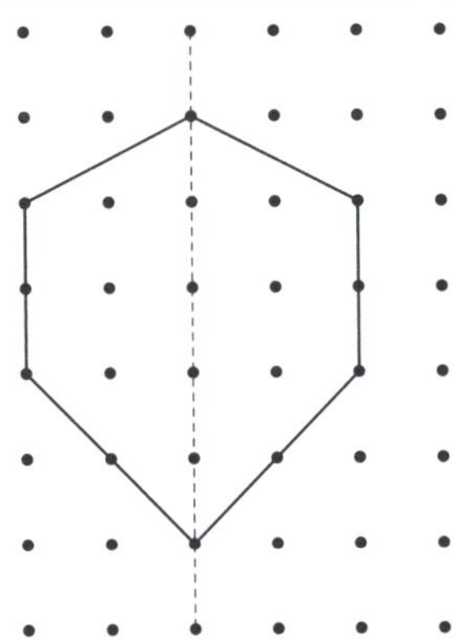	*How do we draw in the missing vertices?*	

Worked example 3	Thinking	Your turn! 3
Draw all the lines of symmetry on this polygon. 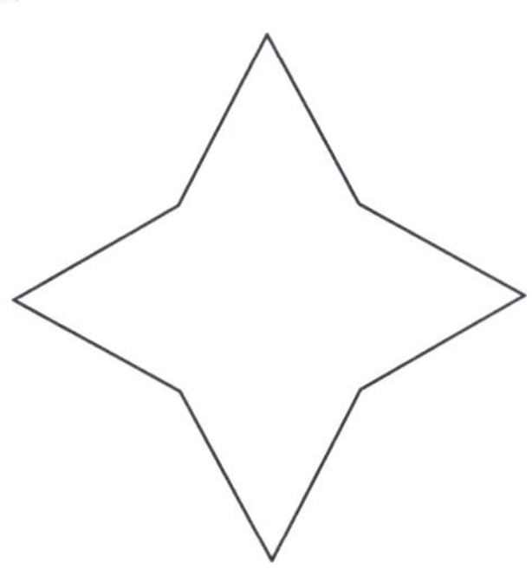	*What is meant by a line of symmetry?*	**Draw all the lines of symmetry on this polygon.** 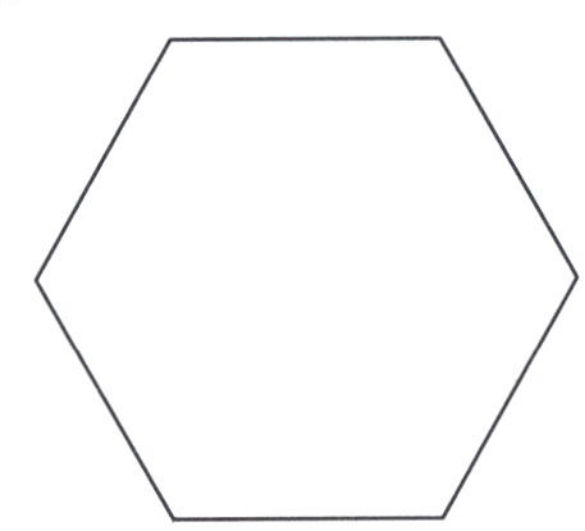
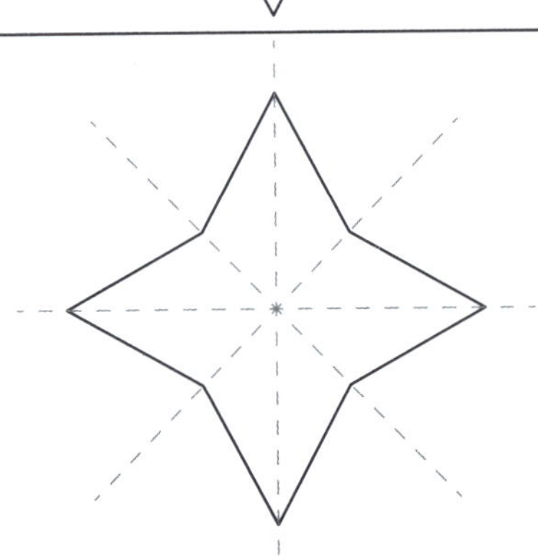		

Worked example 4	Thinking	Your turn! 4
This pentagon has a line of symmetry shown by the dashed line. 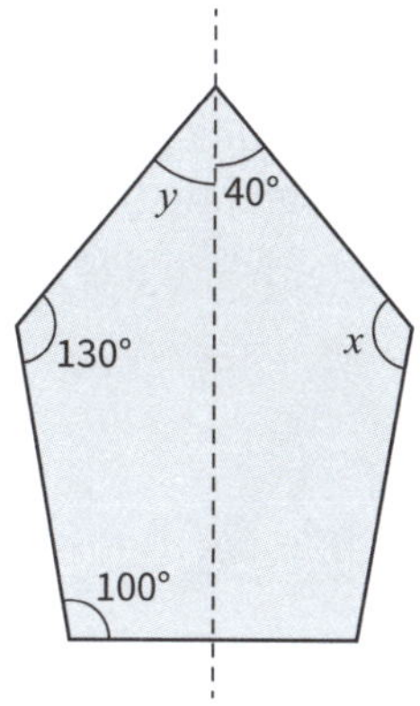 **Write the size of the angles labelled x and y.**	*What does the line of symmetry tell us about the two sides of the shape?* *Which angle is symmetrically opposite each of x and y?*	**This quadrilateral has a line of symmetry shown by the dashed line.** 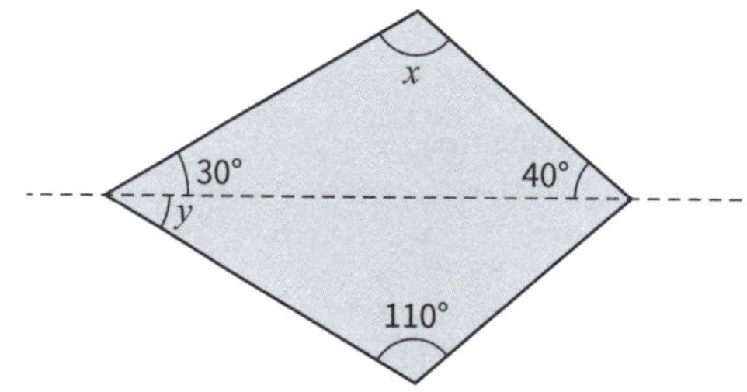 **Write the size of the angles labelled x and y.**
$x = 130°$ $y = 40°$		

8.1.2 Rotational symmetry

Worked example 1	Thinking	Your turn! 1
Here is a parallelogram. Write the order of rotational symmetry. 	*What do we mean by 'order of rotational symmetry'?*	**Here is a polygon. Write the order of rotational symmetry.** 
The shape is the same when the shape is rotated 180° or 360°. So the order of rotational symmetry is 2.		

Worked example 2	Thinking	Your turn! 2
Draw a triangle with rotational symmetry order 3.	*How do we use the order of rotational symmetry to work out the sides and angles?*	**Draw a quadrilateral with rotational symmetry order 4.**
You need to draw an equilateral triangle. Each of the angles will be 60°. 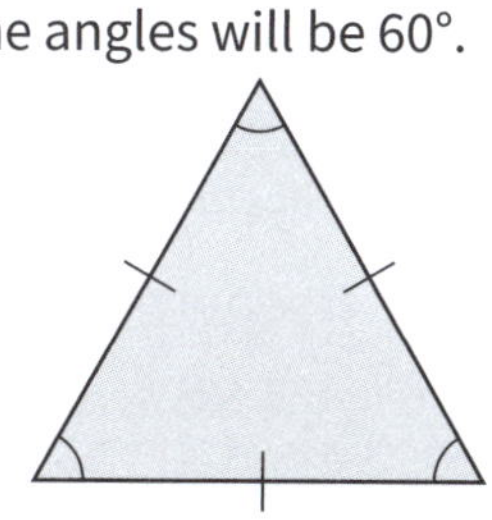	*What kind of triangle must it be?* *What do we use to draw it accurately?*	

Fluency questions

8.1.1 Line symmetry

1 The dashed line is a line of symmetry for three of these four shapes.
Circle the shape for which the dashed line is **not** a line of symmetry.

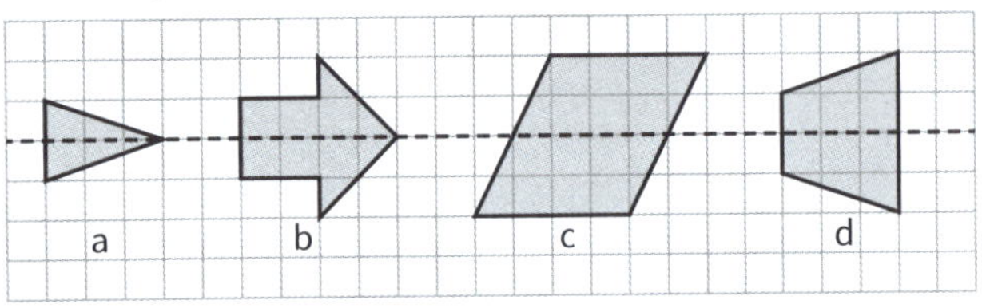

2 Complete these polygons so that each dashed line is a line of symmetry.

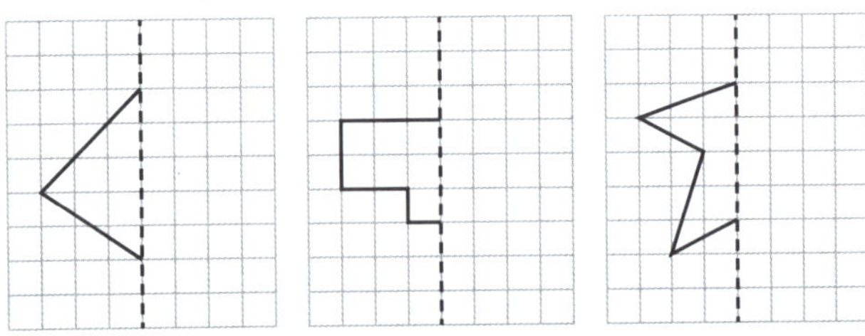

3 Draw all the lines of symmetry on each of these three shapes.

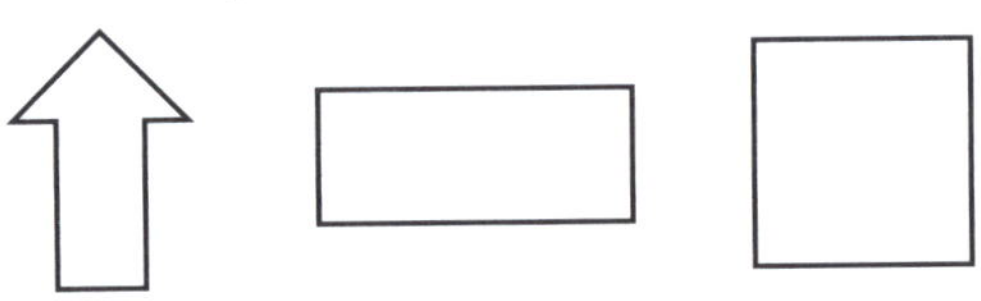

8.1.2 Rotational symmetry

1 The diagram shows a sign, with a dot marked at the top.
Sasha rotates it once through one third of a full turn.
The sign appears the same when it is rotated.

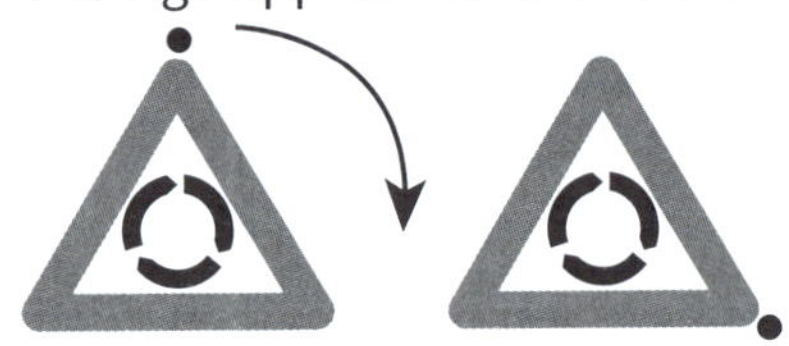

a) In how many ways can Sasha rotate the sign so that it matches the original sign?

b) What is the order of rotational symmetry of this sign?

c) How many lines of symmetry does this sign have?

2 Which of these shapes has **no** rotational symmetry?

3 Three of these shapes have rotational symmetry of order 2.
Which shape does **not** have rotational symmetry of order 2?

8.2 Angle properties

Example-problem pairs

8.2.1 Angles around a point

Worked example 1	Thinking	Your turn! 1
Work out the missing angle, x, in this pie chart. 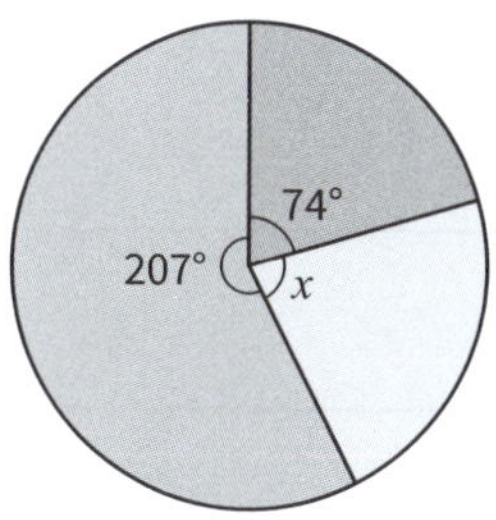 	*What number must the three angles add up to?*	Work out the missing angle, x, in this pie chart. 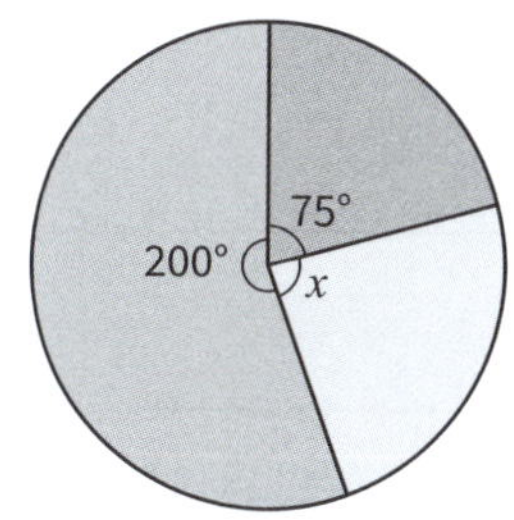
Using the fact that the angles must add up to 360°: $x = 360° - (74° + 207°)$ $= 360° - 281°$ $= 79°$		

Worked example 2	Thinking	Your turn! 2
Find the size of the angles marked x and y. 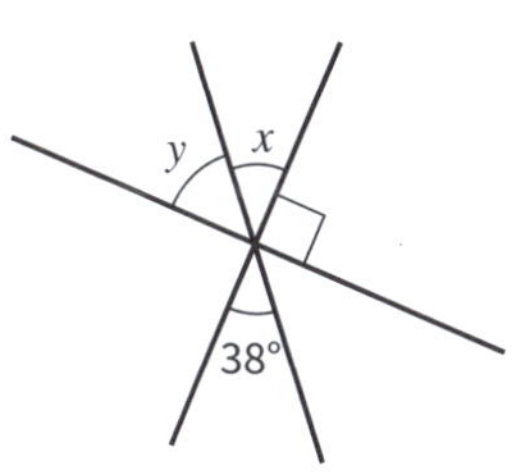 Give reasons for your answers.	*Can we find a pair of vertically opposite angles?*	Find the size of the angles marked x and y. 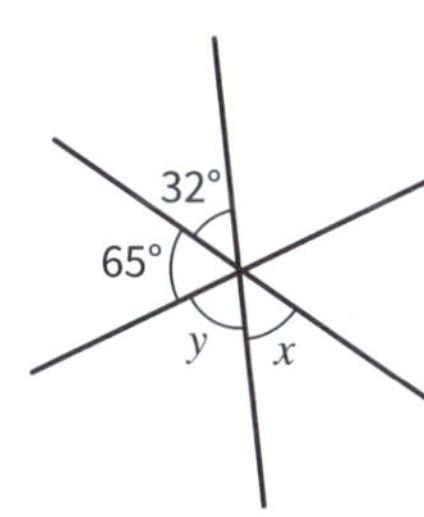 Give reasons for your answers.
$x = 38°$ because vertically opposite angles are equal.	*What do we know about vertically opposite angles?*	
$y = 180° - (90° + 38°)$ $= 280° - 128°$ $= 52°$ Because angles on a straight line add up to 180°,	*What do we know about the angles around a point on a straight line?* *What does the square on an angle mean?*	

Worked example 3	Thinking	Your turn! 3
Work out the value of x. 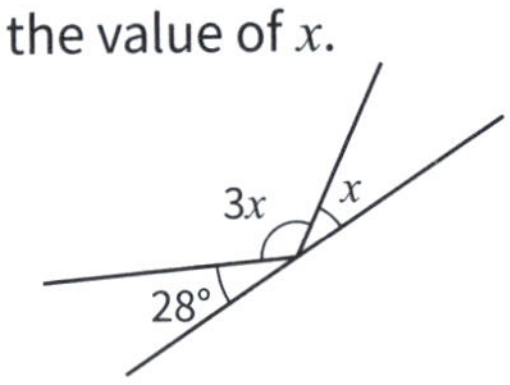 Give reasons for your answers.	*What angle fact can we use here to write an equation?*	Work out the value of x. 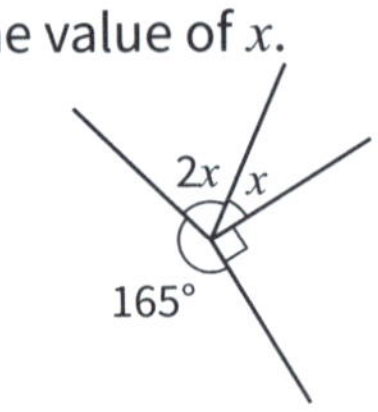 Give reasons for your answers.
$28° + 3x + x = 180°$ because angles on a straight line add up to 180°	*How do we simplify our equation?*	
Simplify equation: $28° + 4x = 180°$	*What operations do we need to apply to both sides of the equation?*	
$4x = 152°$ $x = 38°$		

8.2.2 Parallel lines and corresponding angles

Worked example 1	Thinking	Your turn! 1
Write the angle that corresponds to $\angle EGA$. 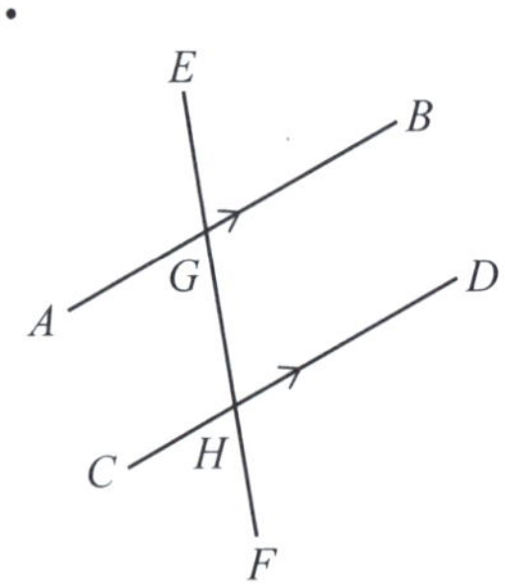 	*What is the definition of corresponding angles?*	**Write the angle that corresponds to $\angle CHF$.** 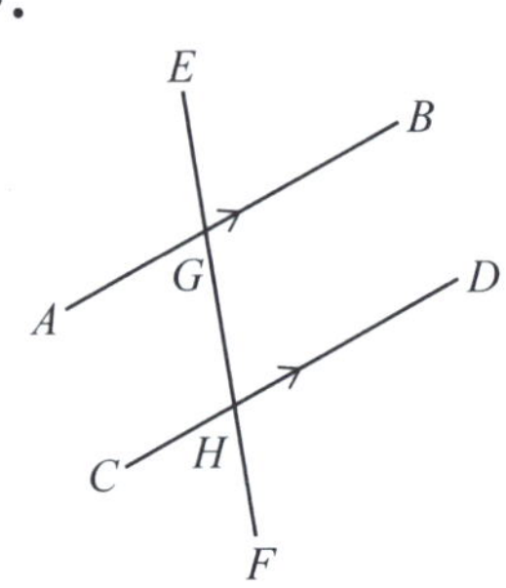
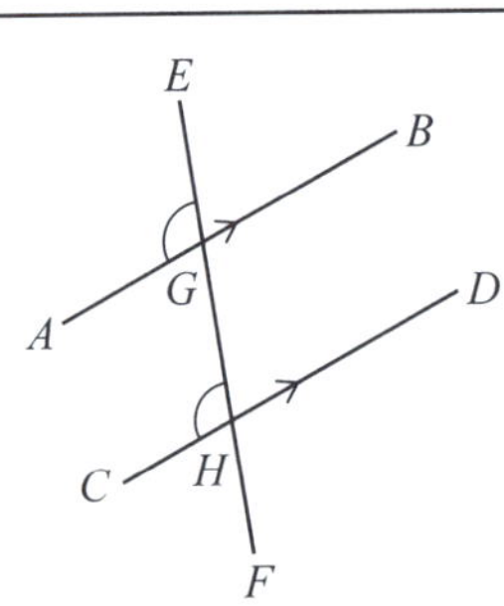 $\angle EHC$ corresponds to $\angle EGA$.		

Worked example 2	Thinking	Your turn! 2
Write the angle that corresponds to $\angle DHE$. 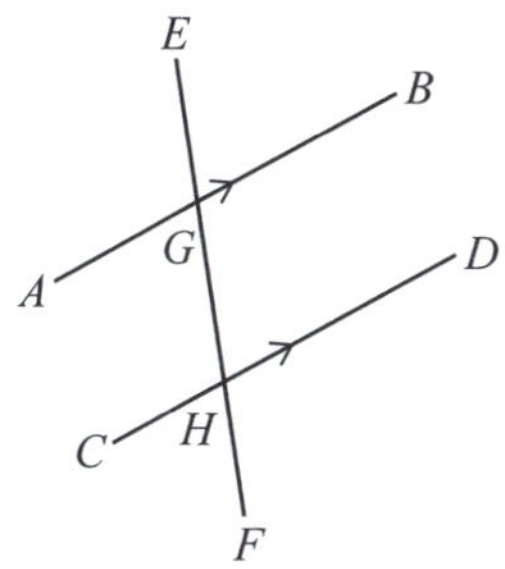	*What is the definition of corresponding angles?*	**Write the angle that corresponds to $\angle FGB$.** 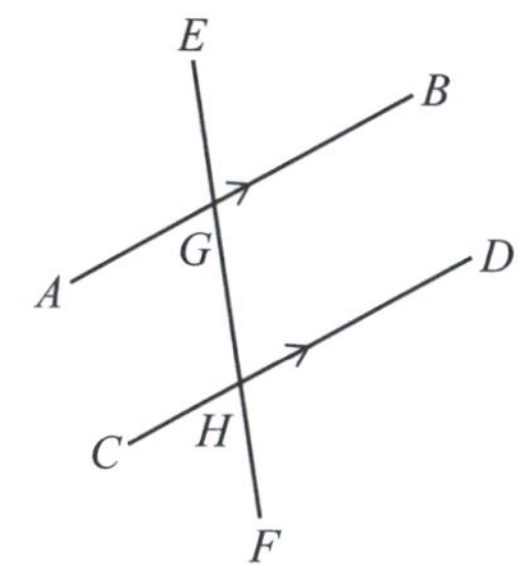
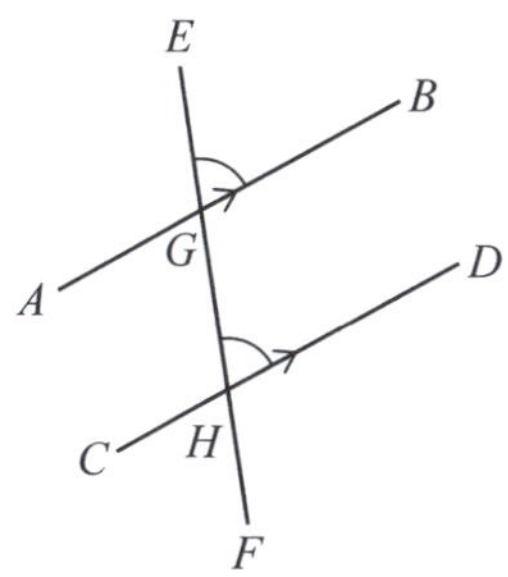 $\angle BGE$ corresponds to $\angle DHE$.		

Worked example 3	Thinking	Your turn! 3
Find the size of angles x and y. **Give reasons for your answers.** 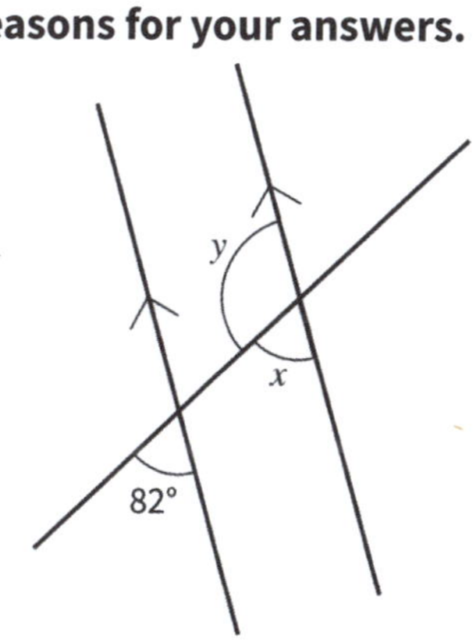	*Can we find a pair of corresponding angles?*	**Find the size of angles x and y.** **Give reasons for your answers.** 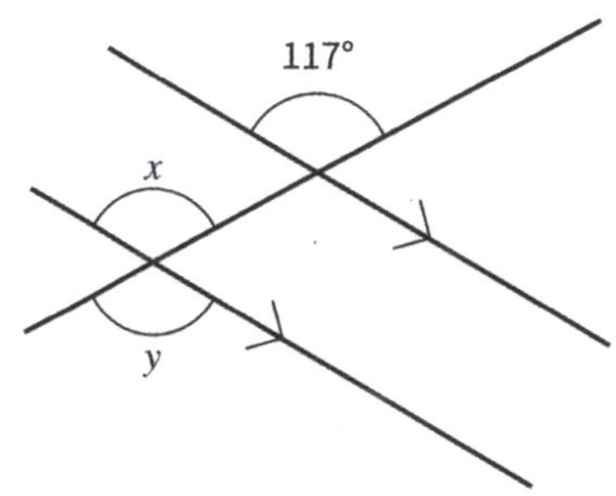
x corresponds to the 82° angle because they are both below the transversal and on the left of the parallel line.	*What do we know about corresponding angles on parallel lines?*	
$x = 82°$ since corresponding angles on parallel lines are equal.	*What other angle rules do we know that may be helpful here to find y?*	
$y = 180° - 82°$ $= 98°$ because angles on a straight line add up to 180°.		

Worked example 4	Thinking	Your turn! 4
Are lines AB and CD parallel? Explain your answer. 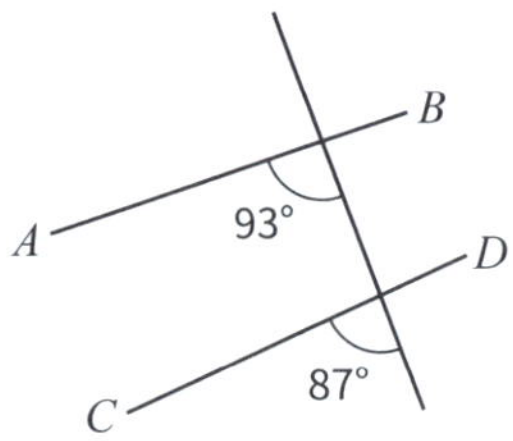	*Can we identify corresponding angles in the diagram?*	**Are lines AB and CD parallel? Explain your answer.** 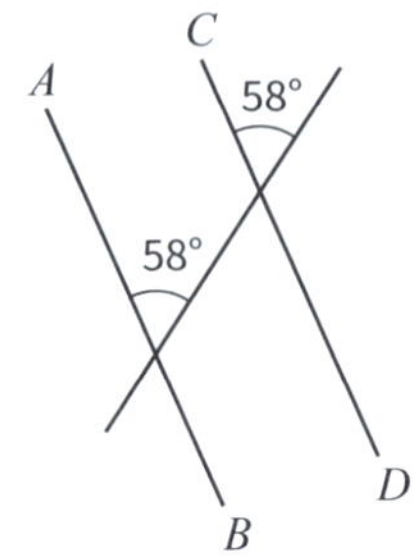
The two labelled angles are in corresponding positions.	*What do the corresponding angles tell us about the lines AB and CD?*	
Therefore the lines AB and CD are not parallel since the corresponding angles are not equal.		

Worked example 5	Thinking	Your turn! 5
Find the size of $\angle BAD$. Give reasons for your answer. 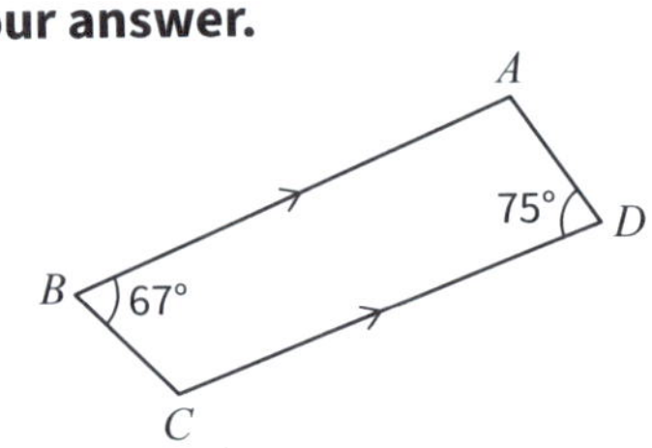	*Can we extend one of the sides to help us find corresponding angles?*	**Find the size of $\angle CBA$. Give reasons for your answer.** 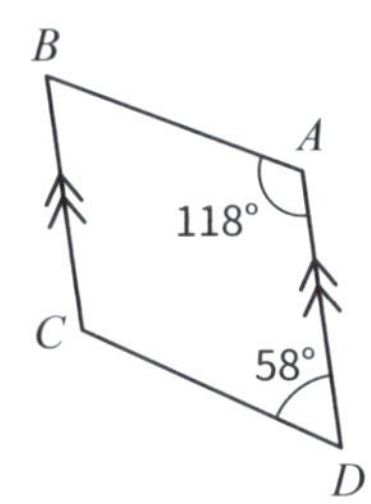
Extend side AD to the point E. 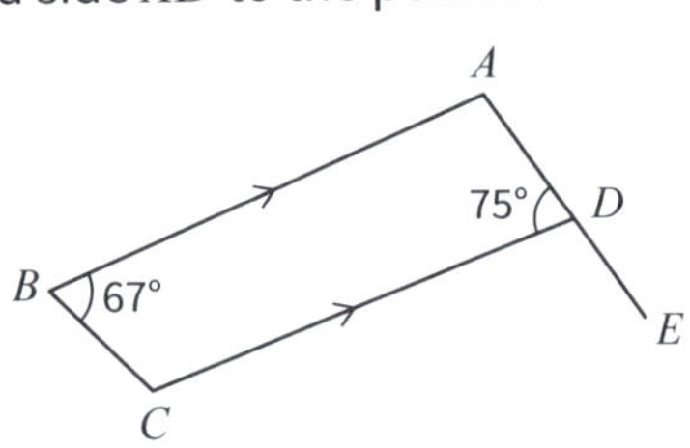	*How can we work out the new angle formed?*	
$\angle CDE = 180° - 75°$ $= 105°$ because angles on a straight line add up to 180°.		
$\angle BAD = 105°$ because it corresponds to the angle of 105° labelled and corresponding angles on parallel lines are equal.	*Can we find a pair of corresponding angles now?*	

8.2.3 Parallel lines and alternate angles

Worked example 1	**Thinking**	**Your turn! 1**
Write the angle that is alternate to $\angle FGA$. 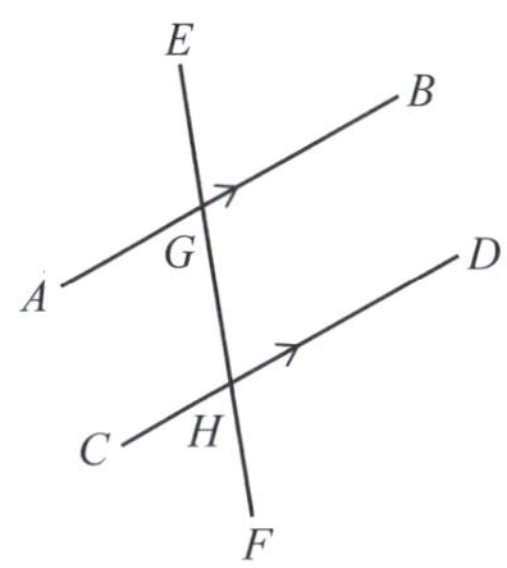	*What does alternate angles mean?*	**Write the angle that is alternate to $\angle BGF$.** 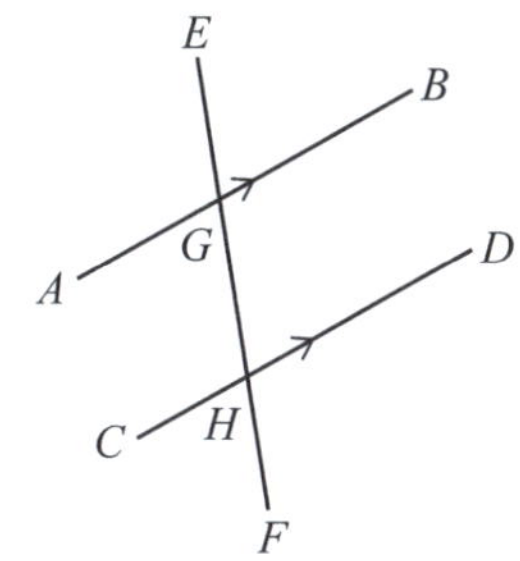
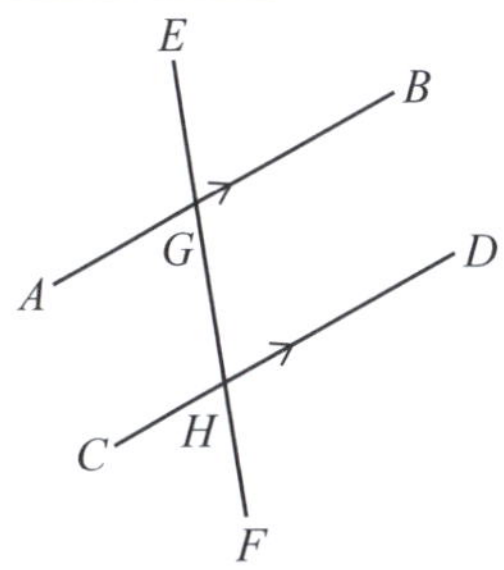 $\angle DHE$ is alternate to $\angle FGA$.		

Worked example 2	**Thinking**	**Your turn! 2**
Find the size of angles x and y. Give reasons for your answers. 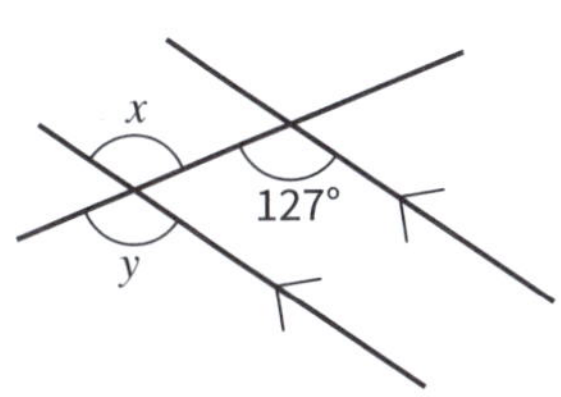	*Can we find a pair of alternate angles?*	**Find the size of angles x and y. Give reasons for your answers.** 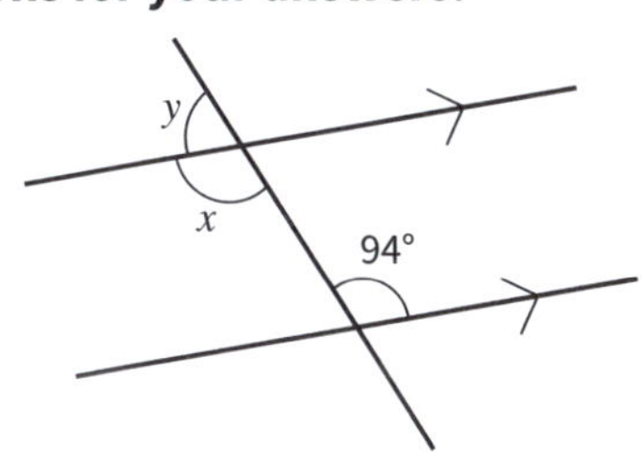
x is alternate to the 127° angle because they are between the parallel lines and on the opposite sides of the transversal.	*What do we know about alternate angles between parallel lines?*	
$x = 127°$ because alternate angles between parallel lines are equal.	*What other angle rules do we know that we can use to find y?*	
$y = 127°$ because vertically opposite angles are equal. Or since corresponding angles on parallel lines are equal.		

Worked example 3	Thinking	Your turn! 3
Find the size of $\angle ACB$. Give reasons for your answer. 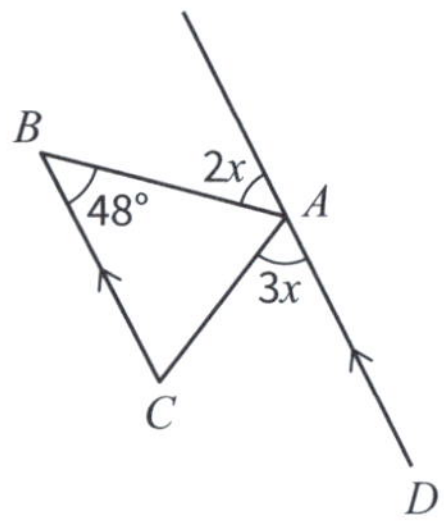	*Can we find any pairs of alternate angles?*	**Find the size of $\angle BCE$. Give reasons for your answer.** 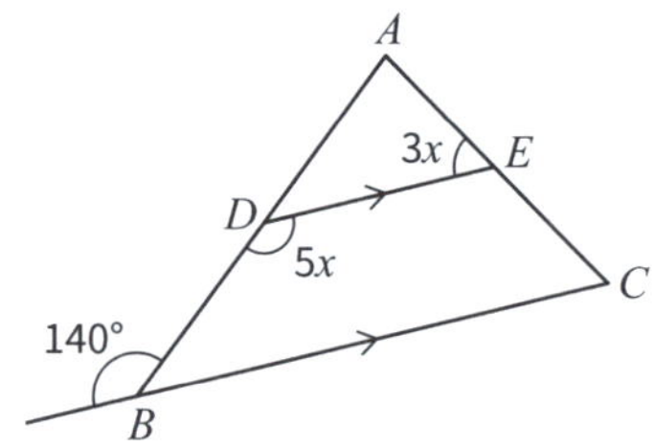
$2x = 48°$ because alternate angles between parallel lines are equal.		
So $x = 24°$.		
$\angle ACB = 3x$ since alternate angles between parallel lines are equal.	*How can we use the value of x to find $\angle ACB$?*	
$\angle ACB = 3 \times 24 = 72°$		

Worked example 4	Thinking	Your turn! 4
Are lines AB and CD parallel? Explain your answer. 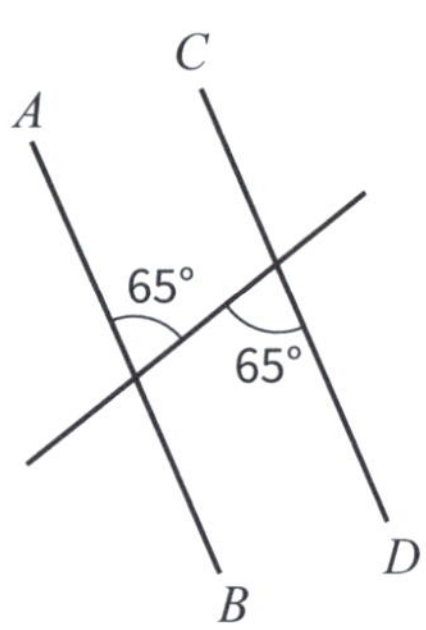	*Can we identify alternate angles in the diagram?*	**Are lines AB and CD parallel? Explain your answer.** 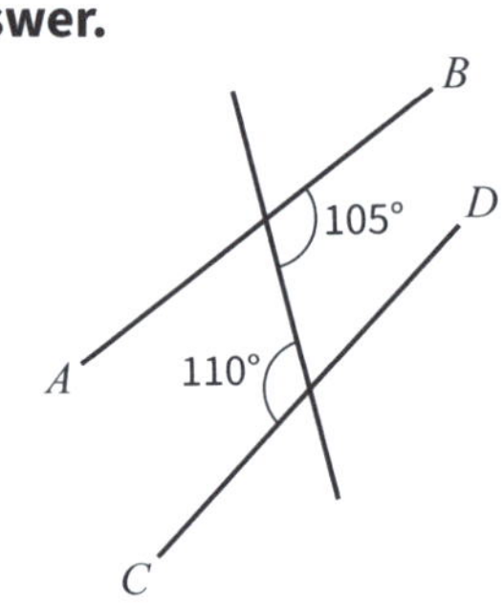
The lines AB and CD are parallel because the alternate angles are equal.	*Are the alternate angles equal?*	

Fluency questions

8.2.1 Angles around a point

1 Complete the sentences.

a) The angles in a full turn around a point add up to ______°

b) The angles at a point on a straight line add up to ______°

2 Work out the missing angles in theses pie charts.

a)

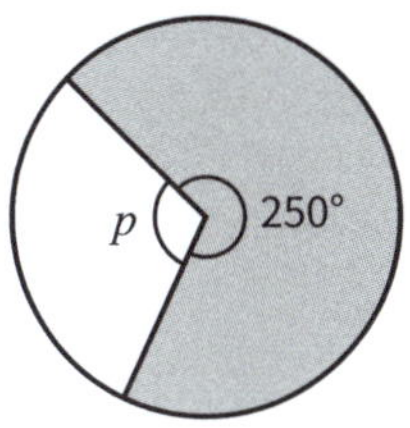

b)

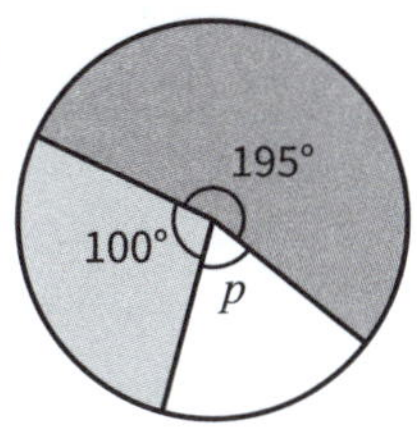

3 Work out the missing angles in these diagrams.

a)

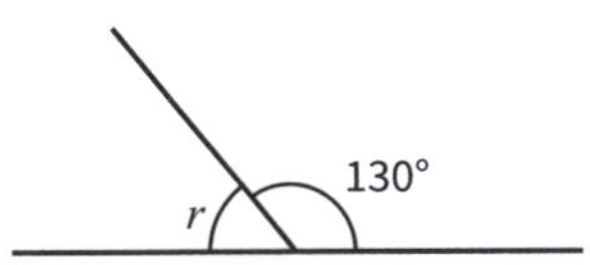

b)

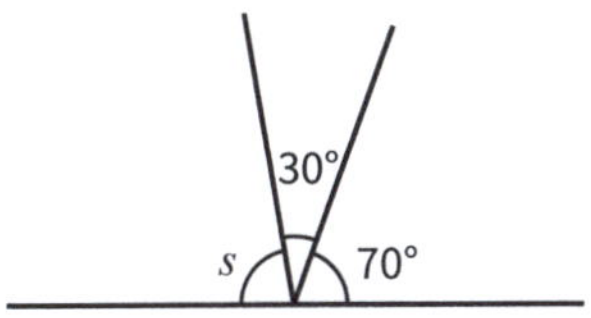

8.2.2 Parallel lines and corresponding angles

1 Which diagrams show a pair of corresponding angles?

a

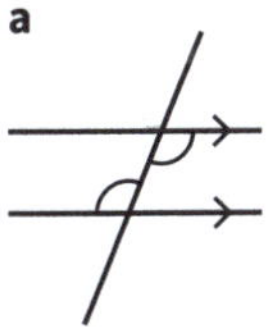

b

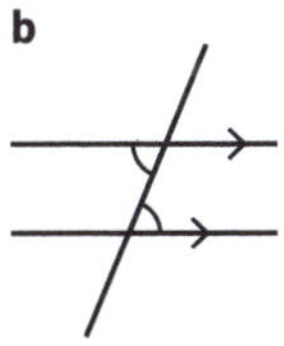

c

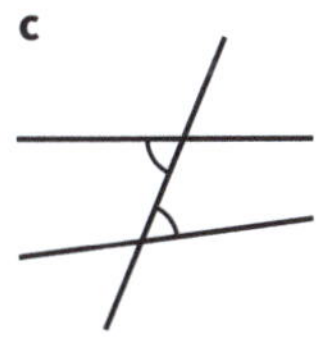

d

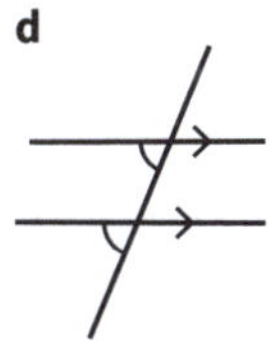

2 Which of angles p and q is corresponding to the 92° angle shown in this diagram? Give a reason for your answer.

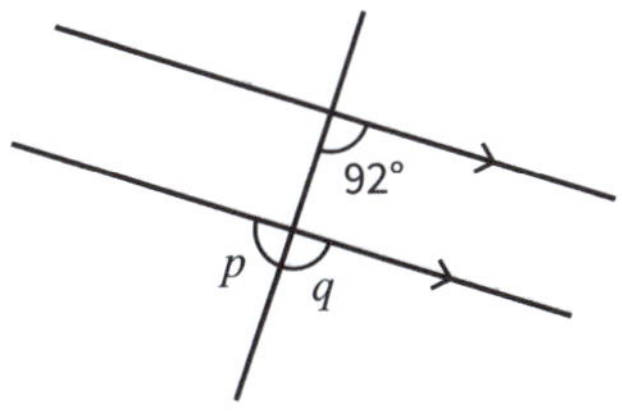

3 Write the value of x in each of these diagrams. Give a reason for each answer.

a)

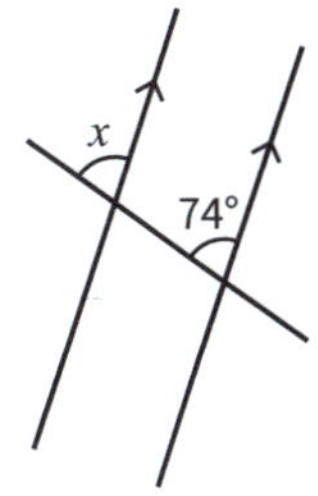

b)

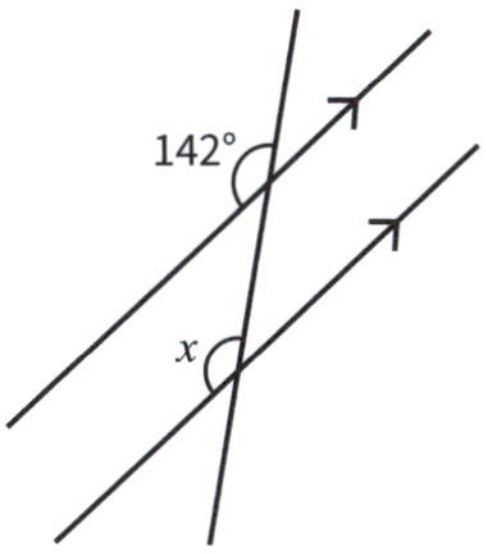

8.2.3 Parallel lines and alternate angles

1 Which diagrams show a pair of corresponding angles?

a

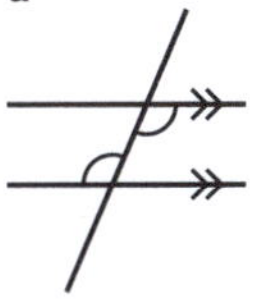

b

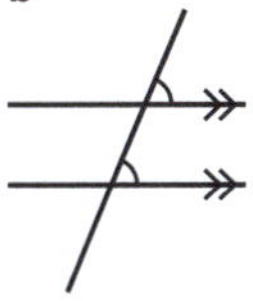

c

d

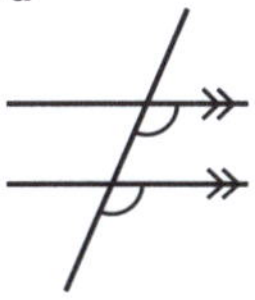

2 Which of angles a and b is alternate to the 93° angle shown in this diagram? Give a reason for your answer.

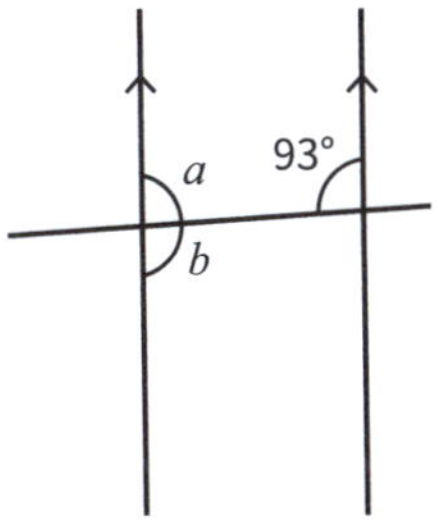

3 Write the value of x in each of these diagrams. Give a reason for each answer.

a)

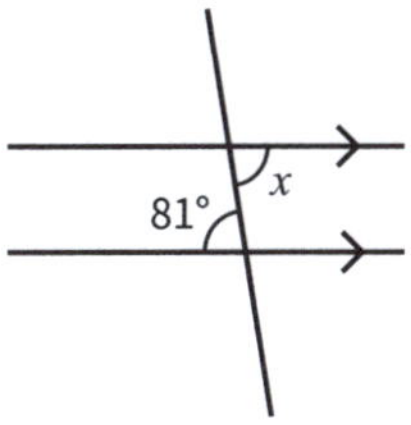

b)

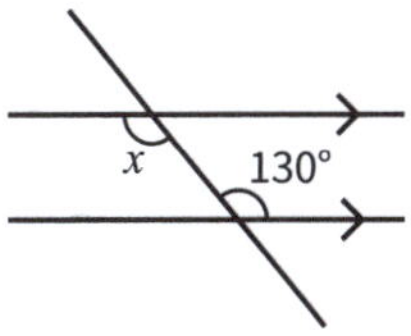

8.3 Angle properties of polygons

Example-problem pairs

8.3.1 Angles in triangles

Worked example 1	**Thinking**	**Your turn! 1**
Find the size of angles x and y. 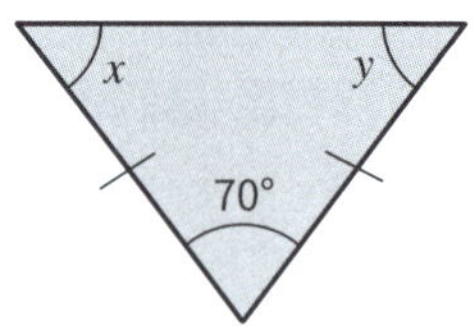	*What kind of triangle is this?* *Which angles are equal in the triangle?* *What fact about the angles in a triangle can we use?*	**Find the size of angles x and y.** 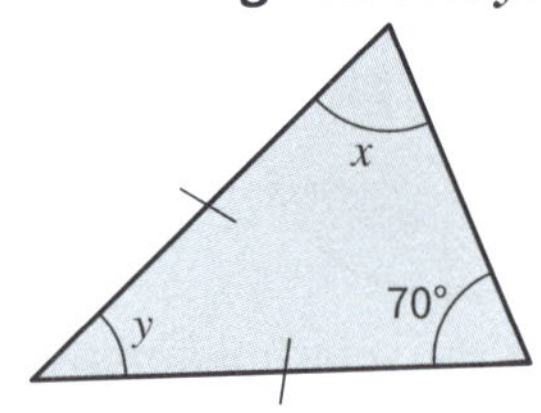
$x = y$		
$2x + 70° = 180°$ $2x = 110°$ $x = 55°$ $y = 55°$		

Worked example 2	**Thinking**	**Your turn! 2**
Find the size of $\angle ACB$. 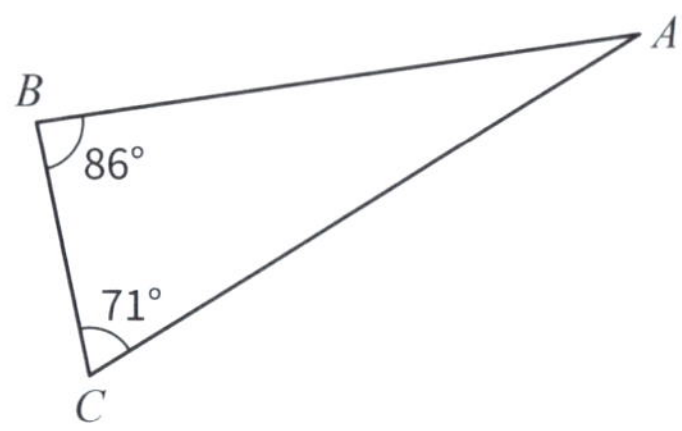	*What do we know about angles in triangles that can help us here?*	**Find the size of $\angle CBA$.** 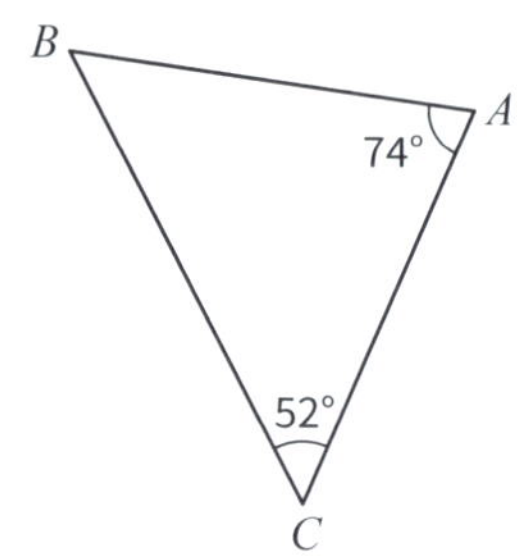
Using the fact that the angles must add up to 180°: $\angle ACB = 180° - (86° + 71°)$ $= 180° - 157° = 23°$		

Worked example 3	Thinking	Your turn! 3
Find the value of x. 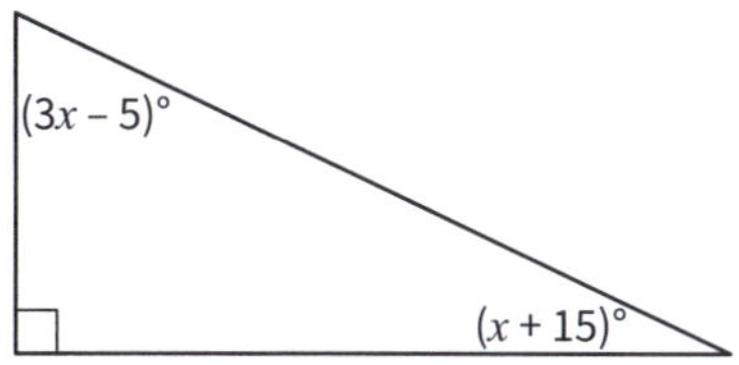	*What fact about the angles in a triangle can we use?*	**Find the value of x.** 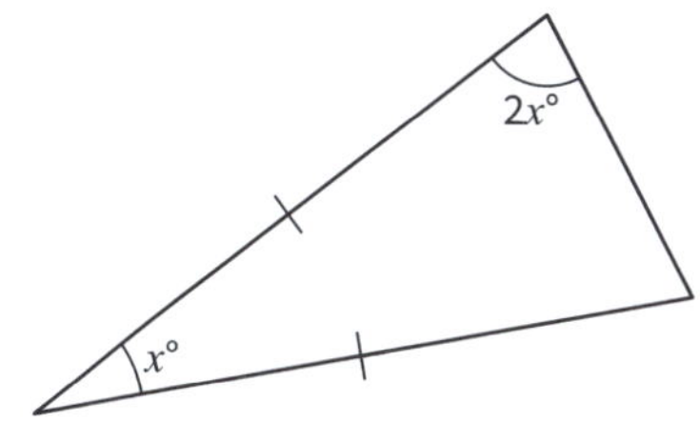
$90° + (3x - 5)° + (x + 15)° = 180°$ because interior angles on a triangle add up to 180°.	*How can we simplify the equation?*	
$100° + 4x = 180°$		
$4x = 80°$ $x = 20°$		

8.3.2 Interior angles of polygons

Worked example 1	Thinking	Your turn! 1
Find the sum of the interior angles of any heptagon. 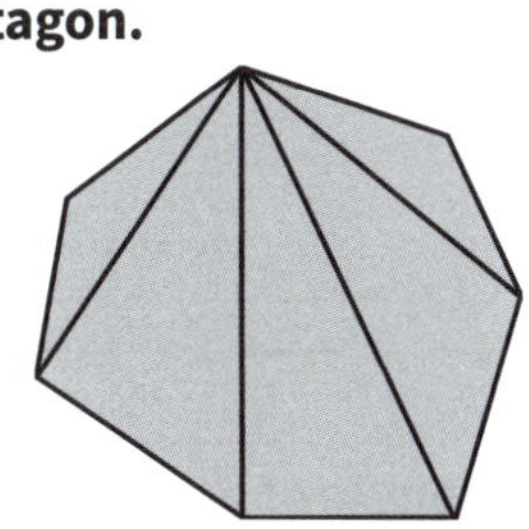	*How many sides does the shape have? How can we split the shape into triangles?* *How many triangles are there?*	**Find the sum of the interior angles of any hexagon.** 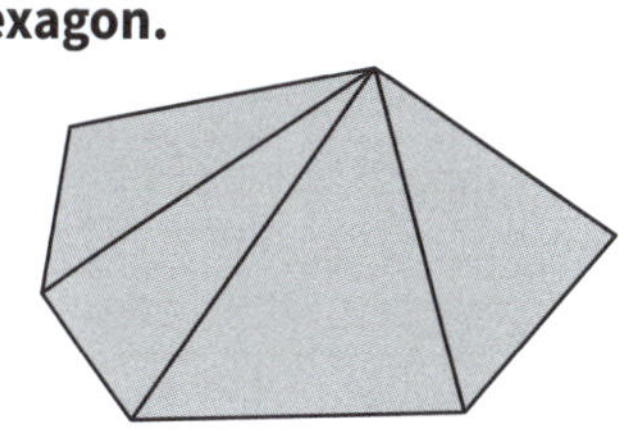
There are 5 triangles inside the heptagon, and the sum of the angles in each is 180°.	*What is the sum of the angles in each of the triangles?*	
Interior angles of heptagon $= 5 \times 180° = 900°$		

Worked example 2	Thinking	Your turn! 2
$ABCDE$ is a regular pentagon. Use the diagram to prove that the interior angle of a regular pentagon is 108°. 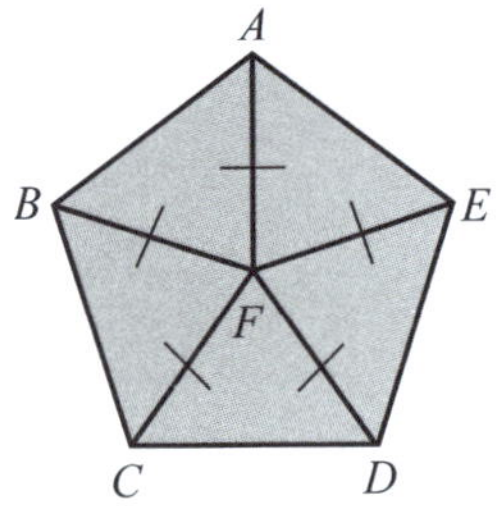	*How can we find one of the angles at the centre?*	**$ABCDEFGH$ is a regular octagon. Use the diagram to prove that the interior angle of a regular octagon is 135°.** 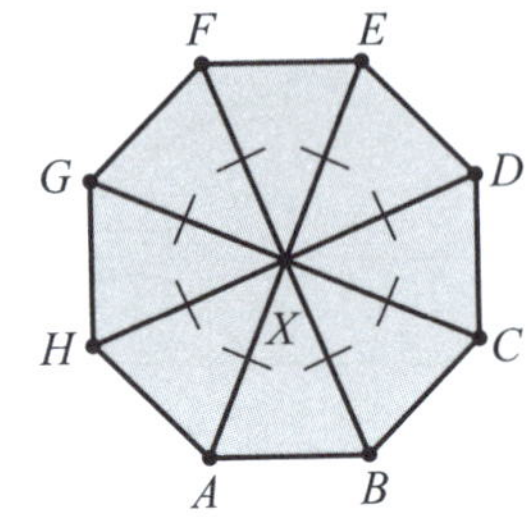
Look at the triangle ABF. $\angle AFB = 360 \div 5 = 72°$, because angles around a point add up to 360°.	*How can we use the fact that the triangles are isosceles?*	
$\angle FBA = \angle BAF$, because base angles of an isosceles triangle are equal. $2\angle FBA + 72° = 180°$ because angles in a triangle add up to 180°. $2\angle FBA = 108°$ $\angle FBA = 54°$ $\angle CBA = 2 \times 54$ $= 108°$ The interior angle is 108°. 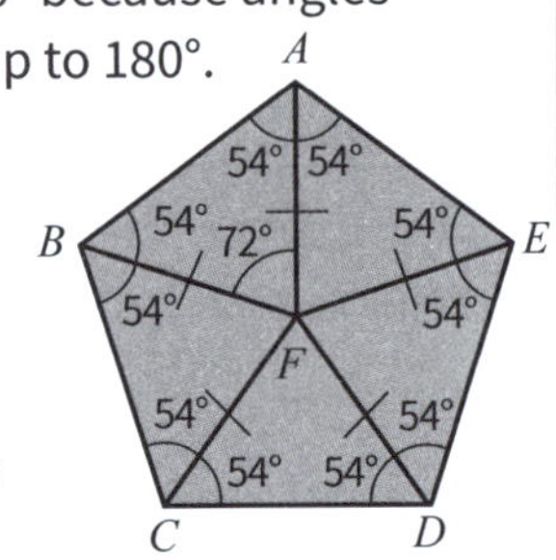	*What does this tell us about the interior angles of the polygon?*	

Worked example 3	Thinking	Your turn! 3
The interior angle of an n-sided regular polygon is 150°. Work out the value of n.	*Imagine splitting the polygon into n isosceles triangles.*	**The interior angle of an n-sided regular polygon is 162°. Work out the value of n.**
The polygon will split into n isosceles triangles. The base angles of each triangle are half of the interior angle of the polygon. So base angle $= 150 \div 2 = 75°$. 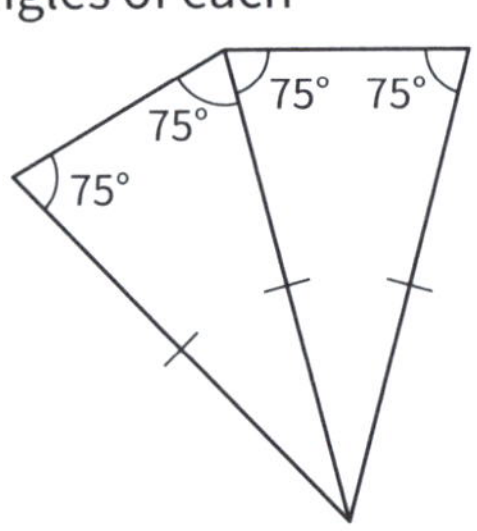	*How can we use the information in the question to work out the base angles of these triangles?*	
Angles in each triangle add up to 180°. Angle at centre of polygon $= 180° - (75° + 75°) = 180° - 150° = 30°$	*How can we work out the angle at the centre of the polygon?*	
$30n = 360$ because angles around a point add up to 360°. So $n = 360° \div 30° = 12$. The regular polygon has 12 sides.	*What do we know about the angles at the centre point of the polygon?*	

8.3.3 Exterior angles of polygons

Worked example 1	Thinking	Your turn! 1
The diagram shows a regular octagon with interior angle x and exterior angle y. The sum of the interior angles is 1080°. 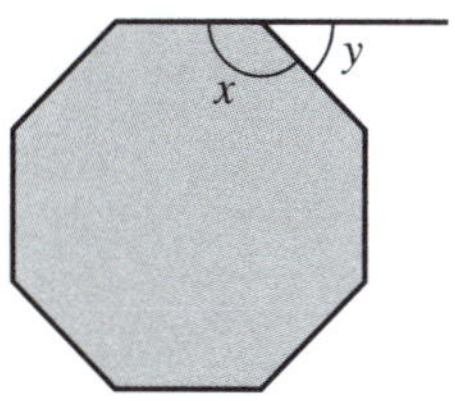 **a) Find the size of angles x and y.** **b) Prove that the sum of the exterior angles is 360°.**	How can we use the fact that the polygon is regular?	**The diagram shows a regular pentagon with interior angle x and exterior angle y. The sum of the interior angles is 540°.** 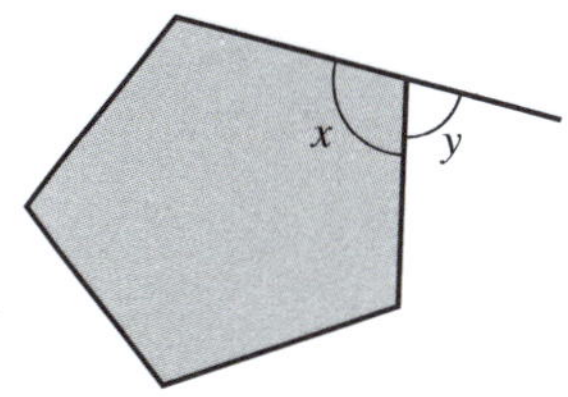 **a) Find the size of angles x and y.** **b) Prove that the sum of the exterior angles is 360°.**
a) $x = 1080° \div 8 = 135°$		
$y = 180° - x$ because sum of interior and exterior angles is 180°. $y = 180° - 135° = 45°$	*What do we know about a pair of adjacent interior and exterior angles?*	
b) Sum of exterior angles of regular octagon $= 8 \times 45° = 360°$	*How can we use this to find the sum of all the exterior angles?*	

Worked example 2	Thinking	Your turn! 2
The diagram shows a regular octagon with interior angle x and exterior angle y. Prove that the sum of the interior angles is 1080°. 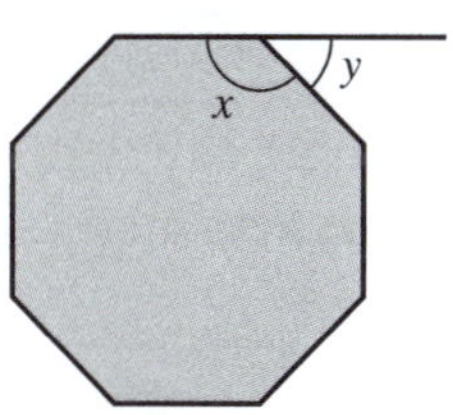	*Can we divide up the shape into smaller ones we know the angle sum for?*	**The diagram shows a regular pentagon with interior angle x and exterior angle y. Prove that the sum of the interior angles is 540°.** 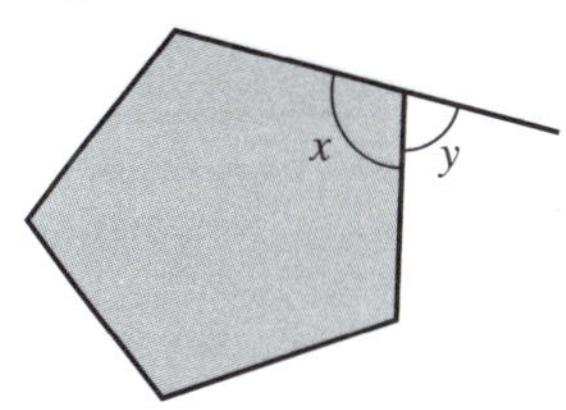
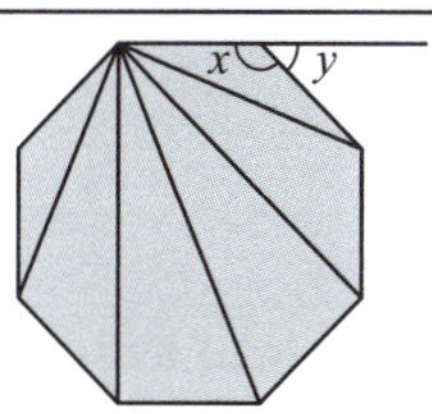	*What do we know about the angles in these triangles?*	
There are 6 triangles and each has an angle sum of 180°. Sum of interior angles of octagon $= 6 \times 180° = 1080°$	*How can this help us find the sum of the interior angles in the polygon?*	

Worked example 3	Thinking	Your turn! 3
Find the size of angle x. 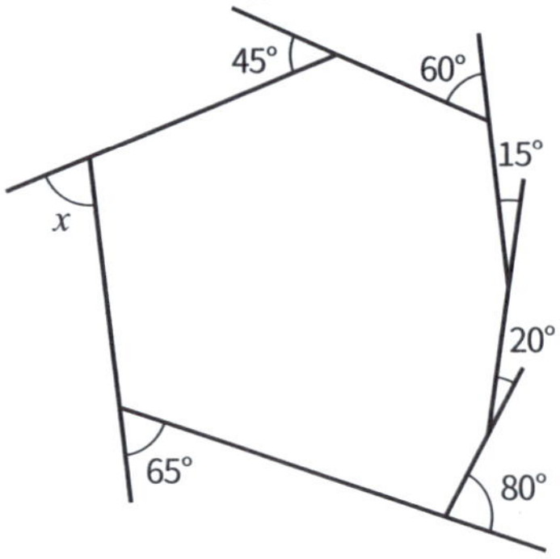	*What kind of angles have we been given?*	**Find the size of angle x.** 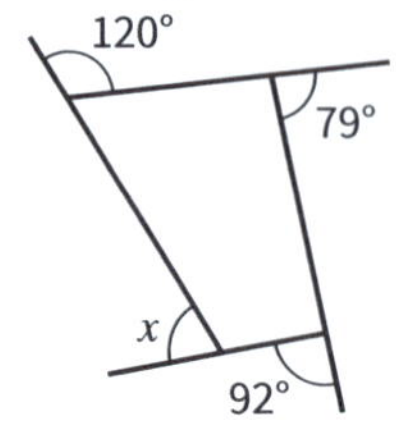
The exterior angles must add up to 360°. $x = 360° - (45° + 60° + 15° + 20° + 80° + 65°)$ $= 360° - 285° = 75°$		

Worked example 4	Thinking	Your turn! 4
a) Find the size of an exterior angle of a regular octagon. **b) Use your answer to part a to find the size of the interior angle of a regular octagon.**	*What does 'regular' tell us about the angles?*	**a) Find the size of the exterior angle of a regular pentagon.** **b) Use your answer to part a to find the size of the interior angle of a regular pentagon.**
a) All the exterior angles are equal in regular polygons. Exterior angle = 360° ÷ 8 = 45° as the sum of exterior angles of a polygon is 360°.	*What do we know about the exterior angles of polygons?*	
b) Interior angle = 180° − 45° = 135° because the sum of interior and exterior angles is 180°.		

Worked example 5	Thinking	Your turn! 5
The exterior angle of a regular polygon is 9°. Work out how many sides the polygon has.	*What do we know about exterior angles of a polygon?*	**The exterior angle of a regular polygon is 20°. Work out how many sides the polygon has.**
360° ÷ 9° = 40 So the polygon has 40 sides because the sum of the exterior angles is 360°.		

Worked example 6	Thinking	Your turn! 6
The interior angle of a regular polygon is 156°. Work out how many sides the polygon has.	*How does the interior angle relate to the exterior angle?*	**The interior angle of a regular polygon is 150°. Work out how many sides the polygon has.**
Exterior angle = 180° − 156° = 24° because the sum of an interior and exterior angle is 180°.	*What do we know about exterior angles of a polygon?*	
360° ÷ 24° = 15 So the polygon has 15 sides because the sum of the exterior angles is 360°.		

Fluency questions

8.3.1 Angles in triangles

1 What do the interior angles of a triangle add up to?

2 Fill in the blanks.

a) 40° + 80° + ______ = 180°

b) 90° + 55° + ______ = 180°

3 **a)** Fill in the blank: 37° + 85° + ______ = 180°

b) Here is a triangle. Write down the size of the angle marked x.

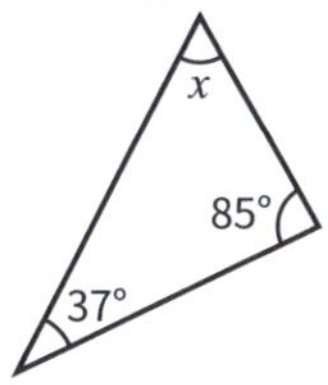

4 Work out the size of the angle marked x in this triangle.

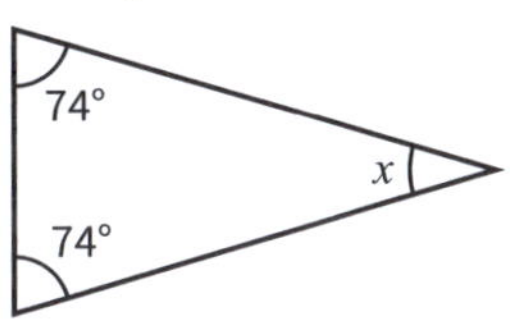

8.3.2 Interior angles of polygons

1 Here is a quadrilateral divided into two triangles.

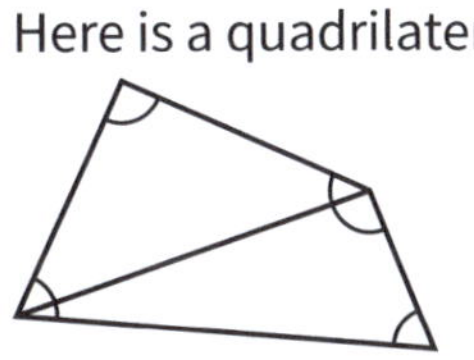

a) What do the interior angles of a triangle add up to?

b) What do the interior angles of a quadrilateral add up to?

2 Here is an octagon divided into six triangles. Use your knowledge of triangles to work out the sum of the interior angles of an octagon.

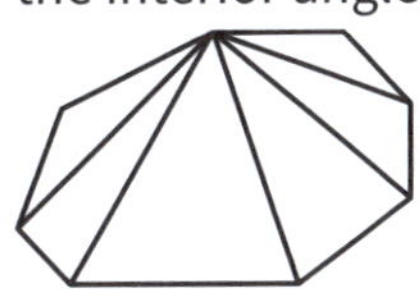

3 Here is a nonagon divided into seven triangles. Use your knowledge of triangles to work out the sum of the interior angles of a nonagon.

8.3.3 Exterior angles of polygons

1 What do the exterior angles of a polygon add up to?

2 Fill in the blanks.

a) 130° + 150° + ______ = 360°

b) 90° + 90° + 140° + ______ = 360°

3 Fill in the blank:

100° + 60° + 75° + 40° + ______ = 360°

Here is a pentagon, with its exterior angles shown.

Work out down the size of the angle marked x.

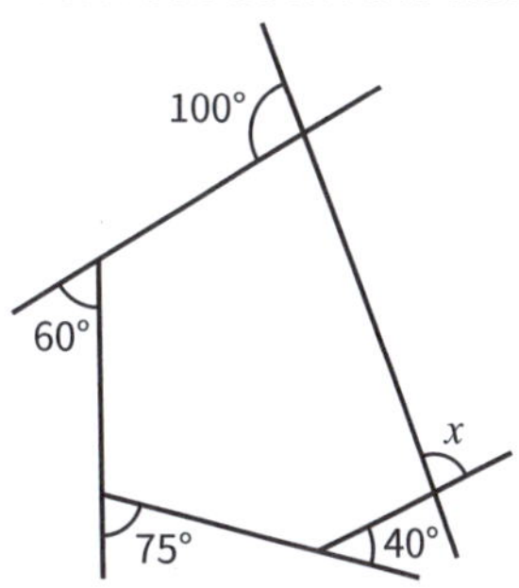

4 Here is a regular hexagon, with its exterior angles shown.

Work out the size of each exterior angle.

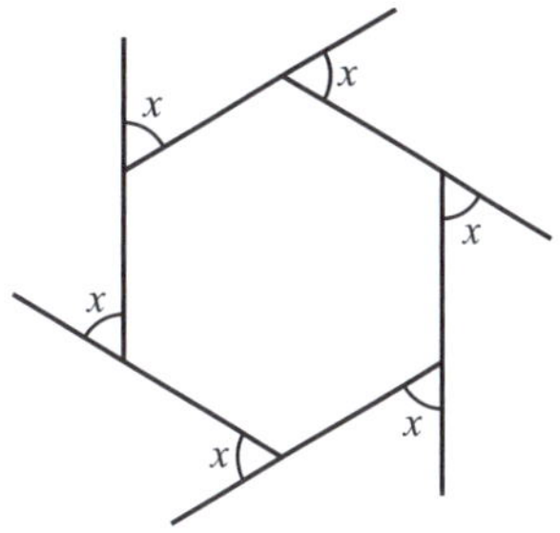

8 Polygons and angles

8.4 Problem-solving with angles

Example-problem pairs

8.4.1 Angle problems

Worked example 1	**Thinking**	**Your turn! 1**
The diagram shows a regular pentagon and a square. Find the size of the angle x, giving reasons for your answer. 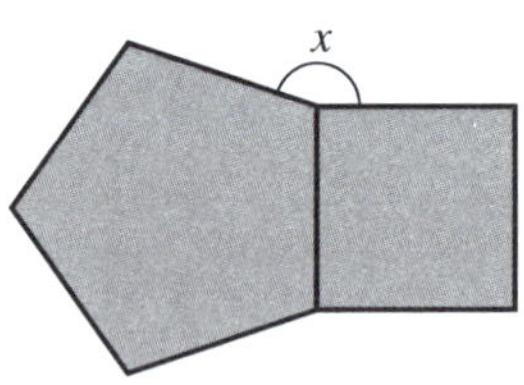	*What do we know about angles around a point?*	**The diagram shows a regular octagon and an equilateral triangle. Find the size of the angle x, giving reasons for your answer.** 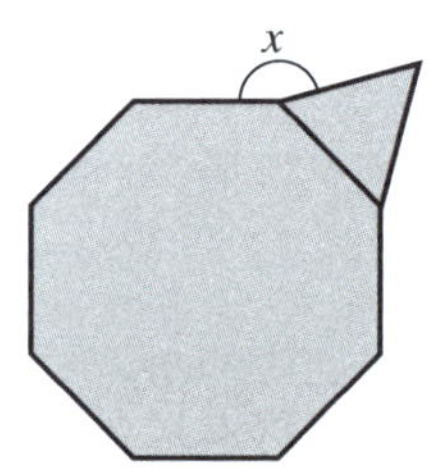
Interior angle of square = 90°	*What is the interior angle of the square?*	
Exterior angle of regular pentagon = 360 ÷ 5 = 72°, because exterior angles of a polygon add up to 360° and they are all equal for a regular polygon.	*What do we know about the exterior angles of a polygon?*	
Interior angle of regular pentagon = 180° − 72° = 108°, because sum of interior and exterior angles is 180°.	*What do we know about pairs of interior and exterior angles that could help?*	
x = 360° − (108° + 90°) = 162° because angles around a point add up to 360°.		

Worked example 2	**Thinking**	**Your turn! 2**
Find the size of the angle x. Give reasons for your answer. 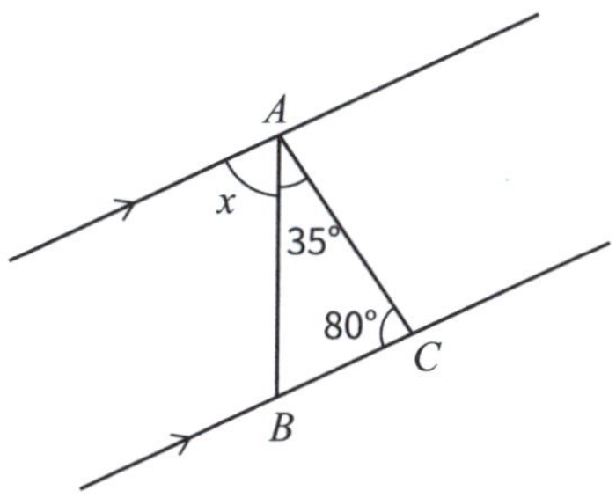	*Can we see an angle that is equal to x?*	**Find the size of the angle x. Give reasons for your answer.** 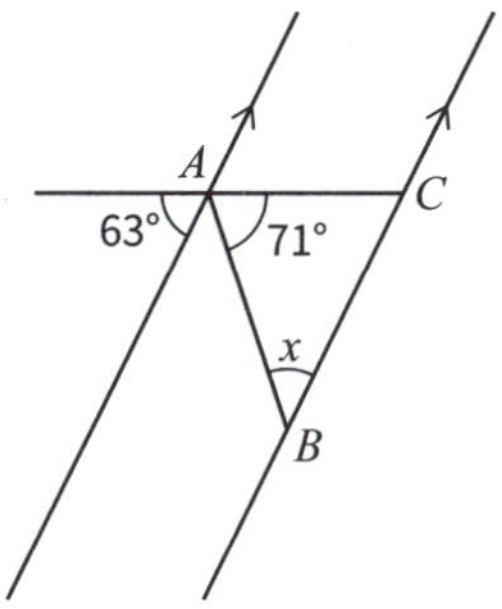
$\angle CBA$ $= 180° - (80° + 35°) = 65°$ because angles in a triangle add to 180°.	*What notation do we use to describe the angle?*	
$x = \angle CBA = 65°$ because alternate angles between parallel lines are equal.	*What angle fact are we using?*	

Worked example 3	**Thinking**	**Your turn! 3**
Find the size of the angle x. Give reasons for your answer. 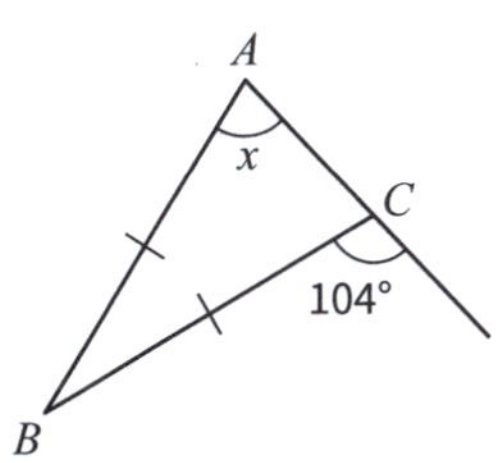	*What do we know about isosceles triangles?*	**Find the size of the angle x. Give reasons for your answer.** 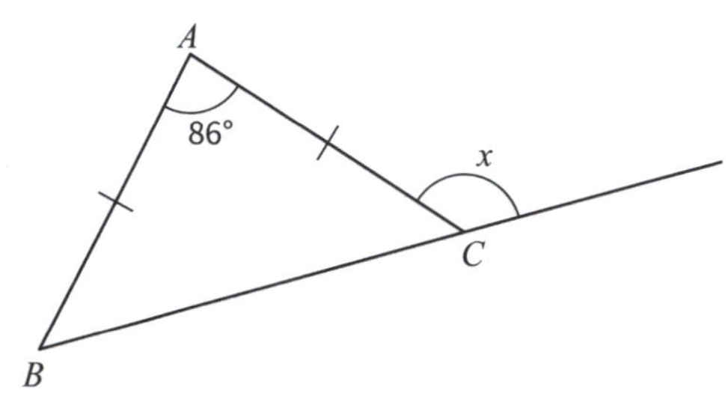
The base angles of isosceles triangles are equal, so $x = \angle BAC = \angle ACB$	*What notation do we use to describe the angle?*	
$x = \angle ACB = 180° - 104° = 76°$ because angles on a straight line add up to 180°. Therefore $x = 76°$.	*What angle fact are we using?*	

Worked example 4	Thinking	Your turn! 4
Find an expression for y in terms of x. Give reasons for your answer. 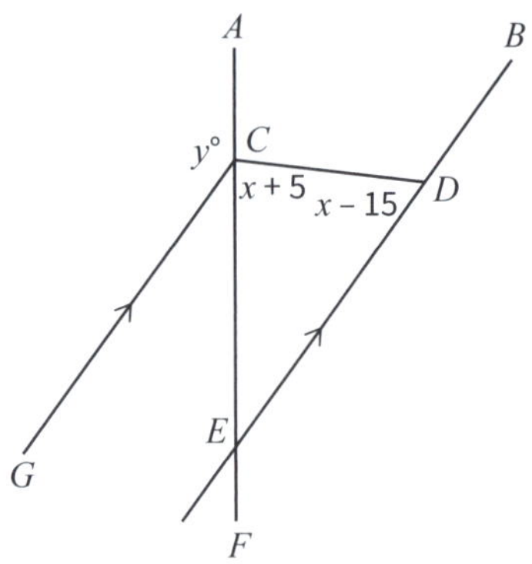	*Notice the parallel lines and the shape between them. What properties do you think we may need to use?*	**Find an expression for y in terms of x. Give reasons for your answer.** 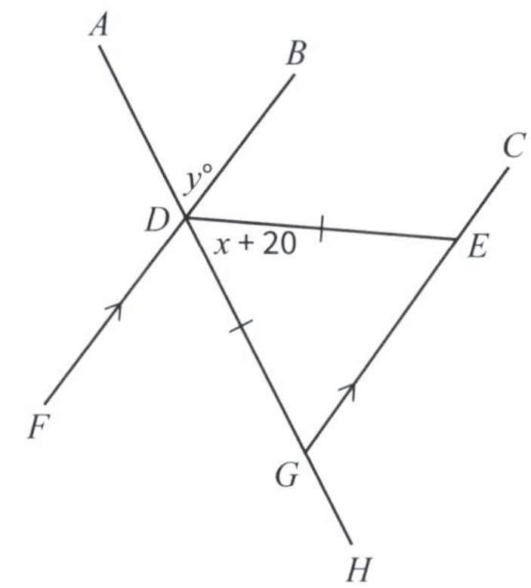
$\angle DEC + (x + 5)° + (x - 15)° = 180°$ because angles in a triangle add to 180°.	*What rule can we use to find the missing angle in the triangle?*	
$\angle DEC + 2x - 10° = 180°$ $\angle DEC = 180° - 2x + 10°$ $\angle DEC = 190° - 2x$	*How can we simplify this expression?*	
$\angle GCE = \angle DEC$ because alternate angles between parallel lines are equal So $\angle GCE = 190° - 2x$	*How can we use the parallel lines to find an angle?*	
$y = 180° - (190° - 2x)$ because angles on a straight line add up to 180°.	*How can we use this to find an expression for y?*	
$y = 180° - 190° + 2x$ $y = 2x - 10°$	*How can we simplify this?*	

Fluency questions

8.4.1 Angle problems

In each of these questions, when asked to give a reason for your answer, choose from one of the following.

- Angles around a point add up to 360°.
- Angles at a point on a straight line add up to 180°.
- Alternate angles between parallel lines are equal.
- The interior angles of a triangle add up to 180°.
- The interior angles of a quadrilateral add up to 360°.

1 a) Find the size of the angle marked x. Give a reason for your answer.

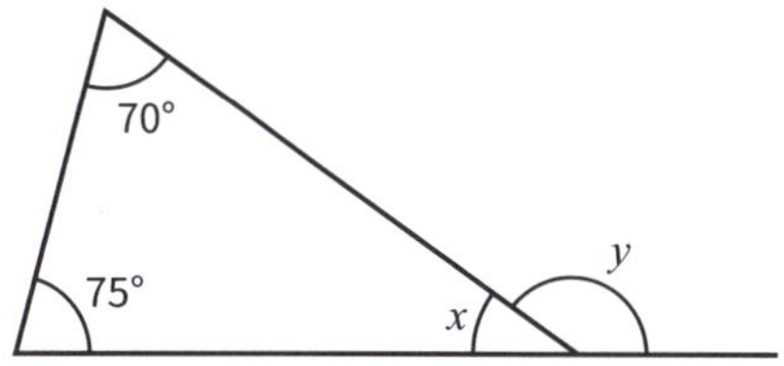

x = ________° – (75° + ________°) = ________°

because ____________________________________

b) Find the size of the angle marked y. Give a reason for your answer.

y = ________° – ________° = ________°

because ____________________________________.

2 Find the size of the angles marked x and y. Give a reason for each answer.

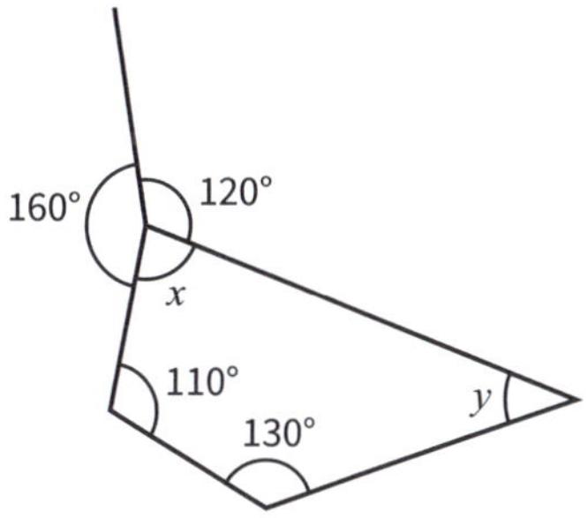

x = ________

y = ________

3 The diagram shows a trapezium and one of its exterior angles.

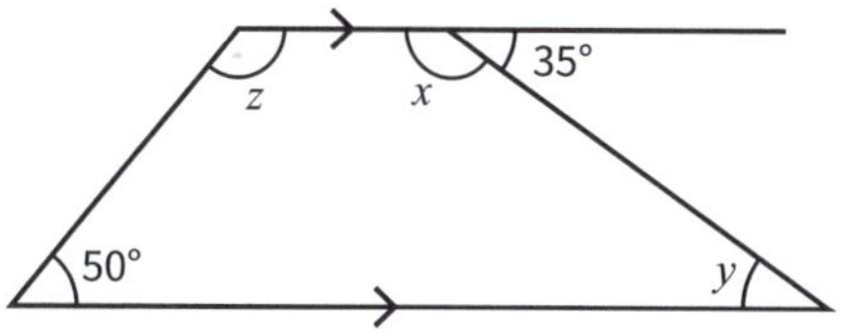

Find the size of the following angles. Give reasons for your answers

a) angle x

b) angle y

c) angle z.

9.1 Construction using circles

Example-problem pairs

9.1.1 Drawing circles

Worked example 1	Thinking	Your turn! 1
Use a pair of compasses to find the points that are 4 cm from A and 3 cm from B. 	*How do we find places 4 cm from A?*	**Use a pair of compasses to find the points that are 2 cm from C and 4.5 cm from D.** 
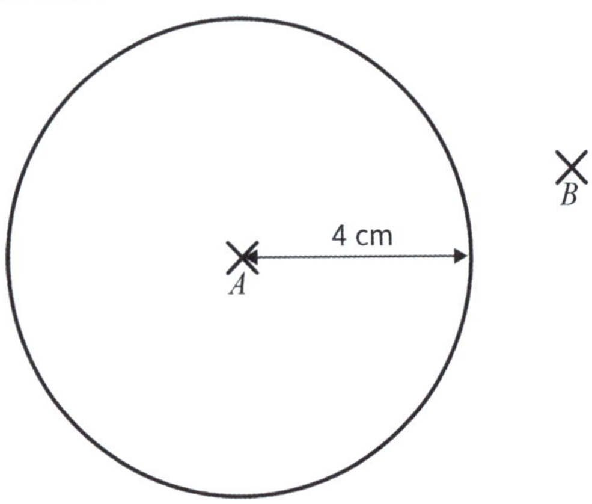	*How do we find places 3 cm from B?*	
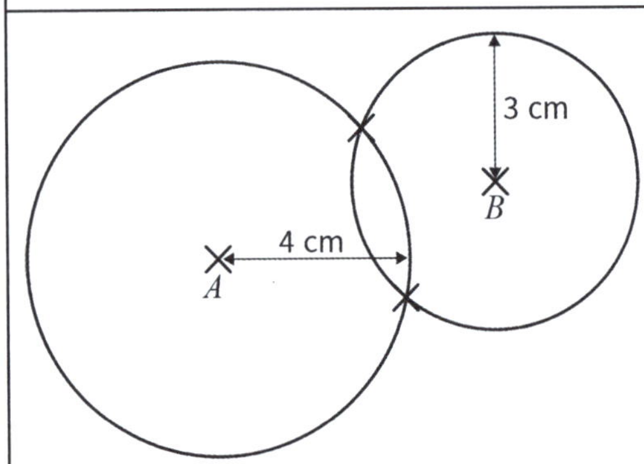	*How do we find the points that are both 4 cm from A and 3 cm from B?*	

Worked example 2	**Thinking**	**Your turn! 2**
Construct the locus of points 4 cm away from a point.	*What point do we mark first?*	**Construct the locus of points 3 cm away from a point.**
Mark the centre point on paper. ✕	*What is the radius of the circle?*	
Measure the compass distance to 4 cm. 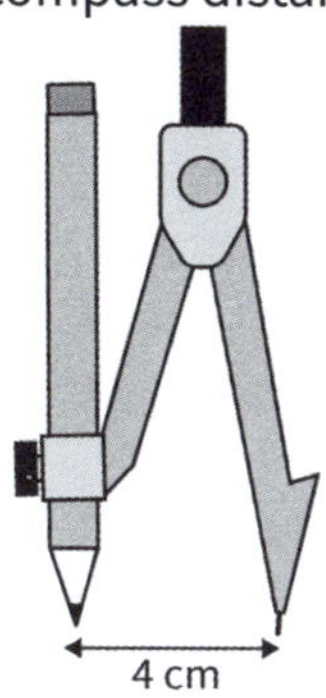	*How do we make sure the circle is accurate?*	
Place the pointed end of the compasses on the centre point and draw the circle. 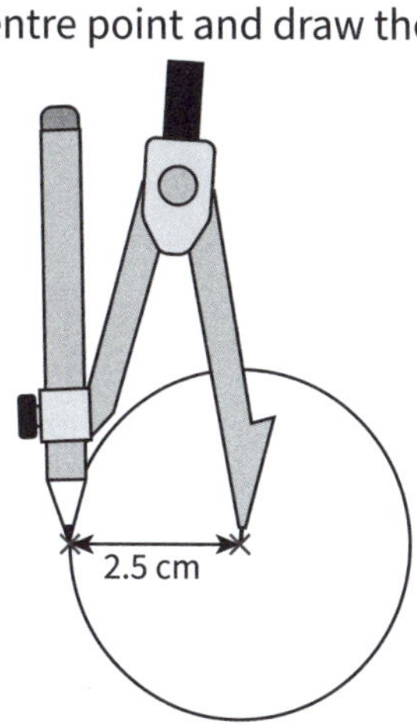		

Worked example 3	**Thinking**	**Your turn! 3**
Construct a circle with a diameter of 9 cm.	*What point do we mark first?*	**Construct a circle with a diameter of 7 cm.**
Mark the centre point on paper. ×	*What is the radius of the circle?*	
Measure the compass distance to 4.5 cm. 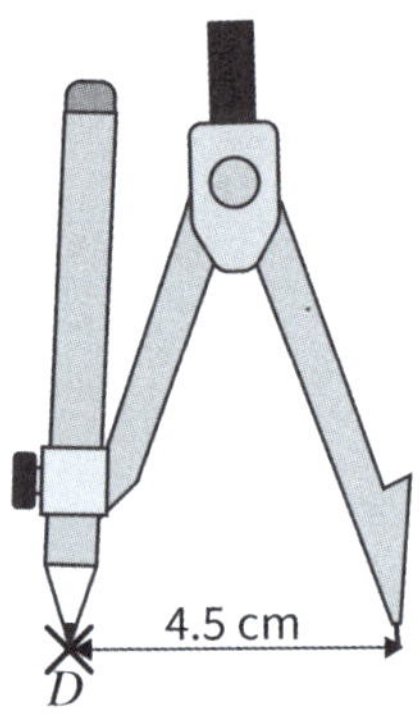 	*How do we make sure the circle is accurate?*	
Line up the pointed end of the compasses and draw the circle. 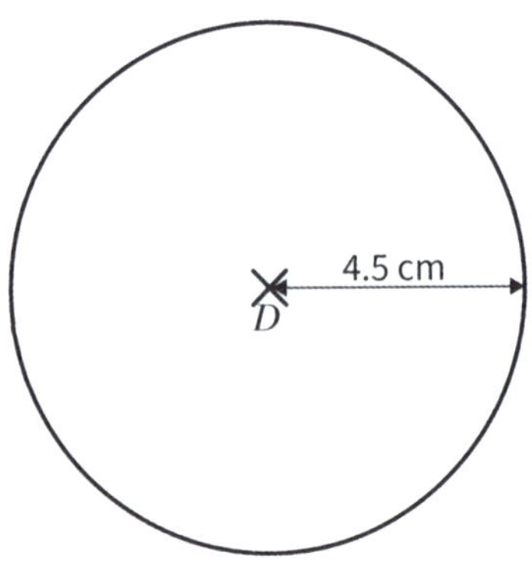 		

Worked example 4	Thinking	Your turn! 4
Use a pair of compasses to find the places that are 5 km from the school and 2 km from the shop using the scale 1 cm = 1 km. 	*How can we find the places that are the given distances from the school and the shop?*	**Use a pair of compasses to find the places that are 2 km from the school and 5 km from the shop using the scale 1 cm = 1 km.** 
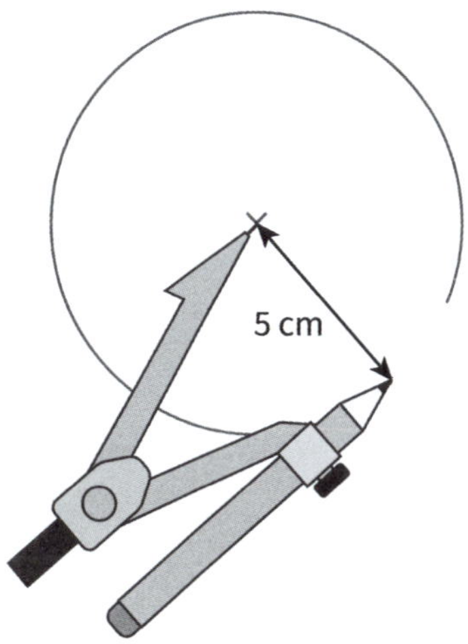	*What scale are we using? How many centimetres do we open the compasses to show the points 5 km from the school?*	
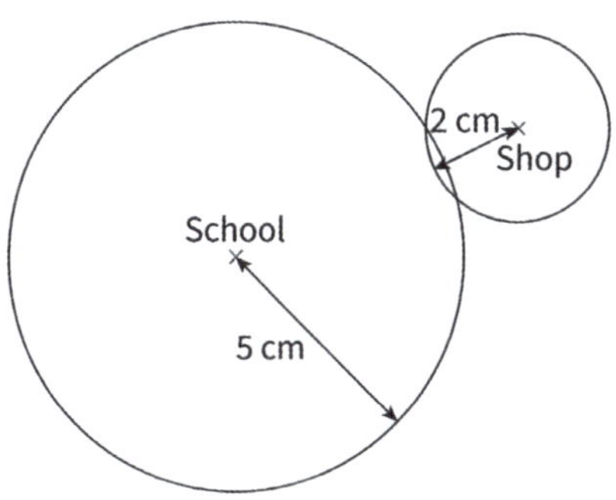	*How do we show the points 2 km from the shop?* *How do we identify the places required by the question? Is there more than one place?*	

Worked example 5	Thinking	Your turn! 5
The circle shown has radius 3 cm. Use a pair of compasses and ruler to find its centre. 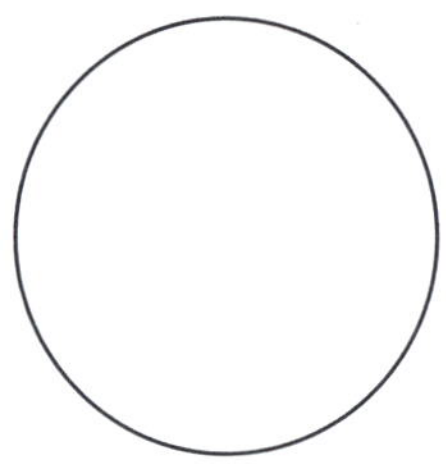	*What is the definition of a radius?*	**The circle shown has diameter 5 cm. Use a pair of compasses and ruler to find its centre.** 
Use a ruler and open the compasses to 3 cm.	*Where should we put the pointed end?*	
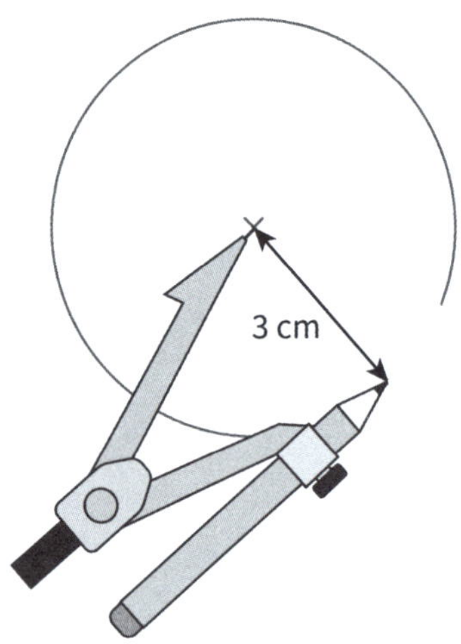	*How can we use the radius to find the centre of the circle?*	

9.1.2 Constructing triangles

Worked example 1	Thinking	Your turn! 1
Construct a triangle with side lengths 9 cm, 7 cm, and 5 cm.		**Construct a triangle with side lengths 5 cm, 7 cm, and 8 cm.**
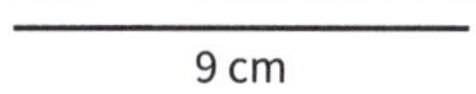	*How do we draw the first side of the triangle?*	
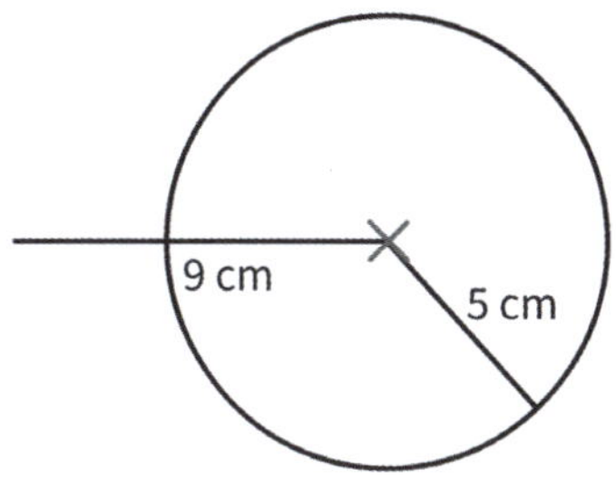	*How do we find all the points that are 5 cm away from one point?*	
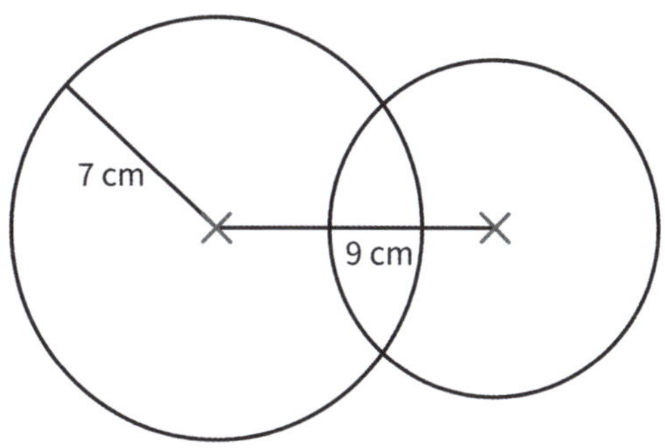	*How do we find all the points that are 7 cm away from the other end?*	
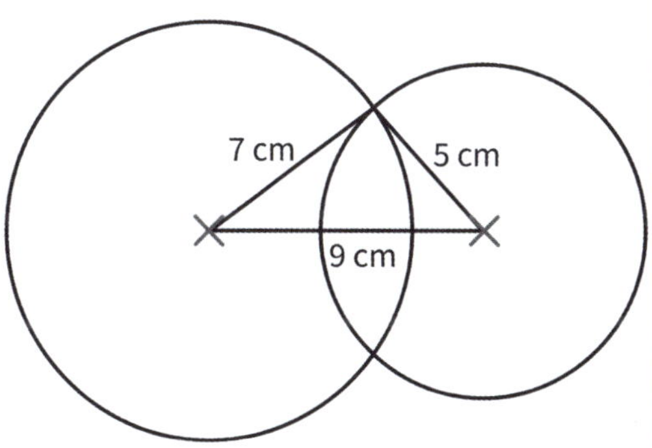	*How do we find the third vertex and complete the triangle?*	

Worked example 2	Thinking	Your turn! 2
Line AB is 6 cm long. The two other sides of triangle ABC are AC = 4 cm, and edge BC = 3 cm. Draw line AB and complete the construction of the triangle. 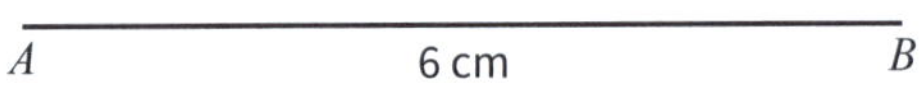	*How do we find all the points that are 3 cm away from one point?*	**Line PQ is 6 cm long. The two other sides of triangle PQR are QR = 8 cm, and edge PR = 8 cm. Draw line PQ and complete the construction of the triangle.** 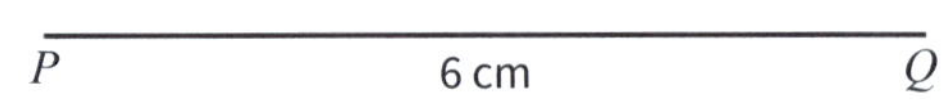
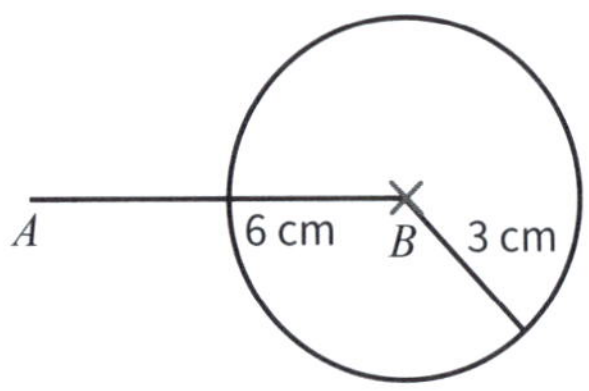		
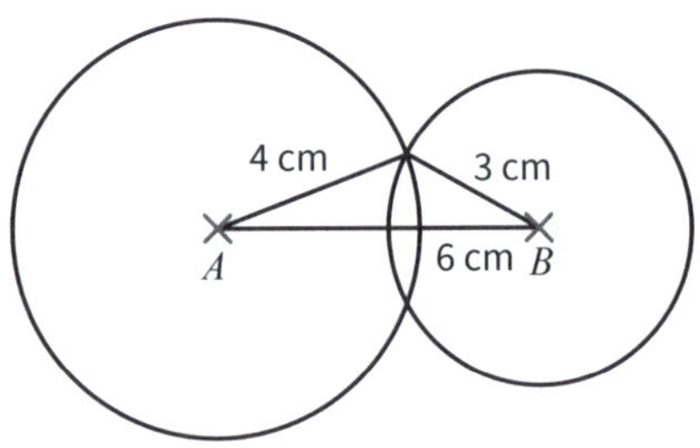	*How do we find the third vertex and complete the triangle?*	

9.1.3 Constructing rhombuses

Worked example 1	**Thinking**	**Your turn! 1**
Construct a rhombus with a diagonal of length 6 cm and sides of length 8 cm.		**Construct a rhombus with a diagonal of length 5 cm and sides of length 6 cm.**
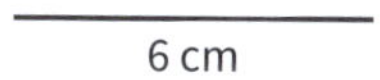	*Which line do we draw first?*	
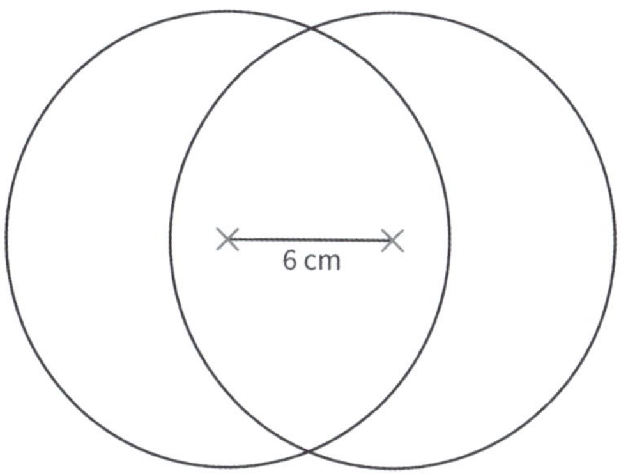	*How do we use the side length in our construction?*	
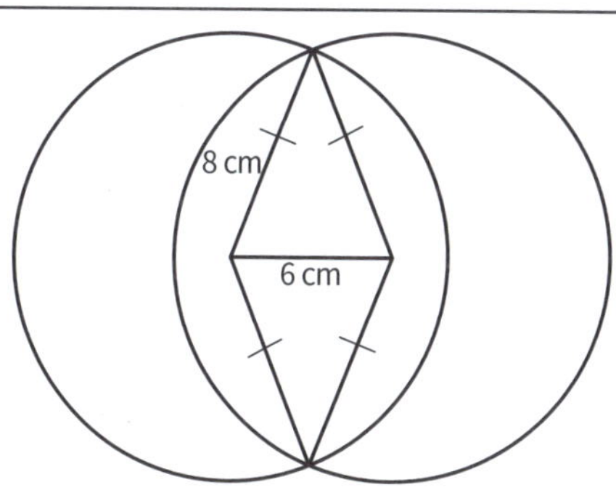	*Which points do we join to complete the rhombus?*	

Worked example 2	Thinking	Your turn! 2
An isosceles triangle has base length 3 cm and equal side lengths of 4 cm. Use a ruler and compasses to draw another triangle to make the shape into a rhombus. 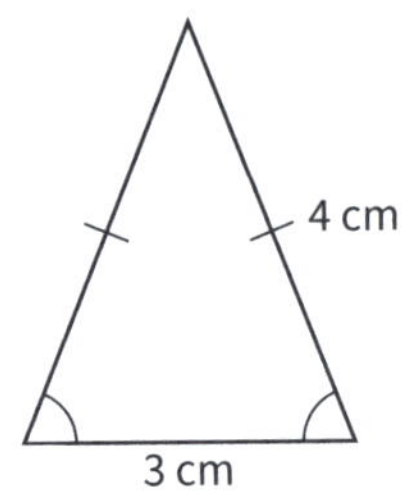	*How do we find all the points that are 4 cm away from one point?* *Which points do we join to complete the rhombus?*	**An isosceles triangle has base length 7 cm and equal side lengths of 5 cm. Use a ruler and compasses to draw another triangle to make the shape into a rhombus.** 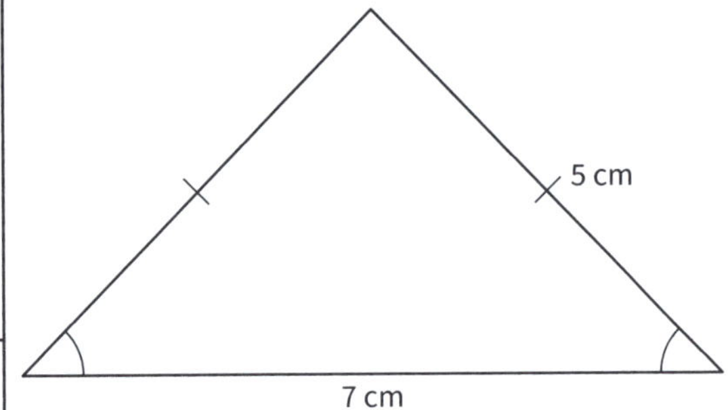
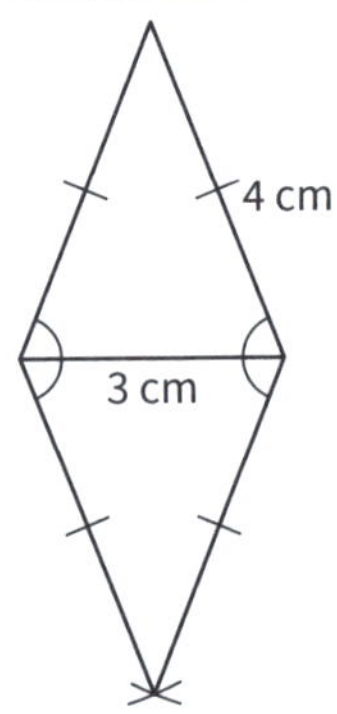		

Fluency questions
Constructions using circles
9.1.1 Drawing circles

1 Use a pair of compasses to draw all the points that are 3 cm from P.

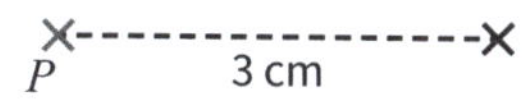

2 Use a pair of compasses to draw all the points that are 7 cm from Q.

3 Mark a point A. Using a pair of compasses, draw a circle with radius 4 cm.

4 Mark a point B. Using a pair of compasses, draw a circle with radius 5.5 cm.

9.1.2 Constructing triangles

1 Line *AB* is 5 cm long.

a) Draw a circle with centre *A* and radius 3 cm.

b) Draw a circle with centre *B* and radius 4 cm.

c) Mark the point of intersection between the two circles drawn in parts **a** and **b** and label it *C*.

d) Complete the construction of the triangle by drawing the sides *AC* and *BC*.

2 Line PQ is 8 cm long.

a) Draw a circle with centre P and radius 7 cm

b) Draw a circle with centre Q and radius 2.5 cm.

c) Mark the point of intersection between the two circles drawn in parts **a** and **b** and label it R.

d) Complete the construction of the triangle by drawing the sides PR and QR.

3 Mark points A and B, where $AB = 6$ cm.

Construct an equilateral triangle ABC with sides of length 6 cm.

9.1.3 Constructing rhombuses

1 Line AC is 5 cm long.

a) Draw a circle with centre A and radius 6 cm.

b) Draw a circle with centre C and radius 6 cm.

c) Mark the points of intersection of the two circles drawn in parts **a** and **b** and label them B and D.

d) Complete the construction of the rhombus by drawing the sides AB, BC, CD, and DA.

2 Line AC is 4 cm long.

a) Draw a circle with centre A and radius 7 cm.

b) Draw a circle with centre C and radius 7 cm.

c) Mark the points of intersection of the two circles drawn in parts **a** and **b** and label them B and D.

d) Complete the construction of the rhombus by drawing the sides AB, BC, CD, and DA.

3 Complete the construction of the rhombus represented in the diagram below.

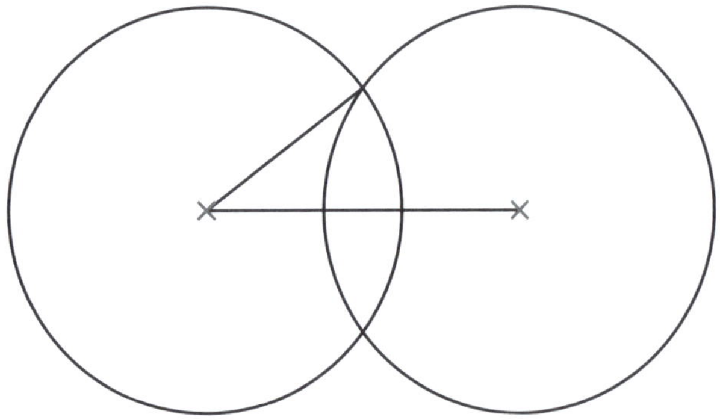

9.2 Construction using rhombuses

Example-problem pairs

9.2.1 Properties of rhombuses

Worked example 1	Thinking	Your turn! 1
***ABCD* is a rhombus. Angle *ABC* is 70°. Without measuring, what is angle *ABD*?** 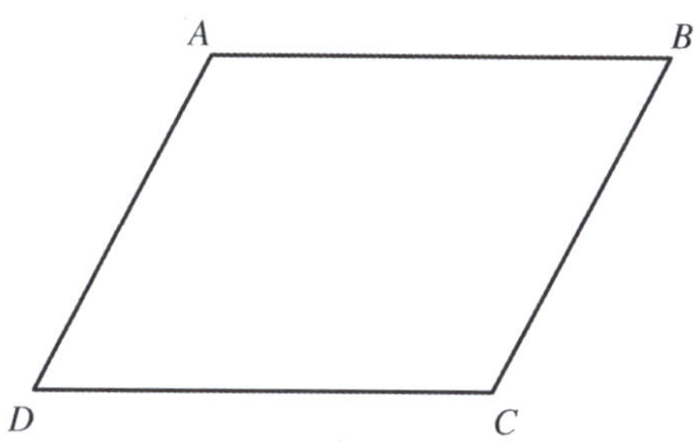 	*What property of a rhombus will help us here?*	***EFGH* is a rhombus. Angle *EFG* is 120°. Without measuring, what is angle *EFH*?** 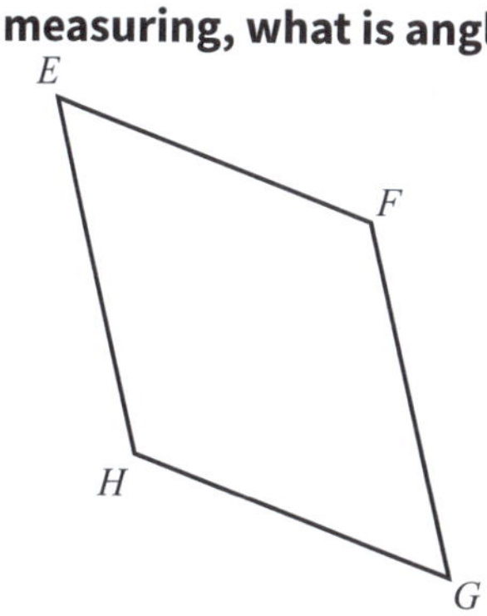
35°		

Worked example 2	Thinking	Your turn! 2
***ABCD* is a rhombus. Without using a ruler, which pairs of isosceles triangles could you make from it using its diagonals?** 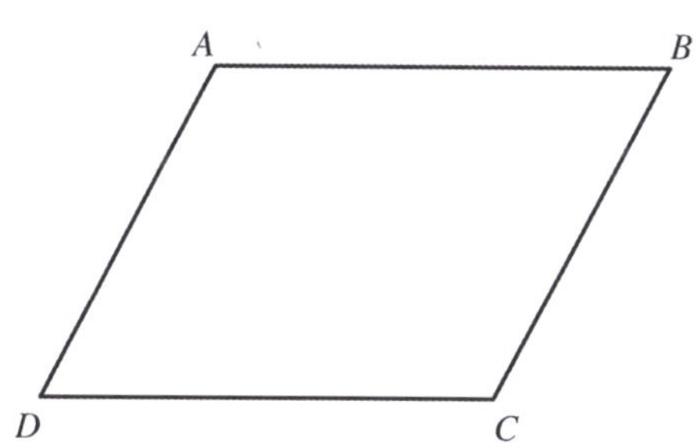 	*What properties of isosceles triangles will help us here?*	***EFGH* is a rhombus. Without using a ruler, which lines would you add to the shape to make four right-angled triangles?** 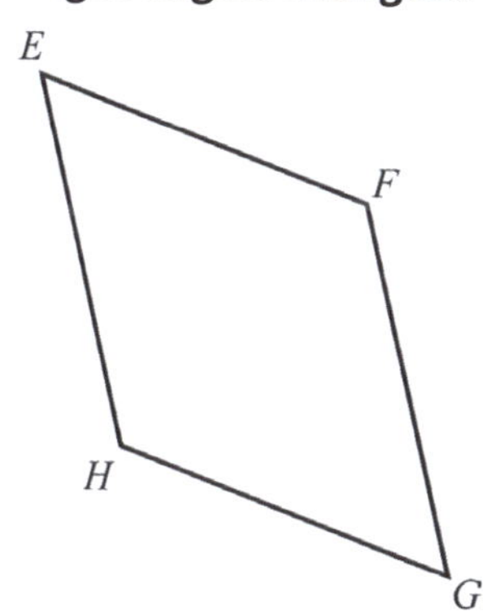
ABC and *ADC* *BCD* and *DAB*		

9.2.2 Constructing the perpendicular bisector of a line

Worked example 1	**Thinking**	**Your turn! 1**
Construct the perpendicular bisector of a 5 cm line. 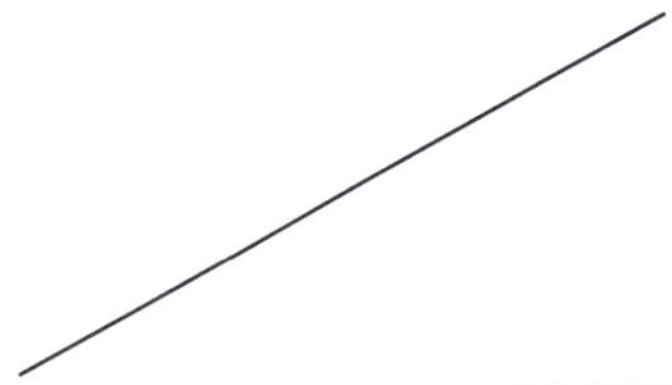	*What line do we draw to start with?*	**Construct the perpendicular bisector of a 7 cm line.** 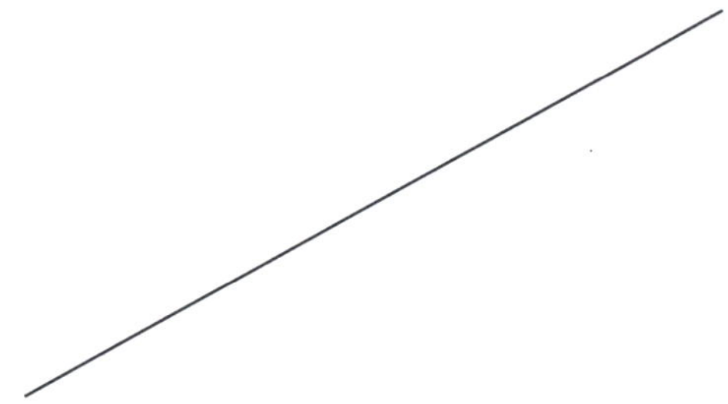
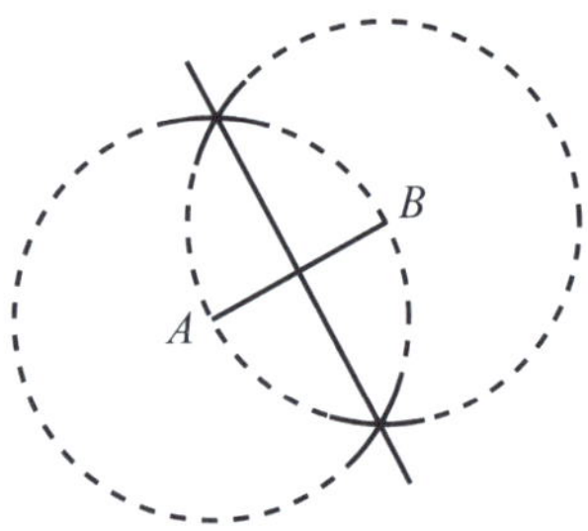	*How do we find the points that we join to construct the perpendicular bisector?* *How do we complete the construction?*	

Worked example 2	**Thinking**	**Your turn! 2**
Construct the perpendicular bisector of this 4 cm line. 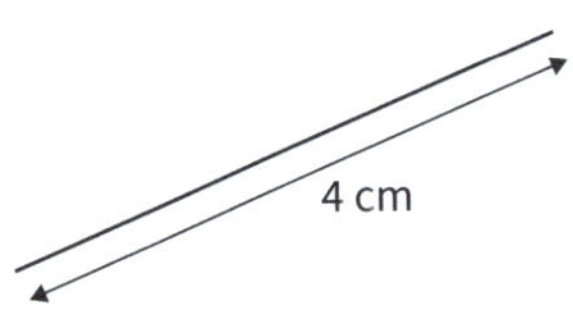	*What equipment will we need?* *What distance must our compasses be set wider than?*	**Construct the perpendicular bisector of a 6 cm line.** 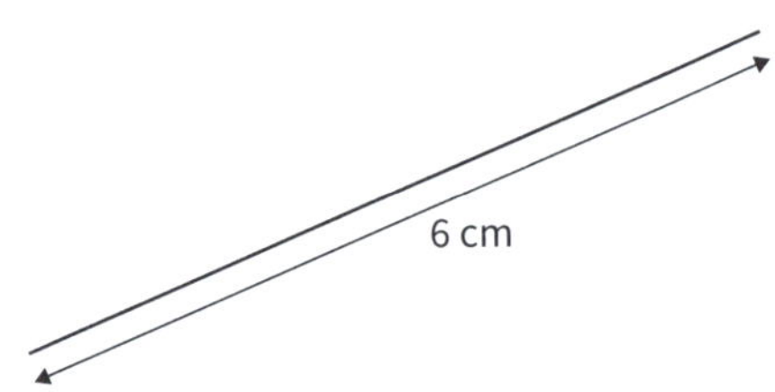
Set the compasses to wider than 2 cm.		
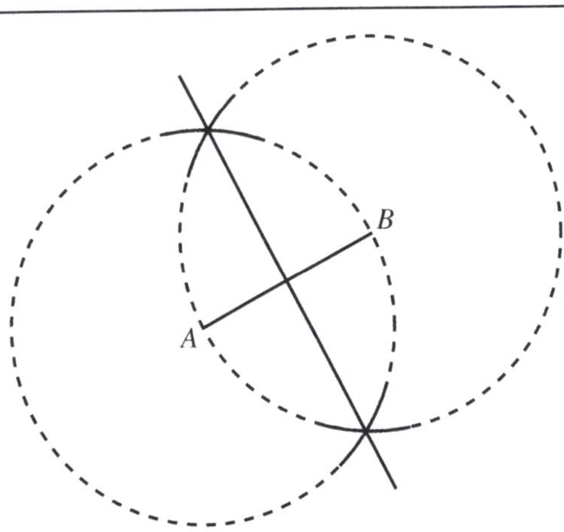	*How do we find the points that we join to construct the perpendicular bisector?* *How many arcs do we need to draw?* *How do we complete the construction?*	

Worked example 3	Thinking	Your turn! 3
Which sides on hexagon *ABCDEF* are bisected by the perpendicular bisector of line *AD*? 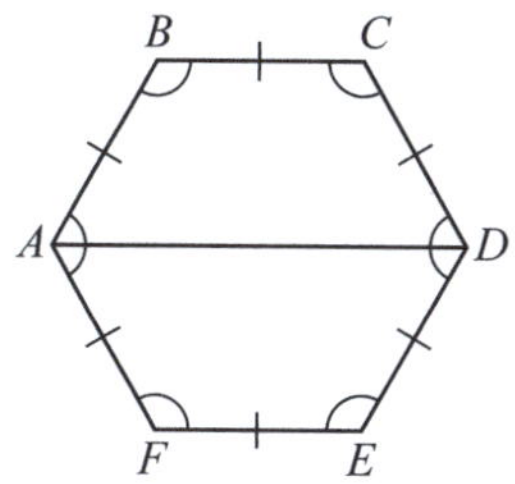	*How do we find the points that we join to construct the perpendicular bisector?*	**Which sides on decagon *ABCDEFGHIJ* are bisected by the perpendicular bisector of line *BG*?** 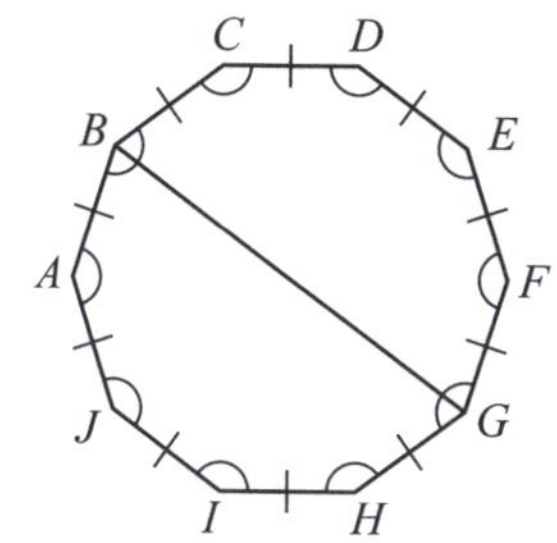
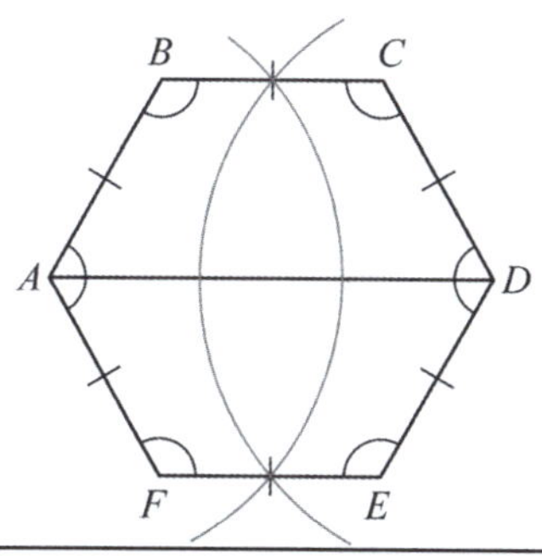	*How do we complete the construction?*	
This is a regular hexagon. *BC* and *EF*.	*What can we say about the polygon?*	

9.2.3 Constructing the perpendicular to a line through a point

Worked example 1	Thinking	Your turn! 1
Construct a perpendicular to this line segment that passes through the marked point. 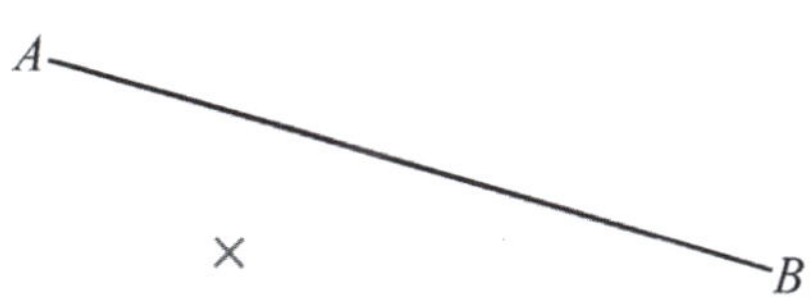	*How can we mark two points an equal distance on either side of the point?*	**Construct a perpendicular to this line segment that passes through the marked point.** 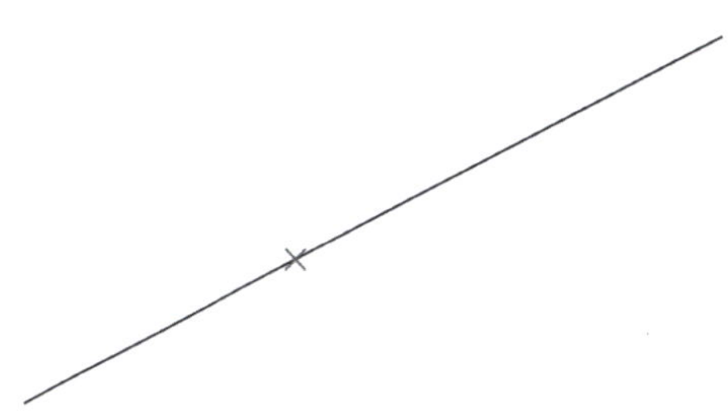
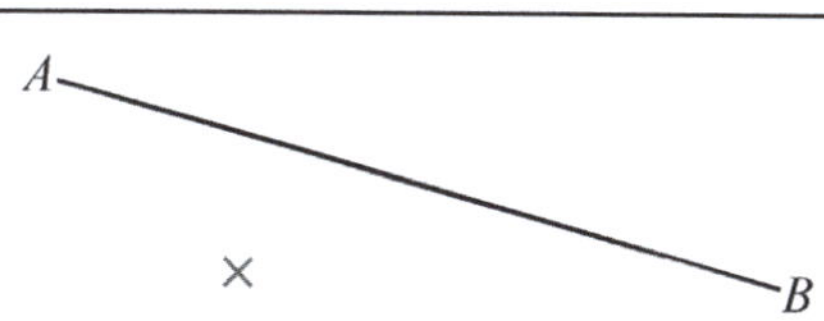	*How does this set up a perpendicular bisector?*	
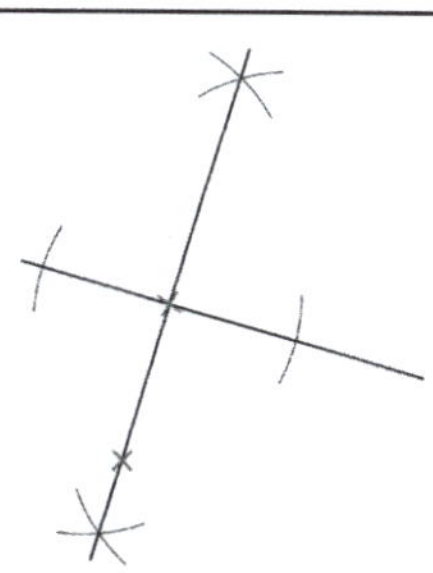	*How can we construct the perpendicular line through the marked point?*	

Worked example 2	Thinking	Your turn! 2
Construct a perpendicular line that cuts through the line AB and passes through the marked point. 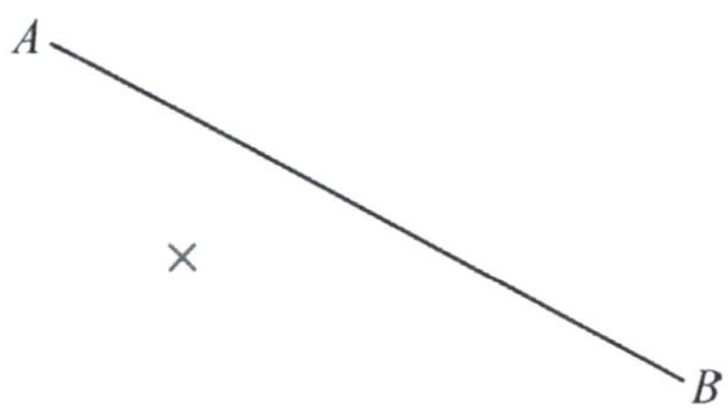	*How can we mark two points an equal distance on either side of the point?*	**Construct a perpendicular line that cuts through the line AB and passes through the marked point.** 
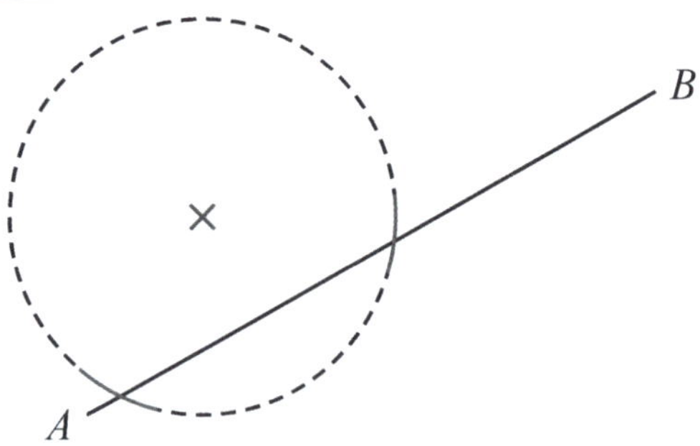	*How can we construct the perpendicular line through the marked point?*	
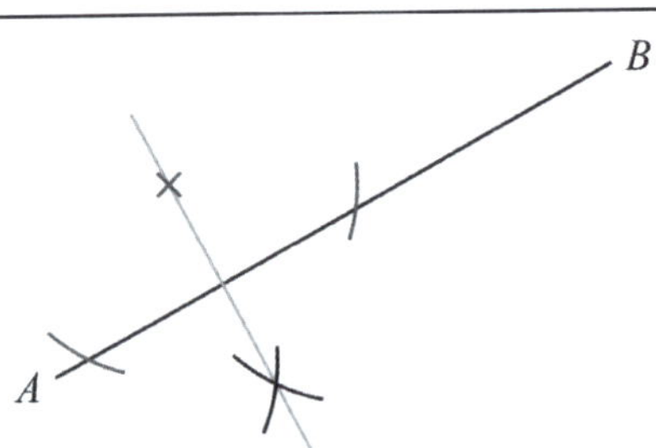	*Why don't we need to draw two pairs of arcs like other perpendicular bisectors?*	

Worked example 3	Thinking	Your turn! 3
Construct the altitude from vertex A of this triangle. 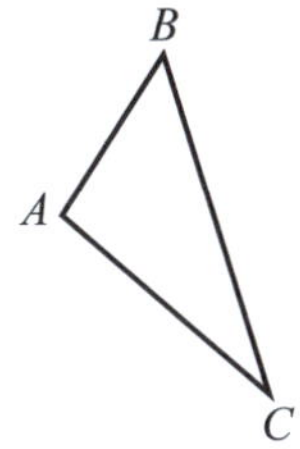	*How can we find a line segment with ends that are an equal distance from the required vertex?*	**Construct the altitude from vertex P of this triangle.** 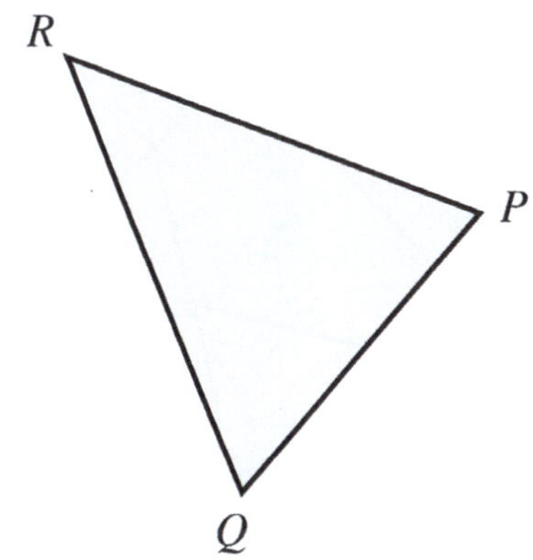
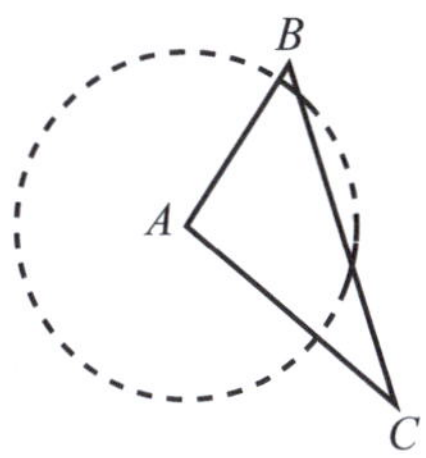	*How can we use these arcs to construct the perpendicular bisector of this new line segment?*	
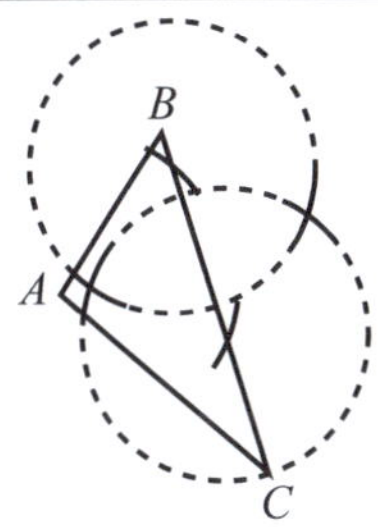	*How do we construct the altitude through the required vertex?*	
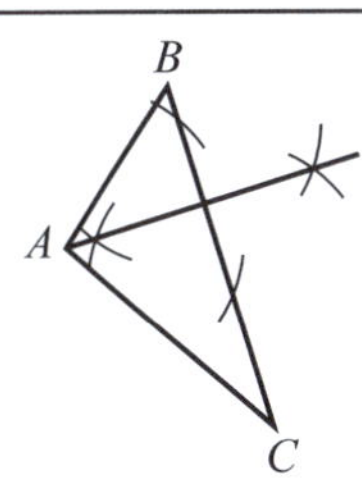		

9.2.4 Bisecting angles

Worked example 1	**Thinking**	**Your turn! 1**
Construct the bisector of angle ABC. 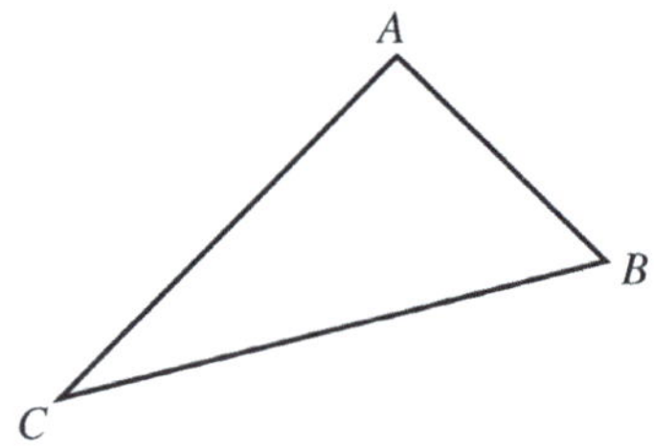		**Construct the bisector of angle EFG.** 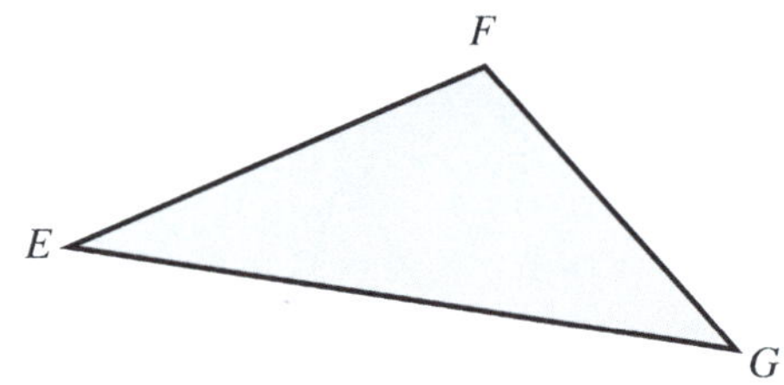
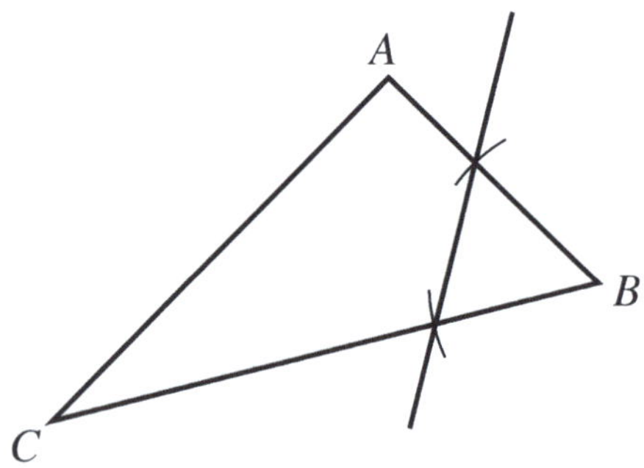	*How can we find a line segment with ends that are an equal distance from B?*	
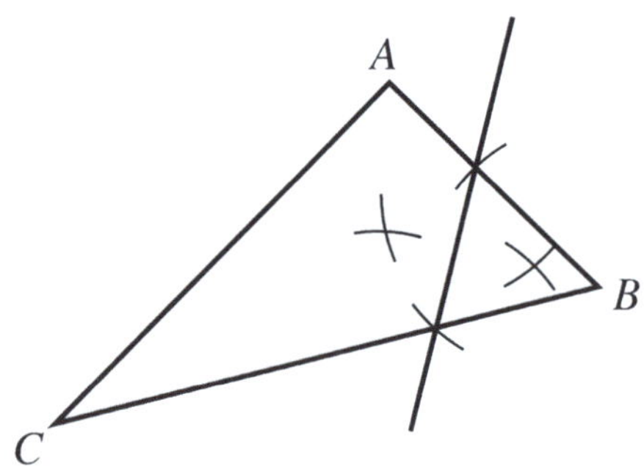 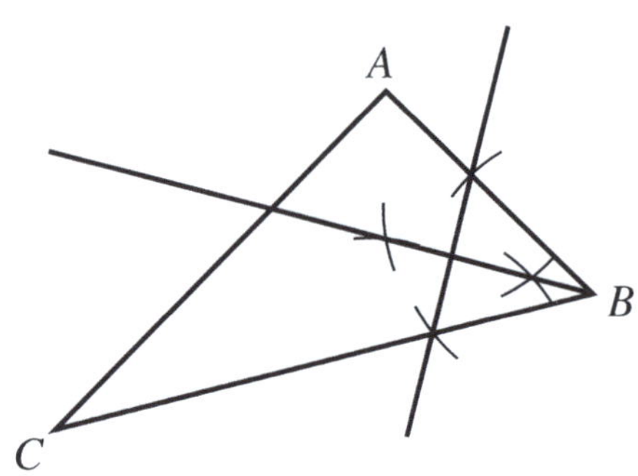	*How do we construct the perpendicular bisector on the unique side of this isosceles triangle?* *How do we construct the bisector of the required angle?*	

Worked example 2	Thinking	Your turn! 2
Construct a 45° angle without a protractor on line *AB*. 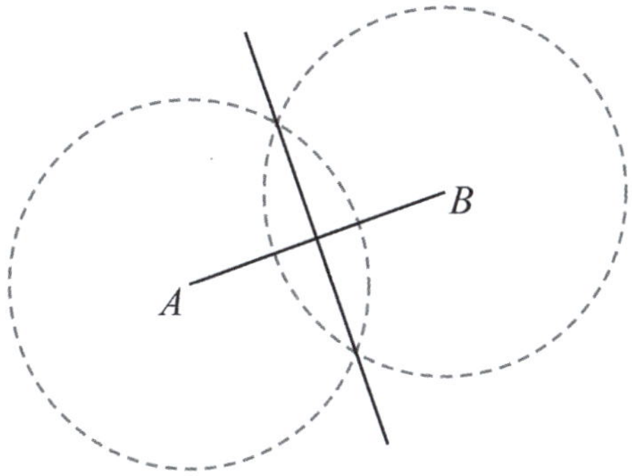	*What angle can we bisect to produce a 45° angle?*	**Construct a 30° angle by bisecting an angle of an equilateral triangle.** 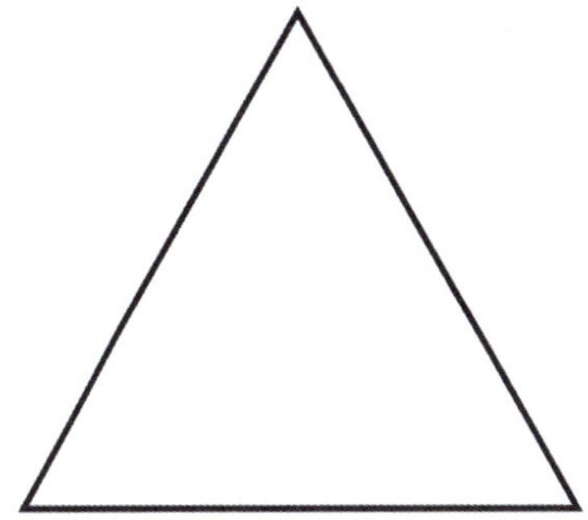
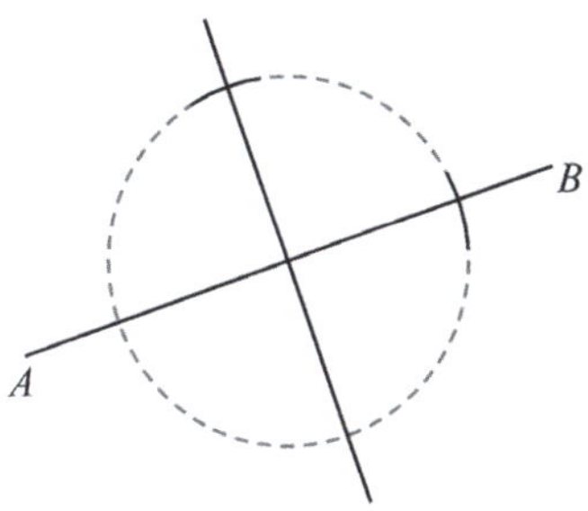	*What do we do first to bisect an angle?*	
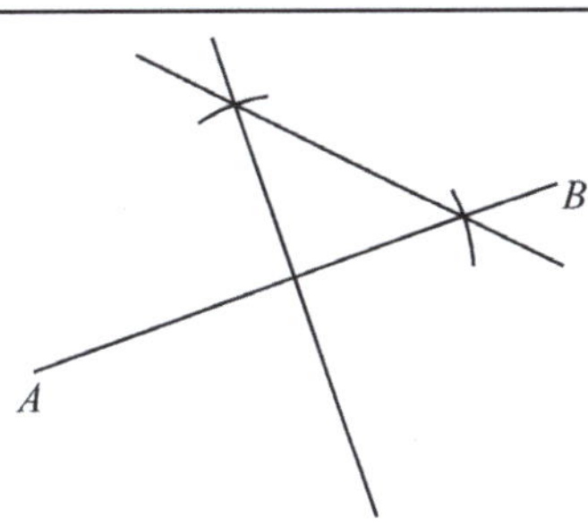	*How do we create the perpendicular bisector on the unique side?*	
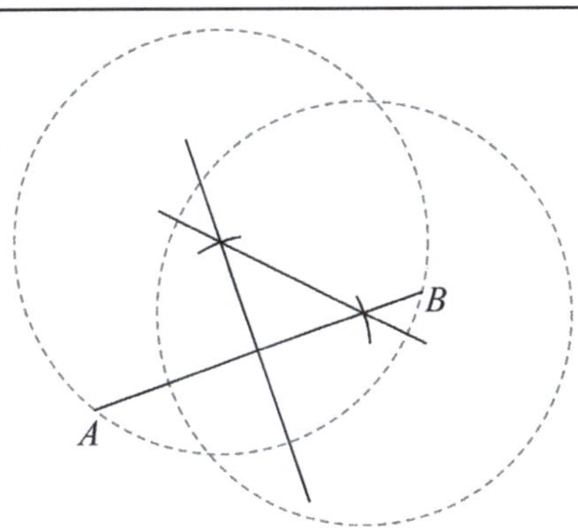 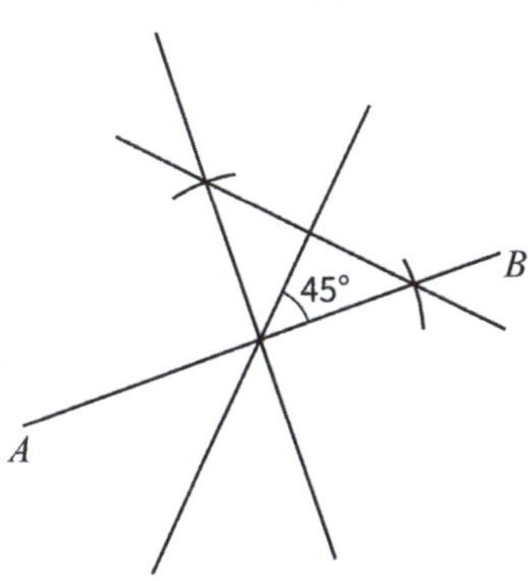	*How do we complete the construction of the angle bisector?*	

Fluency questions

9.2.1 Properties of rhombuses

1 Which of these shapes is a rhombus? How do you know?

a) 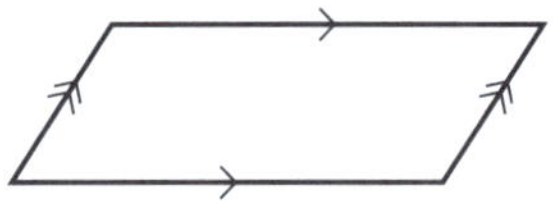 **b)** 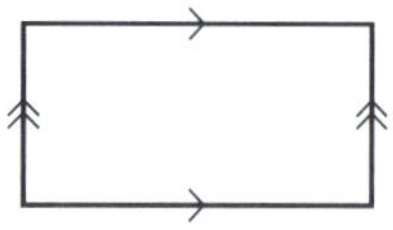 **c)** 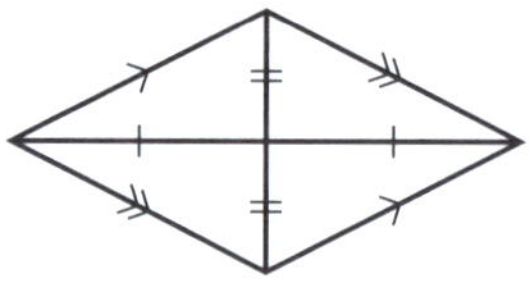 **d)** 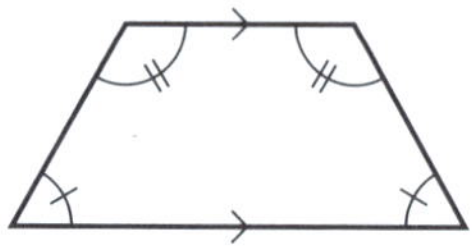

2 Here is a rhombus.

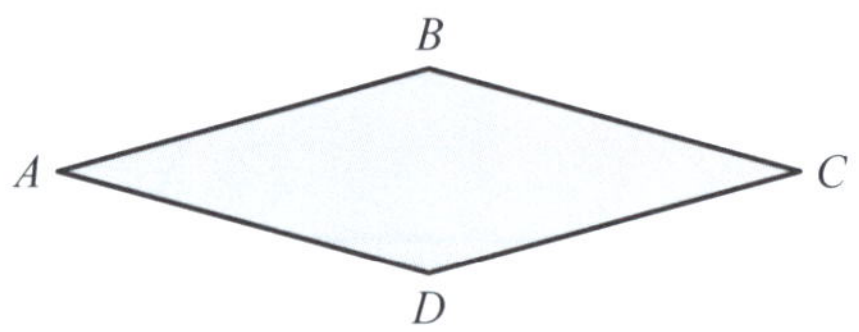

Which of the sides have the same length?

a) AB and BC **b)** AB and CD **c)** BC and CD **d)** All the sides have the same length.

3 Look at the rhombus in question **2**.

Angle ABC is 150°. What is the size of the angle CDA.

4 Here is a rhombus. Angle ABC is 45°. Find the size of the angle ABD.

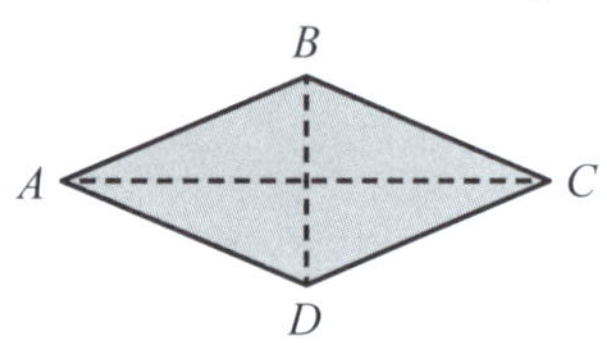

9.2.2 Constructing the perpendicular bisector of a line

1 Line AB is 7 cm long.

Draw two arcs with centre A and radius 4 cm, one above and one below the line segment AB. Draw two arcs with centre B and radius 4 cm, one above and one below the line segment AB. Mark the points of intersection of the arcs drawn in parts **a** and **b**, and label them P and Q. Complete the construction of the perpendicular bisector by drawing the line that passes through P and Q.

2 Line AB is 9 cm long.

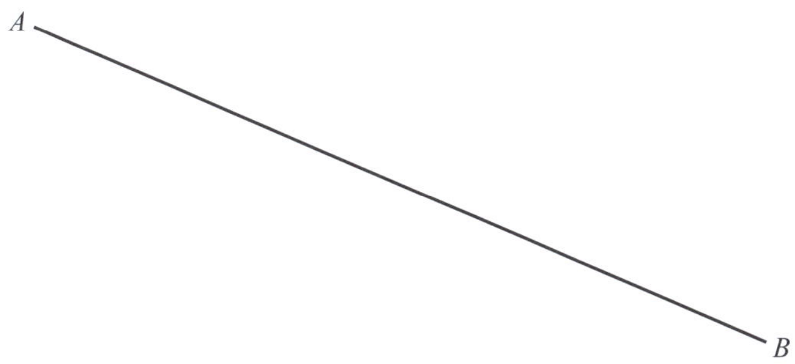

Draw two arcs with centre A and radius 5 cm, one above and one below the line segment AB.
Draw two arcs with centre B and radius 5 cm, one above and one below the line segment AB.
Mark the points of intersection of the arcs drawn in parts **a** and **b**, and label them P and Q.
Complete the construction of the perpendicular bisector by drawing the line that passes through P and Q.

3 Complete the perpendicular bisector in the diagram.

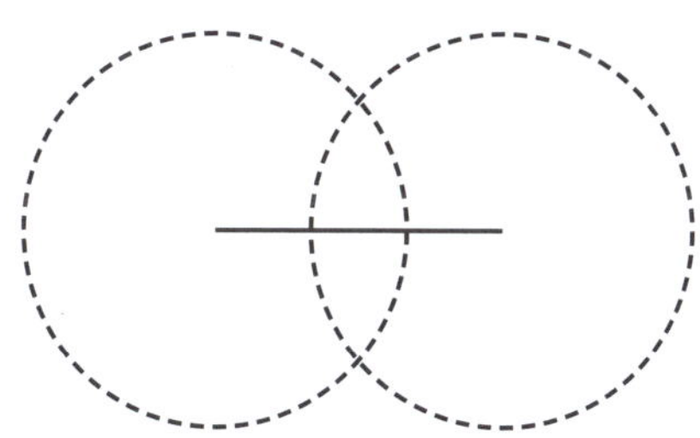

4 Complete the perpendicular bisector in the diagram.

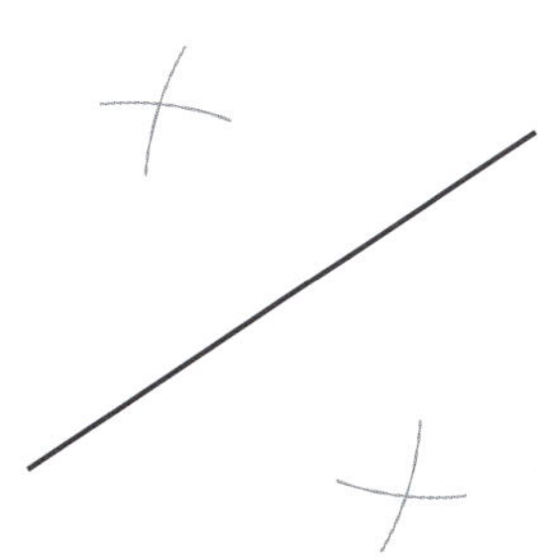

9.2.3 Constructing a perpendicular to a line through a point

1 Consider this line segment with a point marked.

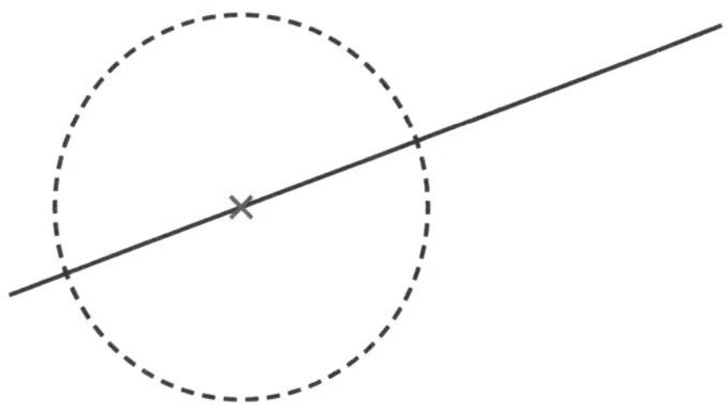

Use the dotted circle centred on the point to draw an arc that intersects the line in two places.
Use a pair of compasses to draw the perpendicular bisector of line segment. You should find that the line passes through the point marked on the line segment.

2 Consider this line segment with a point marked.

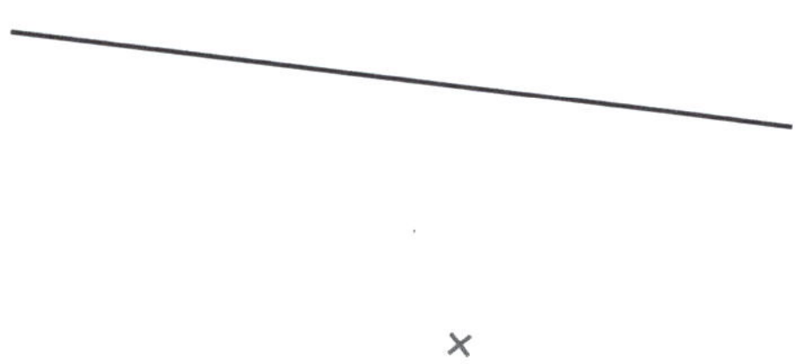

a) Use a pair of compasses, centred on the point marked with a cross, to draw an arc that intersects the line in two places.

b) Use a pair of compasses to draw the perpendicular bisector of line segment. You should find that the line passes through the point marked.

3 Construct the altitude from vertex B of triangle ABC, using the same steps that you used in the question **2**.

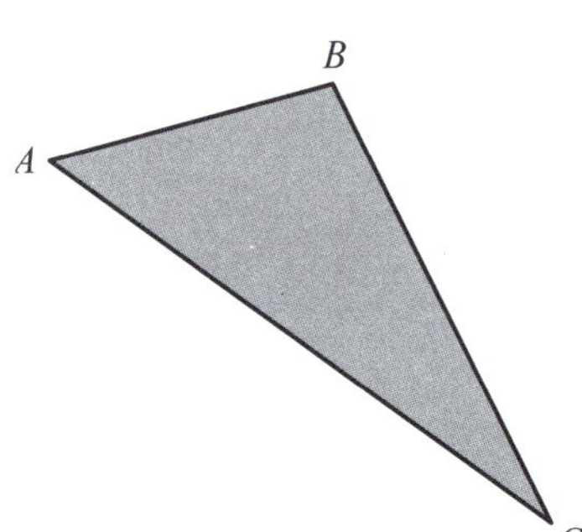

9.2.4 Bisecting angles

1 Here is angle BAC:

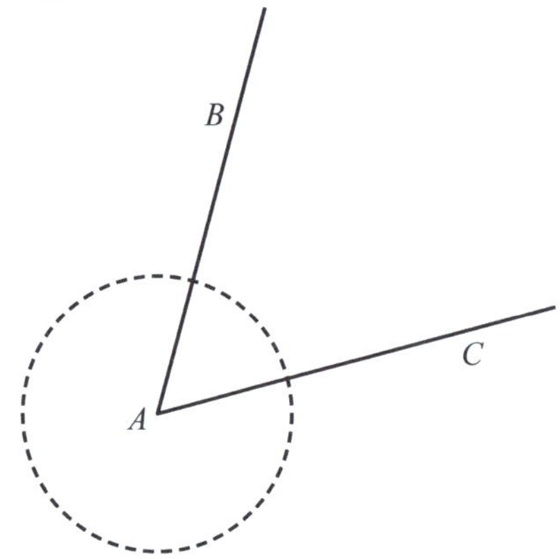

a) Use the dotted circle centred at A to draw an arc that intersects both AB and AC. Mark the points of intersection and label them P and Q.

b) Use a pair of compasses to draw two arcs of equal size, one from P and other from Q, that intersect at point R.

c) Join point A to point R, to draw the angle bisector.

2 Here is an angle:

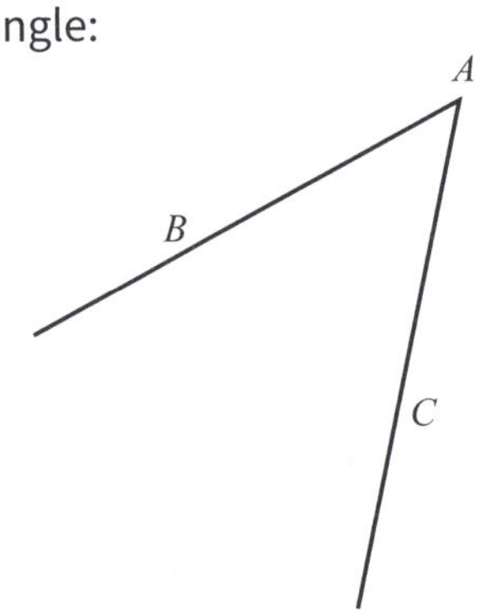

By following similar instructions to question **1**, or otherwise, construct its angle bisector.

3 Here is the triangle ABC:

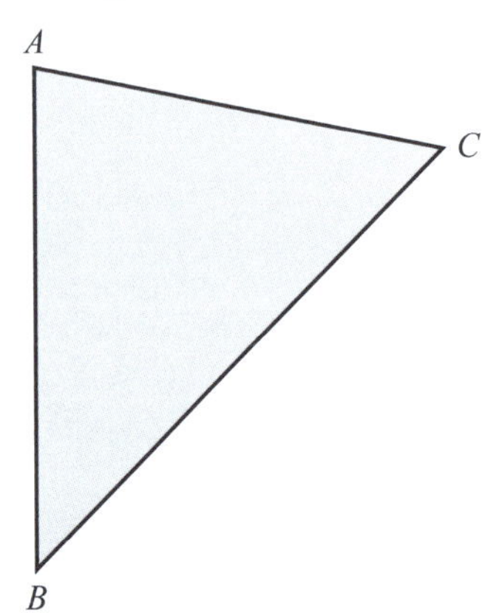

By following similar instructions to question **1**, or otherwise, construct the bisector of angle BAC.

Answers

Example-problem pairs: Your turn!

1.1 Rounding to decimal places

1.1.1 Round integers to the nearest 10, 100, 1000, and higher

1 5 457 901 ≈ 5 460 000 (to the nearest 10 000)

2 412 ≈ 410

1.1.2 Rounding numbers to decimal places

1 0.023 5798 = 0.0236 (to 4 d.p.)

2 340.06 ≈ 340 (to the nearest integer)

3 2.68 ≈ 2.7 (to 1 d.p.)

4 **a)** 0.895 ≈ 0.90 (to 2 d.p.)

b) 25.46921 = 25.469 (to 3 d.p.)

1.2 Rounding to significant figures

1.2.1 What is a significant figure?

1 **a)** The value of the 2 is 200 000

b) The value of the 1 is 0.0001

2 **a)** There are three significant figures: 1, 0, and 3

b) There are two significant figures: 6 and 9

3 **a)** Zero thousandths

b) Zero ones

1.2.2 Rounding integers to significant figures

1 **a)** 8397 ≈ 8400 (to 2 s.f.)

b) 96 420 ≈ 100 000 (to 1 s.f.)

2 The last 2 zeros: 30 000

3 The smallest number that rounds to 3600 to 2 s.f. is 3550

1.2.3 Rounding decimals to significant figures

1 **a)** 0.000 0724 ≈ 0.000 07 (to 1 s.f.)

b) 0.001 042 ≈ 0.0010 (to 2 s.f.)

2 The least number that rounds up to 0.08 to 1 s.f. is 0.075

3 The least number that rounds to 1.000 to 4 s.f. is 0.950

1.3 Estimation

1.3.1 Estimating calculations

1 Area = 14.3 × 27.9 ÷ 2 = 199.485

≈ 199.5 cm^2 (to 1 d.p.) or ≈ 200 cm^2(to 2 s.f.), or ≈ 199 cm^2 (to 3 s.f.)

2 492 × 21 ≈ 500 × 20 = 10 000

3 An estimate gives $\frac{50 \times 2}{10} = 10$

Florence's answer is nearer 1, which means she might have typed 93 instead of 9.3

4 $\frac{781 \times 2.3}{0.502} \approx \frac{800 \times 2}{0.5}$

$= \frac{1600}{0.5}$

$= 3200$

5 $\sqrt{85} \approx 9.2$

1.3.2 Evaluating estimates

1 31 × 712 ≈ 30 × 700 = 21 000

Since both numbers have been rounded down, this is an underestimate.

2 2.34 × 1.78 = 4.1652 m^2 (do not round this yet).

4.1652 × 2.5 = $10.413

It will cost $10.41

3 It is an overestimate.

1.3.3 Error intervals

1 $1.5 \leq y < 2.5$

2 $0.25 \leq x < 0.35$

$1.45 \leq y < 1.55$

Lower bound for xy is 0.25 × 1.45 = 0.3625

Upper bound for xy is 0.35 × 1.55 = 0.5425

Error interval for xy is $0.3625 \leq xy < 0.5425$

3 $0.25 \leq x < 0.35$

$1.45 \leq y < 1.55$

Lower bound for $y - x$ is 1.45 − 0.35 = 1.10

Upper bound for $y - x$ is 1.55 − 0.25 = 1.30

Error interval for $y - x$ is $1.10 < y - x < 1.30$

2.1 Solutions to linear equations

2.1.1 What is a linear equation?

1 **a)** The equals symbol means it is an equation.
x has an exponent of 1, so this is a linear equation.
b) This is an expression.
c) The equals symbol means it is an equation.
Expanding gives: $6x^2 + 2x = 0$
The greatest exponent of x is 2, so this is a non-linear equation.

2 **a)** The equals symbol means it could be an equation or an identity
Simplify both sides: $7x + 7 - x = 6(x + 2) - 5$
$6x + 7 = 6x + 7$
This is an identity because both sides have the same expression.
b) No equals symbol means this isn't an equation.
This is linear a inequality because of the $\geq$ symbol and because the unknown has an exponent of 1.
This is linear a inequality because of the $\geq$ symbol and because the unknown has an exponent of 1.

2.1.2 Solutions to equations

1 Try $x = 2$. $5 \times 2 - 3 = 3 \times 2 + 5$
$7 \neq 11$
Try $x = 3$. $5 \times 3 - 3 = 3 \times 3 + 5$
$12 \neq 14$
Try $x = 4$.
$5 \times 4 - 3 = 3 \times 4 + 5$
$20 - 3 = 12 + 5$
$17 = 17$
so $x = 4$ is the solution to the equation.

2 **a)** Substitute $x = 9$ on both sides.
$9 - 3 = \frac{9}{3} + 2$
$6 = 3 + 2$
$6 \neq 5$
So $x = 9$ is not the solution.
b) Substitute $x = 9$ on both sides.
$3 \times 9 + 10 = 5 \times 9 - 8$
$27 + 10 = 45 - 8$
$37 = 37$
So $x = 9$ is the solution.

3 **a)** Many solutions. There are infinitely many pairs of numbers that sum to 8.
b) One solution, $x = 0$. There is one unknown and one solution.
c) No solutions. You cannot add 12 to a number and get the number you started with.

2.1.3 Maintaining equality

1 **a)** 3 has been subtracted on the left but added on the right. Equality has not been maintained.
b) x has been added to both sides, so equality has been maintained.
c) All of the right side has been multiplied by 4, but only the $5x$ on the left side has been. Equality has not been maintained.

2 For example:
$3a + 5 = 11$
$+3 \downarrow \quad \downarrow +3$
$3a + 8 = 14$

$3a + 5 = 11$
$-4 \downarrow \quad \downarrow -4$
$3a + 1 = 7$

$3a + 5 = 11$
$\times 2 \downarrow \quad \downarrow \times 2$
$6a + 10 = 22$

3 **a)** Both sides have been divided by 5, so equality has been maintained.
b) $5x$ has been subtracted from the left-hand side, but $3x$ has been subtracted from the right-hand side. So equality has not been maintained.
c) 2 has been added to both sides, so equality has been maintained.

2.2 One-step linear equations

2.2.1 Additive steps

1 $8.7 = 3.9 + v$
$8.7 - 3.9 = 3.9 + v - 3.9$
$v = 4.8$

2 $t + 11 = 19$
$t + 11 - 11 = 19 - 11$
$t = 8$

3 $8 = w - 11$
$8 + 11 = w - 11 + 11$
$19 = w$

4 **a)** $b = 5$
b) $p = -7$

2.2.2 Multiplicative steps

1 $x = 3.5$
2 $a = 8$
3 $x = 75$
4 $x = 2$

2.3 Two-step linear equations

2.3.1 Dealing with a negative coefficient of the unknown

1 $x = 2.3$
2 $y = 5$
3 $q = \frac{1}{2}$
4 $d = 4$
5 $y = -8.4$
6 $x = -6$
7 $x = 4$

2.3.2 Solving equations that require more than one step

1 $x = 3$
2 $x = \frac{15}{2} = 7\frac{1}{2} = 7.5$
3 $x = 3$

2.3.3 Unknowns on both sides

1 $x = \frac{4}{3}$
2 $x = \frac{11}{8}$ (or $x = 1.375$)
3 $x = 4$
4 $x = 20$
5 $a = 8$

2.4 Linear equations with brackets and fractions

2.4.1 Deciding how to deal with brackets in equations

1 $x = \frac{13}{5}$ or $2\frac{3}{5}$
2 $x = 2$

2.4.2 Equations with brackets where the unknown is on both sides

1 $x = 2$
2 a) $x = 5$
b) $5(x - 2) = 2x + 5$
÷5 ↓ ↓ ÷5
$x - 2 = \frac{2x}{5} + 1$
No, the equation now involves fractions, because the terms did not have a common factor of 5.

2.4.3 Equations with fractions

1 $x = 8$
2 $x = 8$
3 $x = \frac{55}{12}$
4 $x = -2.5$
5 $x = \frac{11}{12}$

2.4.4 Equations with the unknown in the denominator

1 $x = 4$
2 $x = 2$
3 $x = 8$

3.1 Features of sequences

3.1.1 Continuing sequences

1 a) The first pattern is built using 8 sticks. Each pattern after this needs 7 more sticks than the previous pattern.
b)
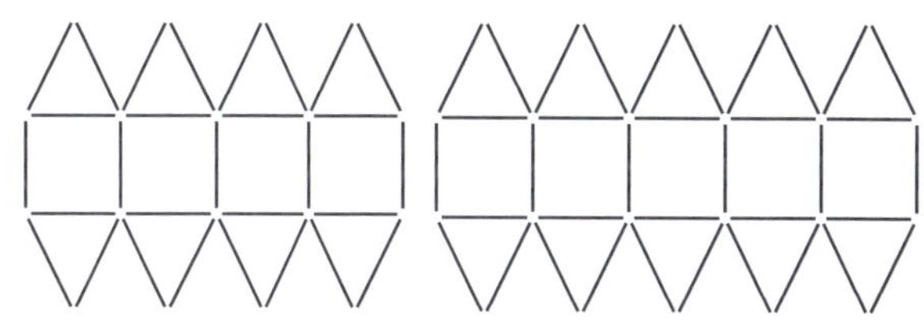

2 a) 3 is subtracted each time.
The next term is 9
b) Each term is 3 times the previous term.
The next term is $27 \times 3 = 81$

3.1.2 Using term-to-term rules

1 Each term is multiplied by 10
The next three terms are 2000, 20 000, 200 000
2 The missing term is 8
The next three terms are 19, 30 and 49
3 2 is added each time
The next three terms are 11, 13, 15
4 For example;
Add 1, then add 3, then add 5, so add the next odd number
The next two terms are 12 and 19
Or add the preceding two terms
The next two terms are 11 and 18

3.1.3 Using position-to-term rules

1 a) The first pattern has 8 sticks.
7 sticks are added with each new pattern, so 9 times altogether.

$8 + 9 \times 7 = 71$

The number of sticks needed is 71

b) Number of sticks

$= 8 + (n - 1) \times 7$

$= 8 + 99 \times 7$

$= 701$

2 a) $-n$

b) $\frac{1}{n}$

3.2 Arithmetic sequences

3.2.1 Identifying arithmetic sequences

1 a) No. There is not a common difference between consecutive terms.

The differences are +2, +2, +4

b) You subtract 3 from each term to get the next term. This is an arithmetic sequence.

c) You add 5 to each term to get the next term. This is an arithmetic sequence.

3.2.2 Working out the *n*th terms of arithmetic sequences

1 nth term is $7n - 3$

2 nth term is $-2n + 9$

3.2.3 Using the *n*th term

1 The sequence is 13, 23, 33, 43, 53, …

2 The sequence is −1, −4, −7, −10, −13, …

3 a) 207

b) 407

c) 411

4 a) 10th term = −9

b) 100th term = −369

3.2.4 Finding terms of arithmetic sequences

1 38 is a term in the sequence.

It is the 8th term.

2 a) The position number is 5

b) $7 - 6n = -77$

$6n = 84$

$n = 14$

n is a positive integer so −77 is a number in this sequence.

4.1 Connect coordinates, equations, and graphs

4.1.1 When to join points on a graph

1 a)

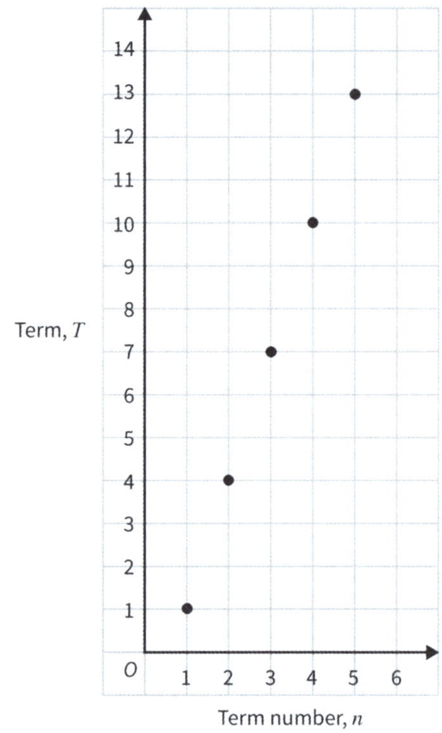

b) No, sequences deal with integer term numbers so you shouldn't draw a line.

4.1.2 Using a rule to find coordinates

1 a)

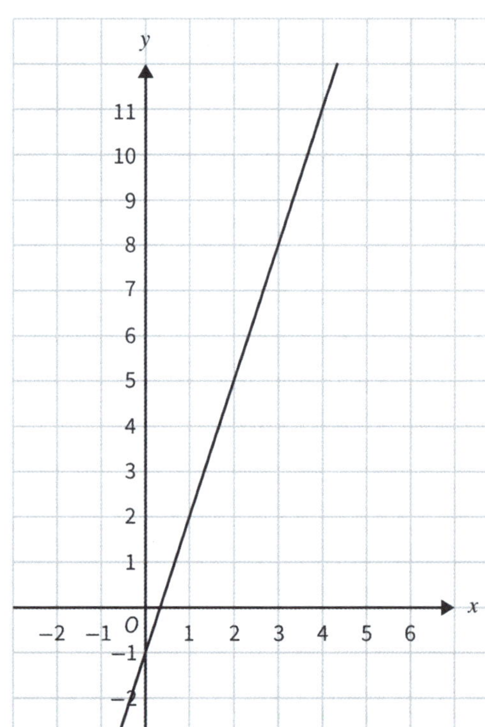

b)

x	0	1	2	3	4
y	–1	2	5	8	11

c) Each y-coordinate is 3 times the x-coordinate minus 1:
$y = 3x - 1$

2 a)

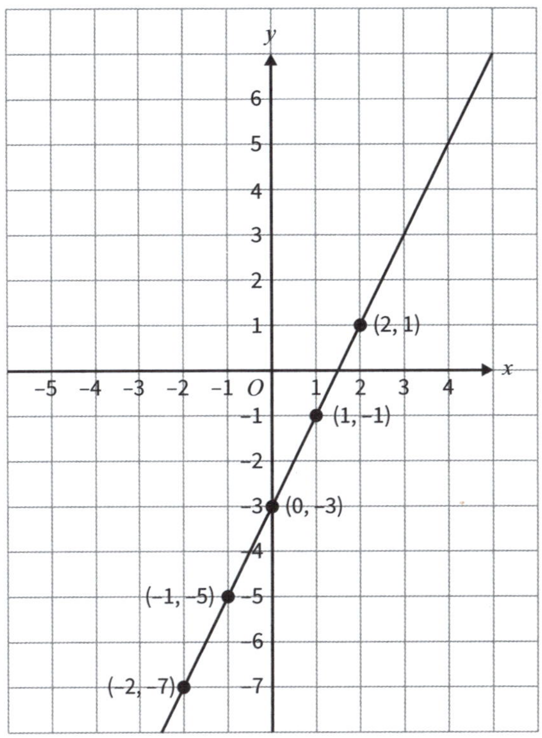

b)

x	–2	–1	0	1	2
y	–7	–5	–3	–1	1

c) The x-coordinate is 10. Using the equation, the y-coordinate should be:
$y = 2x - 3 = 2 \times 10 - 3 = 17$
Therefore, the point (10, 17) does lie on the line.

4.2 Linear relationships

4.2.1 Finding the gradient of a line

1 a) Gradient = 3

2 a) Gradient = 2

b) Gradient $= \frac{3}{6} = \frac{1}{2} = 0.5$

3 a) Gradient = –4

b) Gradient $= -\frac{1}{2} = -0.5$

4 Gradient $= \frac{-9}{6} = \frac{-3}{2} = -1\frac{1}{2} = -1.5$

5 Gradient $= \frac{-8}{10} = -\frac{4}{5} = -0.8$

6 The gradient $= \frac{-10}{2} = -5$

4.2.2 The gradient and y-intercept

1

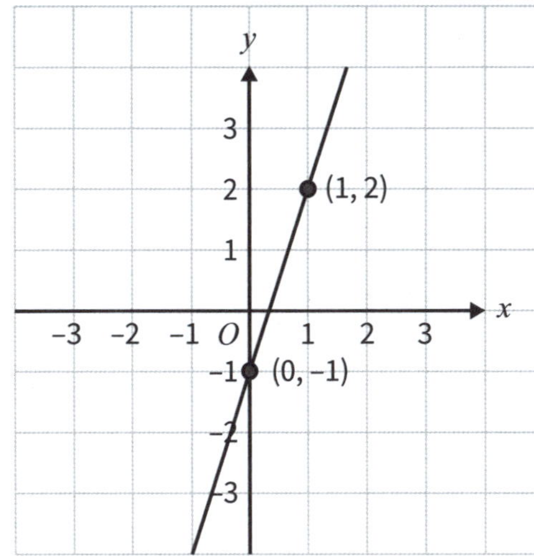

2 Line C has a gradient of zero.
So the rate of change of their distance was 0, meaning it didn't change.
That must mean that they stayed in the same place.
So student C must have stayed at home sick.
Students A and B both changed their distance so must have travelled to school.
Line A is steeper than line B so it has a higher gradient.
So the rate of change of student A's distance was higher.
So, compared to B, they both increased their distance by the same amount but student A did it in less time.
So student A must have been driven to school.
Line B isn't as steep, it has a lower gradient.
So the rate of change of student B's distance is lower.
So student B covered the same distance but in more time.
So student B must have walked to school.

3 The y-intercept is –0.5.

4 The line that matches the first row has a positive gradient and a negative y-intercept.
It must be line *D*.
The line that matches the second row has a negative gradient and a positive y-intercept.
It must be line *A*.
The line that matches the third row has a gradient of 0 and negative y-intercept so it must be a horizontal line that goes through the negative y-axis.
It must be line B.

The line that matches the last row has a positive gradient and a y-intercept of 0 so it must go through the origin.
It must be line C.

5
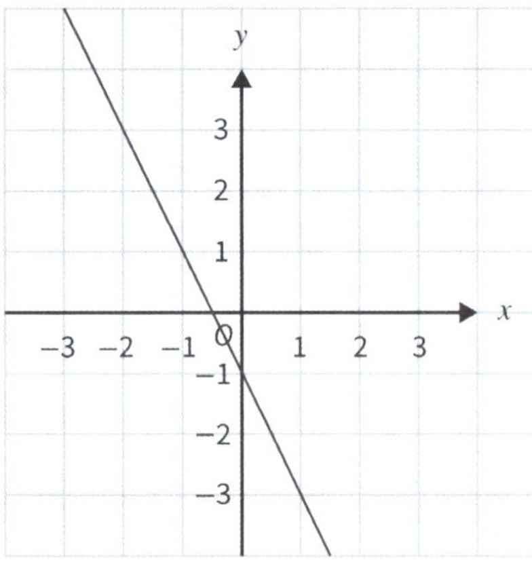

6
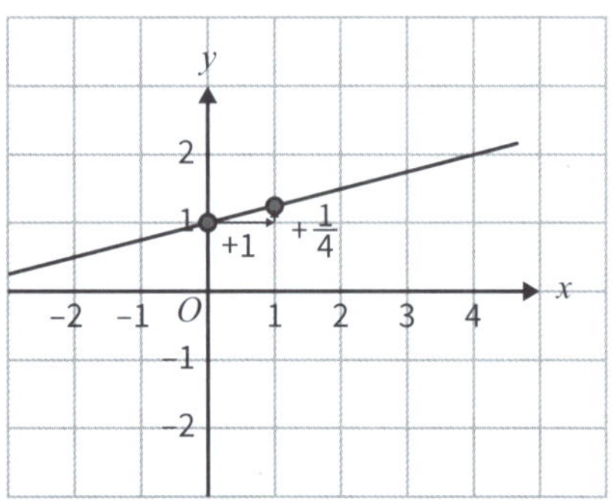

4.2.3 $y = mx + c$ form of linear graphs

1 a) The gradient is 4
The y-intercept is −3
b) The gradient is −8
The y-intercept is 1
2 The gradient is 5
The y-intercept is 3
3 The equation of the line is $y = 2x - 3$

4.2.4 Solving problems involving linear graphs

1 a) The y-intercept is 8
b) The length of the elastic band before any masses are added.
c) Gradient $= \frac{4}{20} = 0.2$
d) For each 1 g in mass added to the elastic band, the length of the elastic band increases by 0.2 cm.
2 a) y-intercept = 2
The base rate at 0 kilometres is \$2.
b) Gradient $= \frac{7}{4} = 1.75$
The cost per kilometre is \$1.75.
3 a) y-intercept = 160
The cost of the materials was \$160.
b) Gradient $= \frac{200}{5} = 40$
The charge per hour is \$40.

5.1 Percentages

5.1.1 Percentages, fractions, and decimals

1 $8\% = \frac{8}{100} = \frac{2}{25}$
$8\% = 8 \div 100 = 0.08$
2 $\frac{7}{8} = 0.875 \times 100\% = 87.5\%$
3 $220\% = \frac{220}{100} = \frac{22}{10} = \frac{11}{5} = 2\frac{1}{5}$
$220\% = \frac{220}{100} = 220 \div 100 = 2.2$
4 $142.05\% = \frac{142.05}{100} = \frac{14205}{10\,000}$
$142.05\% = \frac{142.05}{100} = 142.05 \div 100 = 1.4205$

5.1.2 Comparing quantities with percentages

1 a) $\frac{56}{70} = 56 \div 70 = 0.8$
$0.8 \times 100 = 80\%$
b) $\frac{70}{56} = 70 \div 56 = 1.25$
$1.25 \times 100 = 125\%$
2 Test A: $\frac{40}{50} = \frac{80}{100} = 80\%$
Test B: $\frac{53}{65} = 53 \div 65 = 0.815 = 81.5\%$
Test B is the better score.
3 $175\% = \frac{175}{100}$
$1 \div \frac{175}{100} = \frac{100}{175}$
$\frac{100}{175} = 4 \div 7 = 0.57 = 57\%$

5.1.3 Finding percentages

1 42% of 0.65 = 27.3
2 The number is 440
3 The number is $35 \div 25 \times 100 = 140$
70% of 140 = 98
4 $0.19 \times \$589 = \$111.91$
5 $0.8 \times 0.15 = 0.12 = 12\%$

5.1.4 Percentage increase and decrease

1 a) $100\% - 38\% = 62\%$
$= \frac{62}{100}$
$= 0.62$
b) $0.62 \times \$500 = \$310$
c) $100\% + 38\% = 138\%$
$= \frac{138}{100} = \frac{69}{50}$
$= 1.38$
d) $1.38 \times \$500 = \$690$

2 $100\% - 20\% = 80\% = 0.80$

$= \frac{80}{100} = \frac{4}{5}$

Prices are $\frac{4}{5}$ their original amount.

3 $1.15 \times 0.9 = 1.035 = 103.5\%$

$103.5\% - 100\% = 3.5\%$

The overall change is an increase of 3.5%.

5.1.5 Finding an original amount

1 **a)** \$540 ÷ 0.9 = \$600

The TV originally cost \$600

b) \$183 600 ÷ 1.02 = \$180 000

The house cost \$180 000 last year.

2 \$522.50 ÷ 1.045 = \$500

The computer originally cost \$500

5.1.6 Finding the percentage change

1 The mass of chocolate has increased by 25%.

5.2 Proportionality

5.2.1 Representing multiplicative relationships

1

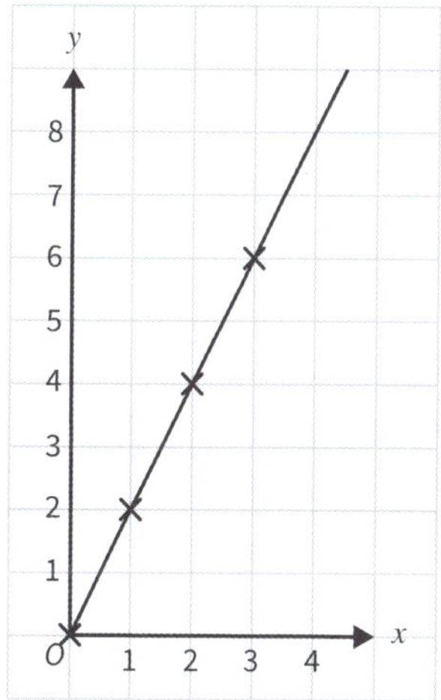

The equation is $y = 2x$

2

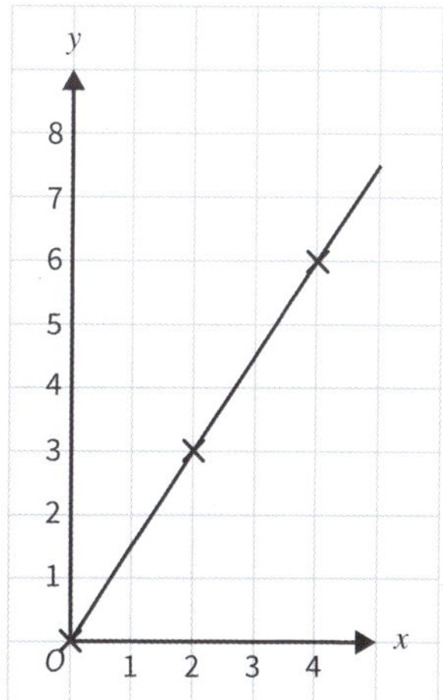

The equation of the graph is $y = 1.5x$

3

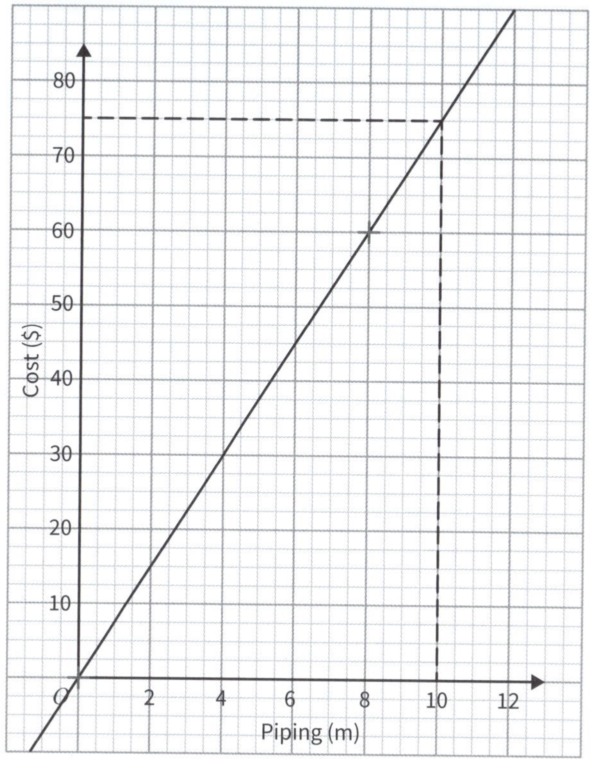

10 metres cost \$75

5.2.2 Direct proportion

1 The formulae showing direct proportion are $y = 6x$, $m = \frac{1}{2}n$, and $a = b$

$x{:}y = 1{:}6$

$n{:}m = 2{:}1$

$a{:}b = 1{:}1$

2 The multiplier is $\frac{-7}{-3}$ or $\frac{-14}{-4}$ or $\frac{-21}{-9}$

3 The formulae showing direct proportion are $y = 5.6x$, $m = (20\%)\,n$, and $\sqrt{3}a = b$

$x{:}y = 1{:}5.6$

$m{:}n = 1{:}5$

$a{:}b = 1{:}\sqrt{3}$

4 The formula is $C = 15n$

The ratio is $n{:}C = 1{:}15$

5 In a ratio table:

x	0	1.5	**3**	4.5
y	0	2.5	**5**	7.5

Example-problem pairs: Your turn!

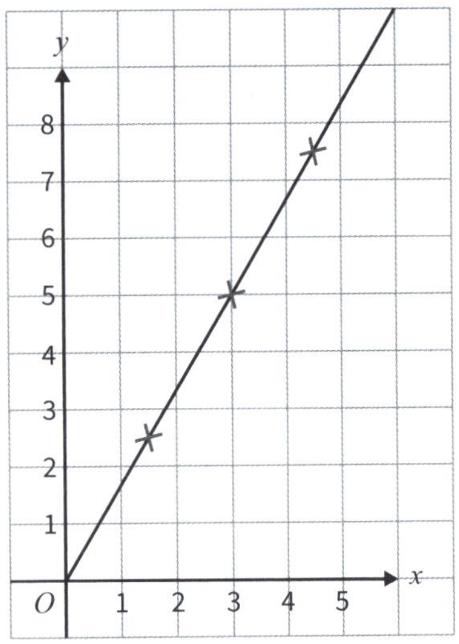

6 $100\,\% + 2\,\% = 102\,\% = 1.02$

$n = 1.02p$

$p:n = 1:1.02 = 100:102$

5.2.3 Solving problems involving direct proportion

1 For 4 people you need 320 g of filling.

2

Tub A	Mass (g)	500	1
	Price ($)	$3.50	$7.00

Tub B	Mass (g)	800	1
	Price ($)	$6.00	$7.50

Tub A is better value for money.

5.2.4 Inverse proportion

1

÷ 3

People	3	1
Days	5	15

× 3

It would take 1 person 15 days.

2

÷ 2.5

Speed (mph)	40	16
Time (h)	2	5

× 2.5

You would be travelling at 16 mph.

3

× 1.5 ÷ 2

x	12	18	9
y	3	2	1

÷ 1.5 ÷ 2

They are not in inverse proportion.

6.1 Representing data

6.1.1 Ungrouped frequency tables

1

Age	Frequency
11	1
12	6
13	7
14	3
15	0
16	1

$1 + 6 + 7 + 3 + 1 = 18$

There were 18 values in the list, so we have recorded all the data

2 Favourite pizza toppings.

How much people would be prepared to pay for pizza.

3 0, 0, 0, 0, 1, 1, 1, 1, 1, 2, 2, 2, 2, 2, 2, 4

6.1.2 Grouped frequency tables

1

Time, x seconds	Tally	Frequency
$10.4 \le x < 10.5$	||	2
$10.5 \le x < 10.6$	|||	3
$10.6 \le x < 10.7$	卌卌	10
$10.7 \le x < 10.8$	卌	5

6.1.3 Bar charts

1 a) Total number of umbrellas = 38 + 42 + 16 + 45 = 141

b) Fewer umbrellas were sold in the summer (July–September) than at other times of the year.

2 The least common result was 2, which occurred 3 times.

3 Friday had the least amount of sunshine. Plymouth had 30 minutes more sunshine than Newcastle.

6.1.4 Pictograms

1 For rugby, $20 \div 20 = 1$, so draw 1 ball.
For cricket, $35 \div 20 = 1.75$, so draw $1\frac{3}{4}$ balls.
For basketball, $25 \div 20 = 1.25$, so draw $1\frac{1}{4}$ balls.
For other, $15 \div 20 = 0.75$, so draw $\frac{3}{4}$ balls.

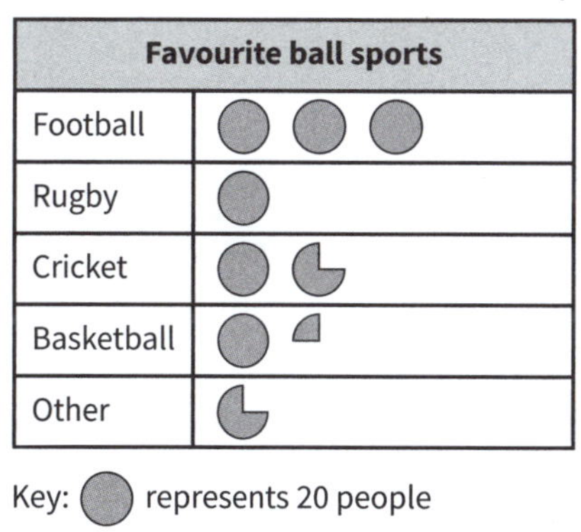

2 Each icon represents 4 posts, so each section of the icon represents 1 post.
Anya = 2 × 4 = 8 posts
Bart = 2 posts
Cleo = 4 + 2 = 6 posts
Dave = 3 × 4 + 1 = 13 posts

6.1.5 Constructing scatter graphs

1

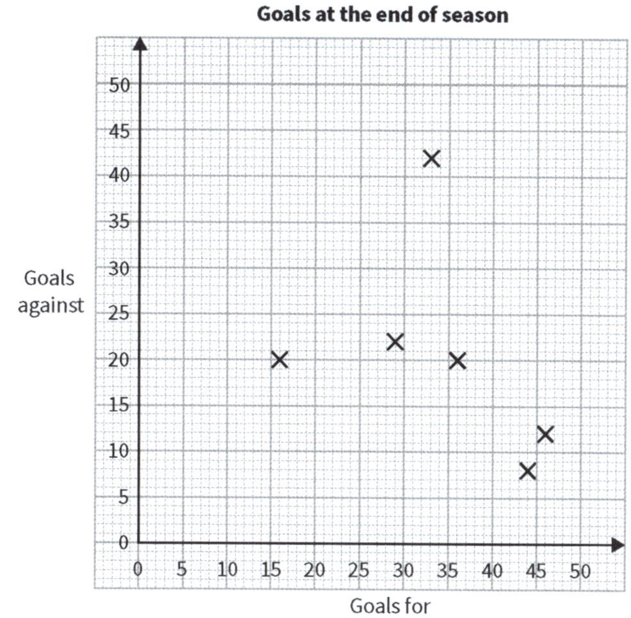

2

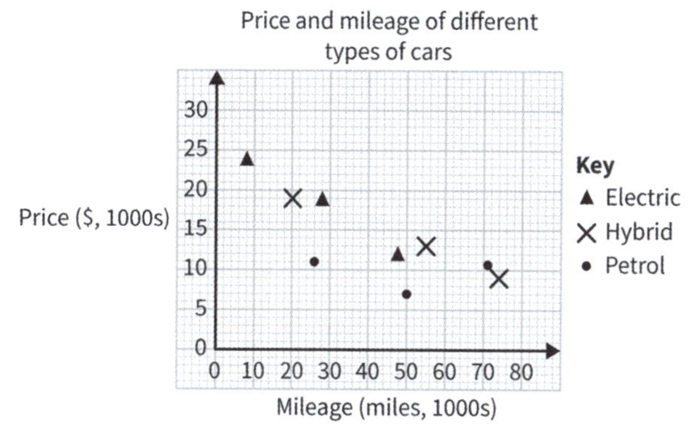

6.1.6 Interpreting scatter graphs

1 Students with a higher score in Test 1 tend to have a lower score in Test 2.

2 a)

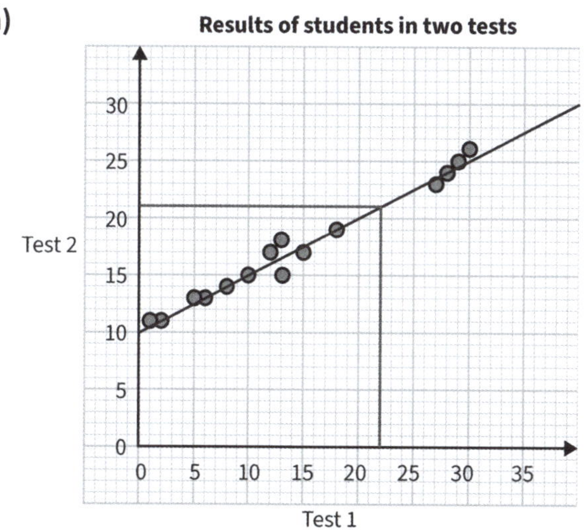

b) 21 marks

6.2 Angles and pie charts

6.2.1 Fractions of circles

1 $\frac{7}{10} \times 360 = 252°$

2 $\frac{1}{8}$ of $360 = \frac{1}{8} \times 360$
$= 360 \div 8$
$= 45°$

3 30% of $360 = 0.3 \times 360$
$= 108°$

4 Angle of shaded sector $= 360° - 115° = 245°$
Proportion shaded $= \frac{245}{360} = \frac{49}{72}$

6.2.2 Constructing pie charts

1

Season	Frequency	Angle
Summer	15	15 × 15° = 225°
Spring	1	1 × 15° = 15°
Autumn	2	2 × 15° = 30°
Winter	6	6 × 15° = 90°

Favourite season of 24 people

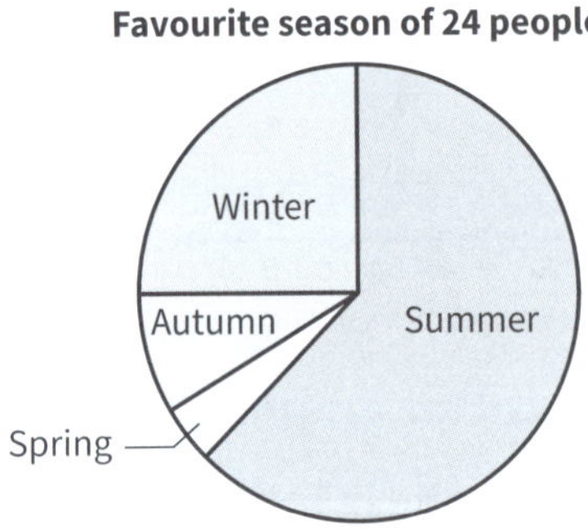

6.2.3 Interpreting pie charts

1 $\frac{1}{60} \times 360° = 6°$
So, each student is represented by 6°.
$72 \div 6 = 12$
So, 12 students study Mandarin.

2 a) Cheesecake = 60°
Sponge pudding = 130°
Ice cream = 360° − 60° − 130° = 170°
The largest sector is for ice cream, so this is the most popular.

b) Fraction preferring cheesecake $= \frac{60}{360} = \frac{1}{6}$

3 a) Afternoon; it has the smaller sector

b) Morning: hot chocolate sector = 45°
Afternoon: hot chocolate sector = 90°
20 hot chocolates sold in the morning.
18 hot chocolates sold in the afternoon.
More hot chocolates sold in the morning

6.3 Measures of average and spread of data

6.3.1 The mean

1 20 children in total, so:
Mean age $= \frac{33 + 24 + 13 + 70 + 135}{20}$
$= \frac{275}{20} = 13.75$ years

2 Total age of football players = 15 × 12 = 180
Total age of netball players = 5 × 16 = 80
Total age of whole group = 180 + 80 = 260
Mean of whole group $= \frac{\text{sum of values}}{\text{number of values}}$
$= \frac{260}{20}$
$= 13$

6.3.2 The median

1 The ordered list is:
5, 14, 14, 15, 29, 31, 40, 42, 71, 75
Median age $= \frac{29 + 31}{2} = 30$ years

2 $\frac{39 + 1}{2} = \frac{40}{2} = 20$
The median is the 20th value.
Median = 28 students

3 $\frac{16 + 1}{2} = \frac{17}{2} = 8.5$
The median is halfway between the 8th and 9th value.
The 8th value and the 9th value are both 4
The median is 4 lessons.

6.3.3 The mode

1 The modal number of pens is 1, as it has the highest frequency.

2 a) The modal restaurant is Pizza Planet, as it has the highest frequency.

b) The modal number of pizzas sold is 75

6.3.4 The range

1 Range = 9 − 5 = 4 hours

2 Range = 11 − 4 = 7 mistakes

6.3.5 Average and range of grouped data

1 a) The modal group is $250 \le h < 260$ since it has the highest frequency.

b) Maximum possible range = 280 − 240 = 40 cm

c) The median lies halfway between the 8th and 9th values.
So, the median lies in the group $250 \le h < 260$

2 Mean $= \frac{735 + 2040 + 1060 + 275}{16}$
$= \frac{4110}{16}$
$= 256.9$ cm (to 1 decimal place)

3 **a)** The modal group is 21–30, as it has the highest frequency.
b) Maximum possible range = 50 – 11 = 39
c) The median lies in the group 21–30
d) Mean $= \frac{0 + 77.5 + 306 + 284 + 227.5}{30}$
$= \frac{895}{30}$
$= 29.8$ (to 1 decimal place)

6.4 Analysing and comparing data

6.4.1 Averages and outliers

1 Mode since they need to know the most popular size of bunch sold.

2 **a)** 99 is an outlier as it is much larger than the rest of the data.
It will increase the range of the data.
b) The outlier does not affect the median, but it makes the mean larger.
So she might choose the mean as it will be bigger.

3 **a)** No mode
Median: $\frac{7+1}{2} = 4$th value
215, 221, 236, <u>302</u>, 305, 308, 310
so median = 302 miles
Mean $= \frac{215 + 221 + 236 + 302 + 305 + 308 + 310}{7}$
$= \frac{1897}{7} = 271$ miles
The company used the median.
b) The mean range is less than 300 miles and 3 out of 7 of the sample are closer to 200 miles than 300 miles.

4 The number 1.04 is an outlier because it is much smaller than the other values.
(i) We might exclude the value because it could be an error (perhaps it should have been recorded as 1.40)
(ii) We might include the value because it could have been correct (1.04 metres height is possible) and we want to include all the correct data values in our calculations.

6.4.2 Effect of changing data on measures of average and range

1 **a)** 1.6 is less than the original mean of 1.7
So the mean will decrease when this value is added to the data set.
b) 1.5 is lower than 15 so the mean will decrease

2 **a)** The median is the middle term, this will not change when the age is corrected.
b) There were 8 employees originally,
$\frac{8+1}{2} = \frac{9}{2} = 4.5$
The median is halfway between the 4th and 5th worker, so $\frac{25+37}{2} = 31$
There are now 9 employees: $\frac{9+1}{2} = \frac{10}{2} = 5$
So the median is the 5th value.
The new value will slot in after the 3rd value of 23
So, the 5th value is now 25
Median = 25 so it has decreased.

3 **a)** mean = 212 median = 218
mode = 212 range = 145
b) mean = 11.2 median = 11.8
mode = 11.2 range = 14.5

6.4.3 Comparing sets of data

1 Ben's mean score is higher than U-jin's.
The range of U-jin's scores is a little higher than Ben's scores.
Ben has a higher mean score and his scores are more consistent, so Ben is the better player.

2 For tennis club, estimate of mean
$= \frac{2853.5}{63} = 45.3$ years
For dance club, estimate of mean $= \frac{3353}{74} =$ 45.3 years
The mean age for both clubs are approximately the same.
For tennis club, maximum range = 69 – 20 = 49 years
For dance club, maximum range = 59 – 30 = 29 years
The maximum range is larger for tennis club than dance club.
The average age for both clubs is the same but there is a greater spread of ages in the tennis club.

3 **a)** outlier is 37.2 seconds
b) Included; it is possible that the 37.2 second measurement is not an error.

6.4.4 Comparing ways of presenting data

1 a) This involves discrete, quantitative data.
A bar chart with the number of tickets bought together against frequency.
b) This involves continuous, quantitative data.
A scatter graph of time of the movie against total cost of refreshments purchased.

2 The pie chart shows this more clearly because 'housing' is more than a quarter of the circle.
To use the bar chart, you would need to find the total spending first.

3 a) A scatter graph of age against the number of number of books borrowed in a month.
b) A bar chart or pictogram showing the frequency of each genre.
Or a pie chart with sectors representing each genre.

6.4.5 Using charts and graphs to compare sets of data

1 Both data sets have 18 values, so the position of the median is given by:
$\frac{18+1}{2} = 9.5$
Median of game A = 7
Median of game B = 4.5
The median score for game A is higher than game B.
Range of game A = 6
Range of game B = 7
The range for game B is larger than for game A.
Riley scored higher in game A on average, but her scores were slightly more spread out in game B.

2 The modal spending category for both years is administration, but the proportion decreased in 2023.
The council spent a greater proportion on community in 2023 than 2022.
The proportion spent on grants was similar.

7.1 Perimeter

7.1.1 Circumference of a circle

1 $C = \pi \times 9 = 28.3$ cm (1 d.p.)

2 $C = \pi \times 12 = 12\pi$ cm

3 Distance travelled = circumference × number of rotations
= diameter × π × number of rotations
Erin and Zayden have the same number of rotations but their wheels are different sizes.
If the wheel diameter is multiplied by 2 then the circumference will be also, and hence so will the distance travelled.
Distance travelled by Erin = 27 × 2 = 54 m

7.1.2 Perimeter of composite shapes

1 Arc length = $\frac{\pi \times 2 \times 2}{4} = 3.14$ cm
Perimeter = 2 + 2 + 3.14 = 7.14 cm (to 1 d.p.)

2 Perimeter = 4.71…+3 + 2 × 8 = 23.7 cm (to 1 d.p.)

3 Diameter = $\frac{37}{\pi} = 11.8$ cm (to 1 d.p.)

4 Length of curved edge = $\frac{\pi \times 13}{2} = 20.42\ldots$ cm
Perimeter = 20.42…+13 = 33.4 cm (to 1 d.p.)

7.2 Area

7.2.1 Area of a circle

1 $A = \pi \times 49$
$= 153.9$ cm^2 (to 1 d.p.)

2 $A = \pi \times 3^2$
$= 9\pi$ cm^2

7.2.2 Problem solving with area of a circle

1 Area of semicircle = $\pi \times 4^2 \div 2$
$= 8\pi$ cm^2

2 Area of quarter circle = $\pi \times 20^2 \div 4$
$= 1256.637\ldots \div 4$
$= 314.2$ cm^2 (to 1 d.p.)

3 Area of semicircle = $\frac{1}{2} \times \pi \times 4^2$
$= 8\pi$ cm^2
Area of rectangle = 20 × 5
= 100 cm^2
Total area = $100 - 8\pi$
$= 74.9$ cm^2 (to 1 d.p.)

4 $r^2 = \frac{37}{\pi}$
$r = \sqrt{\frac{37}{\pi}}$
$= 3.431\ldots$ cm
Diameter = 2 × 3.431…
= 6.9 cm (to 1 d.p.)

5 Area of circle = 2 × 4 = 84 cm^2

$$r^2 = \frac{84}{\pi}$$

$$r = \sqrt{\frac{84}{\pi}}$$

$$= 5.170\ldots \text{ cm}$$

Radius = 5.2 cm (to 1 d.p.)

7.3 Surface area

7.3.1 3D shapes

1 Hexagonal-based pyramid

2 The shape has three rectangular faces:
21 cm by 5.2 cm; 21 cm by 2 cm; 21 cm by 4.8 cm
It has two identical right-angled triangles with sides 2 cm, 4.8 cm and 5.2 cm

7.3.2 Cubes and cuboids

1 Surface area = 2 × (28 + 56 + 32)
= 232 cm^2

2 Surface area = 48 + 16 + 12 + 48 + 16 + 12
= 152 cm^2

3 Area of one face = 54 ÷ 6 = 9 cm^2
Side length = $\sqrt{9}$ = 3 cm

4 Area of cuboid (1) not exposed = 7 × 6 = 42 cm^2
Therefore, exposed surface area of cuboid (1)
= 430 – 42 = 388 cm^2
Five faces of cuboid (2) are exposed.
Exposed surface area of cuboid (2)
= 2 × (20 × 7) + 2 × (20 × 6) + (7 × 6)
= 562 cm^2
Total surface area = 388 + 562
= 950 cm^2

7.3.3 Prisms

1 Area of parallelogram face
= bh
= 8 × 4
= 32 cm^2
Surface area
= 32 + 32 + 120 + 120 + 192 + 192
= 688 cm^2

2 The base is formed from a rectangle and a trapezoid:
Area of rectangle = 4 × 7 = 28 cm^2
Area of trapezoid = $\frac{1}{2}$ × (7 + 12) × 12 = 114 cm^2
Area of base = 28 + 114 = 142 cm^2
Area of other faces:
= length of prism × perimeter of base
= 18 × (4 + 12 + 12 + 13 + 4 + 7)
= 18 × 52
= 936 cm^2
Surface area = 2 × 142 + 936
= 1220 cm^2

7.3.4 Cylinders

1 $C = \pi d$
= π × 12
= 12π cm
Area of curved surface
= 12π × 15
= 180π cm^2
The radius is half of the diameter:
r = 12 ÷ 2 = 6 cm
$A = \pi r^2$
= π × 6^2
= 36π cm^2
Surface area = 2 × 36π + 180π
= 252π cm^2

2 For the cylinder:
Circumference = 2 × π × 3
= 6π cm
Area of curved surface = 6π × 8
= 48π cm^2
For the cube:
Area = 6 × 8^2 = 384 cm^2
For the cylinder:
Area of circular face = π × 3^2 = 9π cm^2
Surface area = 384 + 48π – 2 × 9π
= 384 + 30π
= 478.2 cm^2 (to 1 d.p.)

7.4 Volume

7.4.1 Cubes and cuboids

1 Volume = 5 × 8 × 10
= 40 × 10
= 400 cm^3

2 Volume = 16 cm^3

3 Volume of solid = 8 × 3 × 2 + 2 × 2 × 2
= 48 + 8
= 56 cm^3

4 One possibility is: 3 cm, 3 cm and 11 cm

7.2.2 Prisms and cylinders

1 Area of base $= \frac{1}{2} \times 13 \times 4 = 26\text{ cm}^2$
Volume $= 26 \times 25 = 650\text{ cm}^3$

2 Volume = area of base × length of prism
$= 15 \times 6 = 90\text{ cm}^3$

3 Area of base = area of triangle – area of rectangle
$= \frac{1}{2} \times 23 \times 20 - 4 \times 18$
$= 230 - 72$
$= 158\text{ cm}^2$
Volume = area of base × length
$= 158 \times 19$
$= 3002\text{ cm}^3$

4 $V = \pi \times 9^2 \times 16$
$V = 1296\pi\text{ cm}^3$ (in terms of π)
$= 4071.5\text{ cm}^3$ (to 1 d.p.)

5 3.5 litres will occupy a volume of 3500 cm^3
Radius of cylinder $= 18 \div 2 = 9$ cm
Volume $= \pi r^2 h$
$= \pi \times 9^2 \times h$
$= 81\pi h$
$81\pi h = 3500$
$h = \frac{3500}{81\pi}$
$h = 13.75\ldots$
Height of water = 13.8 cm (to 1 d.p.)

8.1 Symmetry

8.1.1 Line symmetry

1
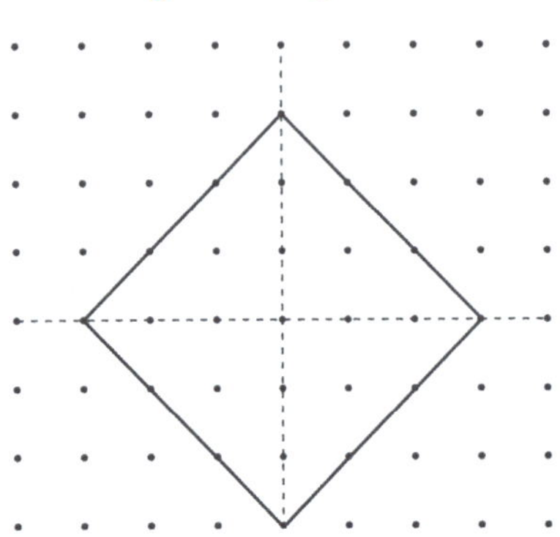

2
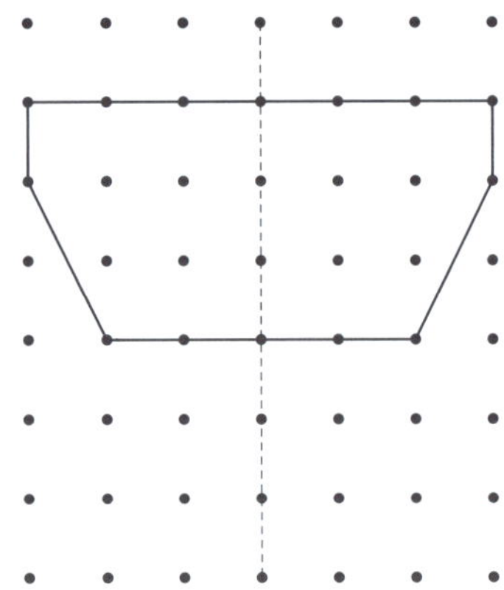

3
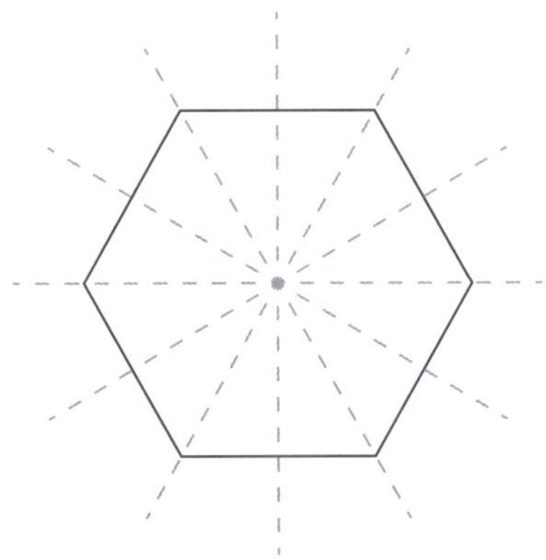

4 $x = 110°$
$y = 30°$

8.1.2 Rotational symmetry

1 The order of rotational symmetry is 4

2 A square. Each of the angles will be 90°

8.2 Angle properties

8.2.1 Angles around a point

1 Using the fact that the angles must add up to 360°:
$x = 360° - (75° + 200°)$
$= 360° - 275°$
$= 85°$

2 $x = 32°$ because vertically opposite angles are equal.
$y = 180° - (32° + 65°)$
$= 180° - 97°$
$= 83°$ because angles on a straight line add up to 180°

3 $165° + 90° + 2x + x = 360°$
since a right-angle is 90° and angles around a point add up to 360°
$255° + 3x = 360°$
$3x = 105°$
$x = 35°$

8.2.2 Parallel lines and corresponding angles

1 $\angle AGF$ (or $\angle AGH$) corresponds to $\angle CHF$.

2 $\angle FHD$ corresponds to $\angle FGB$.

3 x corresponds to the 117° angle since they are both above the transversal.
$x = 117°$ since corresponding angles on parallel lines are equal.
$y = 117°$ since vertically opposite angles are equal.

4 The two labelled angles are corresponding. Therefore, the lines AB and CD are parallel since the corresponding angles are equal.

5 Extend side AB to the point E.

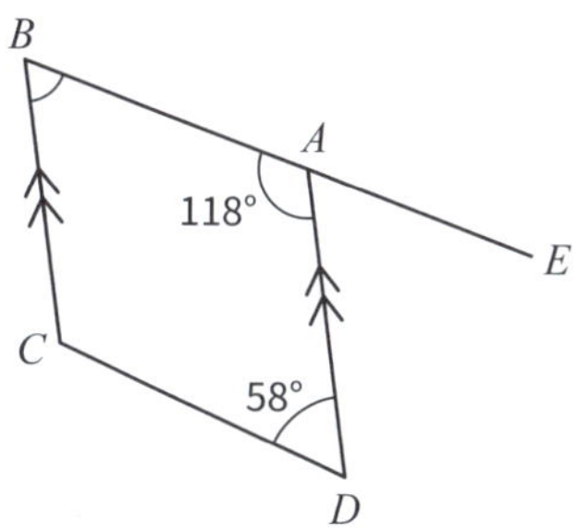

$\angle DAE = 180° - 118° = 62°$ since angles on a straight line add up to 180°
$\angle CBA = 62°$ since corresponding angles on parallel lines are equal.

8.2.3 Parallel lines and alternate angles

1 $\angle CHG$ (or $\angle CHE$) is alternate to $\angle BGF$.

2 x is alternate to the 94° angle since they are between the parallel lines and on the opposite sides of the transversal.
$x = 94°$ since alternate angles between parallel lines are equal.
$y = 86°$ since angles on a straight line add up to 180°

3 $5x = 140°$ since alternate angles between parallel lines are equal.
So $x = 28°$
$\angle BCE = 3x$ since corresponding angles on parallel lines are equal.
$\angle BCE = 3 \times 28° = 84°$

4 No, the lines AB and CD are not parallel since the alternate angles are not equal.

8.3 Angle properties of polygons

8.3.1 Angles in triangles

1 $x = 70°$
$y = 180° - (70° + 70°)$
$y = 40°$

2 Using the fact that the angles must add up to 180°:
$\angle CBA = 180° - (74° + 52°)$
$= 180° - 126°$
$= 54°$

3 $x + 2x + 2x = 180°$
since the base angles of an isosceles triangle are equal
$5x = 180°$
$x = 36°$

8.3.2 Interior angles of polygons

1 Interior angles of hexagon
$= 4 \times 180°$
$= 720°$

2

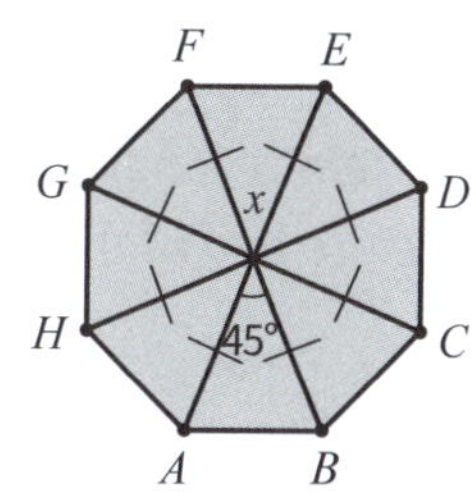

$\angle AXB = 360° \div 8 = 45°$
since angles around a point add up to 360°

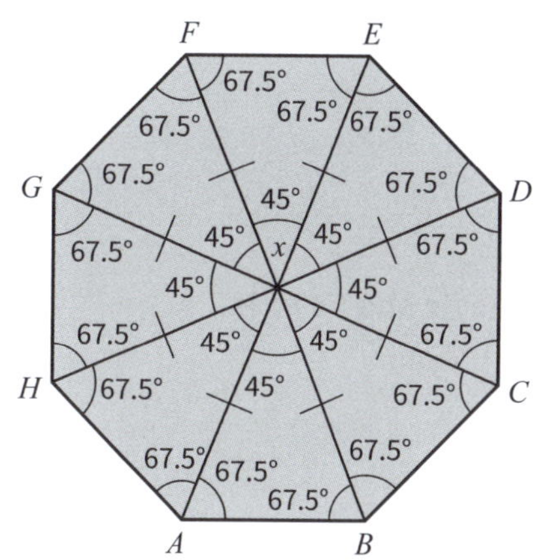

$\angle XBA = \angle BAX$ since base angles of an isosceles triangle are equal

$\angle XBA = (180° - 45°) \div 2$ since angles in a triangle add up to 180°

$= 135° \div 2$

$= 67.5°$

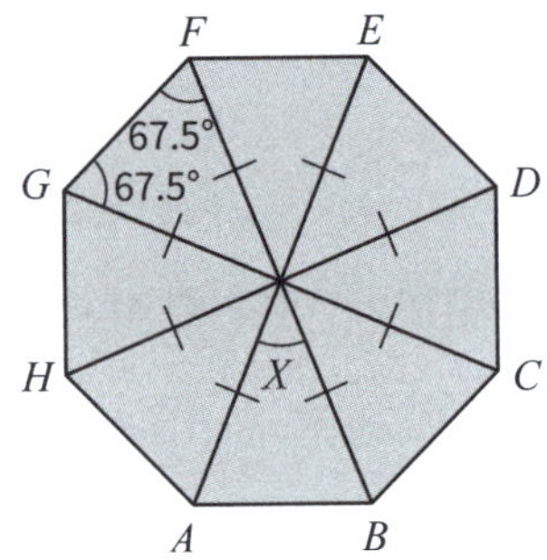

$\angle CBA = 67.5° \times 2 = 135°$

The interior angle is 135°

3

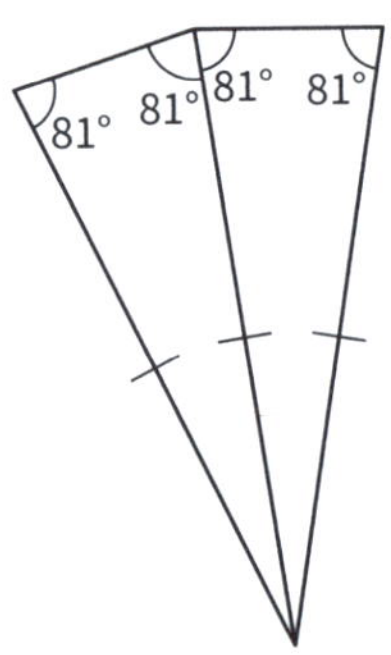

The polygon will split into n isosceles triangles. The base angles of each triangle are half of the interior angle of the polygon.

So base angle $= 162° \div 2 = 81°$

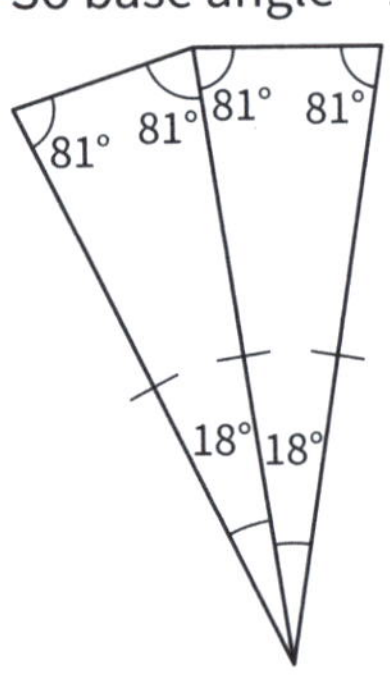

Angles in each triangle add up to 180°

Angle at centre of polygon

$= 180° - (81° + 81°)$

$= 180° - 162°$

$= 18°$

$18n = 360$

since angles around a point add up to 360°

So $n = 360 \div 18 = 20$

The regular polygon has 20 sides.

8.3.3 Exterior angles of polygons

1 a) $x = 540° \div 5 = 108°$ since the pentagon is regular

$y = 180° - x$ since sum of interior and exterior angles is 180°

$y = 180° - 108° = 72°$

b) Sum of exterior angles of regular pentagon

$= 5 \times 72°$

$= 360°$

2

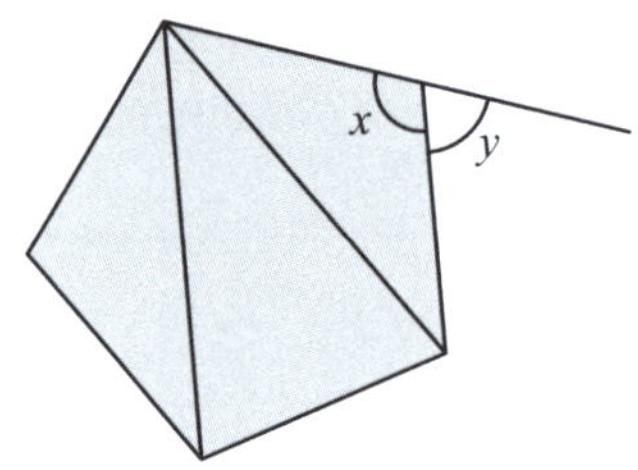

There are 3 triangles and each has an angle sum of 180°

Sum of interior angles of pentagon $= 3 \times 180°$

$= 540°$

3

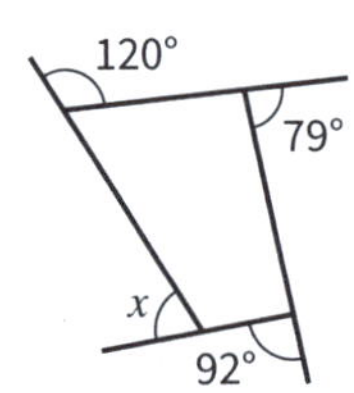

The exterior angles must add up to 360°

$x = 360° - (120° + 79° + 92°)$

$= 360° - 291°$

$= 69°$

4 a) All the exterior angles are equal in regular polygons.

Exterior angle $= 360° \div 5 = 72°$

since the sum of exterior angles of a polygon is 360°

b) Interior angle $= 180° - 72° = 108°$

since the sum of interior and exterior angles is 180°

5 $360° \div 20° = 18$

So the polygon has 18 sides since the sum of the exterior angles is 360°

6 Exterior angle $= 180° - 150° = 30°$

since the sum of an interior and exterior angle is 180°

$360° \div 30° = 12$

So the polygon has 12 sides since the sum of the exterior angles is 360°

8.4 Problem-solving with angles

8.4.1 Angle problems

1 Interior angle of equilateral triangle = 180° ÷ 3 = 60°

Exterior angle of regular octagon = 360° ÷ 8 = 45°, since the sum of the exterior angles of a polygon is 360° and they are all equal for a regular polygon.

Interior angle of regular octagon = 180° – 45°= 135°, since the sum of the interior and exterior angles is 180°

$x = 360° – (135° + 60°) = 165°$, since angles around a point add up to 360°

2 $\angle ACB = 63°$ since corresponding angles on parallel lines are equal.

$x = \angle CBA = 180° – (63° + 71°) = 46°$ since angles in a triangle add up to 180°

3 The base angles of isosceles triangles are equal so

$x = \angle ABC = \angle ACB$

$\angle ACB = (180° – 86°) \div 2 = 47°$

$x = 180° – 47° = 133°$ since angles on a straight line add up to 180°

4

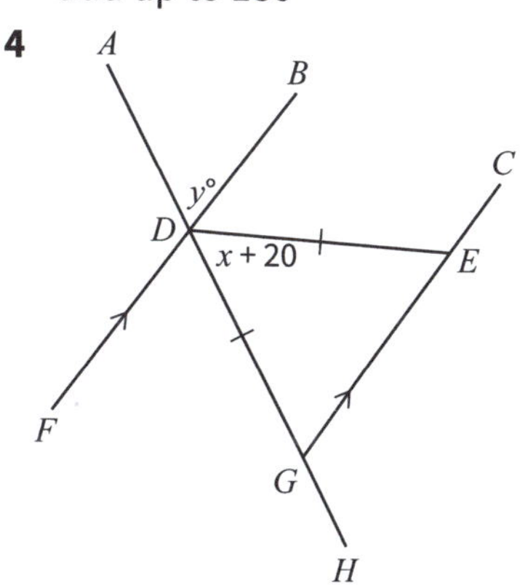

$\angle DGE + \angle DEG + (x + 20) = 180°$

since angles in a triangle add up to 180°

$\angle DGE = \angle DEG$ since the base angles of isosceles triangles are equal

$\angle DGE = (180° – x – 20°) \div 2$

$\angle DGE = (160° – x) \div 2$

$\angle ADB = \angle DGE$ since corresponding angles on parallel lines are equal

So $y = (160° – x) \div 2$

Or $2y = 160° – x$

9.1 Constructions using circles

9.1.1 Drawing circles

1

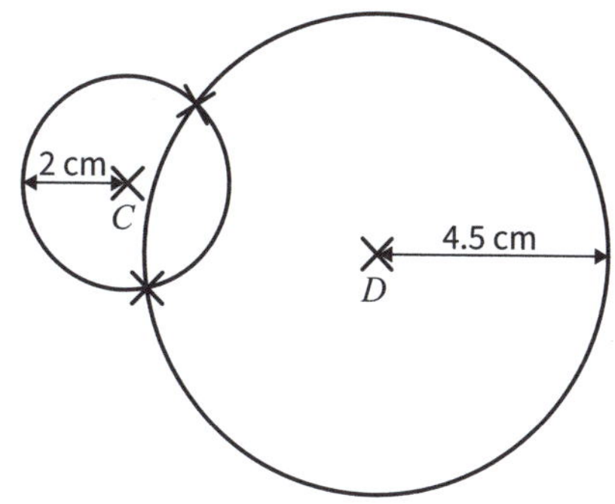

2 Circle with radius 3 cm

3 Circle with diameter 7 cm

4

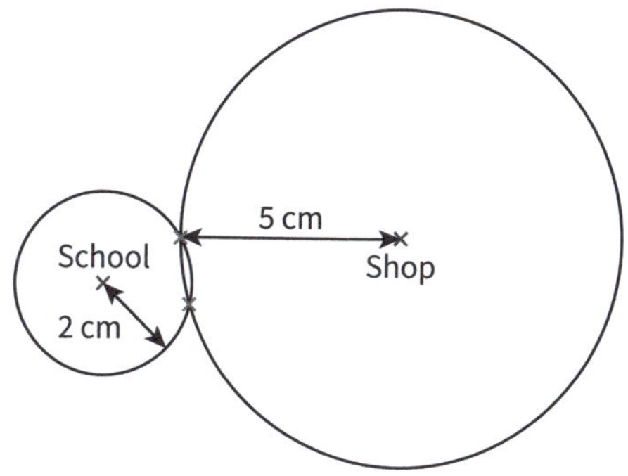

5

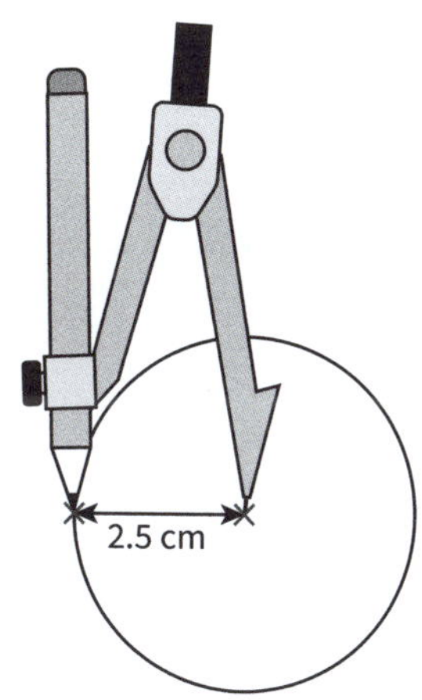

9.1.2 Constructing triangles

1 Triangle with sides 5 cm, 7 cm, and 8 cm.

2

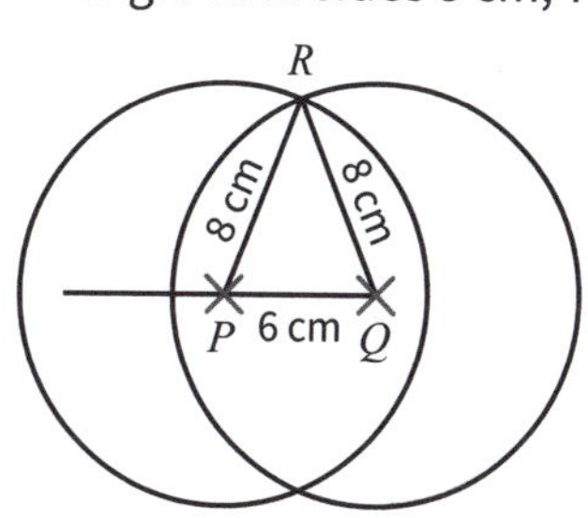

9.1.3 Constructing rhombuses

1

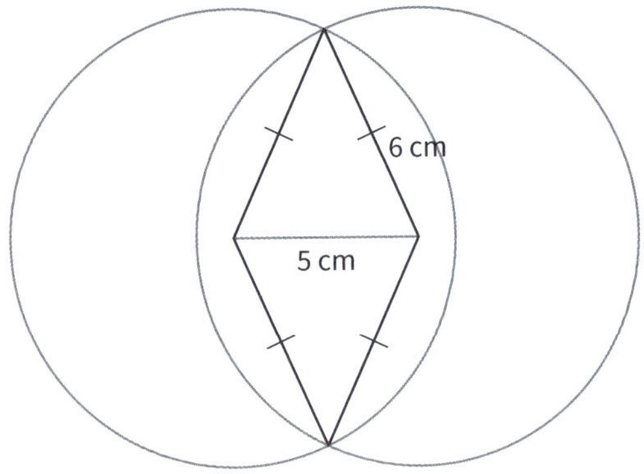

2

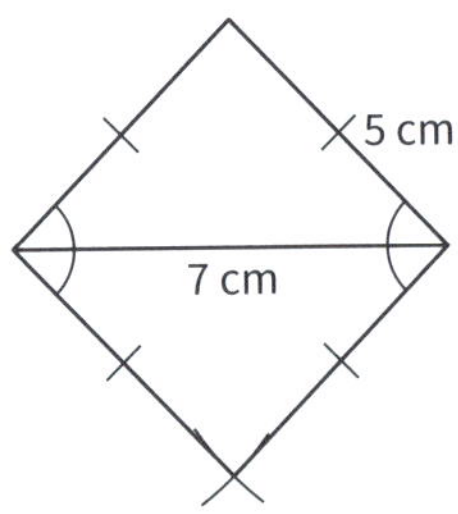

9.2 Constructions using rhombuses

9.2.1 Properties of rhombuses

1 60°

2

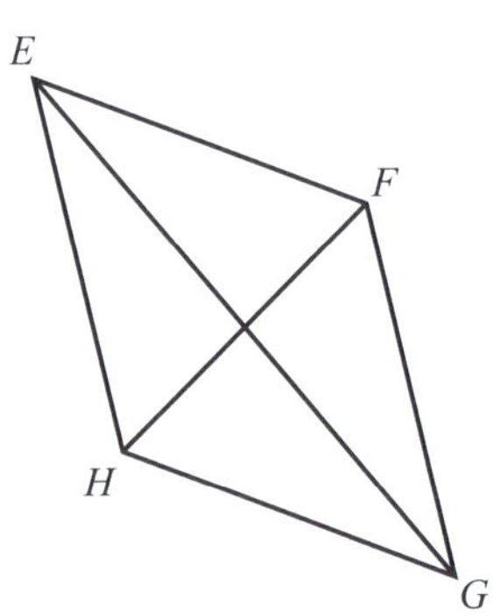

EG and *FH*

9.2.2 Constructing the perpendicular bisector of a line

1

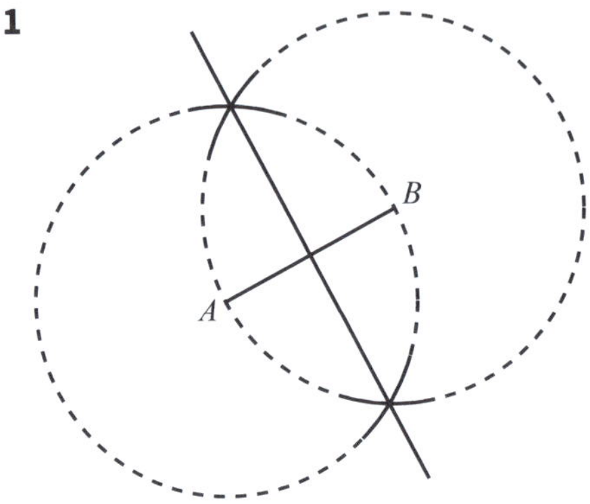

2

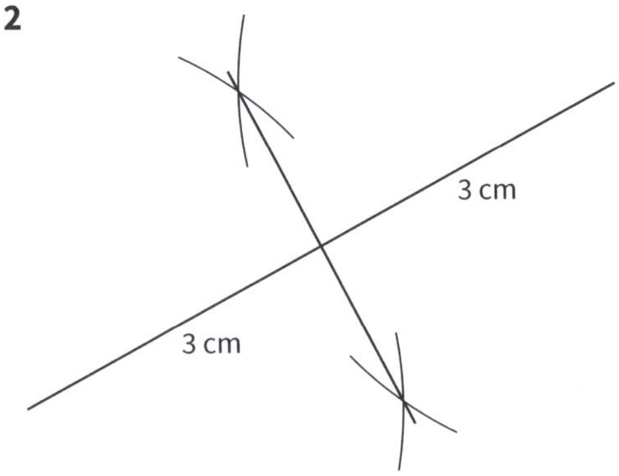

3

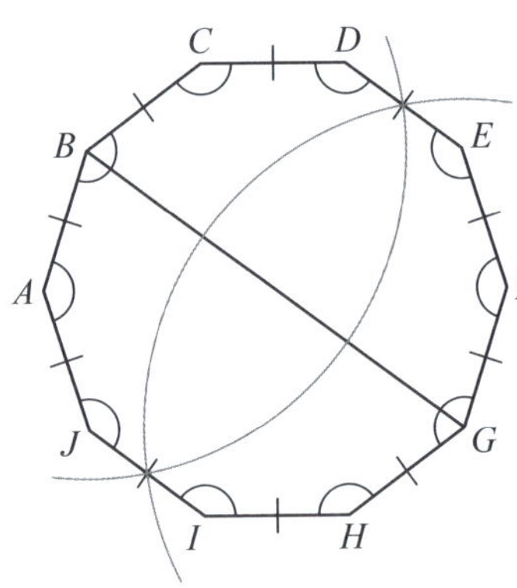

DE and *IJ*. This is a regular decagon.

9.2.3 Constructing a perpendicular to a line through a point

1

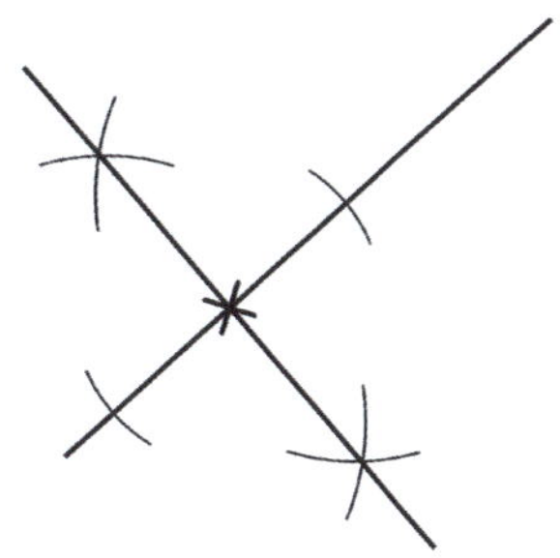

2

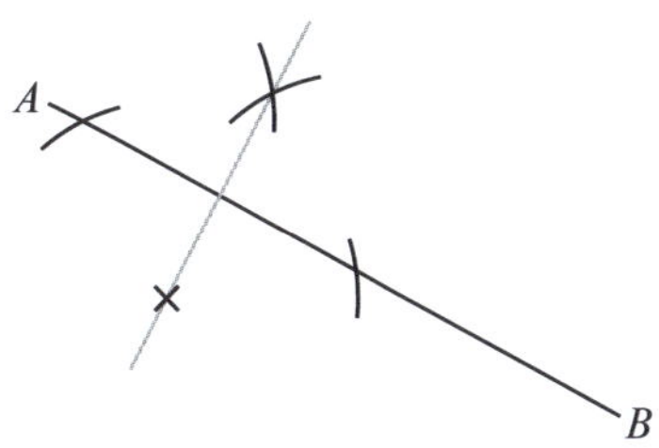

3

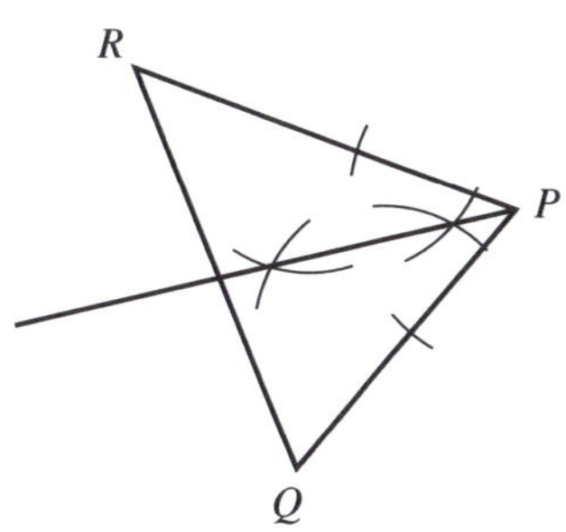

9.2.4 Bisecting angles

1

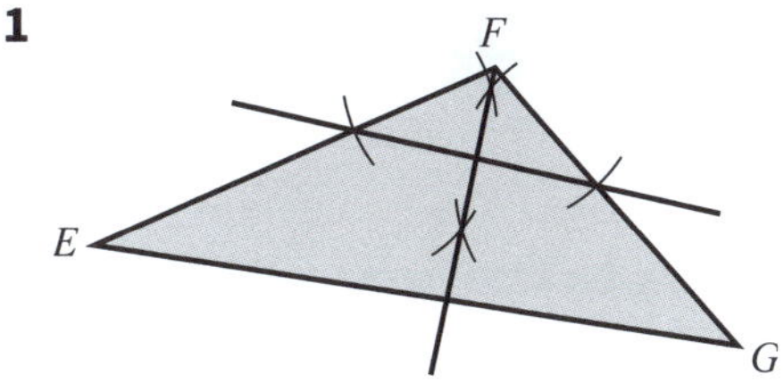

2

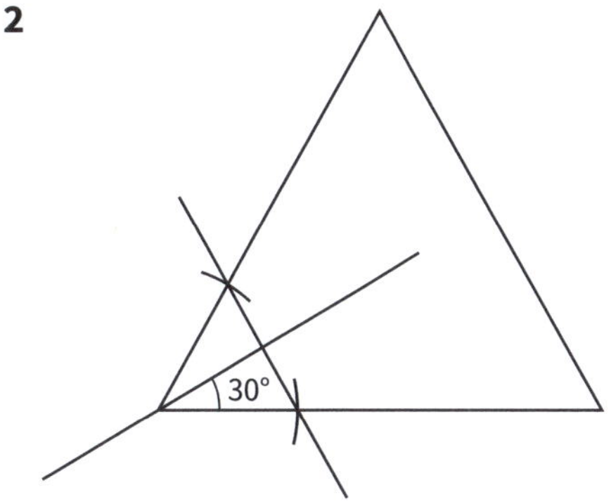

Fluency questions

1.1 Rounding to decimal places

1.1.1 Round integers to the nearest 10, 100, 1000, and higher

1 **a)** 10
b) 470

2 **a)** 100
b) 7400

3 **a)** 1000
b) 12 000

4 **a)** 10 000
b) 850 000

1.1.2 Rounding numbers to decimal places

1 **a)** 3.2
b) 0.9
c) 16.4

2 **a)** 28.37
b) 6.03
c) 0.89

3 **a)** 7.921
b) 0.323
c) 150.429

4 **a)** 0.1896
b) 2.7619
c) 10.4895

1.2 Rounding to significant figures

1.2.1 What is a significant figure?

1 30
2 10 000.4
3 705
4 2.05
5 0.05
6 0.0001
7 0.000 4002
8 0.000 007 502

1.2.2 Rounding integers to significant figures

1 **a)** 700
b) 650

2 **a)** 8000
b) 8100
c) 8130

3 **a)** 10 000
b) 15 000
c) 14 800
d) 14 820

4 **a)** 200 000
b) 220 000
c) 216 000
d) 215 600
e) 215 640

1.2.3 Rounding decimals to significant figures

1 **a)** 30
b) 3
c) 0.3
d) 0.03
e) 0.003
f) 0.0003
g) 0.000 03

2 **a)** 0.7
b) 0.05
c) 1
d) 0.009
e) 2000

1.3 Estimation

1.3.1 Estimating calculations

1 **c)** 14.2 cm, 12.8 cm, 12.1 cm (to 3 significant figures)

2 **a)** 452 ÷ 9.61 ≈ 500 ÷ 10 = **50**
b) 3187 + 9025 ≈ 3000 + **9000** = **12 000**
c) 18.42 × 1201 ≈ **20** × 1000 = **20 000**
d) 581.045 − 249.968 ≈ 580 **− 250** = **330**

e) $1.4983 + 0.5204 \approx \mathbf{1.5 + 0.5 = 2.0}$

f) $8.968 \times 3241.2 \approx \mathbf{9 \times 3000 = 27\,000}$

g) $121.02 \div 19.9983 \approx \mathbf{120 \div 20 = 6}$

h) $74\,925 - 4989.65 \approx \mathbf{75\,000 - 5000 = 70\,000}$

1.3.2 Evaluating estimates

1 a) Overestimate
b) Underestimate
c) Overestimate

2 a) Underestimate
b) Overestimate
c) Underestimate

1.3.3 Error intervals

1 a) i. Yes
ii. No
iii. Yes
iv. Yes
v. No
vi. No
vii. Yes

b) i. 450
ii. 549.99

2 a) i. Yes
ii. Yes
iii. No
iv. No
v. Yes
vi. Yes
vii. No

b) i. 295
ii. 304.99

3 a) i. No
ii. No
iii. No
iv. Yes
v. No
vi. No
vii. Yes

b) i. 799.5
ii. 800.49

2.1 Solutions to linear equations

2.1.1 What is a linear equation?

1 b) =

2 a) $3p + 2 - 5$ ☒ (*this is an expression*)
b) $4y - 2 = 0$ ☑
c) $1.8x = 5x - \frac{1}{2}$ ☑
d) $8z - 2 < 12$ ☒ (*this is an inequality*)
e) $7 \neq 15 - 6x$ ☒
f) $2a = 4b - 3$ ☑

3 a) $-5y$, $8x$
b) No
c) No
d) Yes

4 a) $3x^2$, $4y$, $2xy$
b) Yes ($3x^2$)
c) Yes ($2xy$)
d) No

2.1.2 Solutions to equations

1 a) Yes
b) No
c) Yes
d) Yes
e) No

2 a) 5
b) 3
c) 5
d) 3
e) 2

3 a) 20
b) 4
c) 16
d) 7
e) 32

2.1.3 Maintaining equality

1 a) False
b) True
c) True
d) False
e) True

2 a) Yes
b) Yes
c) Yes

3 a) Yes
b) Yes
c) Yes

4 a) Yes
b) No
c) No

2.2 One-step linear equations

2.2.1 Additive steps

1 a) −7
b) 4
c) 1
d) −12

2 a) I need to add the additive inverse of +4 to both sides:
$x + 4 \underline{- 4} = 9 \underline{- 4}$
$x = \underline{5}$

b) I need to add the additive inverse of −2 to both sides:
$y \underline{- 2} + 2 = \underline{6} + 2$
$y = \underline{8}$

3 a) $x = 1$
b) $y = 18$
c) $x = 24$
d) $y = 20$

2.2.2 Multiplicative steps

1 a) × 9
b) ÷ 2
c) × 10
d) ÷ 12

2 Dividing both sides of the equation by 8 gives:
$\frac{8x}{\boxed{8}} = \frac{32}{\boxed{8}}$
$x = \underline{4}$

3 a) $x = 6$
b) $y = 12$
c) $x = 6.5$
d) $y = 1.5$

4 a) Multiplying both sides of the equation by 3 gives:
$\frac{x}{3} \times \underline{3} = 6 \times \underline{3}$
$x = \underline{18}$

b) Multiplying both sides of the equation by 5 gives:
$\frac{y}{5} \times \underline{5} = 4 \times \underline{5}$
$y = \underline{20}$

2.3 Two-step linear equations

2.3.1 Dealing with a negative coefficient of the unknown

1 a) x
b) −8
c) 15
d) y

2 a) $8 - x = -3$
$(8 \times -1) + (-x \times -1) = -3 \times -1$
$\underline{-8} + \underline{x} = \underline{3}$

b) $-y = 3$
$-y \times \underline{-1} = 3 \times \underline{-1}$
$\underline{y} = \underline{-3}$

c) $-z - 4 = 9$
$(-z \times \underline{-1}) + (-4 \times \underline{-1}) = 9 \times \underline{-1}$
$\underline{z} + \underline{4} = \underline{-9}$

3 a) $x = 12$
b) $-5 = -7 + y$
c) $z + 2 = 8$
d) $x + 20 = -15$

2.3.2 Solving equations that require more than one step

1 a) $3x + 2 + \underline{-2} = 11 + \underline{-2}$
$3x = \underline{9}$

b) $\frac{3x}{\square} = \frac{\boxed{9}}{\boxed{3}}$
$x = \underline{3}$

2 a) $4x - 5 + \underline{5} = 15 + \underline{5}$
$4x = \underline{20}$

b) $\frac{4x}{\boxed{4}} = \frac{\boxed{20}}{\boxed{4}}$
$x = \underline{5}$

3 a) $2x + 7 = 13$
$2x + 7 + -7 = 13 + -7$
$2x + 7 - 7 = 13 - 7$
$2x = 6$

b) $\frac{2x}{2} = \frac{6}{2}$
$x = 3$

4 a) $5x + 10 = 40$
$\frac{5x}{5} + \frac{10}{5} = \frac{40}{5}$
$x + 2 = 8$

b) $x + 2 - 2 = 8 - 2$
$x = 6$

2.3.3 Unknowns on both sides

1 a) i. $x + 12 - \underline{x} = 7x - \underline{x}$

$\underline{12} = \underline{6}x$

ii. $\frac{12}{6} = \frac{6x}{6}$

$\underline{2} = x$

b) i. $8y - \underline{5y} = 5y + 9 - \underline{5y}$

$\underline{3y} = \underline{9}$

ii. $\frac{3y}{3} = \frac{9}{3}$

$y = \underline{3}$

c) i. $2z + 23 - \underline{2z} = 6z + 3 - \underline{2z}$

$23 = \underline{4}z + 3$

$23 - \underline{3} = \underline{4}z + 3 - \underline{3}$

$\underline{20} = \underline{4}z$

ii. $\frac{20}{4} = \frac{4z}{4}$

$\underline{5} = z$

2 a) i. $m + 18 = 4m$

$m + 18 - m = 4m - m$

$18 = 3m$

ii. $\frac{18}{3} = \frac{3m}{3}$

$6 = m$

b) i. $9p = 5p + 16$

$9p - 5p = 5p + 16 - 5p$

$4p = 16$

ii. $\frac{4p}{4} = \frac{16}{4}$

$p = 4$

c) i. $3q + 1 = q + 5$

$3q + 1 - q = q + 5 - q$

$2q + 1 = 5$

$2q + 1 - 1 = 5 - 1$

$2q = 4$

ii. $\frac{2q}{2} = \frac{4}{2}$

$q = 2$

2.4 Linear equations with brackets and fractions

2.4.1 Deciding how to deal with brackets in equations

1 a) $5(x + 4) = 5x + 20$

b) $5(x + 4) = 30$

$5x + 20 = 30$

$5x = 10$

$x = 2$

2 a) $4(2y + 3) = 8y + 12$

b) $4(2y + 3) = 36$

$8y + 12 = 36$

$8y = 24$

$y = 3$

3 a) $3(x - 5) = 3x - 15$

b) $3(x - 5) = 18$

$3x - 15 = 18$

$3x = 33$

$x = 11$

4 a) $2(6y - 1) = 12y - 2$

b) $2(6y - 1) + 5 = 12y - 2 + 5 = 12y + 3$

c) $2(6y - 1) + 5 = 51$

$12y + 3 = 51$

$12y = 48$

$y = 4$

2.4.2 Equations with brackets where the unknown is on both sides

1 a) $2(x + 8) = 2x + 16$

b) $3(x + 4) = 3x + 12$

c) $2(x + 8) = 3(x + 4)$

$2x + 16 = 3x + 12$

$16 = x + 12$

$4 = x$

2 a) $6(y + 2) = 6y + 12$

b) $5(y + 6) = 5y + 30$

c) $6(y - 2) = 5(y + 6)$

$6y + 12 = 5y + 30$

$y + 12 = 30$

$y = 18$

3 a) $4(x + 8) = 4x + 32$

b) $7(x + 2) = 7x + 14$

c) $4(x + 8) = 7(x + 2)$

$4x + 32 = 7x + 14$

$32 = 3x + 14$

$18 = 3x$

$6 = x$

4 a) $10(y + 3) = 10y + 30$

b) $8(y + 5) = 8y + 40$

c) $10(y + 3) = 8(y + 5)$

$10y + 30 = 8y + 40$

$2y + 30 = 40$

$2y = 10$

$y = 5$

2.4.3 Equations with fractions

1 a) $\frac{x}{2} \times \underline{2} = 5 \times \underline{2}$
$x = \underline{10}$
b) $\frac{y}{7} \times \underline{7} = 3 \times \underline{7}$
$y = \underline{21}$
c) $\frac{z}{4} \times \underline{4} = -2 \times \underline{4}$
$z = \underline{-8}$

2 a) $x = 48$
b) $y = 81$
c) $z = -15$

2.4.4 Equations with the unknown in the denominator

1 a) $\frac{10}{x} \times \underline{x} = 5 \times \underline{x}$
$10 = \underline{5x}$
$\frac{\underline{10}}{\underline{5}} = x$
$\underline{2} = x$
b) $\frac{14}{y} \times \underline{y} = 2 \times \underline{y}$
$14 = \underline{2y}$
$\frac{\underline{14}}{\underline{2}} = y$
$\underline{7} = y$
c) $\frac{36}{z} \times \underline{z} = 4 \times \underline{z}$
$36 = \underline{4z}$
$\frac{\underline{36}}{\underline{4}} = z$
$\underline{9} = z$

2 a) $x = 3$
b) $y = 12$
c) $z = 4$

3.1 Features of sequences

3.1.1 Continuing sequences

1 a) Add 2 dots
b) Add 2 dots
c) 7

2 a) Add 3 squares (1 on top, 1 on left, 1 on right)
b) Add 3 squares (1 on top, 1 on left, 1 on right)
c) 13

3 a) Add 4
b) Add 4
c) 14

4 a) Add 5
b) Add 5
c) 18

3.1.2 Using term-to-term rules

1 a) 10, 12, 14
b) 25, 30, 35
c) 30, 36, 42

2 11, 14, 17

3 7, 5, 3

4 16, 32, 64

3.1.3 Using position-to-term rules

1 a) 9
b) 13
c) 19

2 a) 14
b) 20
c) 29

3 a) 26
b) 36
c) 51

3.2 Arithmetic sequences

3.2.1 Identifying arithmetic sequences

1 a) 4
b) 7
c) 3
d) 5
e) 2.5

2 To move from term to term in an arithmetic sequence you…
…add or subtract the same number each time.

3.2.2 Working out the nth terms of arithmetic sequences

1 a) 1
b) 2
c) 3
d) 17
e) n
f) $3n$

2 a) 1
b) 2
c) 3
d) 17
e) n
f) $3n + 1$

3 a) The times table has been shifted by $\underline{+2}$
b) 1st term = 7 = $\underline{5}$ + 2
2nd term = 12 = $\underline{5 + 5}$ + 2
3rd term = 17 = $\underline{5 + 5 + 5}$ + 2
4th term = 22 = $\underline{5 + 5 + 5 + 5}$ + 2

c) 1
d) 2
e) 3
f) 17
g) n
h) $5n + 2$

4 **a)** The times table has been shifted by −1
b) 1st term = 3 = 4 − 1
2nd term = 7 = 4 + 4 − 1
3rd term = 11 = 4 + 4 + 4 − 1
4th term = 15 = 4 + 4 + 4 + 4 − 1
c) 1
d) 2
e) 3
f) 17
g) n
h) $4n - 1$

3.2.3 Using the nth term

1

1st term	2	×	1	+	3	=	5
2nd term	2	×	2	+	3	=	7
3rd term	2	×	3	+	3	=	9
4th term	2	×	4	+	3	=	11
5th term	2	×	5	+	3	=	13

The sequence is 5, 7, 9, 11, 13, ...

2 **a)** $3 \times 1 + 4 = 7$
b) $3 \times 2 + 4 = 10$
c) $3 \times 3 + 4 = 13$
d) $3 \times 4 + 4 = 16$
e) $3 \times 5 + 4 = 19$

3 7, 13, 19, 25, 31

4 1, 4, 7, 10, 13

3.2.4 Finding terms of arithmetic sequences

1 **a)** 10, 16, 22, 28, ... The numbers are all even.
b) 7, 14, 21, 28, ... The numbers are all multiples of 7.
c) 15, 19, 23, 27, ... The numbers are all odd.
d) 1, 6, 11, 16, ... The numbers end in 1 or 6.

2 **a)** They are all even numbers.
b) No; it isn't an even number.

3 **a)** They all end in a 2 or a 7.
b) No; it doesn't end in a 2 or 7.
c) Yes; it ends in a 7.

4 **a)** They are all odd numbers.
b) No; it isn't an odd number.
c) No; the sequence starts at 25 and then decreases so won't go to 43.

4.1 Connect coordinates, equations, and graphs

4.1.1 When to join points on a graph

1 **a)** **i.** Yes
ii. No; sequences only have integer term numbers.
iii. No; sequences only have positive term numbers.
b) No

2 **a)** **i.** Yes
ii. Yes
iii. Yes
b) Yes

3 When a line is used to join the points on a graph, it means that…
c) … any point on that line fits the relationship given in the equation.

4.1.2 Using a rule to find coordinates

1 **a)**

x	1	2	3	4	5
y	5	6	7	8	9

b)

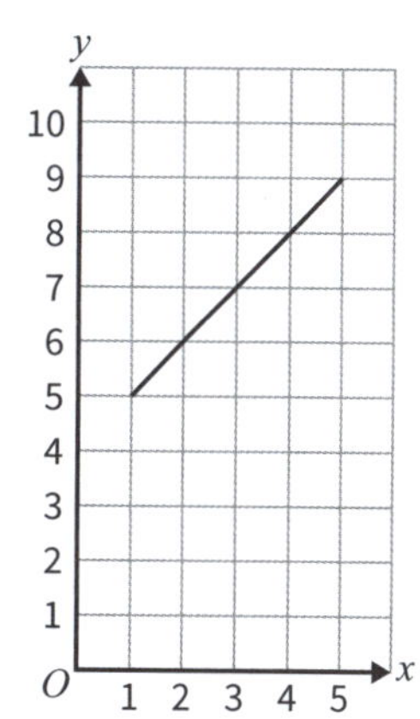

2 a)

x	1	2	3	4	5
y	2	4	6	8	10

b)

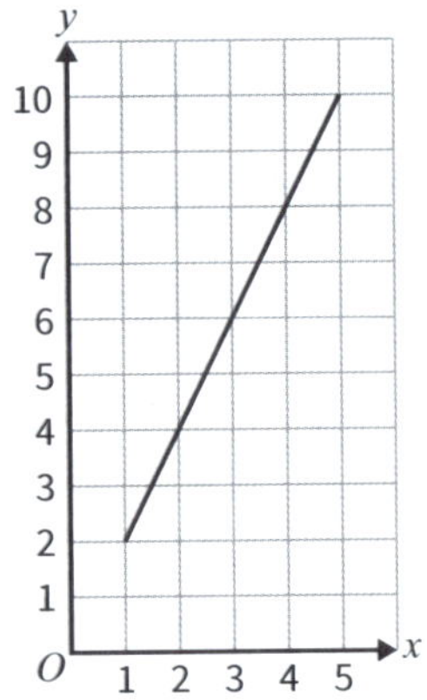

3 a) No
b) Yes
c) No
d) Yes

4 a) Yes
b) No
c) No
d) Yes

4.2 Linear relationships

4.2.1 Finding the gradient of a line

1 a) +3
b) +6
c) $\text{gradient} = \frac{\text{vertical increase}}{\text{horizontal increase}} = \frac{+6}{+3} = 2$

2 a) +4
b) −2
c) $\text{gradient} = \frac{\text{vertical increase}}{\text{horizontal increase}} = \frac{-2}{+4} = -\frac{1}{2}$ or − 0.5

3 a) +9
b) +3
c) $\text{gradient} = \frac{\text{vertical increase}}{\text{horizontal increase}} = \frac{+3}{+9} = \frac{1}{3}$

4 a) +3
b) −8
c) $\text{gradient} = \frac{\text{vertical increase}}{\text{horizontal increase}} = \frac{-8}{+3} = -\frac{8}{3}$

4.2.2 The gradient and y-intercept

1 a) *B*
b) *C*
c) *A*

2 a) *B*
b) $\text{gradient} = \frac{\text{vertical increase}}{\text{horizontal increase}} = \frac{2}{4} = \frac{1}{2}$ or 0.5
c) $\text{gradient} = \frac{\text{vertical increase}}{\text{horizontal increase}} = \frac{5}{1} = 5$
d) *B*

3 a) *A*
b) *A*

4 Arya's line is **steeper**, which means that it has a **higher** gradient. This shows that her distance was changing at a **higher** rate. She covered the same distance in **less** time than Ben.

5 a) *B*
b) *A*
c) *C*

4.2.3 $y = mx + c$ form of linear graphs

1 a) $y = \underline{4}x + \underline{2}$
b) $y = \underline{4}x + \underline{-2}$
c) $y = \underline{4}x + \underline{5}$
d) $y = \underline{6}x + \underline{5}$
e) $y = \underline{1}x + \underline{9}$
f) $y = \underline{5}x + \underline{0}$
g) $y = \underline{0}x + \underline{3}$

2 a) i. $\text{gradient} = \frac{\text{vertical increase}}{\text{horizontal increase}} = \frac{+4}{+2} = 2$
ii. y-intercept = 3
iii. $y = 2x + 3$

b) i. $\text{gradient} = \frac{\text{vertical increase}}{\text{horizontal increase}} = \frac{+4}{+2} = 2$
ii. y-intercept = −1
iii. $y = 2x - 1$

c) i. $\text{gradient} = \frac{\text{vertical increase}}{\text{horizontal increase}} = \frac{+4}{+2} = 2$
ii. y-intercept = 0
iii. $y = 2x$

3 a) i. $\text{gradient} = \frac{\text{vertical increase}}{\text{horizontal increase}} = \frac{+3}{+1} = 3$
ii. y-intercept = 2
iii. $y = 3x + 2$

b) i. $\text{gradient} = \frac{\text{vertical increase}}{\text{horizontal increase}} = \frac{+3}{+3} = 1$
ii. y-intercept = 2
iii. $y = x + 2$

c) i. gradient = 0
ii. y-intercept = 2
iii. $y = 2$

4.2.4 Solving problems involving linear graphs

1 a) Yes **b)** No
c) No **d)** Yes

2 a) C

b) A

c) D

d) B

3 a) y-intercept = 3

b) gradient = $\dfrac{\text{vertical increase}}{\text{horizontal increase}} = \dfrac{6}{3} = 2$

c) ii. $y = 2x + 3$

d) The y-**intercept** represents the cost before any distance has been travelled. That means the taxi driver charges a starting cost of **$3**.

e) The **gradient** represents the cost per kilometre. It shows that the taxi driver charges **$2** for every 1 kilometre travelled.

5.1 Percentages

5.1.1 Percentages, fractions, and decimals

1 a) $70\% = \dfrac{70}{100} = \dfrac{7}{10}$

b) $70\% = \dfrac{70}{100} = 70 \div 100 = 0.7$

2 a) $35\% = \dfrac{35}{100} = \dfrac{7}{20}$

b) $35\% = \dfrac{35}{100} = 35 \div 100 = 0.35$

3 a) i. $\dfrac{1}{10}$ **ii.** 0.1

b) i. $\dfrac{3}{10}$ **ii.** 0.15

c) i. $\dfrac{3}{4}$ **ii.** 0.75

d) i. $\dfrac{14}{25}$ **ii.** 0.56

4 b)

5 a)

5.1.2 Comparing quantities with percentages

1 a) $\dfrac{9}{50} = \dfrac{18}{100} = 0.18$

b) $\dfrac{11}{20} = \dfrac{55}{100} = 0.55$

2 a) $\dfrac{13}{52} = 13 \div 52 = 0.25$

$0.25 \times 100\% = 25\%$

b) $\dfrac{60}{75} = 60 \div 75 = 0.8$

$0.8 \times 100\% = 80\%$

3 a) 85%

b) 82%

c) The Korean spelling test

4 a) 72%

b) 70%

c) 30 ml cup

5.1.3 Finding percentages

1 a)

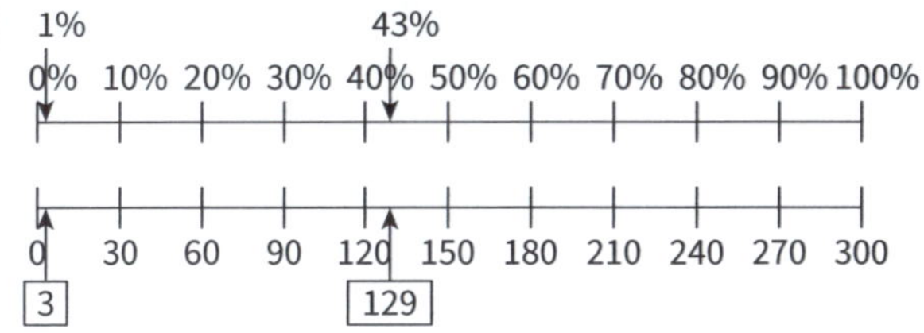

b)

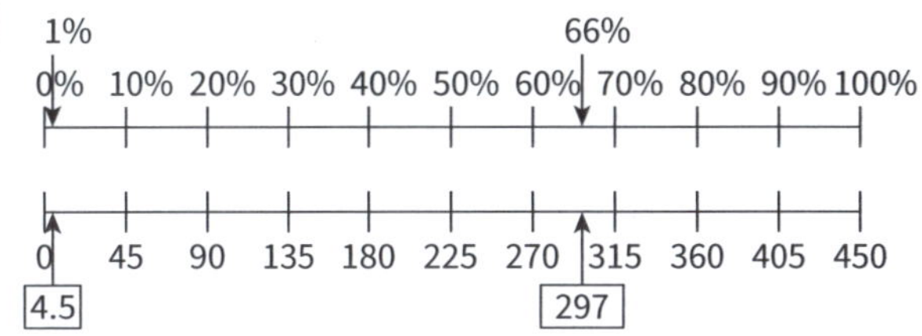

2 a)

Value	11	33
Percentage	25%	75%

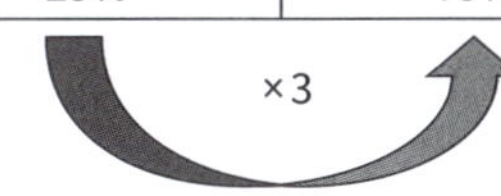

b)

Value	13	65
Percentage	8%	40%

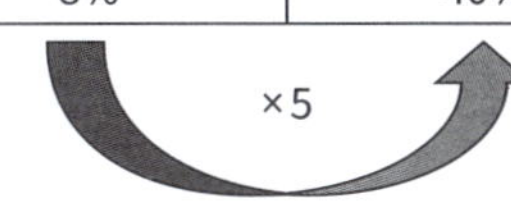

c)

Value	27	9	90
Percentage	30%	10%	100%

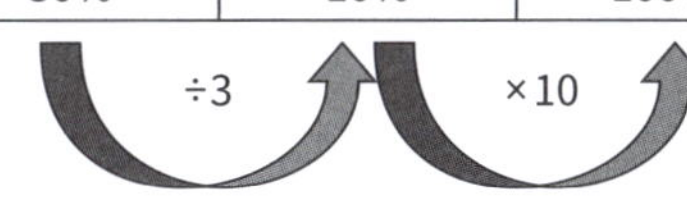

3 c)

5.1.4 Percentage increase and decrease

1 a)

Value	$80	$64
Percentage	100%	80%

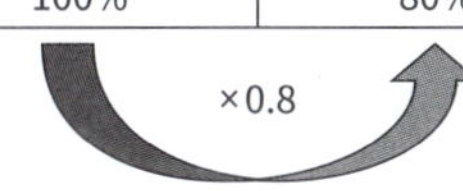

b)

Value	$120	$132
Percentage	100%	110%

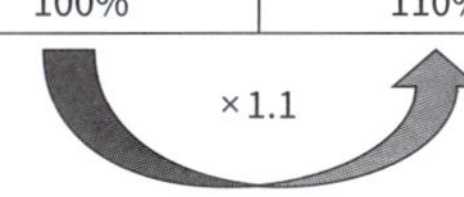

2 a) $100\% - 20\% = 80\% = \dfrac{80}{100} = \dfrac{4}{5}$

b) $100\% - 20\% = \dfrac{80}{100} = 80 \div 100 = 0.8$

3 a) $100\% + 25\% = 125\% = \dfrac{125}{100} = \dfrac{5}{4}$

b) $100\% + 20\% = \dfrac{125}{100} = 125 \div 100 = 1.25$

4 b)

5 d)

5.1.5 Finding an original amount

1 950

2

Value	\$720	\$80	\$800
Percentage	90%	10%	100%

÷9 ×10

3 **a)** 1.2

b)

÷1.2

Value	6630	5525
Percentage	120%	100%

×1.2

c) 5525

4 **a)** 0.7

b)

÷0.7

Value	\$210	\$300
Percentage	70%	100%

×0.7

c) \$300

5.1.6 Finding the percentage change

1 40% increase

2 **d)**

3 **a)** 25% increase = 100% + <u>25%</u> = <u>125%</u> = 1.25

b) 25% decrease = 100% − <u>25%</u> = <u>75%</u> = <u>0.75</u>

4 **a)**

$\times \frac{1500}{1200} = \times 1.25$

Value	\$1200	\$1500
Percentage	100%	125%

The percentage increase is <u>25%</u>

b)

×0.8

Value	1200 m	960 m
Percentage	100%	80%

The percentage decrease is <u>20%</u>

5 **a)** 1.75

b)

×1.75

Value	8 litres	14 litres
Percentage	100%	175%

c) 75%

6 **a)** 0.4

b)

×0.4

Value	15	6
Percentage	100%	40%

c) 60%

5.2 Proportionality

5.2.1 Representing multiplicative relationships

1

x	0	1	2	3
y	0	3	6	9

2 **a)**

x	0	1	2	3
y	0	2	4	6

b)

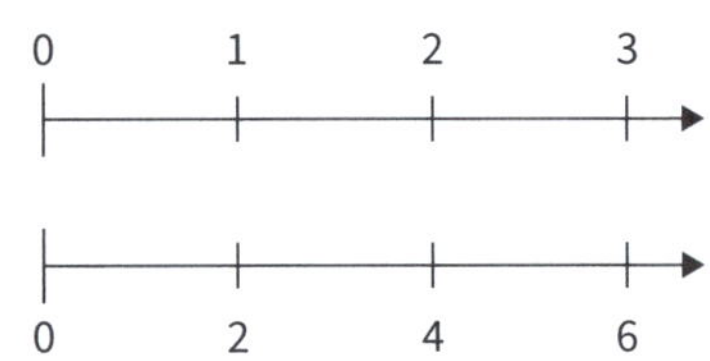

c)

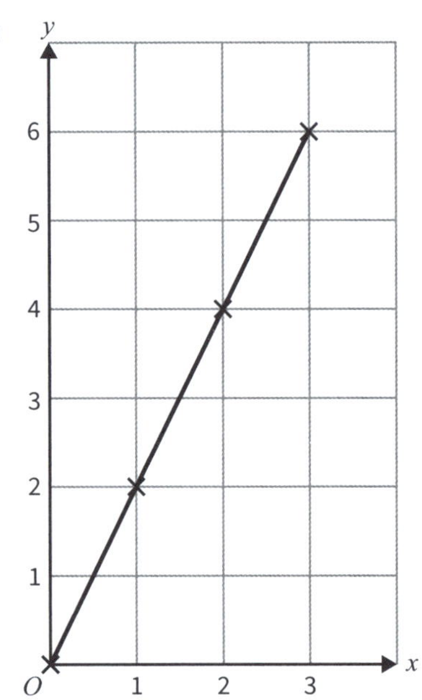

3 **a)**

x	0	2	4	6
y	0	1	2	3

b)

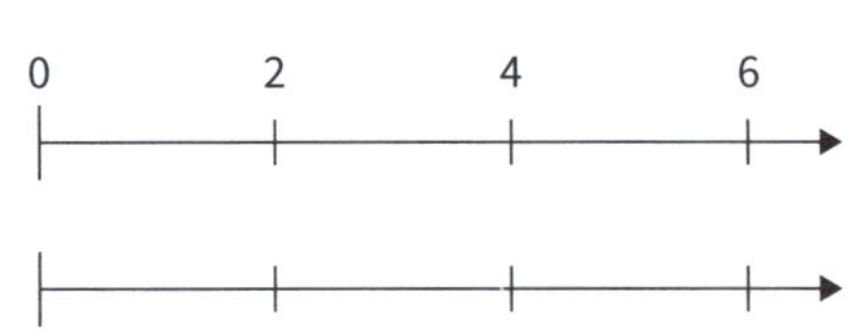

c)

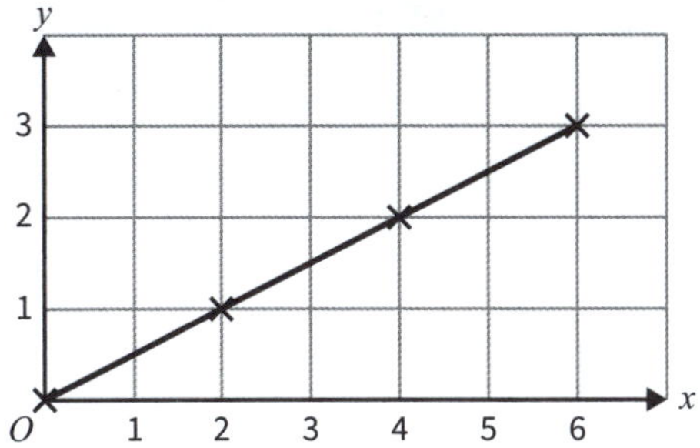

4 b)

5 a)

5.2.2 Direct proportion

1 0

Directly proportional relationship	Multiplier
$y = 4x$	× 4
$y = 3.5x$	× 3.5
$y = 0.8x$	× 0.8
$y = 8x$	× 8
$y = 5.2x$	× 5.2

2 c)

3 c)

4 d)

5.2.3 Solving problems involving direct proportion

1 a)

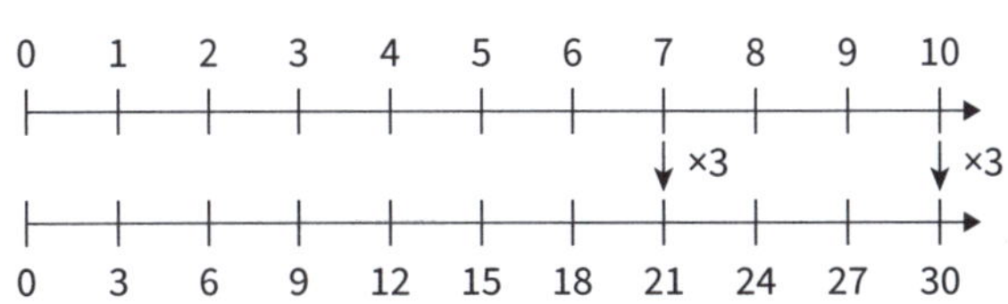

b) $30

2 a)

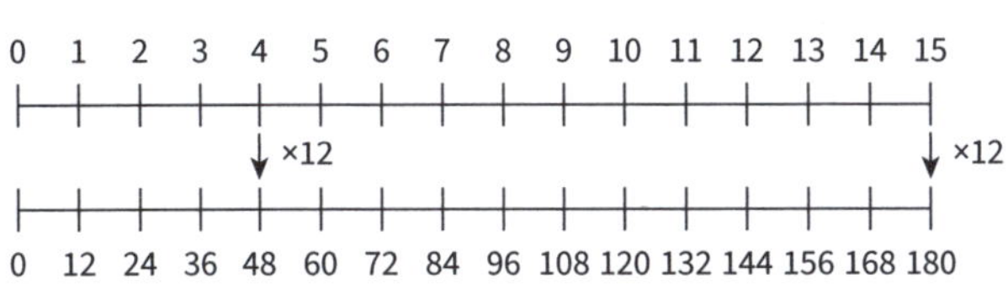

b) 180 square centimetres

3 a) 5 g

b) 60 g

5.2.4 Inverse proportion

1 a)

× 2

Workers	12	24
Days	16	8

÷ 2

b) 16 days

2 a)

÷ 30

Length	450	15
Width	0.6	18

× 30

b) 450 cm

3 a)

÷ 4

Hours	5	1.25
Litres	20	80

× 4

b) 1.25 hours or 1 hour and 15 minutes

4 a)

× 3

Speed (km/h)	30	90
Time (minutes)	42	14

÷ 3

b) 14 minutes

6.1 Representing data

6.1.1 Ungrouped frequency tables

1

Number of cars sold	Tally
0	卌 ||
1	卌 |
2	卌 卌
3	卌 ||

2 a)

Number of goals	Tally	Frequency
0	卌 卌 ||||	14
1	卌 卌 |||	**13**
2	卌 |||	**8**
3	|||	**3**

b) 8

c) 38

3

0	0	0	0	0	0	1	1	1	1
1	1	2	2	2	2	3	3	3	4

4 e.g. Favourite ice cream flavour/number of people who would buy each flavour of ice cream.

6.1.2 Grouped frequency tables

1 a)

Score out of 60	Tally	Frequency
21–30	||||	4
31–40	𝍸	**5**
41–50	𝍸 ||	**7**
51–60	||||	**4**

b) 11 students

c)

Score out of 60	Tally	Frequency
21–30	|	1
31–40	𝍸 |	6
41–50	𝍸 𝍸	10
51–60	𝍸	**5**

2 a)

Height, h (cm)	Tally	Frequency
$100 \le h < 110$	|||	3
$110 \le h < 120$	𝍸 |	6
$120 \le h < 130$	𝍸	**5**
$130 \le h < 140$	𝍸	**6**

b) The $130 \le h < 140$ category

3

Mass, m (grams)	Tally	Frequency
$2000 \le m < 2500$	|||	3
$2500 \le m < 3000$	𝍸 |	6
$3000 \le m < 3500$	𝍸 𝍸 |||	13
$3500 \le m < 4000$	𝍸 |	**6**
$4000 \le m < 4500$	||	**2**

6.1.3 Bar charts

1 Bar with frequency 7.

2 Bars with frequency 4 for Strawberry and 5 for Other.

3 Bars with frequencies 12, 7, 8 for Wednesday, Thursday, and Friday, respectively.

4 **a)** Thursday **b)** Tuesday and Friday

5 **a)** 9
b) 6
c) Wednesday
d) Friday

6 **a)** 2
b) 7
c) 5
d) 6

6.1.4 Pictograms

1 **a)** 4
b) 2
c) 6
d) 14
e) 20

2 **a)** 10
b) 5
c) 15
d) 45

3 **a)** 1
b) 3
c) 7

6.1.5 Constructing scatter graphs

1 Point plotted at (3, 2).

2 Points plotted at (2, 10) and (1, 10).

3 Point plotted at (7, 100).

6.1.6 Interpreting scatter graphs

1 **a)** \$40 million
b) \$11 million
c) 5 weeks
d) \$32 million

2 **a)** 10 scarves
b) 20 sunglasses

6.2 Angles and pie charts

6.2.1 Fractions of circles

1 **a)** 180
b) 120
c) 90
d) 72
e) 60
f) 45
g) 40
h) 36
i) 30
j) 24
k) 20

2 a) $\frac{1}{3}$
b) $\frac{1}{9}$
c) $\frac{1}{5}$
d) $\frac{1}{6}$

3 a) 180
b) 90
c) 36
d) 108
e) 72
f) 288
g) 60

4 a) $\frac{1}{10}$
b) $\frac{1}{20}$
c) $\frac{9}{20}$
d) $\frac{1}{50}$

6.2.2 Constructing pie charts

1 10°
2 6°
3 54°
4 a)

Car colour	Frequency	Angle
White	8	8 × 9° = 72°
Silver	6	6 × 9° = 54°
Red	8	8 × 9° = 72°
Blue	11	11 × 9° = 99°
Other	7	7 × 9° = 63°

b) A correct pie chart showing the above.

6.2.3 Interpreting pie charts

1 a) Banana
b) Orange

2 a) $\frac{1}{2}$
b) 10
c) $\frac{1}{4}$
d) 5

3 a) 60°
b) $\frac{60}{360} = \frac{1}{6}$
c) 12°
d) 10 robins

6.3 Measures of average and spread of data

6.3.1 The mean

1 mean score $= \frac{5+5+8}{3} = \frac{18}{3} = 6$

2 a) 28
b) 4
c) 7
d) 4
e) 11
f) Yes

3 a) 7.5
b) 14
c) 20
d) 16.22

4 a) 1 match
b) 3 matches
c) 6 matches
d) 15 goals
e) 10 matches
f) 1.5 goals

6.3.2 The median

1 a) 6
b) 3
c) 28

2 a) 8
b) 6.5
c) 44

3 a) 7
b) 7.5

4 a) 1
b) 3
c) 2
d) 2
e) 14, 15, 15, 15, 16, 16, 17, 17
f) 15.5

6.3.3 The mode

1 1 car
2 8
3 0 goals

6.3.4 The range

1 7 marks

2 a) 15
b) 42
c) 27

3 a) 6
b) 6.3
c) 107

4 a) 8
b) 53

6.3.5 Average and range of grouped data

1 8th

2 a) 41–50
b) 21. We cannot be sure that a student got 21 because we only know that the lowest score was between 21 and 30 (inclusive).
c) 60
d) i. 25
ii. 13th

3 a) $120 \le h < 130$
b) 17
c) 9th position

6.4 Analysing and comparing data

6.4.1 Averages and outliers

1 a) 6
b) 7
c) 8
d) 5

2 a) 40.72 metres.
b) All the other distances are between 48.59 metres and 51.09 metres.

3 a) \$40 000
b) \$68 000
c) \$59 000
d) \$68 000

4 School B

5 The mean commuting time of people who do listen to podcasts.

6.4.2 Effect of changing data on measures of average and range

1 a) i. 6
ii. 6
b) i. 7
ii. 20
c) i. 7
ii. 46

2 a) i. 15
ii. 15
iii. No, it had no effect on the median.
b) i. 14
ii. 14.2
iii. Yes, the mean increased.
c) i. 6
ii. 7
iii. Yes, the range increased.

3 a) 14.5
b) 13.5
c) 13
d) 6
e) The mean increased.
f) The range increased.

6.4.3 Comparing sets of data

1 a) List 2
b) List 2
c) List 1

2 a) Company 2
b) Company 2
c) Company 1
d) Company 1
e) Company 1

3 a) Team A
b) Team B

6.4.4 Comparing ways of presenting data

1 a) pie chart
b) bar chart
c) scatter graph

2 pie chart

3 scatter graph

4 The pie chart

6.4.5 Using charts and graphs to compare sets of data

1 a) 1
b) 2
c) 0
d) 2
e) 0
f) The modal number of pets in **Stage 8** is higher than in **Stage 7**.

2 **a)** 0
b) 2
c) Yes
d) No
e) 0
f) 3
g) 2
h) The modal number of cars owned by households is higher in the **village** than in the **city**. The range of number of cars owned by households is higher in the **village** than in the **city**.

3 **a)** 6
b) 12
c) 4
d) 10
e) 14
f) 6
g) 8
h) 4
i) The mean number of apples sold **in the mornings** was lower than the mean number sold **at lunch times**. The range in number of apples sold in **the mornings** was lower than **at lunch times**.

7.1 Perimeter

7.1.1 Circumference of a circle

1 **a)** True
b) False
c) False

2 **a)** is true

3 **a)**

	Diameter	Circumference	Circumference ÷ Diameter
A	3 cm	9.42 cm	3.14
B	4 cm	12.57 cm	**3.14**
C	5 cm	15.71 cm	**3.14**
D	6 cm	18.85 cm	**3.14**

b) Circumference ÷ Diameter is always 3.14 (to 2 decimal places)

4

	Radius	Diameter	Circumference
Example	*5 cm*	*10 cm*	*31.4 cm*
a)	4 cm	8 cm	**25.1 cm**
b)	**9 cm**	18 cm	**56.5 cm**
c)	8.5 cm	**17 cm**	**53.4 cm**

7.1.2 Perimeter of composite shapes

1 25.5 cm
2 9 cm
3 5.1 cm
4 **a)** 28.3 cm
b) 9 cm + 14.1 cm = 23.1 cm (to 1 decimal place)

7.2 Area

7.2.1 Area of a circle

1 **a)** An estimate of 28 cm^2 or 29 cm^2.
b) 28.3 cm^2

2 254 cm^2
3 201 cm^2
4 Radius = <u>5</u> cm; $A = \pi \times \underline{8}^3 = \underline{78.5}$ cm^2

7.2.2 Problem solving with area of a circle

1 39.3 cm^2
2 $r = \sqrt{\frac{70}{\pi}} = 4.7$ cm
3 8.9 cm
4 Area of square = <u>36</u> cm^2; Area of whole circle = <u>113</u> cm^2; Area of quarter circle = <u>28.3</u> cm^2; Area of whole compound shape = <u>64.3</u> cm^2

7.3 Surface area

7.3.1 3D shapes

1 **a)** Cuboid (or rectangular prism)
b) Square-based pyramid
c) **i.** face, **ii.** vertex, **iii.** edge

2 **a)** 7
b) 15
c) 10

3 **a)** 8
b) 18
c) 12

4 **a)** 4
b) 6
c) 4

7.3.2 Cubes and cuboids

1 76 cm^2

2 a)

Face	Area
A	15 cm^2
B	**10 cm^2**
C	**6 cm^2**
D	**15 cm^2**
E	**10 cm^2**
F	**6 cm^2**

b) 62 cm^2

3 58 cm^2

4 a) 25 cm^2
b) 6
c) 150 cm^2

7.3.3 Prisms

1 136 cm^2

2 66 cm^2

3 80 cm^2

4 a)

Face	Area
A	130 cm^2
B	**100 cm^2**
C	**130 cm^2**
D	**60 cm^2**
E	**60 cm^2**

b) 480 cm^2

7.3.4 Cylinders

1 a) 66π cm^2
b) 207 cm^2

2 a) 25π cm^2
b) 110π cm^2

3 a) 25π cm^2
b) 10π cm
c) 70π cm^2
d) i. 120π cm^2
ii. 377 cm^2

7.4 Volume

7.4.1 Cubes and cuboids

1 a) 6
b) 6 cm^3

2 15 cm^3

3 30 cm^3

4 60 cm^3

7.2.2 Prisms and cylinders

1 40 cm^3

2 63 cm^3

3 84 cm^3

4 a) 12 cm^2
b) 84 cm^3

8.1 Symmetry

8.1.1 Line symmetry

1 c) (the parallelogram)

2

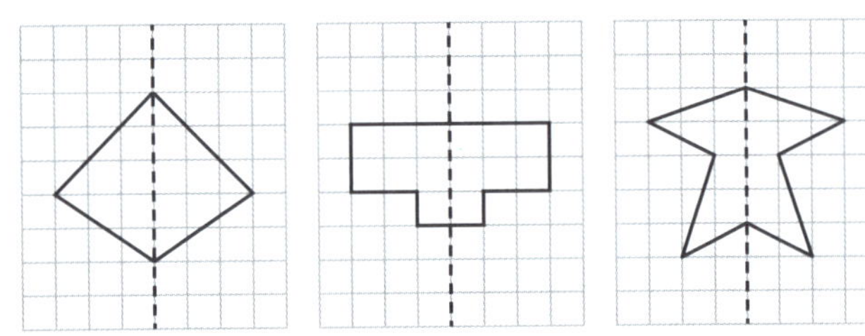

3

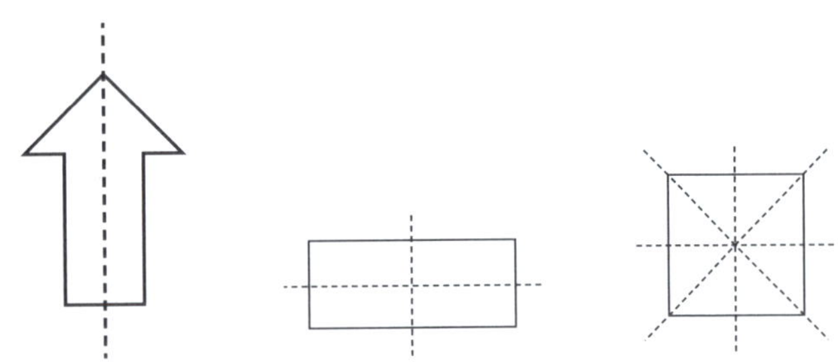

7.1.2 Rotational symmetry

1 a) 3
b) 3
c) 3

2 Isosceles triangle

3 Regular pentagon

8.2 Angle properties

8.2.1 Angles around a point

1 **a)** 360°
b) 180°

2 **a)** 110°
b) 65°

3 **a)** 50°
b) 80°

8.2.2 Parallel lines and corresponding angles

1 Diagram **d**

2 q because it is on the same side of the transversal as the 92° angle, and because both q and the 92° angle are on the same side of the parallel lines.

3 **a)** 74° because corresponding angles on parallel lines are equal.
b) 142° because corresponding angles on parallel lines are equal.

8.2.3 Parallel lines and alternate angles

1 Diagram **a**

2 b because it is on the opposite side of the transversal as the 93° angle, and because both b and the 93° angle are between the parallel lines.

3 **a)** 81° because alternate angles on parallel lines are equal.
b) 130° because alternate angles on parallel lines are equal.

8.3 Angle properties of polygons

8.3.1 Angles in triangles

1 180°

2 **a)** 60°
b) 35°

3 **a)** 58°
b) 58°

4 32°

8.3.2 Interior angles of polygons

1 **a)** 180°
b) 360°

2 1080°

3 1260°

8.3.3 Exterior angles of polygons

1 360°

2 **a)** 80°
b) 40°

3 85°

4 60°

8.4 Problem-solving with angles

8.4.1 Angle problems

1 **a)** <u>180°</u> − (75° + <u>70°</u>) = <u>35°</u>
Because <u>the interior angles of a triangle add up to 180°.</u>
b) <u>180°</u> − <u>35°</u> = <u>145°</u>
Because <u>angles at a point on a straight line add up to 180°.</u>

2 x = 80°. Angles around a point add up to 360°.
y = 40°. Angles in a quadrilateral add up to 360°.

3 **a)** 145°. Angles at a point on a straight line add up to 180°.
b) 35°. Angle y and the 35° angle are alternate angles on parallel lines.
c) 130°. Angles in a quadrilateral add up to 360°.

9.1 Constructions using circles

9.1.1 Drawing circles

1

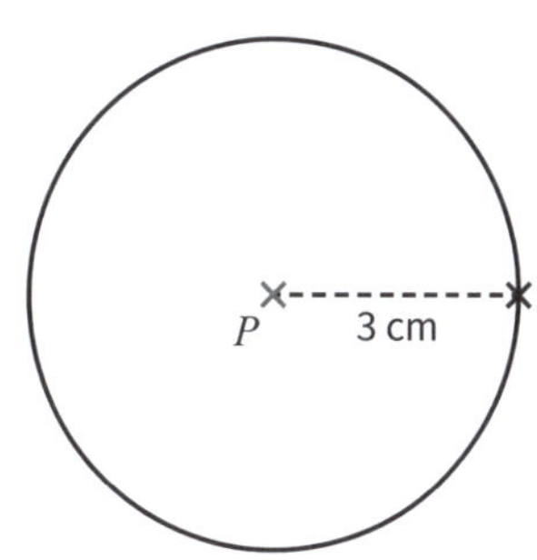

2

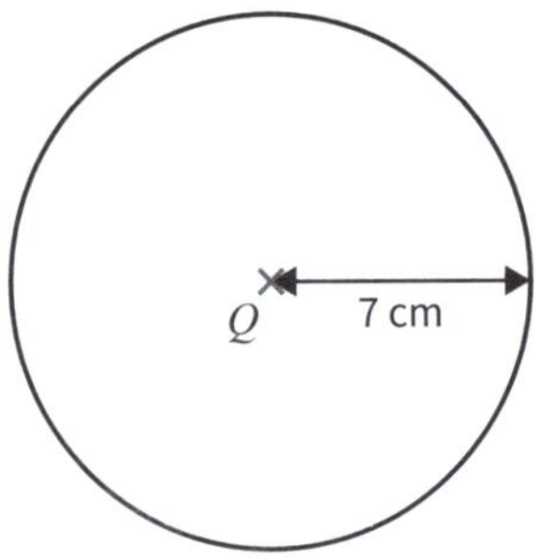

3

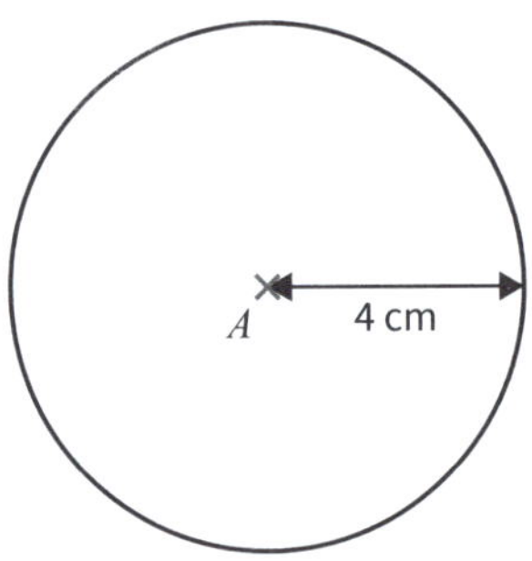

4

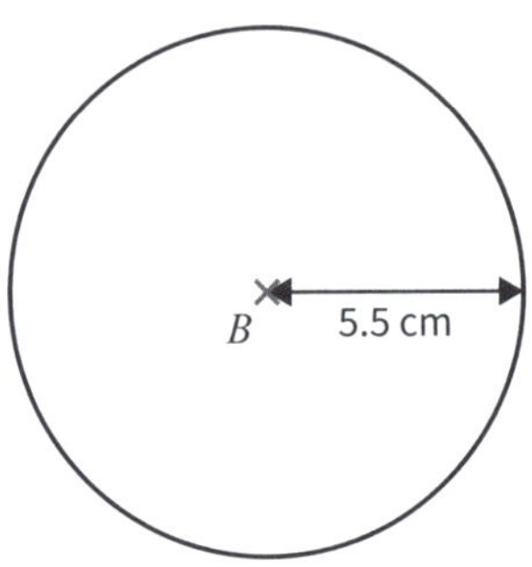

9.1.2 Constructing triangles

1

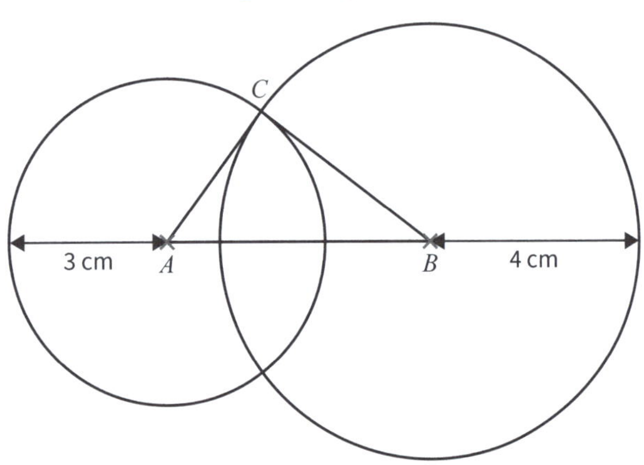

2

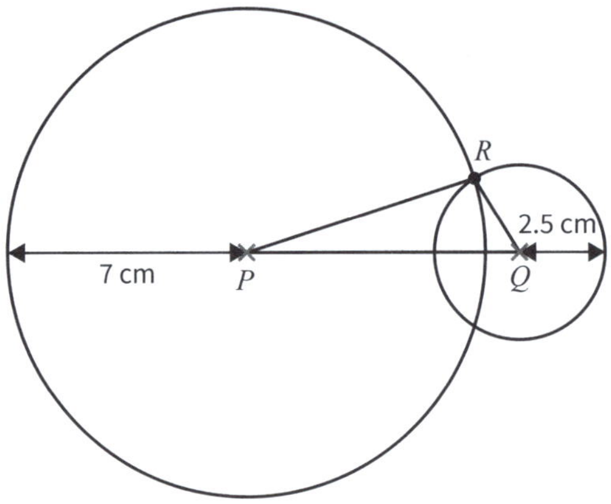

3

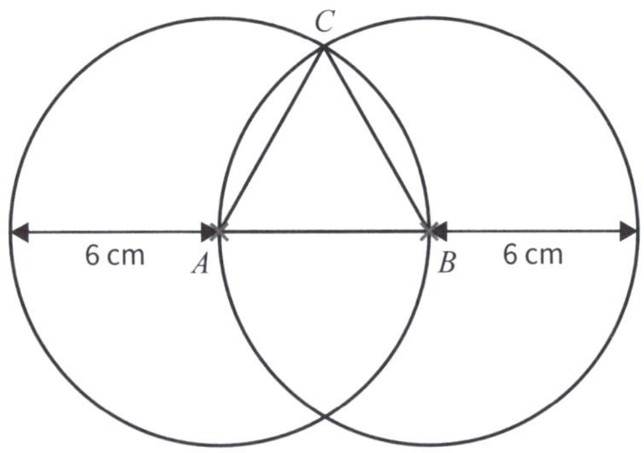

9.1.3 Constructing rhombuses

1

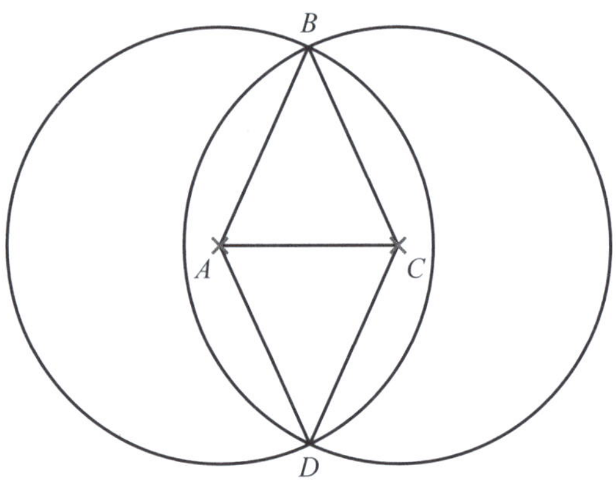

2

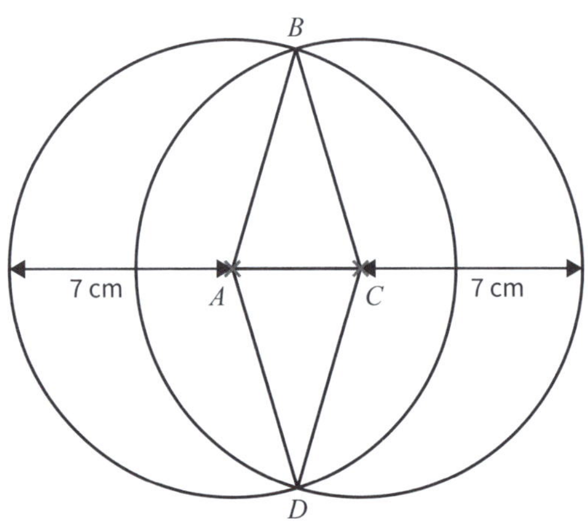

3

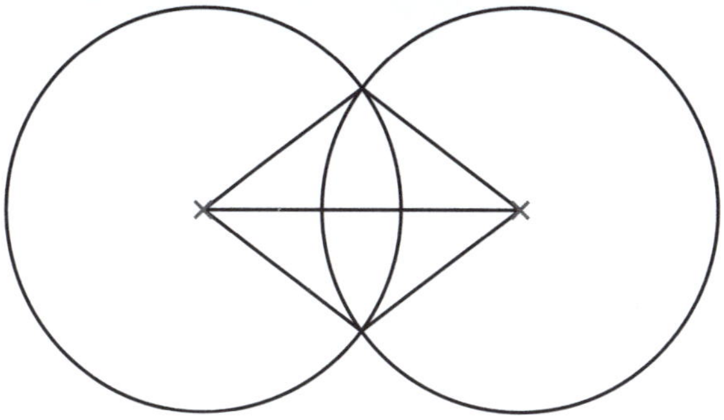

9.2 Constructions using rhombuses

9.2.1 Properties of rhombuses

1 **c)**

2 **d)**

3 150°

4 22.5°

9.2.2 Constructing the perpendicular bisector of a line

1

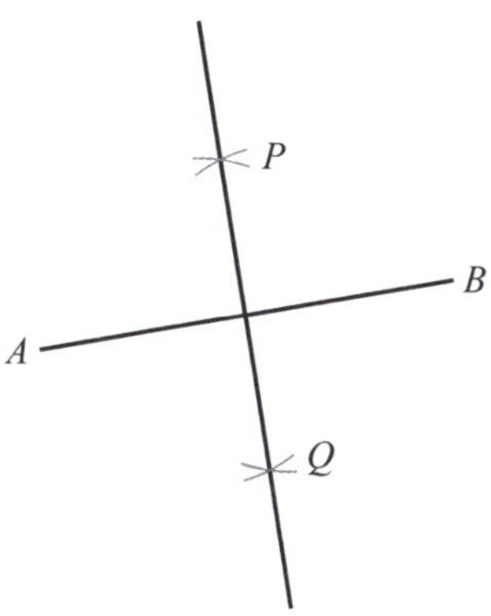

2

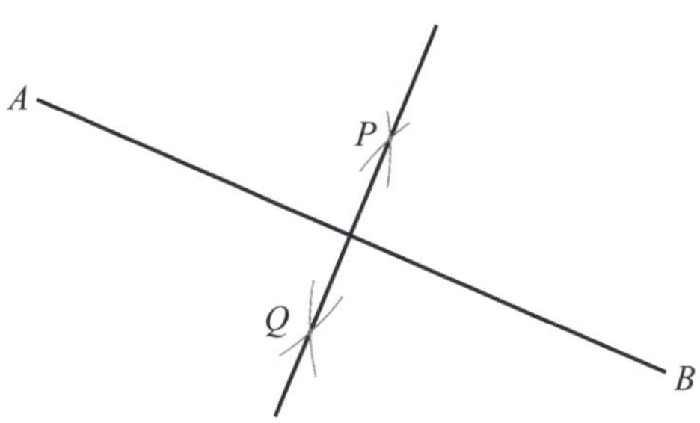

3

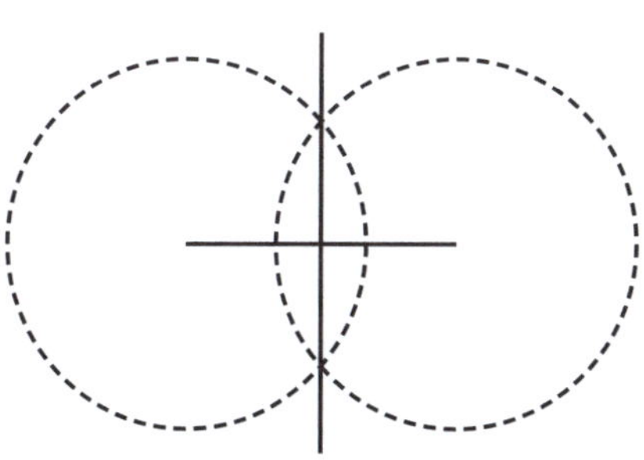

4

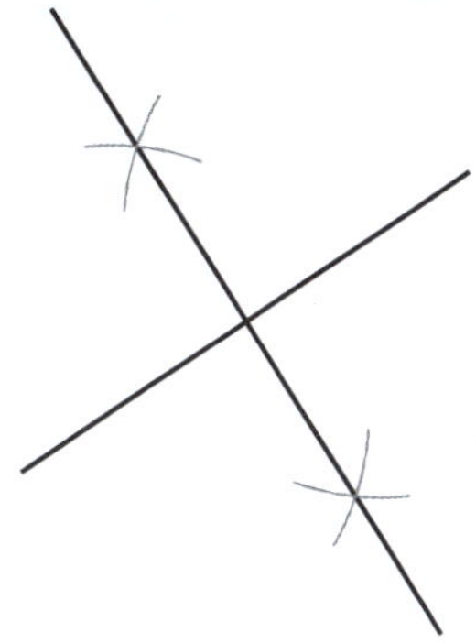

9.2.3 Constructing a perpendicular to a line through a point

1

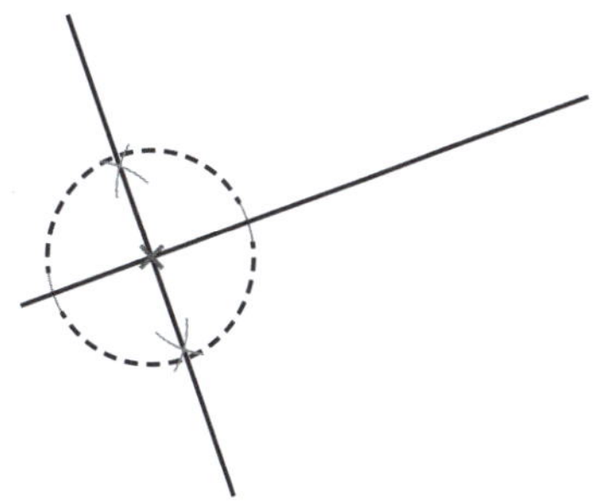

2

3

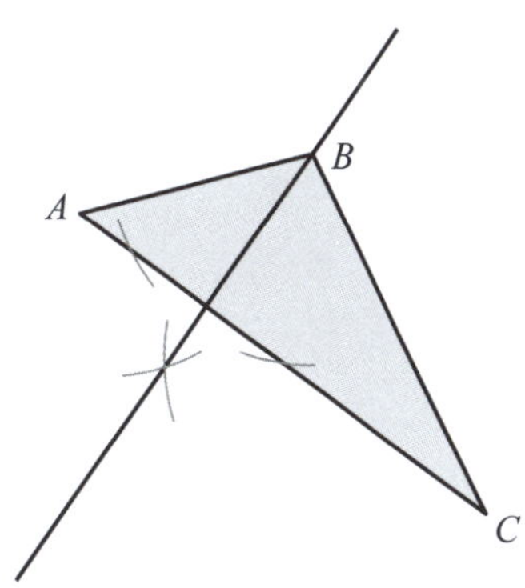

9.2.4 Bisecting angles

1

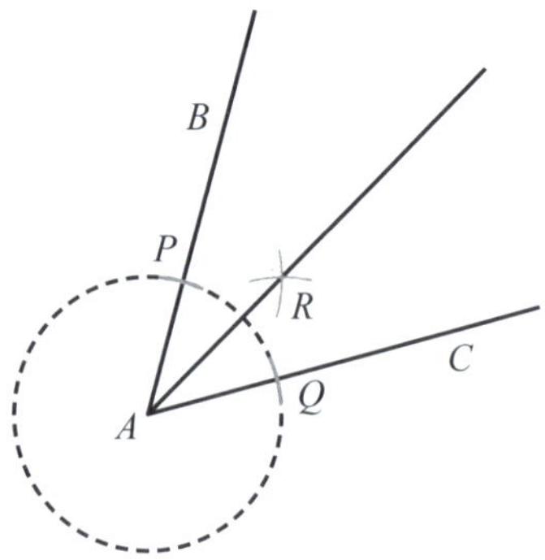

2

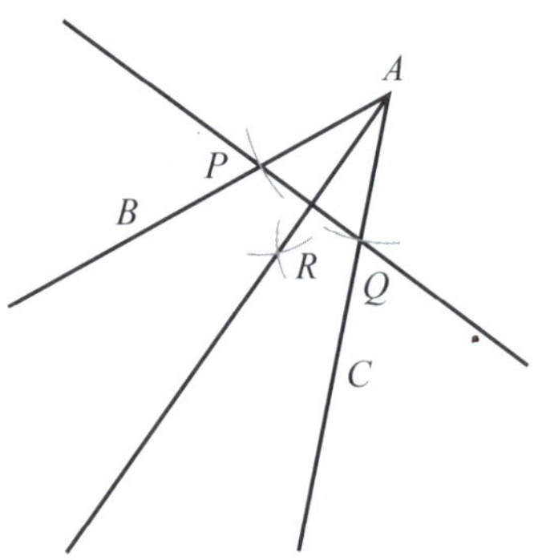

3

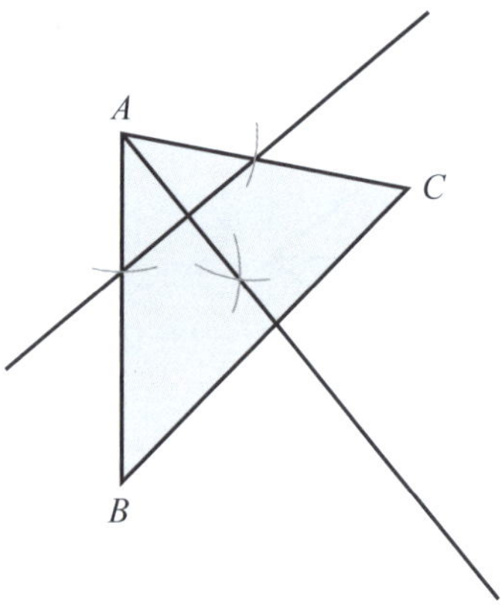